SO-CNO-640

Asheville-Buncombe Technical Institute
LIBRARY
340 Victoria Road
Asheville, North Carolina 28801

DISCARDED

JUN 10 2025

the american consumer ISSUES AND DECISIONS

The Authors

HERBERT M. JELLEY is a professor of business education at Oklahoma State University. In addition to teaching at the high school and university level, Dr. Jelley has also taught courses in life insurance at the home office of a life insurance company. He has served as consultant to business firms and as economic education consultant to the Oklahoma City public schools. His research study, "A Measurement and Interpretation of Money Management Understandings of Twelfth-Grade Students," received the National Business Education Research Award, which is sponsored annually by Delta Pi Epsilon. As a specialist in consumer education, Dr. Jelley has contributed many articles to professional journals and has addressed numerous teachers' groups.

ROBERT O. HERRMANN is an associate professor of agricultural economics at The Pennsylvania State University. Before joining the faculty there, Dr. Herrmann was a member of the Department of Home Economics at the University of California at Davis. Dr. Herrmann has taught courses and conducted research in family economics and consumer behavior, and he is former president of the American Council on Consumer Interests, a national association of professionals in the fields of consumer education and consumer affairs. Dr. Herrmann has contributed many articles to professional journals on subjects such as the development of the consumer movement, consumer behavior of young adults, consumer bankruptcy, and food consumption.

the american consumer

ISSUES AND DECISIONS

Herbert M. Jelley

Robert O. Herrmann

GREGG DIVISION/McGRAW-HILL BOOK COMPANY

New York   St. Louis   Dallas   San Francisco   Düsseldorf   Johannesburg
Kuala Lumpur   London   Mexico   Montreal   New Delhi
Panama   Rio de Janeiro   Singapore   Sydney   Toronto

Senior Editor	Joseph G. Bonnice
Editing Manager	Toby Uger
Editing Supervisor	Wendy L. Hill
Production Supervisor	Maria Winiarski
Designer	John Donnelly
Illustrator	Barron Storey

Library of Congress Cataloging in Publication Data

Jelley, Herbert M
    The American consumer: issues and decisions.

    SUMMARY: A consumer education text which
emphasizes controversial consumer issues and the
daily problems of today's consumers.
    1. Consumer education. [1. Consumer education]
I. Herrmann, Robert O., joint author. II. Title.
TX335.J44 640.73 72-8047
ISBN 0-07-032325-9

The American Consumer: Issues and Decisions

Copyright © 1973 by McGraw-Hill, Inc. All Rights
Reserved. Printed in the United States of America.
No part of this publication may be reproduced,
stored in a retrieval system, or transmitted, in any
form or by any means, electronic, mechanical,
photocopying, recording, or otherwise, without the
prior written permission of the publisher.

56789 DODO 2109876

Preface

Throughout recorded history the consumer has often suffered from the misdeeds of some businessmen and governments—and from his own shortcomings. Today's consumer may have somewhat more protection than his predecessors did, but in many instances he is more vulnerable. The consumer of the seventies is the target of the sophisticated efforts of professional marketers, who use such tools as motivational research, psychologically based sales appeals, and the mass media. The professional marketer is more than a match for the amateur consumer attempting to cope with the variety and complexity of products in the marketplace. Thus, the need for consumer education has never been greater.

Although *The American Consumer: Issues and Decisions* is a new text, it had its origin in a series of consumer education booklets published in the mid-forties that represented the culmination of the Consumer Education Study conducted by the National Association of Secondary School Principals. The study resulted in the recognition by school administrators that consumer education is a vital part of the high school curriculum. In 1951 the booklets were revised and published in textbook form under the title *Consumer Living*. Subsequently, two revised editions of *Consumer Living* were published under the title *Consumer Economics*. These works deeply influenced the authors of *The American Consumer: Issues and Decisions*.

PURPOSE OF THE BOOK

The American Consumer: Issues and Decisions was written to help young people become better consumers. Throughout the book, emphasis is placed on building positive and constructive attitudes, which enable the consumer to approach the marketplace confident of his ability to make the many important decisions required of him.

The importance of forming personal and social goals based on a carefully considered set of values is introduced and stressed in the first two chapters and reinforced throughout the remaining chapters. For example, the aim of the chapters that deal primarily with buymanship is not so much to determine which brand of product may be best as it is to help the student realize what place the product is going to have in his life. By analyzing the usefulness, benefits, and ultimate costs to the consumer of products and services—from furniture and vacation trips to cars and life insurance—*The American Consumer: Issues and Decisions* helps the student recognize his needs, gather pertinent data, and make intelligent buying decisions.

INSTRUCTIONAL CONTENT

The American Consumer: Issues and Decisions includes three main categories of content that many consumer educators agree are essential for a balanced and effective program of consumer education. These categories are as follows:

- Money management—management of personal resources, including credit.
- Buymanship—principles and guides for recognizing product quality and relating it to one's needs and resources.
- Consumer issues—a presentation of the major problems confronting consumers and the steps that have been taken or proposed to correct these problems.

Money management shows how overall plans for spending are developed. Standardized budgets and spending plans are avoided, because sound money management should be based on a consumer's individual values and needs at his particular stage in the family life cycle.

Buymanship provides the background and specific help needed to make wise buying decisions and to carry them out. The text includes chapters on buying food, clothing, cars, housing, furniture, and appliances, and on choosing recreational activities and vacations. Since consumer purchases of these items constitute more than two-thirds of a typical family's total spending, coverage of these topics is essential to a complete program of consumer education.

The study of consumer issues informs the student of the extent to which he may or may not be protected by existing laws, government regulations, and business practices that claim to protect his interests. The presentation of consumer issues also suggests methods consumers can use in demanding better performance from the groups responsible for protecting their interests. The treatment of consumer issues is further enhanced by the inclusion of a chapter that provides a historical perspective of consumer protection efforts. Thus, students can see that current problems are not unique and that the usefulness of consumer education is not limited to the problems of today.

TEACHING AND LEARNING AIDS

The authors recognize that an effective program of consumer education requires more than just up-to-date instructional material. Students must be given the opportunity to review and apply what they have learned, and teachers must be assisted by additional educational materials that support the textbook.

End-of-Chapter Activities

At the end of each chapter are two types of student activities. "Checking Your Reading" is a series of questions that require brief written answers based on recall of information presented in the text. Many of the assignments in "Consumer Problems and Projects" are designed as enrichment activities. Sufficient items of varying difficulty are presented to enable the teacher to provide for students' individual differences. Other activities can effectively be used to promote group discussions, so that students can share their thinking and experiences with other class members.

Student Activity Guide

The *Student Activity Guide for The American Consumer: Issues and Decisions* is designed to supplement and enrich the learning experiences provided in the textbook. The guide offers students an opportunity to review their understanding of new terms, concepts, and principles. The activities in the guide were carefully developed to elicit a full range of intellectual responses.

Teacher's Manual and Key

The *Teacher's Manual and Key* contains answers to all questions in the text and student activity guide and offers suggestions for activities, projects, demonstrations, and discussions. In addition, the *Teacher's Manual and Key* includes transparency masters and achievement tests, ready to duplicate and administer.

ACKNOWLEDGMENTS

Many teachers as well as specialists in business and government generously shared their time and knowledge with the authors, advising them on the development of this book and checking the accuracy of the material presented. Their assistance was exceedingly helpful and is acknowledged with thanks.

Herbert M. Jelley

Robert O. Herrmann

Contents

Consumer planning
and decision making

Part 1

Chapter 1

Consumer problems today

What goods should be manufactured and in what quantities? To whom should these goods go and in what quantities? What services should be provided for people? What type of work should various people do? How much money should be given in exchange for the work done by various people? The answers to these and other questions are determined by the system people use to organize their work efforts in order to satisfy their needs and wants. This system is known as the *economy*.

The objective of our economy can be stated quite simply: to satisfy, as much as possible, the consumer's needs and wants for goods and services. During most of his life, every person in our society is a consumer, of course, because every person is an ultimate user of some of the goods and services that the economy produces. In this book you will read about some of the problems of consumers as well as some of the opportunities for consumers in American society today.

OUR WANTS ARE UNLIMITED

Henry Ford was once asked how much money a person would need to accumulate so that he could stop being concerned about piling up more money. After a moment's reflection, Mr. Ford's answer was, "Just a little bit more." His answer illustrates quite well the fact that all people, even the wealthy, have unlimited wants. When we satisfy one want, we find that others have been created that need to be satisfied.

A new sweater may be just the thing a girl really wants. When she has it, though, she decides that she needs new slacks, too. If she eventually satisfies her desire for new slacks, she might want new shoes. A family might have a strong wish for a television set. When the wish is fulfilled with a black and white set, they may gradually begin wishing for a color set. A boy who has just completed high school might want a car—just any kind of car. What happens after he buys just any kind of car? After a time, he wants a newer, more expensive model. Economists say that human wants are *insatiable,* meaning that our wants are incapable of being satisfied. When we satisfy one want, other wants crop up that we want to satisfy.

The problem, however, is that although human wants are unlimited, the resources (or income) for satisfying those wants are limited. Most of us can understand this problem: we have limited resources and unlimited wants; we can easily dream of scores of things we would really like to have right now. When we think of wealthy people, we may have some difficulty picturing them as having unfulfilled wants. The fact is, though, that everyone has unfulfilled wants, although certainly they are vastly different. One student might be dreaming of a $6 basketball while another is dreaming of a $4,200 car. One man may dream about owning a wristwatch; another man may dream about owning a motorboat.

In the succeeding chapters of this book, you will read how we can go about satisfying as many of our wants as possible with our limited resources (or incomes). You will also read about our obligations as consumers in our society. In the next few paragraphs, let us set the stage by reviewing briefly the consumer environment.

OVERVIEW OF THE CONSUMER ENVIRONMENT

Our nation is rich in natural, industrial, and financial resources, but progress in many areas has been, and still is, so rapid that the world seems to be changing all around us. Our changing economy has brought many problems to consumers. Some of the problems that our ancestors faced are no longer problems to us, but we have new problems that were unknown even a few years ago. As with all problems, the first step in solving them is to know exactly what they are.

The conflicting interests of consumers and producers

Consumers want low-cost, high-quality goods; producers want profits. Consumers should be aware of this conflict of interests.

In an earlier day when a man produced goods for his own use or

Colonial Williamsburg Photograph
Years ago the craftsman was likely to be a friend or neighbor of the user of his product. Thus he felt personally responsible for the product's quality.

for the use of his neighbors, he took pride in the quality of his product, and he knew that if he lowered his standards, the word would soon get around. He would lose not only the respect of his neighbors but also the profit brought by their trade.

Today, however, businessmen seldom have the same kind of pride in quality. The president of a large corporation is sometimes completely unfamiliar with the actual processes of production and knows only a very few of his customers. The highly specialized workers in the automated factory make only a limited contribution to the complete production process. A man who works on one phase of the production line in an automobile assembly plant may be a good, conscientious worker, but he can hardly be expected to feel either great pride or responsibility for the quality of glass used in the windshields of the cars produced in an automated factory.

In a private enterprise economy such as we have in the United States today, the primary motivating force behind business is the desire for profits. Businessmen in recent years have recognized their social responsibilities to society, but still their chief aim is to make the most money they can within their framework of ethics. It is natural and necessary for a businessman to run a profitable business. Fortunately, maintaining high-quality standards frequently results in greater profits in the long run; but sometimes enthusiasm for financial gain can lead businessmen to lower their standards, or it can lead them to use unethical selling techniques.

When we realize that the main purpose for producing goods is ultimately to sell them to consumers at a profit, we will approach our buying tasks with more realistic attitudes.

The complex modern market

Years ago, consumers and producers were well acquainted. They lived in the same community, and the consumer knew how and from what materials his goods were made. He knew what he wanted and gave specific instructions to the producer. The producer, in turn, knew the likes and dislikes of his customers, and he knew just how to go about pleasing them. Today the customer and producer are separated by an intricate market system. Not only does the consumer not know the producer of the goods he buys, he also frequently does not even know the merchant from whom he buys the goods.

At one time, a few simple retail stores constituted a consumer's buying market, but today most communities have a variety of different types of retail stores. The consumer can choose among supermarkets, cooperatives, and independent, chain, department, and specialty stores. Many of these stores will sell identical or similar goods. The consumer must investigate and choose the store or stores that offer the goods and services that will best satisfy his unique needs.

The variety of goods available

Technological advances and improved transportation facilities have brought about a great variety of products, and this means better living for today's consumers. It also means more confusion for today's consumers. The many new food products produced such as frozen meals and prepared "hot" foods available at many food markets are good examples of the variety of items available in today's market, but they are by no means the only examples. New fabrics, new appliances, and new products of every kind have brought better living to the consumer, but they have also brought the problem of choice. Does a consumer really want a snow blower? Should he buy a trash compactor? Does he want a double-knit suit? Or should he buy a worsted wool suit? When the consumer does decide what he wants to buy, he must then determine which manufacturer puts the most workmanship in his product—and whether that manufacturer's expensive or less expensive product is his better buy.

The number of different brands available in the market adds to the confusion. Producers have attempted by means of advertising to establish brand preferences for their products, but as the technique of

Courtesy San Lazaro Diamonds, Tiro Gems Corp.

In today's complex market, consumers must choose among many different types of stores that sell identical or similar products. Without knowing the merchants, the choice is often difficult.

brand advertising has become more widespread, a multiplicity of brand names has resulted. With every seller claiming superiority for his particular brand, the consumer without sufficient evidence to judge the merits of these claims is indeed bewildered.

The confusing selling methods

Selling techniques used by manufacturers and suppliers of consumer goods have been developed so efficiently that many consumers have difficulty buying wisely. Selling has become a highly developed procedure, and the modern salesman knows countless subtle ways to encourage the susceptible consumer to buy. The skillful marketing man often uses emotional and psychological appeals rather than factual information to sell a product, and in most cases the uninformed consumer is no match for him. Thus, the consumer may buy what he does not want and cannot use. As the flood of goods on the market increases, the consumer is forced more and more to rely on the salesman and the advertiser for information.

Various surveys of attitudes have indicated that consumers are not satisfied with the selling methods of advertising; they want more information and less emotional appeal in advertising.

The conflicting interests of certain groups

Consumers want low prices, of course, and low prices are partly a result of high production and efficient distribution. In some cases, production and distribution are hindered by the selfish aims of various economic groups. Groups of businessmen may combine to limit output and increase prices; take advantage of the uninformed consumer by means of deception, adulteration, or even fraud; bring undue pressure to buy; and, in general, promote practices that are contrary to the interests of consumers. Labor groups may make unfair demands on employers that result in production restrictions, high prices, and inefficient production methods.

Groups representing special interests often make selfish demands on the government. Through the procedure known as lobbying, they make their wants (and often demands) known to the lawmakers. Historically, consumers have been largely unorganized and without definite programs. Recently, however, consumer groups have organized and become stronger, and it is hoped that in the future the needs of consumers will be given more attention by government at all levels.

OVERVIEW OF CONSUMER PROBLEMS

The brief overview of the consumer environment just presented shows why consumers have a need for information and knowledge. Being a wise consumer in today's society is not easy. The chapters in this book are written to help you begin a life-long program of learning to be a better consumer. Learning about your role as a consumer is really quite interesting—and often exciting. You will see that learning to be a wise consumer is not only important for you from a selfish point of view; it is also essential if you are to discharge properly your duties as a citizen of the United States.

The next few paragraphs are a short preview of this venture of learning to become a wise consumer. We know that the task of becoming a wise consumer is not easy because of problems that exist. Some problems stem from our relationship to the businessmen from whom we buy goods and services. Some problems we must blame on ourselves. Some problems we make for each other.

Unfortunately, some business firms are guilty of deceptive practices in their dealings with consumers. Deciding when a certain business practice is illegal and should result in prosecution has always been difficult, and as a result of this many merchants engage in practices that fit in that gray area that borders on the illegal. Consumers must be alert to deceptive practices and learn to recognize when they are being treated unfairly.

Some studies have shown that persons living in low-income areas pay prices for food, rent, medicine, and household products that exceed prices paid by persons living in more affluent areas. Even chain stores will charge more for their food in their outlets in low-income areas than in their outlets in middle-income neighborhoods. Studies in other cities, however, have shown little, if any, difference in prices to exist between stores in low-income areas and stores in middle- or high-income areas.

Stores selling furniture and appliances in low-income neighborhoods often charge higher prices than stores in middle- and upper-income neighborhoods, and often the difference is considerable. When it is true that stores charge more in low-income neighborhoods, the business firms often defend the practice by asserting that their operating costs are greater because of higher insurance rates in low-income neighborhoods. In order to earn the same profit they earn in middle- and upper-income areas, therefore, they must pass the higher costs on to consumers. Another reason, unfortunately, that higher prices can be charged in low-income areas is that persons from these areas have been made to feel unwanted in other neighborhoods and thus have had little choice but to patronize the merchants on their own streets and pay the higher prices. Later in this chapter, more will be said about how consumers can help themselves to get more for their money.

In some cases, the quality of goods sold in low-income neighborhoods is poorer than in other neighborhoods. For example, fruit and vegetables may be more often damaged, meat brown around the edges, and milk and eggs occasionally sold past the time recommended by the producer.

When practices such as those described above are true, are the merchants engaging in illegal acts? Certainly in some cases they are wrong. The guilty businessmen should be made aware of the fact that all consumers resent such tactics.

Many consumers have expressed specific gripes about the business community, such as the dining-room table being delivered two weeks late and having a broken leg when it arrived. You might hear about the many defects in a new car just bought. A recent poll by Opinion Research Corporation shows that 68 percent of Americans feel that more consumer protection laws are needed to protect consumers against unscrupulous businessmen.

Complaints about unfair or shoddy business deals poured into the office of the President's Committee on Consumer Interests in Washington, D.C. The Special Assistant to the President for Consumer Affairs indicated that in 1970 about 3,500 letters a month were being received by the Committee. The Special Assistant declared that the deluge of letters was set off because people simply got sick and tired of unsafe products, shoddy merchandise, poor service, meaningless guarantees, shabby repair work, questionable business practices, and outright swindles. What business practices are objectionable to consumers? What products and services cause consumers to become dissatisfied? A glimpse at just a sample of these practices is presented here.

Problems with sales solicitation

Perhaps you have received a telephone call at your home from a young lady with a sweet voice. She asks if the person answering the phone would mind responding to a few questions for a survey being made for the community. Then the call might go something like this:

"Which of the following programs do you watch most frequently: the 'Tonight' show with Johnny Carson, 'Mannix,' or 'The Dean Martin Show'?"

"The 'Tonight' show with Johnny Carson."

"Fine. You know, that is my favorite show, too. I try never to miss it. Who would you like most to see on the 'Tonight' show? Just give me the name of any personality or celebrity."

"Well, probably Bob Hope."

"Yes, that's fine. I certainly want to thank you for being so patient and contributing to our survey. Now I have a very nice surprise for you. If you have watched the 'Tonight' show you have seen *Junque* magazine advertised, I'm sure. The publishers of *Junque* and other magazines would like to thank you for the help you have given them by giving you a gift for your efforts. They will send you a free subscription to any two of the following magazines for only the cost of postage."

At this point the caller would read from a list of magazines from which the survey respondent can choose. Of course, if the consumer later checks the cost of subscribing to the magazines, he may find that it is not really different from the cost of postage for this "free gift" deal, and thus he is angry because he feels that he has been misled.

Other objectionable means of selling magazine subscriptions exist, too, as you may know. For example, there is the young college student who is attempting to get a free trip to Europe by winning a contest for selling the most magazine subscriptions. The young person may say that he has just one more day, and if he can just get one or two more subscriptions he will get the trip. Investigations have shown that these "clean cut" young ladies and gentlemen are really carefully trained for this type of work, know how to play on sympathy, and earn unusually large amounts of money for themselves and their bosses through their deception.

The schemes mentioned above certainly are not large-scale frauds—they are for most persons mainly a terrible nuisance. But some frauds are more serious. A publisher of a mediocre set of encyclopedias once sold sets by training salesmen to visit homes and explain that the owner had been selected to receive a free set of encyclopedias. In return, the publisher wanted permission to use for advertising purposes any quote the owner might like to make later about the set. What was the catch? As an expression of good faith, the owner of the set was expected to agree to buy for a certain number of years the yearbook that updates the set and a research service enabling the owner to request information about topics in which he is interested. In a few years, the yearly price of the research service plus the yearbook adds up to a cost that is more than the worth of the set. Thinking he was really getting something for nothing, the person signed the contract binding him to pay out money for a number of years. Consumers should read contracts carefully before signing them.

Fraudulent sales solicitation through home visits or by telephone can be more serious than paying for a few unwanted magazines or a set of encyclopedias. Entire savings accounts have been wiped out when homeowners have signed contracts for such things as new aluminum siding, new furnaces, or new kitchens.

Problems with products

Consumers often find defects in the products they buy. In 1970 *Changing Times* magazine dug through some of the letters sent to the President's Committee on Consumer Interests to see what people were so upset about. It was found that many letters stressed structural and mechanical defects in products. For example, one owner of a new car said that it had to be towed back to the dealer after only 11 miles because the "rear wheels locked, and I was almost killed." In another case, a station wagon erupted in flames 45 minutes after the car stopped. Investigation showed that the fire was started by defective wiring. The tailgate of another station wagon fell off in the owner's hands, causing him severe back pain.

Many car owners are concerned about whether or not their cars are safe. Manufacturers have recalled certain models of cars when they have discovered a defect common to all, or nearly all, the models sold.

Consumers have had frustrating experiences with such appliances as dishwashers, refrigerators, ranges, and dryers. Some of the appliances are already defective before they are delivered, and some defects may be the result of damage during shipment. In Chapter 15, you will read about buying appliances and learn what consumers should look for when selecting such items.

Other chapters in this book will discuss food buying, advertising, and government assistance for consumers. Manufacturers and suppliers cause some consumer problems, but consumers also cause some of their own problems.

Problems we cause ourselves

Have you noticed that even among people who have about the same incomes there seems to be quite a difference in the money they have available for buying things and going places? Although they may work at the same job and take home the same pay, one man can take his family on a weekend vacation trip, while his co-worker can only dream about it because he cannot afford it. Or, one man can afford to buy a new appliance when it is on sale, while another person with about the same income does not have the cash and must pass up the sale.

The fortunate men mentioned above might have inherited money, of course, but let us say they did not. What accounts for their having more money to satisfy their wants? Several things. And these several things are what make some people wiser consumers than others. In the remaining chapters of this book you will read about many ways to get the most for your money. We will examine a few of them now.

Having a plan for spending income is the starting point for making certain that you get the most from your income. That means you know and record in advance all sources of income for a period of time. Then, you record each week or each month the money you are already committed to spending (rent payments, for example). Next you estimate other expenses. Sounds simple? Surprisingly enough, far too few consumers bother to do this; as a result, they never force themselves to set goals—to think ahead about what they really want in life. So, one man fritters his money away daily on little things that he could really do without, while another man saves money for a vacation trip that will be remembered for a lifetime.

Some people have more because they are shrewd shoppers. The wise housewife knows during what seasons she can buy certain foods at lower prices, so she plans her menus accordingly. When a new appliance is needed, some families take the time to check the quality and safety of different brands before making a decision. Then, the same families know how to compare prices. They also watch for sales. Consumers who do not do these things are paying more money than they should for the value they receive, and thus they are guilty of hurting themselves.

Of course, some consumers live in neighborhoods that make comparison shopping difficult. In certain low-income areas, the stores might charge prices that are quite uniform (and uniformly high), so the only way in which the consumer can shop for lower prices is to leave the area when shopping. This might be difficult for some, but the effort might be quite rewarding. A subway trip to another part of town might be the answer for consumers in New York City, for example. Or, a group of consumers could form a car pool and drive to stores in other neighborhoods.

Courtesy Agricultural Extension Service, University of California

The shrewd shopper who plans the menu and compares prices can save money. This money may be used to buy the luxuries that the family could not otherwise afford.

Another way in which consumers can cause problems for themselves is by borrowing money unwisely. A thorough understanding of interest rates and a knowledge of the different types of lending institutions can make a big difference in the cost of things. Would you not spend a little time checking car dealers' prices if you thought you could save, say, $90 on the price of a new car? Most people do. But then they often finance the car (borrow money for the purchase) at the easiest place to get the financing—probably from the car dealer. On a $3,000 loan, the difference between financing charges (interest) of lending institutions is often $90 or more. The consumer who does not shop for credit is hurting himself.

When we save or invest money, we must be conscious of interest rates paid to us. How important is investing money where the interest will help the money to grow? Did you know that money saved where it will earn just 4 percent compounded annually will double itself in 18 years? If you put $1,000 in a bank paying 4 percent interest, therefore, it will be worth $2,000 when you withdraw it 18 years later. If you could save $100 every half year in an institution paying 6 percent interest compounded semiannually, how much do you think you would have by the end of 15 years? You could buy a car with the money. You would have $4,757.54. People who have no savings and investment plans are not acting as wise consumers, of course; and consumers who do not invest their savings wisely so that they get maximum interest earnings consistent with safety are hurting themselves.

Problems we make for each other

When you receive poor service in a store, do you mention the fact to the clerk who gave the poor service? Do you explain the poor service to the manager of the store? If the poor service persists, do you take your business to another store? You do not have to be cranky and testy—in fact, you should not be. You should explain firmly and politely that you have not been treated properly and that you expect different treatment if you are to continue patronizing the store. The store's management will appreciate your comments, and you will be doing a service for other consumers. By remaining silent you are actually encouraging the continuation of poor service, and both you and other consumers will suffer. A store that offers poor service or sells shoddy merchandise should not be encouraged to continue in business. When you patronize such a store you are casting a vote for that store to stay with such practices.

CONSUMERS' SELFISH PRACTICES Consumers can also hurt other consumers by their selfish practices. Unfortunately, some consumers are guilty of cheating. Here is an example. A young lady has an important date on Saturday night, and she will need an evening gown. On Friday afternoon she visits a dress shop, tries on several lovely gowns, and says to the clerk that she has tentatively decided on one of the garments. She is familiar with the store's policy on returning goods, so she charges the gown and takes it with her to examine further at home. The next night she attends a dance with her escort, and she looks lovely in her new evening gown. What do you think she does on Monday? She returns the gown saying that she has changed her mind about buying one at this time. Clever trick? Not really. She is guilty of deceit, and the price she pays in terms of damage to her self-respect is not worth the free use of the evening gown. Furthermore, she has hurt other consumers indirectly.

The store owners know that some people return used merchandise, but in some cases they do not wish to risk losing goodwill by trying to judge whether or not the return is justified. Probably in the case presented in the previous paragraph, the dress could not be sold—at least not as a new dress. So the young lady has caused the store to lose some money on that particular dress. The owners of the store are in business to earn a profit, so that means they will have to set their prices on all their dresses high enough to cover the costs created by a few dishonest consumers. When other women buy their dresses, they pay more because some people resort to dishonest tactics such as the one described.

Consumers hurt other consumers in many other ways, too, of course. Switching price tags so that an article can be bought cheaper is dishonest, and it means that the store will not make the profit it intended to make on the article. When this happens, the store increases the prices of its merchandise so that it will continue to make a profit.

LACK OF INTEREST IN LEGISLATION Our lawmakers often propose new legislation designed to help consumers. When consumers do not exercise their duties as citizens to support such legislation, they are hurting each other. We can individually, and collectively through consumer interest groups, let our legislators know that we approve of certain legislation or disapprove of certain legislation. We can support with our votes the candidates who are pledged to help us as consumers. It has been said that every time we do not use our vote, we cast a vote for the opposition.

CONSUMER RIGHTS—AND RESPONSIBILITIES

Consumers have rights, and they also have responsibilities. As set forth in the deliberations of three Presidents—John F. Kennedy, Lyndon B. Johnson, and Richard M. Nixon—the "consumer bill of rights" includes the following:

- Consumers have the right to make meaningful choices.
- Consumers have the right to have product information at the point of sale and additional information concerning the use and care of products.
- Consumers have the right to be assured that they are receiving safe products.
- Consumers have the right to be heard—a direct voice to industry.

Each of these rights means a responsibility, too, of course.

In his 1970 State of the Union message, President Nixon said, "The great question of the '70's is: Shall we surrender to our surroundings, or shall we make our peace with nature and begin to make reparations for the damage we have done to our air, to our land, and to our water." Our environment is seriously threatened by the "garbage" of the world's richest economy. The Apollo 10 astronauts could see Los Angeles as a cancerous smudge from 25,000 miles in outer space. Each year, the industrial plants in our nation emit great quantities of smoke and fumes into the air.

Rivers and streams are polluted with chemicals and other waste from industrial plants. The earth has its own waste-disposal system, but this system has limits. For example, the winds, which ventilate the earth, blow only about six miles above the earth. Certain chemical poisons can kill the tiny organisms that normally clean rivers. And, in addition to that, we now have such new things as aluminum cans that do not rust and inorganic plastics that may linger on for years and years. Then, too, man by his sheer numbers is depleting the earth's resources. Consumers must be concerned about the problem.

What are some of the things you as a consumer can do to help fight pollution? You can encourage action taken by business and government as they fight the problem. You can also make contributions as an individual. For example, you can buy gasoline with the least amount of lead required to operate your car satisfactorily. You can form car pools in your neighborhood to cut down on the number of cars on the road. You can support mass-transit systems that pollute less per passenger mile than cars.

Editorial Photocolor Archives, Inc.

Some industrial practices, such as strip-mining, have severely damaged the environment. Consumers must encourage business and government to take action and repair the damage.

You can also avoid excessively packaged products, such as individually wrapped cheese slices and goods in plastic bubble packs. You can use less electric power. The manufacture and use of power pollutes air and water, so cut down on consumption by turning off lights when you leave a room in your home or office. There are other ways that you can help in the fight against pollution. The important thing is to recognize the problem and join in the fight.

Our society will be what we make it. During the past decade or two people in the United States have considered the need for a close look at our society. We have problems to tackle, such as the preservation of the natural resources and the control of environmental pollution. We must learn to use our increased leisure time wisely.

Remember the Preamble to the Constitution? "We, the people of the United States, in order to form a more perfect union, establish justice, insure domestic tranquility, provide for the common defense, promote the general welfare, and secure the blessings of liberty to ourselves and our posterity . . . ." Notice that the statement begins with "We, the people." Not we, the politicians. Not we, the elected officials of the nation. Not we, who have had the opportunity to study the political processes. Just we, the people. We have a big stake in this country.

Checking your reading

1. What is the meaning of the expression "the economy"?
2. What do economists mean when they refer to human wants as "insatiable"?
3. Describe briefly the conflict of interests between consumers and producers.
4. What is the primary motivating force behind a private enterprise economy such as we have in the United States? Why is it important for consumers to be aware of this motivating force?
5. Provide an example of the difference between the market of the past and the market today regarding the relationship between the producer and the consumer?
6. List two developments that have brought about a great variety of products for today's consumers.
7. What is one way producers attempt to establish brand preferences for their products?
8. Discuss how highly developed sales methods have made buying more difficult for consumers.
9. List some of the reasons consumers wrote letters to the Special Assistant to the President for Consumer Affairs.
10. Discuss several ways in which consumers cause problems for themselves.
11. Discuss several ways in which consumers make problems for each other.
12. When you receive poor service in a store, what should you do?
13. List the points covered in the "consumer bill of rights."
14. List several things you as a consumer can do to help fight pollution.

Consumer problems and projects

1. Why do you think the consumer is important in our economic system?
2. There are many types of markets in every community. Select five from your community, and describe what is traded at each.
3. Select from a magazine or other source several examples of advertising that illustrate how producers use emotional appeals in their ads. Briefly explain how each ad makes the product emotionally appealing.
4. Select a product, and prepare a report to be presented to the class on the difference between the way the product was produced 50 years ago and the way it is produced today.
5. Prepare a bulletin board display showing ways in which you as a consumer can help fight pollution.
6. Present as many arguments as you can in favor of studying consumer problems.

7. Some products produced and distributed widely 100 years ago are no longer generally used today. Examples of such products are buggy whips and kerosene lamps.

    a. Why are these two products not so popular today?

    b. Think of two products produced and distributed widely today that probably will not be generally used 100 years from now. Why?

8. When John Whipple saw a carrying case for long-playing records advertised in a music store window at "a special price of $7.99," he went into the store to investigate. While he was examining the cases, a clerk informed him that they were worth at least $10 and were selling very rapidly. Still, John was not sure that he should buy the case until he had examined others. While he was thinking about what he should do, he noticed that the salesman was filling out a sales slip. He asked John for his name and address. Apparently he assumed that John wanted to buy one of the cases.

    a. Analyze this selling technique. Discuss the next move that the consumer should take in this kind of situation.

    b. Give another example of a subtle way salesmen induce customers to buy.

9. During the next two or three days, evaluate one television commercial. Discuss whether or not the commercial gives factual information, and point out any appeals that you consider to be emotional. Why do you consider the appeals to be emotional?

10. The Sands family and the Silverstein family have been friends for quite some time. Mr. Sands and Mr. Silverstein work in the same office and have similar annual incomes. The Sands have been saving their money, and this summer they are going to Europe during Mr. Sand's three-week vacation. The Silversteins, too, have been saving their money, and within the next few weeks they will be moving into a more expensive house in a very nice section of the city. Which family do you think is making the wiser use of its money?

Chapter 2

Values, goals, and choices

One of the first things we discover as consumers is that our ability to get the things we want is limited. The money we have to spend cannot be stretched far enough to get us everything we would like to have. Our money is limited, but our wants seem unlimited. Obviously, some choices are necessary. The whole process of choosing among the different ways we could spend our money is a very important part of being a wise consumer. It is not enough just to learn how to look for bargains and recognize quality. It is also important to know exactly what we want—what our goals are.

Most of this book is devoted to improving your skill as a consumer. This chapter, however, is somewhat different. It is designed to help you think about the things you consider most important and your own goals. Once you have these goals more clearly in mind, the information on consumer skills and buymanship in this book can help you in working toward them. In this chapter we will consider how our wants and goals are formed and how they affect our decisions. We also will consider the resources we have available to use in reaching our goals. Then we will look at the decision-making process.

HOW NEEDS BECOME GOALS

Our basic needs, the things we cannot do without, are common to us all. The basic things we all need are much the same regardless of where we live or what the color of our skin is. Several different lists of needs have been constructed. One of the most widely used lists was developed by the psychologist Abraham Maslow. The list that follows is adapted from Maslow's.[1]

1. Biological needs—food, drink, activity, and rest.
2. Security needs—safety from physical harm, freedom from anxiety, and economic security.
3. Affection needs—the giving and receiving of love, acceptance by others, and a feeling of belonging.
4. Self-esteem needs—feelings of self-worth growing out of confidence in one's abilities and an awareness of social acceptance by others.
5. Self-realization needs—creative self-expression through one's personal and social achievements, satisfying one's curiosity, and understanding the world and one's surroundings.

The list has been referred to as a "hierarchy of needs" because the needs at the top of the list are most pressing. Until the basic needs at the top of the list are satisfied to some minimum degree, an individual has little interest in trying to satisfy other needs such as the need for sports achievement or artistic accomplishment. Once, however, the basic needs at the top of the list are met, energies are released, and individuals are able to seek achievement and accomplishment in school work, on the job, in hobbies, and in recreational activities.

Values—their role in shaping goals

Although basic needs are the same throughout the world, the ways people seek to satisfy these needs are not. People everywhere experience thirst, but the way they seek to satisfy it differs among social and cultural settings. The young American who is thirsty is likely to head for the refrigerator for a soft drink. The young South Sea Islander, on the other hand, may instead look for a coconut palm so he can get some coconut milk to drink. While both experience the same basic need, each has learned to satisfy this need in a way that is characteristic of his society. Each experiences the same need, but the things used to satisfy thirst are different. Goals may be specific objectives or things we want, like a new sweater, a car, or a vacation trip to San Francisco. They can also be intangible objectives such as graduating from technical school or college, getting to be friends with a particular person, or planning to get married.

---

[1] *New Knowledge in Human Values,* Harper & Row, Publishers, Incorporated, New York, 1959.

Values—our own and other's

What we learn from the society in which we live goes far beyond just learning what to drink when we are thirsty. We learn a whole set of ideas about what is good, desirable, and important. Philosophers have labeled these ideas about what is good, desirable, and important *values*. These ideas or values can apply both to objects and to people's behavior. They guide everyday behavior and decisions, and they also guide us when we are in new and unfamiliar situations.

We can begin to get some idea about people's values when we ask them about the things they think are important or desirable. Suppose, for example, that we asked a group of high school students to list what was most important for them. Some might emphasize the importance of continuing their education, while others might talk of marriage and having their own family. Some probably would emphasize becoming financially independent of their parents. A few might talk about having new experiences and seeing the world. Because each of us has a unique background and set of experiences, we have different opinions about what is important. Some of these differences can be seen in the lists of values below. Which list reflects your own feelings? What changes would you make to better represent your own ideas?

LISTS OF THE THINGS DIFFERENT PEOPLE THINK ARE IMPORTANT		
Love	Happiness	Friendship and social activity
Health	Health	Knowledge
Comfort	Rest	Health
Achievement	Recreation	Money
Knowledge	Association with family	Personal appearance
Beauty	and friends	Family life
Religion		Recreation
Recreation		Success
Personal achieve-	Achievement	Living in harmony with nature
ment	Activity and work	and the environment
Security	Service to others	Acceptance of others and
Influence with	Comfort	tolerance of their ideas
others	Freedom and inde-	Humanitarian service
Independence	pendence	Development of one's abilities
Service to others	Acceptance by others	and potential
New experiences	Individuality	Openness to new experiences
Family life	Knowledge	Freedom to develop one's own
Religion	Patriotism	rules and way of life
Wealth		
Skill and competence		
Orderliness		

We can see that many different lists of values are possible. Some may be long and detailed, others short and more general. Since values are abstract ideas which cannot be seen or observed directly, we have little basis for saying how long or short anyone's list should be.

We pointed out earlier that we learn our values from the society in which we live. But just exactly how do we learn them? When we are young, our parents are the people with whom we have the most contact and whom we admire most. We learn our values from them, along with most of our other ideas. As we grow older and enter school, teachers and religious leaders also begin to influence our thinking. As getting along with our classmates becomes more important, friends' and admired schoolmates' ideas influence us greatly. As time goes on, we begin to develop ideas based on our own experiences. We may also be influenced by the media, by the books we read, and by things we see on television.

Goals—the basis for action

Values guide us in the choice of our *goals,* our special objectives and the things we want. Goals, such as saving to buy a car, become a basis for everyday actions and decisions, such as trying to spend less on snacks and clothes. They can also guide us into whole new courses of action; for example, an after-school job to help us build our savings.

In thinking about goals, it is important to recognize that most goals are not ends in themselves. They are instead *instrumental goals,* or steps toward a more important goal. Take the case of Jim Summers, who helped several of his neighbors with odd jobs last winter. Jim was not interested in the money he earned as an end in itself. He wanted it so that he could go on a class trip to Washington, D.C. While one of the main purposes of the trip was educational, Jim's chief interest in going was to be with his girl. Both the money he earned and going on the trip were instrumental goals for Jim.

Sometimes we find that our goals conflict. For example, we may want to save money for college but also want to have money to go to the movies with our friends. Many conflicts in goals grow out of conflicts in our basic values. In this case the problem might be labeled as a conflict between the value of achievement and the value of association with family and friends. When goals and values conflict, we must seek a balance between them that satisfies us. Life without a chance to be with friends is not very satisfying. We have to be sure, however, that we do not give too much emphasis to short-range goals and sacrifice such long-range goals as education that we also want.

Courtesy University of Detroit

A college education is an instrumental goal for many people. It is a step toward a more important goal, such as entering a profession or starting a business.

Sometimes, instead of finding that our values conflict, we may find that several values support the same goal. For instance, the family that wants to buy their first home may conclude that this goal will contribute not only to family life as a value but also to financial security.

We must be careful about trying to use people's goals or their actions to determine what their basic values are. A number of different values may underlie the same goal or action. One family may buy a new house because they want to move to a safer neighborhood. Their next-door neighbors may be more interested in demonstrating their recent financial success. The people across the street, in turn, may have bought their house in hopes of making new friends. The values underlying these three house purchases are all very different even though the behavior we observe is the same.

RESOURCES FOR PURSUING OUR GOALS

Because our resources are limited, it is important to be aware of them all and of the amount of each that we have available. Individual and family resources sometimes are divided into two broad categories, physical resources or physical capital and human resources or human capital. The *physical resources* tend to be more tangible things that we can touch or measure easily, such as a car or a pay check. Physical resources include such things as our incomes, our ability to get credit, our savings, our possessions, and the community facilities we have available to us. *Human resources* are less tangible and are not so easy to measure or evaluate. For this reason, consumers often forget to include them when thinking about their resources. In this category we would include our knowledge and abilities and time and energy.

Using physical resources

The resource we are likely to think of first is our *income,* the money we get from a job, or perhaps from an allowance. For most families, the major part of income comes from the earnings of family members. Many families also receive investment income from savings accounts and stock holdings. Some families depend, at least in part, on social security, welfare benefits, and disability payments distributed by government agencies. These payments are sometimes referred to as *transfer payments,* since they are paid on the basis of need rather than for work or services.

Another important physical resource that can be used in reaching one's consumer goals is *credit*—the ability to borrow against one's future income. By using credit we are able to obtain the use of goods and services and pay for them as we use them. The ability to borrow against future income helps families acquire many things that make their life more pleasant—houses, cars, appliances, and furniture. Although credit is an important resource and a useful one, like most tools it can be dangerous when it is misused or handled carelessly. Every year, thousands of families get into financial difficulty because they have bought on credit beyond their ability to repay.

Savings also can be an important resource in moving toward our goals. *Savings* can provide a fund to meet the expense of unforeseen emergencies such as sickness or to make possible a more specific goal, such as the purchase of a car.

The things we already have, our *possessions,* are also important physical resources because, if they were well chosen, they provide us with a continuing flow of service or satisfaction. This category is a broad one and includes household equipment such as furniture and appliances, other durable goods such as automobiles, the house a family buys, hobby equipment, and the tools needed for making automobile and household repairs.

Another useful physical resource, one that we sometimes forget, is *community facilities*. The services and facilities provided by a community play an important role in helping the members of the community reach their goals. Schools play a key role in helping families reach educational goals. Libraries provide assistance not only toward educational goals but also toward recreational and occupational goals. Swimming pools, parks, and recreation facilities make it easier for community residents to realize their recreational goals. Other services are important, too. Police and fire departments contribute to security goals. What other facilities and services do you have in your community that you would classify as physical resources?

Using human resources

Our human resources include all the things we know and can do, our *knowledge* and *abilities*. Our skills at painting a bedroom, changing a tire, and buying a sweater all help us make the best life for ourselves that we can. Skills and knowledge that help us get a job and advance in it are also important resources. It is these resources and our use of them that provide us with income.

Even if we have knowledge and abilities, we need *time* and *energy* to exercise them. For this reason time and energy have to be included in the list of human resources. Like our other resources, time and energy are limited, too. Time and energy committed to the school yearbook or cheering squad are not available for an after-school job.

Our human resources, or human capital, have not always been fully recognized as important assets. Years ago young people were usually advised to be thrifty and save their money for a "rainy day." This advice was given because savings were regarded as a vital resource and source of security. Nowadays young people are more likely to be advised to develop their job skills and abilities to the fullest extent possible. This course of action often is urged even though it means going into debt for the extra schooling needed. This advice grows out of the idea that knowledge and abilities are the most important resources one can have and can provide a special type of security—the ability to earn a living, make wise decisions, and adjust to economic and social changes.

Substituting one resource for another

Although all the resources that we have are limited in supply, they fortunately have another characteristic—to a certain extent one can be substituted for another. When you are hired as a baby sitter it may

A consumer can substitute his knowledge and abilities for the money that would be required to buy new home furnishings.

Courtesy Family Weekly

seem that all you are doing is taking care of children. In another sense, however, you are substituting one of your resources, your time, for another, money. By giving up some of your spare time you are able to increase the amount of money you have. The mother who hires you is also making a substitution: she is giving up money for time.

The use of time and skill to earn money is one kind of substitution of one resource for another. Another type of substitution is the use of one's spare time to make things or do things you otherwise would have to pay for. An example is a teen-ager using some free time to knit a new sweater in order to save part of the cost of buying one. Another example is a student learning how to do simple plumbing repairs so that his family can avoid the cost of hiring a plumber. In both cases, *home production* of goods and services is going on. These activities can make an important contribution to the way a family lives, since the money saved is freed for use for other wants and goals.

MAKING CHOICES

Even after we have all our resources clearly in mind, we still need to decide how to allocate them to best achieve our goals. Making choices always has been difficult and probably is more difficult today than it used to be. The whole range of products and services from which we can choose is wider today, and the products and services themselves are more complicated. Another factor that makes the choice process more complex is the continued improvement in our understanding of the consequences of our decisions. As scientific knowledge increases, we know more and more about the possible outcomes of our choices and have to bear them in mind as we choose. When little was known about the effect of diet on health, people did not need to concern themselves about vitamins and calories. Nowadays, we must take good nutrition into account along with our food preferences when we decide what to eat.

The decision-making process

The steps in making a choice are much the same regardless of whether the decision is a big one or a small one. The process of purchasing a new notebook will include the same steps involved in purchasing a car. The amount of time and effort devoted to the process of purchasing a car may be far greater, but the process itself will be much the same. The steps in this process include identifying our goal, identifying the alternatives, gathering information, evaluating the alternatives, and making a choice.

IDENTIFYING OUR GOAL   In making choices, we first need to have our goal clearly in mind. We need to think broadly about it. Consumers often think about their needs in terms of a particular product. If they thought about the problem more broadly they would realize that what they need is not a particular product, such as an alarm clock. What they need, instead, is the service that an alarm clock provides— waking them up in the morning.

IDENTIFYING THE ALTERNATIVES   When we set out to identify possible alternatives, most of us already have some information with which to begin. Both our previous experiences and what we have learned from others provide us with useful information about alternatives. Because of what we already know, we usually begin to think of alternatives at once. For example, we would know that key-wound alarm clocks, electric alarm clocks, and clock radios all would provide the service of waking us up.

GATHERING INFORMATION   Once we have some alternatives in mind that seem workable, we can begin to gather information about them. Often, in the course of gathering information, we find new alternatives we had not known about before. These new alternatives can be added to our original list. We may also drop other alternatives we had been considering. We might find, for example, that clock radios cost more than we want to spend and decide that electric alarm clocks are more convenient and reliable than hand-wound ones. For this reason, we might concentrate on collecting information about different brands of electric alarm clocks.

Brand	Features	Price
A	Repeat alarm, lighted dial, brown case	$8.95
B	Repeat alarm, plain dial, white case	$5.95
C	Luminous dial, white case	$3.95

EVALUATING THE ALTERNATIVES   After narrowing the alternatives down to electric alarm clocks we can make an evaluation of our alternatives more easily. In making an evaluation of an alternative, we need to think through its consequences. We might, for example, decide that the repeat feature is very important because we have trouble getting out of bed in the morning and often fall back to sleep. Since Brand C does not provide this feature, we might rank it third in the list of alternatives. We might also decide that a luminous dial is not especially important since we seldom look at our clock during the night. We might also decide that we prefer Brand B's white case to Brand A's brown one, since it would look better in our bedroom. Overall, our ranking of the three brands would be as follows:

Brand A	Second preference
Brand B	First preference
Brand C	Third preference

MAKING A CHOICE   Once we have our preferences clearly in mind we are in a position to make a choice among the three alternatives. In making our decision, we must take both price and our preferences into consideration. The list we have developed would look like this:

Brand A	Second preference	$8.95
Brand B	First preference	$5.95
Brand C	Third preference	$3.95

After reviewing the list, we can see that it is possible to eliminate Brand A from consideration. It is more expensive than Brand B and less preferred. The real choice is between Brand B and Brand C. In making this choice, we must decide whether we prefer Brand B or Brand C plus $2 in savings.

After we settle on an alternative, we still need to put our decision into action. Delays in carrying out decisions can result in lost opportunities or worsen our original problem.

Types of decisions

Certain kinds of choices, such as buying one brand of toothpaste instead of another, come up over and over again. Once we have found a brand that produces satisfactory results we are likely to begin skipping over some steps in the process of choosing a brand of toothpaste. Instead of considering all the possible alternatives each time we buy, we recall that we have been satisfied with the brand we have been using and buy it again. Over time, if our experiences continue to be satisfactory, we are likely to devote less and less effort to the decision as it becomes more and more a matter of habit. In many situations we rely on habit, and, in general, there is nothing wrong with this. Being guided by habit can save decision-making time and energy. There is no reason why we need to give lengthy consideration every day to whether or not we are going to put butter on our breakfast toast. We need, however, to give some thought to our buying habits from time to time to be certain that they are good ones. We may, for example, have gotten into the habit of buying our toothpaste and toiletries at a particular store, forgetting or not realizing that the store down the street sells the same items at lower prices. When we rely on habit we may save on decision-making effort, but we may also be paying higher prices.

In contrast to the problems we resolve by habit, there are certain other kinds of problems that require careful deliberation. These problems require full consideration from beginning to end, and they arise less frequently than those we can resolve by habit. Decisions that require deliberation usually involve some kind of major new commitment and often are part of major changes in the way we live. They may be the result of a move to a new town, a pay raise, an accident, or the unexpected breakdown of household equipment. In all these cases, new action to meet the problem is essential, and this action requires careful consideration. Consumers need to recognize that some decisions are more important than others, and they should give important problems the attention they deserve. Decisions that require deliberation, such as the choice of a job or the decision to buy an expensive new car, may prove to be major turning points in life, and a bad decision may have unpleasant consequences for years to come.

Some decisions, especially major decisions, often involve many smaller decisions. For example, the purchase of a new car involves not only the decision about whether or not to buy but also decisions about equipment, accessories, and colors. In this case, the decision about buying the car could be regarded as the central decision, while the related, smaller decisions can be thought of as satellite decisions. Central decisions are ones that are closely related to important goals and have far-reaching consequences. While satellite decisions are smaller, they also deserve careful thought since the care with which they are made influences how well the central decisions turn out. The decision about what make car we will buy and the equipment we want may have a good deal to do with how satisfied we are with the car.

In addition to making the central decision about whether to buy a car, consumers must make smaller, satellite decisions about accessories and colors.

Courtesy General Motors Acceptance Corp.

Dr. Beatrice Paolucci of Michigan State University has identified another pattern of decision making: the chain.[2] *Chain decisions* consist of a sequence of decisions, with each decision in the chain influencing the decision that comes after it. For example, the decision of a man who has just bought a new suit and is picking out a shirt to go with it will be influenced by the color of the suit he has chosen. His choice of a tie, in turn, will be influenced by the shirt he chooses.

The aim of good decision making is to achieve our own goals, not copy someone else's idea of what our goals should be. Our choices are wise to the extent that they satisfy us and do not create burdens on others.

Checking your reading

1. Into what five categories can our basic needs be classified?
2. What is meant by saying that this list of needs is a "hierarchy of needs"?
3. If people everywhere have the same basic needs, why do their goals, the things they want in order to satisfy these needs, differ so much?
4. What are values?
5. Where do people learn the values they have?
6. What is meant by saying that for many people getting an education is an instrumental goal?
7. Why do our goals sometimes conflict? Is this bad?
8. What are the two general categories of resources? What things are included in each category?
9. Why can home production of goods and services be an important contribution to family welfare?
10. What are the five main steps in making a decision?
11. What are the kinds of decisions that we handle by habit?
12. Is it always a mistake to be guided by habit in making a decision?
13. How do decisions that require deliberation differ from decisions that we handle by habit?
14. What are central decisions? What are satellite decisions? How are they related to each other?
15. What term is used to refer to a sequence of decisions in which each decision influences the one that comes after it?

[2] "Managerial Decision Patterns," *Forum,* J. C. Penny Co., Fall-Winter, 1968, p. 15.

Consumer problems and projects

1.   Collect newspaper and magazine advertisements that illustrate each of the needs in Maslow's hierarchy of needs.

2.   Review the lists of different people's values on page 21, and make up a list that represents the things you think are important.

3.   Suppose you unexpectedly won $50 in a contest. How would you spend it? What do you think this shows about your values?

4.   What do you regard as your major goal right now?

    a. What resources will you need in order to reach this goal?

    b. What resources do you now have available?

    c. How do you plan to get the additional resources you will need? What substitutions can you make between the resources you have and those you need?

5.   Several kinds of substitutions of one resource for another were mentioned in this chapter. In each of the following cases what resource or resources are used (or given up)? Which ones are gained?

    a. Tom takes money out of his savings account and buys a motorcycle.

    b. Instead of buying a book on auto racing that he wants to read, Jack borrows it from the public library.

    c. Carol opens a charge account and buys a new fall jacket on credit.

    d. Jane helps repaint a friend's bedroom, and in return the friend teaches her how to knit.

6.   The kinds of decisions that we handle by habit and the decisions that require deliberation differ in several ways. What kinds of differences do you see between the following examples of a habitual decision and a decision that requires deliberation?

    Habitual: Susan has just bought another can of her favorite hair spray for $1.47. She expects it to last for four weeks.

    Deliberation: John has just bought a new car and hopes he has made the right decision. He has agreed to pay for it in 36 monthly installments of $95 each.

7.   How does the amount of resources you have affect the range of alternatives you can consider when making a decision?

8.   Do you think that protecting the beauty of the environment is likely to be an important public goal in a poor country where most of the population lacks food? Can you use Maslow's hierarchy of needs in developing your answer?

Chapter 3

Financial planning and budgeting

Consider three families, each made up of a father, a mother, and two children. The three families are remarkably similar in many ways: their ages are comparable, the educational attainment of the parents is about equal, their incomes are almost identical, and they live in the same neighborhood. The Able family, the Baker family, and the Cruz family have had dissimilar experiences, however, in handling family finances.

■ The Ables never seem to be able to stretch the monthly family income long enough to last until the next payroll check arrives. As a result, Mr. Able has had to borrow money from a bank twice during the past two years so that certain bills could be paid on time. This year, the Able family is facing the prospect of forgoing a vacation trip because the little money they have on hand should be used to help pay a few large bills, one of which is the cost of last year's vacation.

If we examined the way in which the Able family has been handling its financial affairs (like viewing a television replay of the family's financial actions during the past year or two), we would learn that no attempt has been made to plan the use of income. No person in the family knows how much money has been spent on food, clothing, transportation, or entertainment. Mr. Able simply deposits most of his monthly payroll check in a checking account, and when items such as food or clothing are needed, he or Mrs. Able writes a check.

The Able family has never prepared a budget to plan spending for the future. When the family "needs" some new item, it is simply bought. For example, three months ago, the Ables bought a new television set because, as the television repairman said, the old set was finally worn out. Because they had only a few dollars in their checking account at the time, they bought the new television set on an installment plan arranged by the dealer.

The Able family has not saved money in any systematic way. All the family income is needed for fixed expenses (such as mortgage payments, insurance premiums, taxes, utility bills, and installment payments for various purchases) and for a seemingly endless list of things, such as groceries, gasoline, entertainment, and clothing. As indicated earlier, the family income does not stretch far enough.

■ The Baker family got together one day several months ago and discussed the fact that despite their reasonably good income, they did not seem to be doing well financially. They had trouble making ends meet, and they decided that the problem was lack of careful financial planning. Mrs. Baker volunteered to go to the library and check out books on family recordkeeping and budgeting. Among the materials Mrs. Baker discovered in the library were charts showing how much families with different incomes spend on various categories of expenses such as housing, food, transportation, clothing, and entertainment. The Baker family then made up a detailed list of expenses, covering every item they could think of, and assigned to each item the amount of money they would spend on it each month.

As the Bakers spent money, they recorded the purpose and the amount in a ledger, no matter how small the amount (even 10 or 15 cents for coffee). Mr. Baker spent time every three or four days going through the book and adding the amounts spent on the various expense categories. He found, first, that the family was spending too much on some of the categories, and long before the month ended they often had exceeded the amounts allowed. The decree was issued that no more was to be spent on certain items, but such decrees were met with cries of anguish by certain family members. Second, he discovered that some family members (possibly including himself) were forgetting to record the amounts spent on some items. The system was not working well, so for the following month a change in the plan was instituted.

For the second month, an envelope was used for each category. The amount of cash needed for a week's expenditures would be placed in each envelope. When money was needed, it could be removed from the appropriate envelope. Several minor problems were encountered. For example, when the proper change was not available in an envelope, some quick shuffling of money in other envelopes was necessary. Often the money available for the week was not enough, and money had to be borrowed from one or more of the other envelopes. When money was borrowed in this way, IOU notes were placed in the envelopes from which the money was taken. In many cases the amounts placed in the envelopes were not adequate.

Mr. and Mrs. Baker attempted almost daily to shuffle money from one envelope to another to settle the IOUs, and as the weeks went by they felt harassed and uncomfortable; tempers often flared. Following an agonizing two-hour session of budget work one evening, Mr. Baker emptied the cash from all the envelopes and then threw the envelopes into the fireplace. He decided that budgeting was a diabolical scheme developed to take the joy out of living.

■ The third family, the Cruzes, always seem to have enough money to take advantage of cash sales for big-ticket or expensive items. For example, just a week or two before the Able family bought a new television set, a discount store, selling for cash, advertized a sizeable discount on a name-brand television set at their warehouse. The Cruz family had been watching for a bargain such as this because they wanted to replace their old set. So the Cruz family paid cash for a new set.

The Cruzes are able to save money systematically for several different purposes. They successfully match their expenditures with their income. When cash is needed for emergencies, they have the money available. Next month, the Cruz family is taking a one-week camping vacation—they have been planning the trip for a long time now, and they have the money for the trip in a savings account in their bank.

Although the family incomes in these three cases are almost identical, only the Cruz family seems to be experiencing the peace of mind that results from successful matching of outgoes with income. Why the difference? What do the Cruzes do that makes it possible for them to save money so they can take advantage of cash sales for big-ticket items such as television sets? How do they control their income so well? On the other hand, what have the Ables and Bakers done wrong?

The Ables have no plan for spending their money, and without some careful planning, as you will see later in this chapter, most of us cannot reach the goals that we consider important. Our money will be frittered

Courtesy Starcraft Co.

Planning family finances can mean the difference between being able to afford a vacation each year and having to borrow money to meet regular expenses.

away on things that we would not have chosen had we taken the time to consider the alternatives. The Bakers made a valiant attempt to plan their family finances, but they became bogged down with plans that were too elaborate and detailed—plans that took the fun out of life, in other words. Also, the Bakers made the common mistake of thinking that their spending habits had to be patterned too precisely after "average" budget figures. The Cruz family had examined their interests and their goals in life. They knew what they wanted before they started financial planning. Then, keeping their records as simple as possible, they let their budget plan help them spend their money for the things that bring them the most satisfaction.

WHAT A BUDGET CAN DO FOR YOU

The reason budgeting is necessary, of course, is that most of us must live on fixed incomes. We never have enough money to do all the things we would like to do and to buy all the things we would like to buy. So we must learn to apportion our funds in order to meet our needs and achieve our goals. Perhaps you have already learned that you must do some careful planning if you are to have enough money left for things that really count for you.

Suppose that within a year or two you attend a college in another city and that you have a steady income of $200 a month from an allowance and a part-time job. This is the amount you know you can count on receiving—no more, no less—each month of the school year.

With this monthly income, you know that you must pay for your room and board, buy your clothing, books, and other school supplies, and reserve some money "just for spending." How can you be sure that your $200 will last you through each month? Obviously, if you do not have some scheme for apportioning your income, the last few days of each month are going to be lean indeed.

During your first month in college, for example, you spot a sweater in your school colors that you would like to own. While looking at the sweater you also see an attractive college pennant that would look nice in your room. Before you know it, you have spent $20 in the campus store. Later that day, some friends ask you to go out with them to dinner and a movie. This night out costs you another $8. Later in the month when you want to attend an important football game, you do not have enough money to do so. Yet this is the one big event you had looked forward to. You realize then that you should have had a plan that would have forced you to spend your monthly income more wisely. Such a plan is called a budget.

Budgeting is essentially the same for a family as for an individual. The difference lies in the things budgeted for. The family is a basic economic unit, and its spending is planned in terms of the family group as a whole. The Cruz family plans each month's expenditures so that they will not find themselves short of money for things they have decided are important or essential.

After considering some basic principles of financial planning for individuals and families, we will examine in some detail the way in which the Cruz family keeps its records and maintains its budget.

PLANNING PRINCIPLES

Neither an individual nor a family will likely earn enough to satisfy all desires. As our incomes increase, so do our wants.

The young man who gets a substantial salary increase suddenly decides that he can join the golf club or buy a new house or a fancier car or invest in more expensive clothing. When he makes one of these decisions, he has the same financial problem he had before the salary increase. He must still plan his spending carefully—perhaps even more carefully than before.

The purpose of planning a budget is to help you decide what to do with your money. The decisions you make when you spend your money determine your whole way of life. These decisions, if made wisely, can make your dreams and ambitions realities. On the other hand, if they are made unwisely, they can lead you even further away from your goals.

Business firms and government agencies prepare budgets to serve as guides for expenditures. Churches, clubs, and other organizations also make budgets to control their financial transactions. Millions of our most competent individuals regularly make budgets. So if you decide to make a budget, you will be in good company.

An individual's budget or a family's budget may not look much like the budget prepared by General Motors, yet the two are basically the same. No matter who prepares a budget, three important steps are necessary: (1) establishing goals, (2) estimating income, and (3) planning the use of income. The latter two steps, estimating income and planning its use, cover a set period of time, usually a month or a year.

A *budget,* then, is a plan for allocating income during a set period based on an estimate of the funds available.

To determine whether to budget by the week or by the month, you should use as a guide the period covered by your regular allowance, wage, or salary.

Establishing goals

To begin with, decide what goals you wish to reach. Working out the details of a budget makes sense when you know precisely what to expect from your work. Stated differently, you are budgeting for a purpose. In the case of family budgets, setting a goal should be a group project, with every member old enough to participate doing so. If all suggestions are considered, it is more likely that everyone will be satisfied with the results. The most important goals should, of course, be given priority. Income, both present income and future estimates, should be considered carefully so that goals will be realistic.

Many individuals or families find it easiest to begin recording goals by thinking first of long-range goals—those they hope to achieve in 15, 20, or 25 years. Then goals for the next 5 or 10 years can be decided upon. Finally, short-term goals—goals for the coming year and the next five years—are planned.

Long-term goals may include a debt-free home. They may include a vacation cottage on a lake or a houseboat. A long-range goal may also include a sum of money for retirement days.

Intermediate goals may include a vacation trip to Europe, or education for the children, or a new house in another neighborhood.

Immediate goals for the coming year might include the purchase of a home movie camera or a short vacation trip. Immediate goals might simply be to reduce or pay off certain debts.

Establishing goals is an important first step in the budgeting process, and because individual and family goals change from time to time, they should be reviewed periodically. No special form is needed for recording goals. Simply writing out the goals under such headings as these will suffice:

- Goals—long-range (15 years and longer)
- Goals—intermediate (5 to 15 years)
- Goals—short-range (coming year to 5 years)

Estimating income

The next step to follow in preparing a budget is to estimate all income expected during the period covered by the budget. Most people can be fairly certain of what their income will be during any given period. Even a person who works irregularly can, from his past experience, do a fairly good job of estimating future income.

For families, the main source of income is ordinarily salary or wages. An employer withholds from salary or wages income tax and FICA (social security) taxes and, often, insurance and other deductions. It is much simpler for budgeting purposes to consider only the net wages, or take-home pay, that the employee receives after deductions. Then, when listing expenditures, only those items that are spent out of take-home pay are recorded.

In estimating income, it is necessary to include everything that will be received—dividends, interest, bonuses, and any other sources of income. Probably the best way to estimate miscellaneous sources of income is to assume that they will be the same as in the past year. It is best to be conservative in an estimate. If you are not sure that you will get an extra $100 bonus at the end of the year, do not include it. If you do get the bonus, you can easily take it into account; but if you include the $100 and then fail to get it, your whole budget will fall apart.

Planning the use of income

Most of the money spent by families goes for fixed, committed expenses that are relatively out of their direct control (for example, mortgage payments set by a bank). The amount of money remaining after these fixed, committed expenses are allowed for can be used for savings and for variable living expenses.

To summarize, individuals and families use their incomes for these three purposes: (1) fixed, committed expenses; (2) savings; and (3) variable living expenses.

FIXED, COMMITTED EXPENSES   Much of our incomes go for expenses that are relatively large and that remain the same size, or about the same size, month after month. Included in this category are such things as rent or mortgage payments, insurance premiums, utility bills, installment payments, and taxes. Once these items exist in our budgets, we are committed to make the payments. When a color television set is purchased on an installment plan, the monthly payment represents a large expense item added to the budget for several months. Once the debt is incurred, it must be paid unless the item can be sold. Careful planning of financial resources may force us in the future to examine carefully whether we should make these large purchases.

When planning the use of income, then, these committed expenses must be considered. If you do not prepare for them, they can cause a great deal of hardship when payments are due.

The allowances for large, committed expenses should be spread out so that each monthly allotment of income includes a share of them. For example, if a $300 life insurance premium is due twice a year, the family should put aside $50 every month to meet these semiannual premium payments. By doing this the family will not run the risk of spending the money for the insurance premiums on a desired but unnecessary item.

If you were a college student with a monthly allowance or income, you should, for example, put aside a certain amount of money for the textbooks that you would have to buy at the beginning of each semester. If you estimated that twice a year you would have to spend $45 for textbooks, then you would put aside $9 a month during each of the ten months you were in school.

SAVINGS   Any person who desires security and independence must save systematically, but no reasonable person advocates saving simply for the purpose of piling up money. We save money so that we can take advantage of sales. We save money so that we can pay cash and avoid paying interest charges on installment plans. We save money for vacations, for travel, for clothes, for gifts, for education, and for emergencies. The list is endless, just as our wants are endless.

After planning for fixed, committed expenses, we should plan a savings program. For most people, the first fund to be established is an emergency fund. The chief purpose of this fund is to provide for the unexpected expenses that always arise but cannot be anticipated. Some financial counselors recommend that a family should maintain an emergency fund the equivalent of two months' income.

VARIABLE LIVING EXPENSES After deducting from his net income money for fixed, committed expenses and an amount for savings, the budget planner has remaining an amount that can be allocated for variable living expenses, such as food, clothing, transportation, gifts, household operation expenses, and personal allowances. These expenses must be covered, but because no advance commitment has been made for them, it is possible to restrict expenditures here—to tighten one's belt, so to speak.

Therefore, the immediate job of managing income and expenditures becomes one of watching closely the money available for variable living expenses. It is these uncommitted dollars that the individual or the family must watch carefully and apportion wisely. On the other hand, the fact that possibly only a third of one's income is available for such apportioning should impress upon consumers the importance of planning carefully and wisely the large expenditures in the area of fixed, committed expenses.[1]

THE CRUZ FAMILY BUDGET

The Cruz family wanted a budget to do three things: (1) tell them how much money they would receive each month from various sources; (2) enable them to provide first for the necessities of life, then for the comforts of life, and then—whenever possible—for the luxuries of life; and (3) give them a plan for saving money.

In order to plan such a budget, the Cruzes devised three different record forms: one form to estimate income for a year; a second form to estimate the family's variable living expenses for about three months; and a third form to record fixed, committed expenses and proposed savings for a year.

Estimating income

Form I on page 43 is the one that the Cruz family devised to show their estimated income for a year.

Mr. Cruz's take-home pay for his job as a technical engineer at a

---

[1] According to the National Industrial Conference Board, on a national average, the consumer has available to him for savings and for uncommitted spending just 34.7 cents out of each dollar of income.

television station is $965 a month, or $11,580 a year. In addition to his salary, Mr. Cruz can count on a bonus of $200 at the end of the year. He repairs radio and television sets in his basement workshop, and this work brings in about $40 every month, except August, when he does not accept any repair jobs. Mrs. Cruz receives $25 every month, except August, for directing a church choir. Finally, Mr. Cruz owns a bond that pays $60 interest twice a year. Notice that the monthly income varies from $965 in August to $1,290 in December. The total annual income is $12,615. Thus, the average monthly income is $12,615 divided by 12, or $1,051.25.

Estimating variable living expenses

Form II on page 43 is the one that the Cruz family devised to show their variable living expenses.

From past experience, the Cruz family knows that monthly food costs average about $190. Similarly, they know that expenses for the other items listed (car expense, personal allowances, clothing, and the like) can be estimated at certain amounts. The estimates are filled in for three months in advance; then, as each month's expenses are recorded in the "Spent" spaces, estimates for an additional month are added. For example, the month of February has just passed, and the amounts spent have been recorded. At this time, estimates are recorded for May. At any time, the estimates for any of the items can be changed.

Recording fixed, committed expenses and proposed savings

Form III on page 45 is the one that the Cruz family devised to show their fixed, committed expenses and proposed savings.

The Cruzes make semiannual premium payments on three different life insurance policies; premium payments are due in February, April, May, August, October, and November. The car insurance premium is due in March and September, and the license plates must be renewed in March. Notice that the expenses are recorded in the months in which they must be paid; then the total is entered in the Yearly Total column.

Several years ago, the Cruz family borrowed money from a savings and loan association to purchase the house in which they live. Each month a payment of $175 is made to the savings and loan association. Part of the $175 is used to reduce the amount owed, part of it is interest on the loan, and part of it is used to purchase insurance on the home.

About a year ago, the family bought a new car, and to help finance this purchase, Mr. Cruz borrowed money from the First National Bank. The monthly payment on this debt is $72.

FORM I

Income

Source	Jan.	Feb.	Mar.	Apr.	May	June	July	Aug.	Sept.	Oct.	Nov.	Dec.	Yearly Total
Take-Home Pay Bruce	965.-	965.-	965.-	965.-	965.-	965.-	965.-	965.-	965.-	965.-	965.-	965.-	11,580.-
												200.-	200.-
Interest						60.-						60.-	122.-
TV & Radio Repair	40.-	40.-	40.-	40.-	40.-	40.-	40.-		40.-	40.-	40.-	40.-	440.-
Chair Income	25.-	25.-	25.-	25.-	25.-	25.-	25.-		25.-	25.-	25.-	25.-	275.-
Totals	1030.-	1030.-	1030.-	1030.-	1030.-	1090.-	1030.-	965.-	1030.-	1030.-	1030.-	1290.-	12,615.-

FORM II

Variable Living Expenses

Items	Jan.	Feb.	Mar.	Apr.	May	June	July	Aug.	Sept.	Oct.	Nov.	Dec.
Food	190.-	190.-	190.-	190.-	190.-							
Spent	171.-	188.-										
Car Expense	40.-	40.-	40.-	40.-	40.-							
Spent	48.-	55.50										
Personal Allowance	65.-	65.-	65.-	65.-	65.-							
Spent	52.-	55.75										
Clothing	60.-	60.-	60.-	60.-	60.-							
Spent	125.-	0										
Entertainment	20.-	20.-	20.-	20.-	20.-							
Spent	12.50	22.-										
Appliances & Furniture	30.-	30.-	30.-	30.-	30.-							
Spent	0	0										
Bridge & Grounds	12.-	12.-	12.-	12.-	12.-							
Spent	0	0										
Gifts & Contrib.	25.-	25.-	25.-	25.-	25.-							
Spent	25.-	14.75										
Books & Magazines	8.-	8.-	8.-	8.-	8.-							
Spent	6.-	6.-										

As part of their regular, systematic savings program, the Cruzes are now investing $60 each month in a mutual fund (Chapter 17 discusses mutual funds and other means of investing). In addition, Mr. Cruz contributes to a retirement fund through his employer; his contribution is withheld each month from his salary check, so it does not have to be recorded on the budget sheets. Through July of the current year, the family will add $30 a month to their vacation fund. Beginning in August (the month during which they will take their vacation), their monthly contribution to this vacation fund will be decreased to $10.

The Cruz family maintains an emergency fund of about $3,500. The fund is used for unexpected expenses and for seizing certain buying opportunities, such as the chance they had recently to buy a color television set at a bargain price. During the current year, they are contributing to the fund $10 a month through July and then increasing the contribution to $30 a month for the remaining months of the year. Both the vacation fund and the emergency fund are kept in a savings account in their bank.

Through a group plan at Mr. Cruz's place of business, the Cruz family has hospital, surgical, and major medical insurance coverage. Mr. Cruz's contribution to this health insurance coverage is deducted from his salary checks, so the budget forms do not have to show this expense. However, to cover health expenses not included in the group plan, including dental services, the Cruzes set aside $40 a month.

Notice that Form III has rows labeled "Spent" following the major categories. During January, utility bills totaled $70.50, and this amount has been recorded in the appropriate row in the January column. The payments in January to the savings and loan association ($175) and to the bank ($72) total $247, and this figure has been recorded in the "Spent" row under "Debts" in the January column.

The fixed expenses and savings for each month vary from $452 to $838. The yearly total of $7,186 divided by 12 is $598.83—the amount that must be set aside each month so that money will be available to make the payments when they become due.

Elasticity of the budget

The Cruz family budget has a feature that is quite important for all budgets—the feature of elasticity. If money for a certain item is not used one month, it will accumulate and can be used for the same purpose the following month. For example, Mrs. Cruz used only $171 for food during the month of January instead of the allotted $190

FORM III

Fixed, Committed Expenses and Proposed Savings

Items	Jan.	Feb.	Mar.	Apr.	May	June	July	Aug.	Sept.	Oct.	Nov.	Dec.	Yearly Total
Life Insurance													
Mr. Cruz		362.-						362.-					724.-
Mrs. Cruz					38.-						38.-		76.-
Family Policy				76.-						76.-			152.-
Spent	362.-	362.-											
Car Insurance			79.-						79.-				158.-
Spent													
Taxes													
Real Estate				310.-						310.-			620.-
Auto License			32.-										32.-
Spent													
Utilities	65.-	65.-	65.-	65.-	65.-	65.-	65.-	65.-	65.-	65.-	65.-	65.-	780.-
Spent	10.50	68.-											
Debts													
*Savings & Loan	175.-	175.-	175.-	175.-	175.-	175.-	175.-	175.-	175.-	175.-	175.-	175.-	2,100.-
1st Nat'l Bank	72.-	72.-	72.-	72.-	72.-	72.-	72.-	72.-	72.-	72.-	72.-	72.-	864.-
Spent	247.-	247.-											
Medical	40.-	40.-	40.-	40.-	40.-	40.-	40.-	40.-	40.-	40.-	40.-	40.-	480.-
Spent	14.-	8.-											
Savings													
243 Ins. Fund	60.-	60.-	60.-	60.-	60.-	60.-	60.-	60.-	60.-	60.-	60.-	60.-	720.-
Spent		60.-											
Vacation Fund	30.-	30.-	30.-	30.-	30.-	30.-	30.-	10.-	30.-	30.-	30.-	30.-	260.-
Spent	30.-	30.-											
Emergency Fund	10.-	10.-	10.-	10.-	10.-	10.-	10.-	30.-	10.-	10.-	10.-	10.-	220.-
Spent	10.-	10.-											
Totals	452.-	814.-	563.-	838.-	490.-	452.-	452.-	814.-	531.-	838.-	490.-	452.-	7,186.-

* Mortgage on Home

(perhaps she used many of the canned goods she had stored). The unused $19 could be added to the February allotment. The family may plan to cut food costs; but they realize they cannot do it merely by changing a figure in their budget.

If unusual circumstances cause the Cruzes to spend more on an item during a month than has been allocated for it, the difference can be deducted from the allotment for the same item for the following month. If it develops that the allotment for that particular item is too small in the following month, the family will have to increase the allotment for succeeding months and find some account from which they can deduct the difference.

COMPARING BUDGETS

The amount of money spent by an individual or a family depends on the money available to spend, or income. The way in which the available money is spent depends on how the individual or family wishes to live. For this reason, some families put a greater part of their income into vacations. Other families may wish to put more money into housing, or food, or cars. What is good consumption for one family is not necessarily good consumption for another family.

There is an advantage to be gained, on the other hand, from examining the amounts other families with similar incomes spend on various items. Such an examination may be a signal to the family that it should reexamine its goals and perhaps make some changes here and there. Several popular magazines regularly publish family budgeting articles showing what "average" families in different income brackets spend on food, housing, clothing, entertainment, and other items. The Bureau of Labor Statistics establishes guidelines for the use of families wishing to make comparisons. Information of this type is available in libraries and can provide valuable examples to which a family can relate its situation. But always, the family should form its budget according to its goals, and these goals may be quite different from the goals of the average family.

FAMILY FILES AND RECORDS

To do a realistic job of estimating expenses, a family must keep adequate records. One of the most valuable recordkeeping tools is the checkbook. When checks are written, certain information that will be useful later can be added to the check stub or register. For example, "clothing," or "food," or "gift" can be added to the stub or register to indicate for what purpose the money was used. At the end of the month, the amounts spent for various items can be determined by simply flipping through the check stubs or register and adding the figures. In addition, the canceled checks are both proof of payment and another record of expenses.

Other valuable record information can be added to the check stubs or register. When paying for a magazine subscription, for example, you can indicate the date on which the new subscription will expire. Such a record may be useful as you plan expenditures for such things in the future. Furthermore, if the publisher should bill you early, you have a record to refer to.

A family that is just beginning to budget its money may find value in keeping a rather detailed record of all expenses on a large columnar worksheet. Some families have found that good check-stub records plus placing notes of cash expenditures in a large envelope or shoe box is sufficient. Periodically, the notes and the check-stub information is summarized.

Families usually need two places to keep records: a home file and a safe-deposit box at a bank. If a regular file cabinet is too large for

Editorial Photocolor Archives, Inc.

Some families rent a safe-deposit box at a bank, because it is a safe place to keep valuable items such as marriage and birth certificates, wills, and insurance policies.

the home, accordian-type file jackets made from heavy paper are available in many stores. A safe-deposit box can be rented for a few dollars a year, and it is the safest place for valuable items.

Among the records that should be kept in a safe-deposit box are all legal records of birth, marriage, citizenship, death, and military service. One copy of wills should also be kept in a safe-deposit box (the original should be retained by your lawyer). Other items that should be kept in a safe-deposit box include a list of insurance policies and their numbers and an inventory of household items.

A file at home should be used for such things as canceled checks, insurance policies, automobile records, tax records, investment records, income records, debt records, guarantees, and instruction sheets.

Keeping accurate records for income tax purposes is essential. Thus, receipts, canceled checks, and other evidence to prove amounts claimed as deductions must be retained. Records that support an item of income or a deduction appearing on the income tax return must be kept until the statute of limitations for the return expires. The statute of limitations expires three years from the date the return was due or filed, or two years from the date the tax was paid, whichever occurs later. Despite the three-year statute of limitations, however, some property and stock records should be kept longer because of the possibility of deferring capital gains.

One easy and convenient way to keep papers so they can be stored and retrieved easily is to buy a supply of file folders. All records pertaining to the family car, for example, can be inserted in the folder marked "19--, Aardvark." A guarantee and pamphlets containing information pertaining to a television set owned by the family can be filed in a folder marked "Color TV, 19--."

Checking your reading

1. Explain why budgeting is necessary.
2. What is the purpose of planning a budget?
3. When preparing a budget, what three important steps should be followed?
4. Give a one-sentence definition of a budget.
5. Give several examples of long-term, intermediate, and immediate goals.
6. How can one best go about estimating miscellaneous sources of income?
7. For what three general purposes do individuals and families use their income?
8. Describe what is meant by "elasticity" in a budget.

9. What should determine the way an individual or a family spends its money?
10. Explain why a checkbook is a valuable recordkeeping tool.
11. List some of the records that should be kept in a safe-deposit box.
12. List some of the records that should be kept in a file at home.
13. How are accurate records helpful for income tax purposes?
14. When does the statute of limitations expire for income tax returns?
15. Explain a way to keep papers so they can be easily stored and retrieved.

Consumer problems and projects

1. Two families of the same size and with the same income have two entirely different budgets. What might be some of the reasons for these variations?

2. Prepare and present a skit showing a family situation in which there is a need for budgeting. If possible, record the skit on audio tape or video tape for playback.

3. Jim Keating, who just finished college, plans to be married in a few days. He does not intend to keep a budget. Jim's father had systematically saved money over the years in order to provide a college education for Jim. During Jim's 4 years in college, his parents paid for his tuition and books and major supplies directly and sent him $160 a month. Jim paid $110 a month for room and board in a dormitory. He spent about $15 a month for clothes and used the remainder of the money for miscellaneous expenses. Now Jim will be working in the purchasing department of a manufacturing firm at a salary of $810 a month, an increase of $650 over the monthly income he had been receiving from his parents. "I got along without budgeting before, so why should I begin now when my income is higher?" asks Jim. Answer Jim's question.

4. Susan and David Buffett would like to trade in their 7-year-old car for a new one, but they do not know whether or not they will be able to make the monthly payment of $97 over a 2-year period. The Buffetts, who have two children, have had difficulty making ends meet on David's annual income of $8,900. A friend suggests that budgeting might help them to cut down on their expenditures and make the car payments.
   a. Outline the steps that the Buffetts could take to set up a workable budget.
   b. How will a budget help the Buffetts to solve their problem?

5. The members of the Wimer family estimated their future income, and now they want to complete an income form similar to the one shown on page 43.
   a. Make out an income form for the Wimers. Include the following information:
      Mr. Wimer's income. Mr. Wimer's monthly take-home pay for 8 months of the year is $780. The months of April, May, September, and October are busy months at the manufacturing plant where he works, and so, during those months, he works additional hours for overtime pay. In previous years, his take-home pay for the months of April and May has been 10 percent higher than his regular take-home pay; his take-home pay for the months of September and October

has been 20 percent higher than his regular take-home pay. Mr. Wimer can count on receiving a $300 bonus in December.

Mrs. Wimer's income. Mrs. Wimer works part time for a tax consultant during the first 4 months of the calendar year. Her take-home pay during these months is as follows: January, $108; February, $148; March, $148; April, $80.

Other income. The Wimers receive a check for $137.50 twice each year (March and September) for the interest on a Series H bond that they hold.

b. What is the average monthly income of the Wimer family?

6. Prepare for the Wimer family a form for fixed, committed expenses and proposed savings similar to the one shown on page 45. Include the following information:

Insurance. Mr. Wimer's annual life insurance premium of $230 is due on September 15. Mrs. Wimer's semiannual life insurance premium of $12 is due on January 10 and on July 10. Their automobile insurance is paid three times a year—in February, June, and October. The amount of each automobile insurance payment is $69.

Taxes. The Wimers' automobile registration fee of $45 is paid in January. The Wimers estimate that in addition to the income tax withheld from their payroll checks, they will have to pay a tax of $140. Federal income tax is due on April 15, but they intend to file their return sometime in March.

Debts. The Wimers make a payment of $180 to their bank each month. This amount covers their mortgage payment, real estate taxes, and a homeowner's insurance policy. For the next 12 months, the Wimers will also be making monthly payments of $31 for a new washer and drier that they purchased from Field's Department Store.

Savings. The Wimers have been accumulating money in their checking account, and they now have $2,300. Thus, no provision need be made for saving for an emergency fund. They would, however, like to put aside enough money each month to accumulate $360 for a vacation trip in the summer. In addition, Mr. Wimer wants to save another $40 a month for what he calls "the big chance."

7. The monthly estimates of the Wimer family's living expenses are as follows: food, $205; household operations, $57; personal allowances, $50; automobile, $40; charity, $35; clothing $30; magazines and newspapers, $10.

a. Prepare for the Wimer family a form for variable living expenses similar to the one shown on page 43. Include their estimated expenses for three months.

b. What are the family's total estimated variable living expenses for one month?

c. If estimated monthly income exceeds estimated monthly expenditures, as is the case for the Wimer family, what should be done with the excess?

Chapter 4

Principles of wise buying

Doing a good job of managing your money is something like planning a trip. First you need to decide where you want to go. Even after you have decided on a destination you still need to decide how you will get there. Decisions have to be made as to how you will travel, what route you will take, and what stops you want to make on the way. A good job of planning will help make the trip easy and pleasant and will help to ensure that you get to your destination successfully.

Just like the traveler, consumers need to consider both their goals and a buying plan for reaching them. In Chapter 2 we talked about deciding on one's goals. But even after goals are decided on, consumers still need a plan to help them reach their goals. Many questions still will have to be considered. Suppose, for example, that your goal is to buy a car and that, at last, you have enough money saved to buy one. With the help of the product-testing magazines and a friend who knows something about cars you first settle on two makes that look like good prospects. You still will need to decide exactly how to go about shopping for your car. Which models should you consider—only two-door hardtops? What dealers should you check? How many dealers should you visit before you make a decision? What factors should you take into account before deciding on buying from a particular dealer? Wise decisions on these questions are likely to be important in determining how pleased you are with your final choice.

PLANNING AHEAD FOR PURCHASES

In order to ensure that they will reach their goals, consumers must make long-range plans. Without careful plans they may end up without the things they need most and with too many things for which they really have no great need. This would be like the situation of the newlyweds who spent all the money they received as wedding gifts on an expensive sofa and found they did not have enough money left for kitchen equipment and utensils.

Determining your situation and needs

The first step in making a long-range plan is deciding exactly what you need. This involves getting your goal clearly in mind and deciding just where you are in relation to it. For example, take the problem of getting together the clothes needed for a part-time job at a nearby supermarket. First, you would need to know what clothes your employer expects you to wear. Once you know this you could go through your wardrobe and determine exactly what you have that meets the rules and what extra things you still need. For many kinds of purchases, including both clothing and food, an inventory of what you already have on hand is important in determining exactly what you need to buy.

Editorial Photocolor Archives, Inc.

Taking an inventory of what you have is an important step in deciding what you need to buy.

Shoppers also need to consider exactly which product characteristics are most important to them. Are durability and quality most important? What about style and color? What about novelty and uniqueness? And finally, what about economy? When you think about it, you realize that it may be impossible to find all these characteristics in one product. A durable, high-quality item is likely to be expensive. A novel, one-of-a-kind, high-style article of clothing may not be suited for hard wear and is almost certain to be expensive.

Planning a purchasing program

With a long-range plan, the consumer often can break down a major purchasing project into smaller, more manageable steps. One man with a thin pocketbook and a great love of fishing decided to buy tackle with a long-range plan in mind. The first large piece he bought was a tackle box, even though at that time he had almost nothing to put in the box. He said he wanted to be sure he could keep whatever he bought in good shape and not lose it. Then he decided on a list of supplies and equipment he wanted to own and began buying the things on the list a few at a time. It was amazing how quickly he acquired the equipment he wanted.

Many kinds of goals involve a succession of smaller purchases that are steps toward a goal. Few families are able to furnish a house all at once; instead, they must proceed one item at a time. For this kind of program to work, the initial plan must be a good one, and the plan must be kept in mind at each succeeding step. If the plan is neglected or proves to be a poor one, the individual is likely to end up with an assortment of things that really do not go together.

Anticipating opportunities for special purchases

For many kinds of purchases, shoppers can save money by learning when special sales or purchase opportunities occur and consequently planning ahead to take advantage of them. Certain kinds of sales have become traditional and are held at the same time every year, so it is easy to plan for them. The January white sales, featuring specials on bed linens and bath towels, are examples of annual sales.

Seasonal items may be available at special prices either in preseason or postseason sales. Sometimes dealers for seasonal items make special offers well ahead of the season to attract early shoppers. Sales of snow tires in September are one example of this kind of sale. In many cities, Columbus Day and Veterans Day are occasions for preseason sales of winter coats and outerwear. Postseason sales are used to clean out stocks of unsold items that the merchant does not want to keep on hand. Postseason sales on fall and winter clothes and footwear typically come just after Christmas, and the summer sales come just after the Fourth of July. Price reductions on preseason sales are smaller than those for postseason sales, but preseason sales offer better selections.

Not all sales occur at regularly scheduled times, however. Smart shoppers should watch advertising and in-store signs for unusual buys. These sometimes may come at unexpected times, even at the peak of the season. Such sales may be held when business is slow.

An understanding of retailing terms will help you know better what to expect at sales events. The National Retail Merchants Association suggests the following use of terms to its members:

- *Sale* is used when articles are offered at a reduction from the advertiser's own bona fide prices. The seller should make it clear whether the "sale" claim is based on the advertiser's own regular prices or on local prices for identical or comparable merchandise. When the term "regularly" or "regular price" is used, it is understood that the merchandise will return to the regular price after the sale period. For merchandise that will not be marked up again after the sale, the terms "were," "formerly," or "originally" should be used.

- *Clearances* or *Clearance Sales* are sales used to clear out leftover items; prices are reduced from the previous or the original prices. When price comparisons are made, the previous or original price should be clearly indicated. The term "regularly" should not be used for price comparisons for clearance items, since unsold items are not to be returned to their previous prices, but are instead marked down until they sell.

- *Special Purchase* or *Closeout* is properly used to refer to merchandise purchased from the manufacturer on unusually favorable terms and offered to the public at lower prices than they ordinarily would expect to pay in their area.

In planning ahead for sales it helps to build up some extra savings that you can draw on for your purchases. Staple items you use everyday are especially good bargains at sales. You know you will always be able to use some more of your favorite brand of underwear or shampoo. Caution is required for major purchases of clothing and luxury items. Here you will need to consider whether you really like the item on sale or are paying too much attention to the fact that it is cheaper than it used to be.

DECIDING WHETHER OR NOT TO SHOP AROUND

Shopping costs prospective buyers both money and time. Because of these costs they must decide whether shopping is likely to produce sufficient savings to make their efforts worthwhile. These savings may either be in the form of a better product for a particular price or a better price for some particular product.

Cases in which shopping pays off

Shopping around is most worthwhile when substantial differences in prices and quality exist within a particular market. If prices and quality do not vary much, the easiest-to-find product or the nearest store is the best choice. If, however, different brands of a product do not all perform equally well, and if prices differ among outlets, shopping for the best price-quality combination will produce worthwhile returns for the shopper. These returns will be largest for big-ticket or expensive items such as cars, appliances, and furniture and for items that are purchased regularly, such as gasoline, food, and toiletries.

One study has pointed out some of the situations in which price and quality variations are likely to be large.[1] One instance is a situation in which the seller, because of the nature of his product, is able to charge different customers different prices for the same item. This is the same as saying that he is able to practice *price discrimination* among different customers. This happens sometimes when customers find it difficult to compare the deals that each has been offered. It is, for example, difficult for car buyers to compare deals because of differences in trade-ins, differences in models, and the variety of options offered. Price discrimination among different shoppers can also occur when resale of a good or service is impossible or is prohibited. Dentists, for example, can charge different patients different prices since one patient cannot sell another a filling or a check-up.

The second instance in which price and quality variations are likely to be large is when products or services are *differentiated*. In these cases, similar products or services have unique features that keep them from being fully comparable. For many products or services these differences may be relatively minor, but they still may be sufficient to complicate shoppers' efforts to make comparisons. Examples of differentiating features include the "miracle ingredients" in toothpaste. The addition of these ingredients creates differences among toothpaste

---

[1] E. Scott Maynes, "The Payoff for Intelligent Consumer Decision-Making," *Journal of Home Economics,* Vol. 61, pp. 97–103, February, 1969.

brands that make evaluation of the price and performance difficult. Differentiating features may exist for stores, as well as for products and services. For example, one store may provide free alterations while another makes no credit charges on accounts paid within 90 days. Faced with the same price for the same suit in these two stores, the shopper must decide which of these two features is most valuable to him before he purchases the suit from either store.

Cases in which shopping is of no benefit

For certain products and services the price is fixed and is the same at all outlets. In these cases, shopping provides no advantages, since the price is the same everywhere. This may be the result of efforts by a manufacturer to ensure that his product is sold at the same price everywhere. Certain manufacturers of popular, heavily advertised items are able to insist on this and keep dealers in line by threatening to drop those who cut prices.

In certain cases there is no benefit to shopping because there is only one seller in a particular locality. This is the situation for utilities such as telephones, electricity, water, and public transportation for which there is only one seller whose rates are regulated by the state.

Cases in which shopping costs can be reduced

Even in cases in which shopping is likely to be worthwhile, shoppers still will want to hold the amount of time and money that they spend to a minimum. One way to save both time and money is to substitute other methods of collecting information for store-to-store shopping trips. Information on availability and prices can be obtained from newspaper ads. Phone calls also can be used to determine where a particular item is available and its price. Smart shoppers can use part of the time they spend out shopping to collect information about purchases they are planning in the future.

KNOWING WHAT TO LOOK FOR IN A PRODUCT

We have suggested that one of the initial steps in buying something is deciding which characteristics are most important for the use you have in mind: quality and durability, economy, style and color, or uniqueness and novelty. Even after you have decided on the relative importance of these different characteristics, you still will need to know just how to recognize the features that indicate durability and quality, for example, and how to determine whether a less expensive item is likely to be a poor bargain because it requires frequent and expensive repairs or wears out quickly.

An examination of the product itself may provide the shopper with a number of pieces of information—the price, the brand name, the product's composition or ingredients, and suggestions and instructions for use. The shopper needs to learn how to interpret this information and determine its usefulness in answering his questions.

Price

One of the first things we are likely to notice when we examine a product is its price. Our interest in price is twofold. First, we want to know whether the product is something we can afford. Second, we may look at the price as an indication of the quality of the item compared to the other items available. Studies of consumer behavior have found that consumers often rely on price as an indication of quality. They seem most inclined to use price as an indication of quality for products whose performance is difficult to evaluate but which they think vary widely in quality. An example might be stereo hi-fi equipment. Most of us are convinced that there are important differences in quality among different models and brands, but we are not sure just how to go about detecting them. In such a situation we might be inclined to think that the more expensive models are better.

Consumers may be too convinced of the old saying "you only get what you pay for." This statement seems to be true for some products, but not for others. Studies of the relationship between the product-testing ratings developed by Consumers Union and actual product prices indicate that, in general, price is *not* a very reliable indication of quality. For many products, lower-priced brands have been almost as likely to get high ratings as the expensive ones. This means that paying a high price does not necessarily assure you of getting a high-quality product. High-quality products have been found at various price levels. The shopper must look for other kinds of information instead of relying solely on price. It should be noted that these studies made comparisons within groups of similar products. Color TV sets were compared with each other, not with black-and-white sets; Chevolets were compared with Fords and Plymouths, not with Cadillacs.

Brand name

A key piece of information about a product is its brand name. Brand names have developed over the years because manufacturers want to create an identity for their products and build up a group of customers who will look for their products in the market and buy them again and again. With a brand name to distinguish his product from others, the manufacturer can try to build up a reputation for it both through the quality of the product itself and through advertising that emphasizes the brand name.

Although most manufacturers try to build up a reputation for the reliable quality of their brand, the quality ranking of particular brands does change over time. Products with a high ranking one year may later lose position while others gain. When the Consumers Union product ratings of electrical appliances in different years were compared, it was found that brands that had a high ranking in one year's tests were only to a certain extent the same ones that received high rankings in later tests.[2] It was also found that there was a good deal of variation, over time, in the relative rankings of sunburn lotions.[3] From this we can conclude that a good experience in the past with a brand should be taken into account in making a purchasing decision, but such experience cannot be counted on too heavily.

In considering the full range of brands available, shoppers need to be aware of store brands (sometimes also called private-label brands) as well as the more familiar nationally advertised brands, since they often provide good quality at reasonable prices.

For most products, the brand names of large manufacturers who advertise heavily are familiar to us all. We all are familiar with such nationally advertised brands of aspirin as Bayer and St. Joseph. We may be less familiar with the store brands—products made especially for a retail store or chain, to its specifications, and sold only by the store under its own brand name. Most drugstore chains carry their own brand of aspirin as well as the nationally advertised brands. Rexall drugstores, for example, carry Rexall Aspirin. Other examples of store brands are Ann Page food products, which are available only at A&P supermarkets, and Kenmore appliances, which are available only at Sears, Roebuck and Company.

Most store brands are made by major manufacturers who also produce their own nationally advertised brands. For instance, Kenmore washers are made for Sears, Roebuck and Company to its specifications by a washing machine manufacturer that also produces its own brand.

---

[2] Ruby T. Morris and Claire S. Bronson, "The Chaos of Competition Indicated by Consumer Reports," *Journal of Marketing,* Vol. 33, pp. 26–34, July, 1969.

[3] Ruby T. Morris and Betty Block, "The Instability of Quality: As Revealed in 10 Consumers Union Studies of Sunburn Preventatives 1936–1966," *Journal of Consumer Affairs,* Vol. 2, pp. 39–60, Summer, 1968.

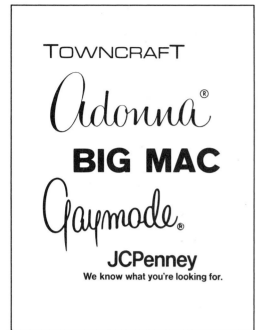

Courtesy J. C. Penney Co., Inc.　　Courtesy Sears, Roebuck and Co.

Many large retailers offer products, often at significant savings, with their own brand names rather than with manufacturers' brand names.

One way to tell whether a product is a nationally advertised brand or a store brand is to check the label to see whom the product is made or distributed by. Nationally advertised brands use such phrases as "made by" or "processed by" while store brands use the terms "made for" or "distributed by."

Store brands are of special interest to consumers because their quality is often comparable to that of nationally advertised brands, yet they sell at a lower price. This lower price is possible partly as a result of the elimination or reduction of advertising costs. Although the price of a store's own brand often has to cover some expenses for local newspaper advertising, it does not have to cover expensive national television, radio, or magazine advertising.

The savings possible through buying store brands are illustrated in a recent study that compared the quality and prices of nationally advertised brands and store brands of sheets and pillow cases.[4] The

[4] Mary Wager and Rachel Dardis, "Does the Consumer Gain from White Sales?" *Journal of Consumer Affairs,* Vol. 5, pp. 186–195, Winter, 1971.

researchers found no significant differences in quality between the nationally advertised brands and those sold under a store brand. They did find price differences, however. The nationally advertised brands of sheets were 12 percent higher in price than store brands during white sale periods and 28 percent higher in nonsale periods.

Label information

Consumers do not always use one helpful source of product information that is readily available to them—the product label. In addition to the brand name, a good label may provide a wide range of information. Although there probably is no single label that provides all the items of information consumers might wish, at a minimum a good label should provide the following information:

- Quantity and/or size
- Composition (ingredients or contents)
- Directions for use and care
- Name and address of the manufacturer or distributor

Completeness of label information varies greatly among products and manufacturers. Opinions on exactly what information should be provided also differ greatly. The information that must be provided for food products and textiles is closely regulated by the federal government. For other products, manufacturers make most of the decisions about what label information will be provided. What kinds of information do you feel should be made available? Many critics of present labeling practices feel that information on the expected life of appliances should be included on labels. How would you feel about this?

More detailed label information is one of the major goals of the consumer movement. A particular area of concern is product performance. Some proposals call for wider use of *informative labeling* that provides information on the performance of the product under standard tests. This information may be provided in the form of test scores or ratings. For example, stainless steel tableware might be tested for resistance to chemical attack, bending strength, and the durability of the cutting edge, with performance in each of these three areas scored on the basis of 100 points. Such a system would provide consumers with a great deal of useful information. For such a system to work, however, agreement has to be reached on exactly which characteristics will be tested, and then appropriate test procedures have to be devised. Performance-test information is available for many industrial products but is seldom made available for consumer products. One piece of performance data that is readily available to automobile buyers is the engine's horsepower rating. Other information, however, such as the expected mileage life of the tires or the car itself, is not available.

Grade labeling goes one step beyond informative labeling. With *grade labeling,* the results of the whole set of standard performance tests are taken into account and an overall quality rating or grade assigned to the product. The grades used for food products, such as the U.S. Choice grade for beef, are the ones most familiar to us.

The development of a system of grade labeling, such as one for stainless steel tableware, requires some decisions about the relative importance of different product characteristics. In assigning an overall grade, should each product characteristic be weighted equally, or are some characteristics more important than others? In the case of stainless steel tableware, for example, just how much weight should resistance to chemical attack have relative to bending strength?

Proposals urging wider use of grade labeling have been attacked by those who argue that different people have different needs and preferences and that a system that assigns a single grade to each product cannot take all these differences into account. The problem of weighting different product characteristics for grade labeling is a difficult one. The problems of establishing performance standards for individual products and the provision of test results on informative labels are a good deal less complicated. There would seem to be few good arguments against more informative labels. Informative-labeling systems for a number of consumer products already are in use in several Western European countries.

Construction and workmanship

The shopper's inspection of the product should go beyond the price, the brand name, and label. It should include the product itself. Even less-experienced shoppers can learn a good deal about a product by examining it closely. Is the workmanship good? Is it neatly finished? What are the key points of wear—hinges, buttonholes, springs? Are they reinforced and well made?

Quality control for many consumer items is poor. Clothing items, in particular, have been the subject of many complaints in recent years. Smart shoppers will do well to closely examine every item they buy before completing the purchase. Is the fabric free of defects? Are the seams fully sewn and strong? Are the buttons well secured?

Guarantees and warranties

The words "guarantee" and "warranty" are both used to describe the written statement given by a seller or a manufacturer that promises repair, replacement, or refund if a product fails to perform as specified at the time it was sold.

Warranties are provided for a wide variety of items, ranging from automobiles to electrical appliances. Warranties differ among brands for many items, and these differences may be an important consideration in choosing a brand or a place to buy. Even without a written guarantee, the manufacturer is responsible for providing a product that works as it is supposed to—a record player, for example, should play records. Under the law every product should perform as it is intended to. The fact that a manufacturer offers an item for sale for a particular use is regarded as evidence that he is guaranteeing its suitability. In legal terms, his offer to sell the item for a particular use creates a "warranty of merchantibility."

Many guarantees are complicated and full of legal fine points. At a minimum you should know what to look for in a guarantee. The salesman who tells you the product is "guaranteed," is not telling you anything. You need to know what the written guarantee really covers. A good guarantee should be clearly worded and include the following information:

- The name and address of the firm that is giving the warranty. (Is it the manufacturer or the retail dealer?)
- The person to whom the warranty is given. (Does the warranty apply only to the original purchaser?)
- The product or parts covered and the duration of coverage.
- The parts and repair work not covered and other exceptions. (Who pays for labor charges? Shipping charges?)
- A statement of what will be done in case of a defect or breakdown, at whose expense the work will be done, and the period of time within which it will be done. (Does the warranty promise repair, replacement, or a full refund?)
- A statement of the obligations of the purchaser. (Does the purchaser have to provide normal maintenance? Does he have to return the product to the factory if it breaks down?)

Under Federal Trade Commission rules sellers who promise "satisfaction guaranteed or your money back" or "10-day free trial" should mean that the purchase price will be refunded in full on request by the purchaser. If any conditions are attached to the guarantee, they must be made clear at the time of purchase. If there are conditions that are not made clear, the seller is considered to be engaged in a deceptive practice and is subject to FTC action. So-called "lifetime" guarantees also sometimes cause confusion. The FTC specifies that the seller must indicate clearly if the lifetime referred to relates to a life other than the purchaser's. For example, an auto supply dealer selling a muffler with a "lifetime guarantee" must indicate that the guarantee applies to the life of the car, not the buyer, if that is what he means.

Consumers often have a difficult time cutting through the complex language of guarantees. In response to this problem, some business firms have made their guarantees into models of simplicity. New laws also have been proposed to help consumers better understand the provisions of warranties. One proposal requires that any warranty that does not provide for full repair or replacement without charge and within a reasonable time be labeled a "partial warranty" to distinguish it from a "full warranty," which provides for full repair or replacement without cost. Other proposals would provide additional help for consumers who have difficulty in getting sellers to live up to the terms of their warranties.

Every consumer should make a habit of saving the guarantees, instructions, and sales receipts that come with the items purchased. The file does not have to be an elaborate one; it can be just a big envelope or a small box. Such a file will save time and problems if difficulties do occur with a product.

Other sources of product information

After looking over the package, labels, and the product itself, consumers may still conclude that they do not have all the information they would like. There are a number of sources to which the perplexed shopper can turn: government publications, business and trade associations, and consumer-supported product-testing agencies. These sources are so varied and numerous that they are discussed in the next chapter.

COMPARING PLACES TO BUY

Shoppers in larger cities and towns have several choices about where to shop for clothes, records, and appliances. In some cases, their choice is between two different stores of the same type—for example, two different men's clothing stores. Often, however, the item they want is available in a number of different types of stores. Records, for example, are available at discount stores, drugstores, variety stores, record shops, and department stores. The policies, services, and prices of these different types of stores vary widely. These differences make the decision about a place to buy a complicated one.

Comparing prices among stores

The types of stores range from large discount stores with low prices and a high sales volume to small neighborhood stores with a low sales volume and higher prices. Discount stores gain large sales by emphasizing low prices. They hold costs down by buying in large quantities and limiting the variety of items, the number of clerks, and other services. Smaller stores that cannot compete in terms of price alone survive by providing their customers with other services. Neighborhood stores provide convenience of location and perhaps other services such as easy credit and free delivery. Other smaller shops may emphasize specialized selections of merchandise, unusual decorations, ample clerk assistance, or other special services. In order to make wise decisions, shoppers need to know about the whole range of sellers for each item they want and about the extra services each seller provides. Without this knowledge they may not obtain the combination of product, price, and extra services that would suit them best.

Many businesses are able to offer low prices by eliminating services. Consumers have to decide what services they are willing to pay extra to obtain.

Courtesy The Plaza   Editorial Photocolor Archives, Inc.

The process of comparing the products, prices, and service offerings of different stores is called *comparative shopping*. It is a good habit to form, especially for larger, more important purchases. Consumer research studies have found that high-income shoppers visit more stores before making a purchase than do low-income shoppers. Low-income shoppers seem to prefer to stick closer to neighborhood stores where they are known, where they can be certain about how they will be treated, and where they are certain they can get credit. This is unfortunate because prices in stores serving low-income areas often are substantially higher than those in stores serving the general market. An FTC study in Washington, D.C., a few years ago estimated that a television set with a wholesale price of $100 would sell for $131 in a store serving the general market but would sell for $187 in a store serving the low-income market. Poor families were, in a sense, forced to buy at these prices because they needed credit to make the purchase and could only obtain it from stores in the low-income market. The high prices in the low-income market stores studied were not found to be due to unusual profits. They were a result of higher bad-debt losses and higher outlays for salaries and commissions to salesmen.

Comparing price levels among different stores may be difficult because of the frequent use of "specials." Specials are used by many stores to focus attention on their offerings and to help them differentiate themselves from their competitors. Such stores constantly shift prices as part of their promotional efforts. Prices of some items are shifted down and emphasized in store ads, while the prices of other items are raised. This procedure, which is common in supermarkets, is called *variable price merchandising*. As a result of it, we should not judge a store just by its specials. Some studies have indicated that supermarkets with the best specials have higher average prices for other items. Some shoppers take advantage of these specials and do their regular shopping elsewhere. This can be worthwhile if the extra time and travel costs involved are not too great.

Another problem that complicates price comparisons among stores is the fact that some stores give trading stamps, while others do not. The stamps given have a definite value, but it is difficult for shoppers to determine exactly how much. The value of stamps varies among companies. It also varies over time and with the particular items selected when the stamps are redeemed; some items are a "better buy" than others. A recent study to determine the value of S&H Green Stamps, estimated their redemption value at an average of $3.25 per book. Since the stamps in a book represent $100 worth of purchases, the stamps given with each dollar spent are worth $3\frac{1}{4}$ cents. The value of stamps to the consumer is, however, reduced by the limitations placed on the way they can be spent. Stamps are, in a sense, a discount paid in a special currency that can be spent only at redemption centers, with choices limited to the particular merchandise carried in stock. Because of these restrictions on the way they can be spent, stamps are less useful than regular money, which can be spent in any way the consumer chooses or saved.

Understanding what services are provided

In order to fully evaluate the price asked for an item, the shopper needs to know exactly what extra services are included in the price and the cost of the other services that may be available. In some stores delivery costs, alterations, and installation charges are included in the price. In others, there are charges for some of these services.

Another important aspect of a store's services is the policy on returned goods. In general, by law all sales are final unless some serious defect is discovered in an item. In order to maintain customer goodwill, however, most stores do not insist on the letter of the law. Some stores permit returns for a full refund, while others permit exchanges or give credit on returns. A few permit no returns or exchanges—this may be the policy for sale merchandise even in more liberal stores. Department stores and specialty shops usually are the most liberal in permitting returns. This is one of the extra services these stores provide in return for the somewhat higher prices they charge.

Consumers should be fair and reasonable in asking stores to accept returned merchandise. Handling returned items can be costly and may involve a substantial loss if the customer has damaged an item. Most retailers have a full set of stories about unreasonable requests for returns. One story that crops up frequently is about the shopper who returned a coat one Monday morning in the fall because "it didn't fit right." On checking the coat over, the storekeeper found mustard stains on the collar and football stubs in the pocket.

Checking other sources of goods

Stores are not the only source for the merchandise that consumers buy. Other possible sources include mail-order houses and door-to-door salesmen. Like regular retail stores, these nonstore sources offer both advantages and disadvantages. It is well to be aware of both the advantages and disadvantages of buying from these sources.

Mail-order houses offer consumers an opportunity to obtain specialized merchandise that may not be available in a local community because the market is too limited to support a specialty store. This often is the situation for hobby and sports items such as stamps, hi-fi equipment, or special clothing styles or sizes. The large book and record clubs offer the shopper an opportunity to share in the benefits of large-scale purchasing in return for a promised number of purchases per year. Because of the distance that separates the buyer and the seller and because of the communication problems involved, mail-order purchases have been a frequent subject of consumer complaints. The most frequent complaint is that merchandise ordered and paid for has not been received. Consumers should be aware of these problems and deal with established and reputable firms.

Door-to-door salesmen offer a variety of items including housewares, cosmetics, and cleaning supplies as well as home-improvement products such as aluminum siding. The consumer must proceed especially carefully in door-to-door purchases because of the repeated frauds and abuses that have occurred. Door-to-door salesmen place consumers in a position in which they are especially vulnerable to sales pressure. Most of us find it difficult to end a sales presentation and get rid of the salesman. Sales pitches are, in some cases, cleverly devised scripts designed to arouse the emotions and interest of the prospective customer. In addition, salesmen often try to force the consumer into making an immediate decision, neither giving him time to think over the purchase nor letting him compare prices from other sources. To give consumers a chance to think over purchases, an increasing number of states now allow consumers a two- or three-day "cooling-off" period within which they can cancel a door-to-door sales contract. In order to protect themselves, consumers should insist on being allowed time to check other sources, prices, and the reputation of the sales firm. They should never give in and sign a contract just to get rid of a salesman or let him stay so long that he begins to wear them down—if it is necessary, they should threaten to call the police.

In this chapter we have discussed some of the things consumers can do for themselves in choosing products and the stores in which to make their purchases. Often, however, shoppers will have to turn to other sources for additional information about products or stores. They also may need extra help in handling their complaints. Special sources of information and assistance for consumers are discussed in Chapters 5 and 27.

Checking your reading

1. Why is an inventory of what you have often an important first step in planning new purchases?

2. How do clearance sales and special purchase sales differ?

3. In what kinds of buying situations are consumers most likely to use price as an indicator of quality?

4. Why does the existence of price discrimination among customers create a situation in which it is important to shop around?

5. What is meant by saying that products or services are differentiated?

6. What techniques can consumers use to reduce the time and expense of shopping around?

7. Why do manufacturers label products with brand names?

8. What are store brands? Why are store brands usually lower in price than manufacturers' brands?

9. How do informative labeling and grade labeling differ?

10. What kinds of information should be included in a guarantee?

11. Why do shoppers need to know the whole range of sellers for the item they want, along with the prices charged and the extra services provided?

12. What is comparative shopping?

13. Why does variable price merchandising make price comparisons among stores difficult for consumers?

14. How do trading stamps complicate price comparisons among stores?

15. Do buyers always have the right to exchange or return goods they have purchased? Why do stores differ in their policies on returns and exchanges?

Consumer problems and projects

1. Long-range planning frequently involves purchasing merchandise during off-season sales. List five articles or types of goods that can be purchased at a saving at certain times of the year. List also some of the disadvantages of this kind of buying. Example: Buying Christmas cards in January. Disadvantage: The cards and envelopes might become discolored during the year before you can use them.

2. What store brands are offered in the drugstore or grocery store where you usually shop? Make a list of five product categories in which the store offers both store brands and manufacturers' brands. Some likely categories to check are canned peaches, frozen peas, frozen orange juice concentrate, ice cream, cola beverages, aspirin, and rubbing alcohol. Note all the brands offered in each of the five product categories, along with the price and whether the brand is a store brand or a manufacturer's brand.

Have you ever compared any of these store brands with the manufacturer's brands? How would you rate them?

3. Make a collection of five labels from different products you and your family use. Make your collection as varied as possible—paint, dog food, canned food, toothpaste, clothing, laundry detergent, etc. What are the good and bad features of each label? What other information would you like to see included?

4. What are the arguments for and against grade labeling? What kinds of products are suited to a system of grade labeling? What kinds are not?

5. Obtain a copy of the guarantee for a product in which you are interested. (If necessary, visit a local store, and request permission to copy the guarantee.) Does the guarantee provide *all* the information needed? Is it clear? What exactly is covered by the guarantee—the entire product or particular parts? Who pays for replacement parts? Who pays the labor costs for repairs?

6. Choose a product you would be interested in buying or buy frequently and that is sold in several different stores in your area. A hit record or tape, toothpaste, shampoo, or some other toiletry or cosmetic would be a good choice. Prepare a list of places in which the item is offered, along with the price in each store. Also make note of whether trading stamps or special services are provided. If you were to buy the item, where would you make your purchase? Why?

7. Prepare a report on the arguments for and against trading stamps. Visit your library to obtain references. Such indexes as *Reader's Guide to Periodical Literature, Business Periodicals Index,* and *Public Affairs Information Service* will help you locate useful articles.

Chapter 5

Sources of information for consumers

In the last chapter we discussed the use of a number of items of product information to which the shopper has easy access. These include product price, brand name, label information, and guarantee information. As we saw, the information provided by these sources can be useful but does have its limitations. The careful shopper needs more information than these sources are likely to provide. Where can he turn for impartial advice based on technical and scientific knowledge? Sources of useful information will be discussed in this chapter.

Consumer-supported product-testing organizations, government agencies, business firms, business trade associations, and business-sponsored informational and educational organizations all provide advice that can be useful in buying. Each of these sources has its uses and its limitations. In reading the following sections, you should try to get an idea of just what strong points each source of information has and just what shortcomings those who use it should bear in mind.

PRODUCT-TESTING ORGANIZATIONS

During the 1920s, more and more consumers bought new durable goods that were just coming into widespread use. Sales of autos, refrigerators, vacuum cleaners, and radios were brisk. Consumers were flooded with advertising from billboards, electric signs, newspapers, magazines, and the new medium—radio. As the decade passed, consumers grew more and more aware that they had little information to use other than what they could gather from the torrent of advertising to which they were subjected.

At the same time all this was happening, interest was developing in using the latest scientific and engineering techniques to determine product quality. During the 1920s a number of large companies set up laboratories to perform certain standardized tests on the materials they bought. A few large retail stores adopted the idea, too, and began to use testing to guide them in selecting the merchandise they offered to their customers. In 1927, Stuart Chase and F. J. Schlink proposed the idea of a consumer-supported organization that would perform product testing and provide consumers with the technical information they needed to make purchasing decisions.

The stream of inquiries from readers of their book, *Your Money's Worth,* soon convinced Schlink that the local Consumers' Club he had organized should be expanded. In 1929, Consumers' Research, Inc. (CR) was organized to perform product testing on a national scale. CR now has its headquarters in Washington, New Jersey, and has about 100,000 members and a full-time staff of around 80 people. CR has been outpaced by Consumers Union of United States, Inc. (CU), which split off from CR in 1936 as the result of an employee labor dispute. Now CU is by far the larger organization, with a staff of over 300 people. Its headquarters are in Mount Vernon, New York. Both CR and CU issue monthly publications: *Consumer Bulletin* is published by CR, and *Consumer Reports* is published by CU. In the early 1970s, *Consumer Reports* had a monthly circulation of over two million copies.

Both organizations engage in comparative testing. In *comparative testing,* a group of products is subjected to a set of standardized tests, with test conditions carefully controlled to ensure that all the products are treated in the same way. The performance of each individual product on each test is recorded. On the basis of test results and the test engineers' estimate of its overall quality, each brand is assigned a rank.

Both CU and CR know that their reputations depend on the accuracy, reliability, and fairness of their tests. Both organizations make every effort to preserve their independence from other organizations and special interests, including product manufacturers. To help them maintain their financial independence of business, neither organization's magazine accepts advertising, and neither permits manufacturers to cite their findings. Although both organizations have been accused at various times of playing favorites, no convincing proof has ever been offered to support such accusations.

What kinds of products are tested?

Not all products lend themselves to the product-testing approach used by CU and CR. Product testing works best with products that consumers can readily identify by brand name and, if necessary, model number. To be useful, the ratings must also include the brands that are most widely available and widely used throughout the country. Certain kinds of products do not meet these requirements very well. For example, fresh meat, which is for the most part sold unbranded, would not meet such requirements. In contrast, canned hams and other processed meat products are identified by brand name, and rating information by brand is a useful guide to consumers in making a choice.

In choosing products to be tested, particular attention is given to items that make up an important part of family budgets—food, automobiles, appliances, and clothing. But attention is also given to hobby and sports items, including a number of items that would be of special interest to young adults. CU has tested a variety of sports, camping, and fishing gear. CU also notes that it is guided by the requests of its members in choosing products to be tested. One of the special interests of many CU members is hi-fi equipment, and CU has, over the years, built up a reputation for expertise in this area. Certain products are tested frequently, even annually if necessary, to keep up with model changes. Because of annual model changes, autos are tested each year.

Courtesy Consumers Union

Consumer-supported product-testing organizations use scientific test procedures to evaluate products.

How are products tested?

Both organizations use standard testing techniques recognized by both industry and government. In some cases, however, special new tests have to be devised when existing procedures do not cover a situation. To test hair sprays, CU puts sprayed swatches of human hair into a high-humidity chamber and measures how much and how quickly each curl drops. Each organization does testing in its own laboratories. CU has elaborate special equipment for testing, including a special chamber that shields TV sets from stray electronic signals during testing and a special muffled acoustic chamber to test hi-fi and other audio equipment. When special tests or information is required, outside testing laboratories with the necessary equipment and special consultants are called on. In addition to being tested in a laboratory, products may also be tested under conditions of actual use by panels of consumers who report their experience with the product. One such panel, working for CU, recently wore and reported on men's hair pieces.

The products that are tested by CU are bought in various cities throughout the country by shoppers who do not reveal that the items are to be used for CU tests. For some products, only one sample of a particular brand is tested; in other cases a number of samples are used. Some critics have argued that it is unfair to test only one sample of a brand, since the particular sample tested may not really be typical of the brand. CU has replied that most consumers cannot afford repeat purchases if a product does not work well the first time they buy it; they deserve to know if some units of the product are faulty. CU does, however, do repeat tests if test results seem unusual or if a particular brand gets an unusually high or low rating. CR, because of its more limited budget, has been unable to use all the precautions used by CU in obtaining product samples for testing.

What ratings are given?

Products are rated on the basis of overall quality. To calculate the rating, the results of the individual tests conducted are weighted and added together for a comprehensive score. CR rates products on the basis of quality or performance. Products fall into three categories: (1) recommended, (2) intermediate, and (3) not recommended. CR also assigns price ratings. Thus it could rate a product high in quality but also indicate that it is relatively high-priced.

CU assigns products to two broad categories: acceptable and not acceptable. The products in each category are listed in order of estimated overall quality. Products that are significantly superior to others in the "acceptable" category are indicated with a check rating. Products that are rated "not acceptable" usually fail because of some safety hazard, such as danger of shock in electrical appliances. CU does not assign price ratings but does indicate a "best buy" when a product is rated high and is relatively low in price.

In using the ratings developed by the two product-testing organizations it is important to be aware of the characteristics on which a product has been rated. To develop the overall ratings, scores on particular tests are weighted and added together. These weights assume that consumers' needs are fairly similar and that most consumers would assign about the same importance to a particular product characteristic. Consumers with special needs may want to study the test reports to determine which of the top-rated products best meets their requirements.

Test results are published as quickly as possible. Keeping test information up to date is a continuing problem as new models replace old ones and entirely new products appear. Out-of-date information is, of course, of only limited use at best. CU has considered a number of means of keeping test information more current. One proposal calls for putting test information in a computer, with new test results replacing old ones when necessary. Remote printers hooked up to a computer would be placed in shopping centers throughout the country. Shoppers interested in the latest information on a product—color TVs, for example—could put a few quarters into the printer and receive a print-out of current test results.

What impact have the product-testing organizations had?

The product-testing organizations have had an important impact on government and business, as well as on consumers. Consumers have benefited directly from the money-saving advice offered. Evidence has been provided that haphazard buying that ignores product-testing information may be more costly than most of us would imagine.[1] After comparing the prices of products given the poorest ratings by CU with the prices of products given the best ratings, it was estimated that, on the average, the products with the poorest ratings cost 27 percent more than those with the best ratings. Consumers who bought the lowest-rated products not only spent considerably more but also lost out on quality as well.

---

[1] Ruby Turner Morris and Claire S. Bronson, "The Potential Loss in Money Income to the American People by Haphazard Purchasing," *Journal of Consumer Affairs*, Vol. 4, pp. 103–112, Winter, 1970.

Both CR and CU deal with consumer problems that go beyond product testing, and both have published special articles on such issues as pollution and the use of pesticides—issues that are of concern to us all as consumers and as citizens. Both CR and CU also have educational departments that assist schools by providing educational materials. CU, in particular, has made a substantial effort to help schools develop new consumer education programs. Despite continuous efforts, CU has had little success in reaching one group of consumers that needs product information—low-income families.

Manufacturers are well aware of how they stand in the product ratings, and they are sometimes forced to make needed improvements when their products receive unfavorable publicity because of poor test results. They are also influenced by the effect of ratings on sales. Many small and new companies have received their big break when favorable ratings have brought their products to the public's attention. Even the large car manufacturers can observe the effects of the ratings of different models on their sales.

The government also is affected by the activities of the consumer-supported product-testing organizations. Test results may provide evidence of the need for new laws on product safety or other new legislation. CU has actively assisted in the development of new consumer legislation by helping draft new bills and providing expert testimony on consumer problems. In contrast to CU, CR does not engage in any legislative activities.

AGENCIES OF THE FEDERAL GOVERNMENT

As part of its regulatory and educational activities, the federal government issues a wide variety of consumer information publications. These range from Department of Agriculture pamphlets on food buying to Department of Interior booklets on recreation facilities in the national parks.

The number of publications is so great that it is difficult both to discover what information the government already has available and to keep up with new publications as they appear. Recognizing the problem, President Nixon in 1970 ordered the organization of the Consumer Product Information Coordinating Center. The Center was given responsibility for making existing publications more easily available to consumers. It was also given responsibility for encouraging the development of new publications based on product testing done to guide government purchasing and based on government research activities. The first *Consumer Product Information* catalog issued by the Center included over 200 publications selected because of their special interest to consumers. Copies of the current catalog are available free from the U.S. Product Information Distribution Center, Washington, D.C. 20407. Along with the Consumer Product Information Coordinating Center in Washington, the General Services Administration now operates Federal Information Centers in a number of major cities. The Centers are staffed by people who are prepared to answer or get answers to consumers' questions about federal government services, programs, and publications. When problems do not fall into federal jurisdiction, callers are referred to the appropriate local or state agency. In 1971, Federal Information Centers were operating in 26 major cities, and another 16 cities had free long-distance telephone service linking them to a Center. The phone numbers in all 42 cities are included under the "U.S. Government" listings.

An even more complete list of consumer publications is prepared by the Government Printing Office. It is Price List No. 86, "Consumer Information," available for 10 cents (check or money order) from the Superintendent of Documents, Government Printing Office, Washington, D.C. 20402. Over 600 items were included in the most recent edition of this price list.

The government's consumer information publications generally have avoided comparing and evaluating products by brand name. Only in the last few years has information that identifies products by brand name been published. Automobiles, cigarettes, and hearing aids were among the first product categories for which brand names were provided along with the other information. Instead of providing product information by brand name, federal publications typically emphasize general tips on buymanship, including product characteristics to look for and product features that are useful for particular purposes. For example, *Adhesives for Everyday Use,* a consumer information guide prepared by the National Bureau of Standards, reports that vegetable glue "paste" is suitable for use only with paper and paper products and has "poor moisture resistance and low strength," but that casein glue has "good strength, better moisture resistance than vegetable glues" and is suitable to use with cardboard and wooden items.

Department of Agriculture

One of the largest groups of government publications for consumers has been produced by the Department of Agriculture. The publications discuss foods and food buying as well as menu planning and nutrition.

The federal government publishes booklets that provide helpful information about a wide variety of consumer topics.

Other topics include clothing selection, sewing, and housing. The Yearbooks of Agriculture often are of particular interest to consumers. The 1969 Yearbook, *Food for Us All,* discussed all aspects of food beginning with its movement from the farm to the market and ending with its preparation for family meals.

National Bureau of Standards

In recent years there has been a lot of effort to translate technical research findings by government agencies into terms that will be useful to consumers. The feeling has been that consumers, as taxpayers, have helped pay for developing this information and that it should be made readily available for their use. The Consumer Product Information

Coordinating Center, recently mentioned, was formed to coordinate and encourage such publications.

The National Bureau of Standards is a scientific and technical agency that has begun a publication series especially for consumers. Its reports are based on its experience in developing product-testing procedures and on actual tests of certain products purchased by the government. The first three reports that it published were *Fibers and Fabrics, Tires—Their Selection and Care,* and *Adhesives for Everyday Use.* There are a great many other products for which the National Bureau of Standards undoubtedly could provide useful information. One such product is automobile batteries.

National Highway Safety Bureau

The National Highway Safety Bureau of the Department of Transportation also has developed a consumer information publication series. Its publications provide information on safety aspects of automobile performance. One of the Bureau's first publications was *Performance Data for New 1971 Passenger Cars and Motorcycles.* It includes information on acceleration and passing times and distances, on tire reserve loads (the capacity of tires to bear additional weight), and on stopping distances. The publication is based on data provided by manufacturers to comply with government regulations. The data are listed according to make, model, and equipment option. This publication was one of the first to actually include brand names and model designations. The tables in this report indicate a great deal of variation in performance among makes and models, even for such an important safety factor as stopping distance.

Federal Trade Commission

The consumer education program of the Federal Trade Commission (FTC) is an outgrowth of its responsibility for controlling misleading advertising and deceptive business practices. The publications of the FTC aim to alert consumers to common types of fraudulent claims and deceptive practices. Some of the FTC's concerns are reflected in the titles of its publications: *Mail Order Insurance, Unordered Merchandise—Shipper's Obligations and Consumer's Rights,* and *Advice for Amateurs Who Expect to Breed Chinchillas for Profit.* The first paragraph of the publication on raising chinchillas notes that the ads recruiting prospects "present a glowing picture of large sums of money easily made through the breeding of chinchillas at home. Most such ads have one serious disability. They are false."

COOPERATIVE EXTENSION SERVICE

The Extension Service is a cooperative federal, state, and county program of education in agriculture and home economics. It is administered by the land-grant university in each state, such as Cornell University in New York, The University of Illinois, Oklahoma State University, and the University of California. Extension Service programs are carried to the public by field personnel in individual counties throughout each state.

The original goal of the Extension Service was to improve the income and well-being of rural families by providing information on better farming and homemaking practices. As the American population has become more and more urban, the Extension Service has expanded its programs to serve urban as well as rural families.

One of its important services to consumers is its bulletin series. The publications provide information on such varied topics as food selection, sewing, and lawn care. Like the federal government publications, the Extension Service publications do not mention brand names but instead emphasize buymanship techniques. A current catalog of the Extension Service's consumer publications for your state is available from the Cooperative Extension Service Bulletin Office at your land-grant college or university. Some titles selected from recent catalogs are as follows:

- *Food Facts for Young Athletes* (Ohio State University)
- *Be a Better Shopper* (Cornell University, New York)
- *Refinishing Furniture* (Michigan State University)
- *Selection and Care of Sweaters and Knit Apparel* (University of Illinois)
- *Wet Weather Wear* (University of California)

Your local extension service office, usually located in the county seat, has a staff that can answer a wide range of questions.

BETTER BUSINESS BUREAU

The sources of consumer information that we have discussed so far all have provided product information. They provide relatively little help to the consumer who is trying to decide where to buy. There is, however, a source of information on firms in a local market—the better business bureau. In addition to providing information on local firms, the better business bureaus provide booklets with useful buymanship tips and many warnings on fraudulent schemes. There are, it should be noted, certain kinds of information the better business bureaus are not set up to provide, including product endorsements and ratings and information on the least expensive places to buy particular items. Another service of the better business bureaus is handling consumer complaints. This part of the work of the better business bureaus will be discussed in Chapter 27.

The beginnings of the better business bureaus date to 1912, when the first local groups were organized by businessmen to combat exaggerated claims and fraudulent schemes that they felt damaged the public's faith in advertising. There now are over 140 local better business bureaus throughout the United States. These local organizations are all nonprofit and are supported by contributions from businesses.

The local better business bureaus are self-governing and operate independently but are joined together in a national organization, the Council of Better Business Bureaus, Inc. Some local bureaus have made outstanding records for their service and information efforts. Others have been less forceful either because of lack of funds and personnel or perhaps because of fear of pressure from local member firms. In 1970, the national BBB association reorganized with the goal of improving the services of all the local bureaus. The new national organization has sought funds to assist the local organizations and is encouraging them to take a more active role in assisting consumers. The goal of the new national organization is to create a consumer program so effective that new government programs will seem less necessary.

When providing information on local firms, the better business bureaus will not advise the individual making an inquiry about whom to deal with. They instead give facts from their complaint and information file and leave it up to the individual to interpret the information and make his own decision. For example, someone concerned about the reputation of a particular wig sales firm might be told:

We have had 25 complaints about this firm in the past three months. We have had complaints that the wigs sold failed to live up to the claims made and that the firm did not live up to its money-back guarantee. The firm has advertised wigs as originally $29.95 when there is no evidence that any were ever sold at this price.

In this particular instance, the decision about where not to buy a wig is not very difficult.

The BBB pamphlet series includes a wide variety of subjects, with information on both product choice and kinds of frauds that occur frequently. Two titles from the series are *Color TV—What You Should Know About Purchase, Installation and Service* and *Facts You Should Know about Health Quackery*. The pamphlets are available through local better business bureaus.

Many small cities and towns do not have better business bureaus. Those who do not live in an area served by a better business bureau may request publications from the national organization: Public Affairs Division, Council of Better Business Bureaus, Inc., 1150 17th Street, N.W., Washington, D.C. 20036.

TRADE CERTIFICATION PROGRAMS

Several groups of business firms concerned with improving the durability and safety of consumer goods have joined together to support a testing organization that certifies products that conform to the standards set by a particular organization and awards those products identifying seals. In cases where the organizations have set high standards that are carefully regulated, their seals have real meaning for consumers. In cases where standards are low or are not enforced, the seals awarded have little significance. Three of the best-known seals are those of the Underwriters' Laboratories, Inc., the American Gas Association, and the International Fabricare Institute.

Underwriters' Laboratories, Inc.

Perhaps the most familiar of these seals is the "UL" symbol of the Underwriters' Laboratories, Inc. Over 1 billion UL seals are used each year on new appliances and other products that the Underwriters' Laboratories checks. UL is a nonprofit organization supported by insurance companies; it checks not only electrical appliances but also automotive and boat safety equipment and burglar and fire alarms. UL checks product designs in its own laboratories, visits factories, and checks products purchased in the retail market. Products that are certified have been checked for safety from fire, electric shock, and other hazards. UL does not, however, judge product quality or performance. While UL's testing program performs a valuable service, some consider its standards for electric current leakage too low. Consumers Union has higher standards for preventing electric shock hazards than UL. Nevertheless, shoppers are well advised to look for UL seals when they buy. They should check to be certain that the seal is on both the appliance itself and the cord. Some appliances have cords with seals but do not themselves carry a seal.

American Gas Association

The star seal seen on gas appliances is the symbol of the American Gas Association (AGA). This seal indicates that the product has been built according to standards set by the AGA to ensure durable construction and safe, efficient operation. The AGA is supported by manufacturers of gas appliances and by gas companies. The AGA checks products in its own laboratories, visits factories and stores, and checks product performance under conditions of actual home use. Most gas appliances are reported to carry the AGA seal. Shoppers should double-check for it before buying.

International Fabricare Institute

Because of their concern that the items they handle stand up well to cleaning, members of the cleaning industry have developed a certification program for clothing, household linens, and other fabric items. This certification program is conducted by the International Fabri-

Trade certification seals can be an important source of information for consumers.

Courtesy associations shown

care Institute. After a thorough check proves an item's ability to stand up under typical professional cleaning techniques, the manufacturer is granted permission to use the Institute's "Certified Washable" or "Certified Dry Cleanable" seals. These seals are displayed on hang tags, labels, and in advertising.

Manufacturers interested in obtaining certification send samples to the Institute for testing. The samples are run through a wide range of tests and are cleaned using commercial laundry or dry cleaning equipment and accepted techniques of the laundering or dry cleaning industry. A Dacron-cotton blend dress shirt, for example, is subjected to 20 launderings. Measurements are taken before and after launderings to check that shrinkage is within allowable limits. Special attention is given to collar and sleeve measurements. The fastness of dyes is checked along with the resistance of colors to perspiration and crocking (the transfer of color by rubbing). Buttons and closures are checked to ensure that they have stood up well. The breaking strength of the fabric and seams also is checked. Since the ability of garments to stand up well to repeated cleanings is an important part of satisfactory performance, the Institute's seals can be a useful guide to consumers.

OTHER BUSINESS SOURCES

Individual firms and business trade associations publish a wide variety of booklets and other informational materials about their products and ways to use them. These materials typically are listed in ads. Some home magazines carry special sections listing available informational materials.

Catalogs issued by business firms also may be useful references. In describing items in print, the seller has to point out the quality differences that justify differences in prices. As a result, catalog descriptions can help the consumer identify key quality factors. Mail-order catalogs are a particularly useful reference for product descriptions and also are a useful reference against which local prices can be checked.

MASS MEDIA SOURCES

Until a few years ago consumer problems and issues were given only occasional coverage in either the print media—magazines, newspapers, and books—or in the electronic media—radio and television. More recently all the mass media have come to appreciate the public's great interest in the whole variety of issues that affect them as consumers. Nowadays consumer issues and problems are considered news by the mass media and are the subject of special feature stories, regular columns, and television shows. Stories appear in general-audience magazines such as *Reader's Digest,* home magazines such as *Better Homes and Gardens,* women's magazines such as *McCall's,* and special-interest magazines such as *New York.*

The new coverage of consumer problems supplements the consumer information that the mass media have provided for years. Such items as movie and play reviews, TV and book reviews, and tips on food buying and recipes have been familiar for many years. The mass media have moved into other consumer areas more hesitantly, apparently because they fear the reaction of their advertisers and in some cases open pressure and advertising cancellations. Most publications still avoid mentioning brand names and retailer names when discussing products.

The growing group of consumer reporters is finding a variety of topics that interest its audience. Some reporters have conducted investigations of the local marketplace, including the practices of employment agencies and sanitation in local restaurants. Others have written about government actions affecting local consumers, such as recalls of contaminated food by the Food and Drug Administration. Reporters have done local follow-ups on national issues such as the relation of particular products to pollution problems. Only a few publications have attempted to evaluate products, apparently because of fear of law suits. Francis Pollock of Consumers Union points out that this hesitation to evaluate consumer products is difficult to understand since newspapers have never hesitated to evaluate movies, stocks, basketball teams, and even political candidates.

Consumers should be aware that one of the sources of material for consumer news stories is press releases and photos prepared by public relations experts for manufacturers and trade associations. All the media receive large quantities of this material daily. They are free to ignore it, use it as received, or adapt it to their special needs. Material supplied by heavy advertisers is given special attention in some publications. This practice is said to be especially common on the food and travel pages.

If you took a critical look at your local newspapers and the magazines you read, how would they rate as sources of consumer news? Do they mention brand names and the names of retailers? Do they provide balanced coverage of consumer topics, reporting bad points as well as good points? Do they cover local market conditions? Do they consider the implications of national issues for consumers? Do their stories appear to be free of the influence of special interests?

Consumer-oriented magazines

Two magazines that are devoted exclusively to consumer topics deserve special mention among mass media sources of consumer information. The first is *Changing Times*. This monthly magazine is devoted chiefly to money management and family finance topics, such as "Buy an Old House and Fix It Up?" Some attention is also given to buymanship topics, but no product-testing results or brand ratings are given. Another useful magazine is *Everybody's Money,* which is distributed by many credit unions to their members and is also available by individual subscription. This quarterly publication covers current consumer problems and issues, money management topics, and buymanship information. Neither of these two publications carries advertising.

Magazine seals of approval

Several magazines maintain testing laboratories or employ independent testing agencies to examine products submitted for advertising in their pages, and give a stamp of approval to goods meeting their standards.

Good Housekeeping magazine maintains the Good Housekeeping Institute, which administers a program of study and testing of the products discussed or advertised in its pages. To carry on this program the Institute maintains laboratories and workshops and a staff of more than a hundred persons. Consultants and outside laboratories are sometimes used to supplement the Institute's own work.

Good Housekeeping will not advertise a product until the Institute has investigated it and satisfied itself that the product is a good one and that the advertising claims made for it in the magazine are true. To the products it accepts for advertising, *Good Housekeeping* awards its Consumers' Guaranty Seal, which bears the legend "If product or performance defective, Good Housekeeping guarantees replacement or refund to consumer." The Guaranty Seal does not indicate sweeping approval or recommendation; rather, it is a simple guarantee that if the product is not as advertised in *Good Housekeeping* the magazine will replace the merchandise or refund the purchase price.

Parents' Magazine also awards seals to advertisers whose products meet specific standards. Each advertiser must apply for use of the seal and may not use it until the magazine's Consumer Service Bureau has studied the product and the claims made for it. If necessary, laboratory tests and tests under conditions of actual use of the product may be conducted before approval is given.

Consumers should be aware of several things about the value of magazine endorsements. First, the seal simply says to prospective buyers that the article performs satisfactorily; it does not indicate that it is the best article available. Second, the consumer has little knowledge of the standards by which products are tested. If standards were set extremely high, the number of potential advertisers would decline, and the magazines would lose revenue. Finally, no information is given concerning the comparative value of the product. The tests might very well indicate that the quality of the product justifies its advertising claims, but at the same time, the price of the product might be higher than it should be.

Checking your reading

1.   What was the basic idea that motivated the founding of the consumer-supported product-testing organizations?

2.   What is comparative testing?

3.   What kinds of products do not lend themselves well to the type of testing performed by Consumers' Research and Consumers Union?

4.   How are overall product ratings developed by CR and CU?

5.   In what ways do the product ratings of CR and CU affect manufacturers?

6.   Why was the Consumer Product Information Coordinating Center organized?

7.   How does the list of consumer publications published by the U.S. Government Printing Office differ from that prepared by the Consumer Product Information Coordinating Center?

8.   What topics are the chief concern of the FTC publications?

9.   How can you contact the cooperative extension service in your state?

10.   What kinds of information about local firms do better business bureaus provide? What kinds of information are not provided?

11.   What factors are considered before the Underwriters' Laboratories grants use of its "UL" seal? What factors are not taken into consideration?

12.   What do the International Fabricare Institute's seals "Certified Washable" and "Certified Dry Cleanable" signify?

13.   Why are catalog descriptions of products useful sources of information?

14.   How has concern about the reaction of their advertisers affected the mass media in their handling of consumer news?

15.   What do magazines' seals of approval tell consumers? What type of information do these seals of approval not provide?

1.   Go to the library, and look through some recent issues of *Consumer Bulletin* and *Consumer Reports*. Read carefully about a product that interests you, and prepare a report on your findings. How was the product tested? Which of the characteristics tested seem to have been assigned greatest importance? If you were going to buy the product, what brand and model would you choose? Why?

2.   Jim Munson was talking to his neighbor about how he had used information from Consumers Union and Consumers' Research in choosing a car. The neighbor said, "I wouldn't believe a word either of them says. You can tell they're taking bribes by the way they always rate the same brand at the top." What could Jim reply?

3.   Prepare a report on the activities of either Consumers Union or Consumers' Research, using your library as a source of references. You should use both the publications of the organization itself and discussions about the organization in recent periodicals. Such indexes as *Reader's Guide to Periodical Literature, Business Periodicals Index,* and *Public Affairs Information Service* will be useful in locating articles in magazines and trade journals. What are some of the criticisms of the organization, and what responses have been made to these criticisms? What other activities besides product testing does the organization carry on?

4.   Check the catalog of one of the large mail-order firms, and select a product that interests you and that is offered at several different price levels. Some possibilities are men's T-shirts, jeans, sweat shirts, sneakers, latex interior wall paint, AM-FM table radios, and electric alarm clocks. Make a list of the different items offered by product number. List the materials used and the features, price, and shipping weight of each item. What are the basic differences among the items offered? Which one would best suit your needs? Why?

5.   The consumer-supported product-testing organizations, agencies of the federal government, the Cooperative Extension Service, better business bureaus, the mass media, and trade certification programs all provide consumers with useful information. Make a table listing each of these sources, the kinds of information that each provides, and the strengths and weaknesses of each as a source of useful, unbiased information for consumers.

6.   Examine a recent issue of your local newspaper. Make a list of the headlines of all the articles that contain useful information for consumers. (For this project you can ignore such other useful sources as ads, radio and TV listings, stock market reports, and classified ads.) What important information is included in each article?

7.   We noted in this chapter that the content of the columns and articles in some magazines is influenced by heavy advertisers. Check some recent copies of magazines read by young people to see if you can find any references to particular products or brands in articles and columns. Are these products or brands also advertised in the magazine? What do you conclude from your findings?

The consumer
in the marketplace

Part **2**

Chapter 6

Understanding the effects of advertising

A great deal of money is being spent by business to inform and influence American consumers. The information provided by salespeople, public relations offices, and advertising all are part of this effort to influence consumers. Advertising is a major part of this effort. In the early 1970s American business was spending $20 billion a year on advertising. This figure sounds impressively large, and we can begin to get a better idea of what it means when we realize that this is almost $100 for each person in the country. Because advertising is such an important force in the marketplace and in our everyday lives, it is important for consumers to understand how advertising affects us all. In this chapter we first will discuss how and why business uses advertising as a marketing tool. Next we will consider the extent to which we are influenced by advertising and the kinds of appeals that are used in advertising. We then will consider some of the major criticisms of advertising and some types of deceptive advertising appeals and claims that appear frequently. In the final section we will consider how advertising is regulated.

THE ROLE OF ADVERTISING

Advertising plays an important role, from the standpoint of both business and consumers, in informing the public about new products. It provides information on product features, prices, and availability.

In general, advertising has been the most successful when it has been promoting new products with unique features. Advertising also serves an important function in informing consumers about new ways they can use older and more familiar products and services.

Maintains sales of existing products and services

Advertising is used by business to help maintain the sales of existing products and services. While people outside business sometimes view these ads as attempts to win customers away from other brands, businessmen often talk about advertising as a way to "defend" their share of the market. Both groups probably are right. Advertising is both an offensive and a defensive device, one that can be used to win customers away from other brands and hold the customers one already has. Advertising of existing products and services also serves the function of recruiting customers who only recently have become interested in the product or service. Young men are likely to pay little attention to life insurance ads while they are bachelors but are much more likely to read them after they get married, especially after their first child arrives. Life insurance companies advertise continuously since they know people may become interested in life insurance every day. The Yellow Pages of the telephone book are used to attract customers who are looking for a product or service for the first time.

Provides support for mass media

Advertising plays an important role in our lives since it provides support for the mass media, including newspapers, magazines, radio, and television. While consumers pay part of the cost of producing magazines and newspapers, advertisers pay an even larger share. Without advertising revenue to pay part of its operating costs, a newspaper that now costs the consumer 10 cents might cost 40 cents. Advertising pays the entire cost of operating commercial radio and television. While the broadcast media do have free use of the airwaves, which are public property, the other costs of transmitting programs are borne by the advertisers who use these media. Consumers, of course, pay the costs of buying and operating the radio and television sets that receive these programs. Some people have expressed concern about the dependence of the mass media on advertising and are afraid it may give advertisers too much power over media content. In Chapter 5 you have already seen that advertisers sometimes have been guilty of trying to use their great financial power in order to dictate the content of the mass media.

THE INFLUENCE OF ADVERTISING

It is hard to ignore advertising. We find it everywhere—in the magazines we read, on television, and in the newspaper. Even when we get in our cars and drive off to get away from it, we find advertising on the car radio and on the billboards we pass. Then when we finally get home, we look at the mail and find that it is mostly advertising circulars. There have been a number of attempts to estimate the number of ads to which a consumer is exposed in a given day. One of the most recent and most carefully made studies undertook to determine how many ads people actually do notice in a day.[1] A group of consumers was asked to click a counter each time they noticed an ad during the day. The people in the study reported noticing about 76 ads a day. This estimate of our contact with advertising is impressive when we remember that this exposure occurs day after day and year after year. Such a force could have an important effect on our behavior.

How much can advertising influence behavior?

Until about 30 years ago advertising men were convinced that a series of ads that hammered continuously at the consumer would eventually produce the desired reaction. The problem of influencing the consumer was regarded as mostly one of finding the most effective "sales pitch" and then finding a way to deliver it to the consumer.

More recent research has shown that advertising must be related to the needs and concerns of the audience in order to be effective. If it is not, it will be ignored. The audience no longer is viewed as a passive target for whatever the advertiser throws at it. The modern view is that the audience interacts with the ad. Depending on whether or not the ad interests them, they may either ignore it or look at it. If they look at it, they may either understand the message or misinterpret it. They then may either remember the message or forget it, and, finally, they may choose either to act on the message or disregard it.

Advertising must work within the broad outlines set by a society's values and its wants and goals. No amount of advertising is ever likely to produce many sales for products that do not fit into our way of life. It seems unlikely that advertising would ever produce many sales for chopsticks in this country. Advertising also has little effect on maintaining sales of products outmoded by new technology. It seems unlikely that the manufacturers of old-fashioned ice boxes could ever

---

[1] Raymond A. Bauer and Stephen A. Greyser, *Advertising in America: The Consumer View*, Division of Research, Graduate School of Business Administration, Harvard University, Boston, 1968.

The Bettmann Archive, Inc.

Advertising has little effect on maintaining sales of products such as iceboxes, which have been outmoded by new technology.

have successfully competed in the market with manufacturers of electric refrigerators, no matter how much they advertised.

We can conclude that advertising is not as powerful a force in changing behavior as it sometimes has been pictured. Claims about the possibility of "brainwashing" the public with advertising are greatly exaggerated. The fact that advertising is not all-powerful does not make misleading advertising any less undesirable. Advertising is an important source of information for consumers, and consumers need and deserve to have it kept honest.

What are the appeals used in advertising?

Those who write about advertising usually classify ads as either "rational" or "emotional." Ads that supply basic facts and information about product features, prices, and availability are labeled "rational." Those that provide no facts but instead stress the feelings produced by use of the product are labeled "emotional." These two categories of ads usually are viewed as direct opposites—either an ad is rational or it is emotional. With a little thought we can see that "rational" and "emotional" are not really opposites. For example, an ad may be rational and still arouse strong feelings. An ad that says "Accidents

Are the Leading Cause of Death Among Young Adults—Drive Safely" would seem to have both rational and emotional content. Another problem with classifying ads as either rational or emotional is that, as we saw in the previous section, not all readers respond to an ad in the same way. An ad that some view as emotional may produce little reaction in others.

In studying the appeals used in advertising it may be more useful to focus on the content of an ad and avoid attempting to guess what reaction it will arouse in those who see it. One research team has suggested that ad messages can be grouped into two broad categories: rational appeals and irrational appeals.[2]

- *Rational appeals*—the content of the ad has a direct, natural link to the product. An example would be an ad that describes particular product features, such as the automatic transmission in a new car.
- *Irrational appeals*—the content of the ad makes an arbitrary association between the product and something that has no essential connection with it. An example is an ad that links a soft drink with a baseball game. While soft drinks are often consumed at ball games, they are more frequently consumed in other types of situations.

The researchers identified two different kinds of irrational appeals. One type they call an *internal association*. In this type of appeal an arbitrary association is made between the product and something within the reader, perhaps his need for success or some other personality characteristic. This kind of association is seen, for example, in an ad that reads, "We want this to be the finest car you've ever owned." In this example, the car is associated with the reader's desire for quality and reliability. The other type of arbitrary appeal is an *external association*. This is an association between the product and things within the reader's environment. An example is an ad showing a new-model car as part of a picnic scene, thus linking it to enjoyable activities.

ADVERTISING—PRO AND CON

There have been many criticisms of advertising over the years and many responses to these criticisms. In this section we will examine some of the most frequent criticisms. Some critics have gone so far

[2] Ivan L. Preston and Lawrence Bowen, "Perceiving Advertisements as Emotional, Rational and Irrational," *Journalism Quarterly,* Vol. 48, pp. 73–84, Spring, 1971.

as to take the position that no advertising should be permitted at all. This suggestion seems contrary to our basic ideas about freedom of speech. Certainly the businessman has the right to make his wares known to the public. What is in question is not his right to promote his wares but the manner in which he promotes them.

Should ads be more informative?

One of the most frequent criticisms of advertising is that it provides little useful information on which consumers can base their buying decisions. This problem grows out of the basic nature of advertising. Its goal is to persuade rather than inform. Ads may contain many facts or only a few facts, but in either case the facts presented are chosen to put the product in the best possible light. Even ads that seem basically informative, such as "Home-Grown Tomatoes—35 cents a pound," have a desired reaction in mind: a sale.

Since the advertiser is the one who is paying for the ad, some businessmen argue that he should be allowed to say whatever he wishes as long as what he says is factually correct and the ad is not deceptive or misleading. Some critics of advertising say that we need to go even further than this and require *full disclosure* of all the facts about a product—its good points as well as its bad ones.

It does not seem reasonable to expect the advertiser to discuss the limitations of his product unless it is to his advantage to do so—or unless he is required to. In some cases advertisers may find it desirable to emphasize the kinds of uses for which their product is not suited in order to ensure proper use and safety and to help avoid consumer disappointment.

There are certain facts, some of which may be negative, that sellers are required by law to disclose. Failure to disclose these important facts about a product is considered deceptive and makes the seller subject to action under Federal Trade Commission rules or similar state laws. The kinds of information that must be disclosed include changes in the nature or composition of a product—for example, the substitution of a new ingredient for one that had been used for years. Sellers must also provide information on a product's composition when its appearance is deceptive. For example, a belt made of plastic that could be mistaken for leather must be labeled "imitation leather." Sellers must warn about dangers in the use of products; for example, poisonous vapors, flammability, electric shock, and harmful effects resulting from the misuse of drugs and cosmetics. Sellers must inform buyers if the items offered are not new and if they are of foreign origin. The warning on cigarette packages informing users of the possible harmful effects of smoking is another example of negative product information for which disclosure is required.

Is advertising wasteful?

A frequent criticism of advertising is that it is wasteful and makes the things we buy more expensive than they otherwise would be. In considering this criticism, we should begin by thinking about what advertising really does cost us. Advertising is not as costly as is often thought, and many consumers greatly overestimate the portion of a product's price that goes for advertising. What would be *your* estimate?

Some estimates of advertising's share of product price run as high as 25 and even 40 percent. In general, however, advertising's share is far below these figures. Food processors, on the average, spend about 2.5 cents of each dollar of sales on advertising. Manufacturers of cosmetics and toiletries are among the heaviest spenders and lay out almost 11 cents of each dollar they receive. In contrast, expenditures by motor vehicle manufacturers are only a little over 1 cent for each dollar of sales and are more typical of the outlays of all manufacturing firms taken together. Of course, even this 1 percent becomes substantial when we consider the prices of new cars—advertising would account for about $40 of the cost of a new $4,000 car. We can see, however, that the prices of most products would be reduced relatively little if advertising disappeared altogether. We also should bear in mind that the consumer eventually must pay the bill for advertising, regardless of its size.

Supporters of advertising frequently argue that advertising reduces prices by replacing more costly methods of providing product information. Most of us probably would agree that it is less costly than relying on door-to-door salesmen and large numbers of store clerks to promote goods and services to consumers and provide them with product information.

Spokesmen for advertising have also claimed that instead of raising prices, advertising helps lower them. They argue that advertising expands the market for products and thus permits large-scale production, which lowers the cost of each unit of output and therefore makes lower prices possible. This argument seems valid for products produced by smaller companies and for new products. However, it probably is not valid for established products produced by larger companies. Most economists believe that after companies reach a certain size, they exhaust all possible ways of improving efficiency and cutting costs. Moreover, as companies become very large, problems of communications and management actually may begin to reduce efficiency and increase costs.

Some critics of advertising argue that advertising is wasteful because ads for one brand only cancel out those for others without producing any real increases in total sales. For certain types of products, such as presweetened cereals, consumers have little continuing loyalty to particular brands and are easily switched to others. As a result, cereal manufacturers rely heavily on toys, contests, and advertising to attract and hold customers. Most of us would probably agree this battle for customers is wasteful. There is little question that these expenditures for advertising and promotion do increase the prices that consumers pay. One way to reduce this waste would be to limit the number of brands offered. The dangers and undesirable features of this type of regulation probably would far outweigh the benefits.

Supporters of advertising often argue that advertising is not wasteful because it adds value to products that are advertised. That is, because of advertising, consumers value products more highly than they otherwise might and gain more satisfaction from them. This argument does have merit. Part of our enjoyment in consuming most products is a result of the feelings they produce. If a particular shade of lipstick makes a woman feel more beautiful, it actually may give her the self-confidence and poise that will, in fact, make her more attractive. This effect is something like the *placebo effect* of the sugar pills doctors sometimes give patients. While the sugar pill has no real physical effect, its psychological effect helps to relieve the patient's symptoms. It should be noted, however, that while advertising adds value to new products it also may help to destroy the value of things we already own. Ads for new clothing styles may make us value last year's clothes less and may make us more willing to discard them. Thus, ads may increase the *psychological obsolescence* of things we have, causing us to value them less, even though they still are perfectly usable.

Does advertising distort our values?

We have noted that advertising techniques are not powerful enough to "brainwash" us into accepting products or ideas that conflict with our basic values. Some critics, however, claim that even though advertising may not be able to completely change our values, it is capable of distorting them. These critics argue that advertising leads us to want the kinds of things we see advertised rather than seek other possibilities. This, they say, leads us to spend more than we might otherwise spend on advertised articles and less on unadvertised things such as public recreation facilities and libraries. This argument was developed in detail by the noted economist John Kenneth Galbraith in his book *The Affluent Society.* Galbraith contrasted the sizable stock of private goods that most of us enjoy with our poor public services, noting that: The family which takes its . . . air-conditioned power-steered, and power-braked car out for a tour passes through cities that are badly paved, made hideous by litter . . . they pass on into a countryside that has been rendered largely invisible by commercial art . . . they picnic on exquisitely packaged food from a portable icebox by a polluted stream and go on to spend the night at a park which is a menace to public health and morals.[3]

A frequent response to this argument is that a consumer's wants have meaning regardless of where they come from. A want created by advertising may be just as strong and just as important to a consumer as one growing out of more direct experience. One can still wonder, however, what our wants and needs would be like if the idea of good nutrition were promoted as strongly as food brands, or if the idea of providing more public parks and swimming pools were promoted as heavily as new motion pictures are.

The Advertising Council, Inc.

The advertising profession has worked to enlist concern on a number of important public issues.

---

[3] John Kenneth Galbraith, *The Affluent Society,* 2nd ed., rev. 1969, Houghton Mifflin Company, Boston, p. 223.

It should be recognized that the advertising profession actually has worked to enlist public interest for some important national concerns such as better schools, protection of the environment, and sales of savings bonds. Campaigns dealing with these concerns have been developed by the Advertising Council, a nonprofit organization founded and supported by business to conduct public-service advertising campaigns. Ads for the Council's campaigns are created without charge by advertising agencies, and time and space are donated by the media. Millions of dollars' worth of free ads are run each year as a result of the Advertising Council's efforts.

Does advertising interfere with competition?

Questions about the effect of advertising on competition in the marketplace are heard less often than the questions that we have just discussed. They are, however, important ones. Some economists have expressed concern that advertising gives an unfair competitive advantage to larger firms and makes the situation of new firms and small firms more difficult. These economists believe that the advertising costs of launching new products are so high that small firms have difficulty raising the necessary funds. Without advertising, small companies cannot win needed customers, since in the absence of other information shoppers are likely to rely on familiar brand names. In contrast, larger companies have ample funds available to promote new products and have the added advantage that their company name already is widely known. Larger companies that are high-volume advertisers also have the advantage of getting significant discounts on the time and space they buy in the mass media. Some economists believe that these advantages have been an important factor contributing to the growth of larger firms and their increasing control of the market for many consumer goods.

Critics of advertising have also pointed out that advertising diverts the consumer's attention from the product's price to other aspects of the product. They argue that this tends to reduce competition among companies on the basis of price. Spokesmen for advertising admit this and continue by arguing that competing on the basis of price is easy. Price cuts by one company can be matched quickly by others but may result in a price-cutting war that destroys weaker firms. Supporters of advertising argue that competition that emphasizes product features, service, and warranties also benefits the consumer and avoids the problems created by price wars. Most advertisers emphasize differences in product features and services in the hopes of building a group of customers who will continue to be loyal to their brand. They hope that by using this technique, *product differentiation,* they can insulate themselves from some of the competitive pressure of other brands.

RECOGNIZING DECEPTIVE APPEALS AND CLAIMS

Certain kinds of deceptive advertising appeals and claims appear over and over again despite continued efforts to stop them. These claims often are used by advertisers who are fully aware that their claims are deceptive and that they may result in government action or pressure from local better business bureaus. Advertisers who use such claims generally have found them so successful that they can make a great deal of profit from them before any action can be taken to force them to stop. Because ads employing deceptive appeals appear repeatedly, consumers need to learn how to recognize them.

Meaningless claims and misrepresentation

Ads are full of phrases such as "lasts longer!" that, at first glance, appear to supply useful facts. Some ads even supply statistics such as "lasts 40% longer!" to give their claims an authentic ring. On closer consideration, however, it is unclear just exactly what the performance of the product is being compared to. Is the comparison being made between present performance and the performance of the previous version of the brand, before it was "improved"? Or is the product's performance being compared to that of other similar products? Statements of this type can be regarded as *unclear claims,* claims that cannot be evaluated because of uncertainty about what they really mean. Advertising that says that a product is "guaranteed" is making another unclear claim, since uncertainty remains about what exactly is being guaranteed.

Problems also arise from the use of *vague terms,* ones that cover a wide degree of meaning or performance. The term "washable" on the label of a woman's delicate blouse, for example, could be considered vague. Does "washable" mean machine-washable and at regular temperatures or does it mean hand-washable? Other examples of terms that cover a wide degree of performance are "stain-resistant," "rust-inhibiting," and "wrinkle-resistant."

Another problem is claims that misrepresent important facts about a product. The Federal Trade Commission has acted in a number of cases where exaggerated or false claims about a product's durability and performance were made. These actions provide consumers with some protection against exaggerated claims. Consumers should recognize, however, that the FTC has not checked, and cannot possibly check, all advertising claims. Consumers still need to be on their guard, especially when they hear claims such as "you may never need to buy socks again—unless the laundry loses these."

Bait advertising

Bait advertising is an insincere offer to sell a product or service that the advertiser does not really wish or intend to sell. The offer is, instead, used as "bait" to lure customers to the advertiser's place of business. Once he has the customer in his store, the advertiser tries to switch the customer to a more expensive, and more profitable, item than the one he advertised. This technique of luring customers with an ad for one item and then trying to switch them to another item sometimes is referred to as *bait and switch*. The practice is outlawed by many states and is considered a deceptive practice by the FTC.

Examples of the technique are ads by furniture retailers offering "3 Rooms of Furniture—Only $129." Once in the store, the potential customer may find that the items offered include only a bed, a sofa, and a dining table with two chairs, all of which are scratched and in poor condition. The disappointed shopper is quickly diverted by the salesmen to more expensive items in better condition. Shoppers who actually are interested in buying the advertised items typically find that they are "already sold" or are not available for some other reason.

The bait and switch technique should be distinguished from attempts by salesmen to "trade up" shoppers from advertised models to higher-priced lines. *Trading-up* is considered a legitimate sales technique in cases where the advertised item is capable of doing the job and where the advertiser has a reasonable supply that he is willing to sell.

Referral sales schemes

Advertising plans that offer purchasers bonuses for providing the seller with the names of other prospective buyers have been labeled *referral sales schemes*. These plans have been a repeated source of problems and disappointment for consumers. Under such a scheme, a builder of swimming pools would, for example, offer a pool buyer $50 for each prospective purchaser he refers to the builder who buys a pool. However, referral sales schemes usually require the purchaser to pay the full price and in the sales contract promise bonuses for referrals. Most purchasers find that under these terms they can produce few real prospects. Referral sales schemes are frequently used in promoting sales of aluminum house siding, storm windows, and other items for remodeling, but they are also used to promote such items as carpeting, encyclopedias, sewing machines, and vacuum cleaners. Although some attempts have been made to outlaw referral sales schemes, they are legal. They have been considered deceptive only when the seller refuses to make the promised bonus payments or when he advertises a "special introductory price" that is really his regular price. Consumers would be well advised to consider contracts with referral sales promises with care and should not count heavily on receiving bonuses.

Fictitious pricing

Another deceptive practice that appears regularly is the overstatement of the "list price" and "manufacturer's suggested price" in order to convince shoppers that advertised prices offer special bargains. Often manufacturers collaborate with retailers by "preticketing" goods with these prices. The list price used is high enough so that most retailers can discount it and point to the price tag as evidence of what a good buy they are offering.

Not all list prices are fictitious, and thus offers of price reductions cannot automatically be considered deceptive. The advertising of list-price claims is, however, considered deceptive by the FTC unless the price stated is one at which a substantial volume of sales actually occurred. A clearly deceptive practice would be a watch manufacturer's offer to preticket his watches with any price the retailer wanted.

Meaningless claims, misrepresentation, bait advertising, referral sales schemes, and fictitious pricing are only a few of the deceptive advertising appeals of which consumers need to be aware. We will have an opportunity to discuss some others later in this book. Consumers need to be aware of them all.

REGULATING AND IMPROVING ADVERTISING

In the last section we examined some of the many different kinds of appeals that deceive consumers. Legal authorities have, in general, taken the position that as long as an ad does not misrepresent the facts, it should be permitted. The line between exaggerated claims (or puffery, as it is sometimes called) and deliberate misrepresentation is hard to draw. It partly is a matter of degree: minor misstatements may escape legal action while clear exaggerations may not. Some laws require proof that the advertiser intended to deceive. It usually is very difficult to establish this.

Federal Trade Commission

The government agency that has the major responsibility for regulating advertising is the Federal Trade Commission. It has the responsibility of taking action against most kinds of deceptive claims appearing in almost any medium, from television to sales brochures and sales talks. The FTC originally was established in 1914 to control unfair methods of competition among business firms. Later its powers were broadened to include deceptive actions as well. Attention was given to deceptive ads because of the unfair competitive advantage they give dishonest businesses and the financial injury received by the consumers.

In deciding whether an ad is deceptive the following factors are taken into account:

- Even though every statement in it is factually correct, the ad must not create any misleading impressions.
- Important facts about the product or service advertised must not be concealed.
- Attention must not be diverted from the actual terms and conditions of the offer.
- False or misleading comparisons with other products are not permitted.

Even in cases where there is no evidence of actual intent to deceive, the FTC can rule an ad deceptive if it is judged to have a tendency to deceive.

When individual firms employ practices that the FTC considers deceptive, the FTC has the power to order them to "cease and desist" from these activities. The FTC can also go into the courts to obtain injunctions to temporarily restrain firms from using false advertising appeals until it has time to hold a regular FTC hearing to decide whether the ad is deceptive.

The FTC relies heavily on the voluntary cooperation of business and tries to help individual firms and entire industries understand how their activities can be brought within the legal guidelines set by the FTC. As part of this effort the FTC issues *trade regulation rules,* which are its interpretation of the kinds of actions required of firms under the laws that the FTC enforces. Violations of these rules are likely to result in FTC action. An example of a rule, issued in 1971, is the trade regulation of grocery store specials. This rule makes it a violation of the law for any retail food store to advertise food or other merchandise at a stated price unless the products advertised are in stock and readily

The Federal Trade Commission found this advertisement deceptive. In the advertisement, the top photograph was accompanied by the following text: "This is ordinary safety glass made of window glass. It puts a wiggle in the things you watch." The Federal Trade Commission found that the picture at top was taken with a telephoto lens (which magnifies the distortion in the foreground).

The picture at bottom was accompanied by the following text: "This is safety plate glass. It takes the wiggle out of what you watch." However, this photo was taken with a regular lens through an open window (that is, with no glass).

available to customers during the days indicated in the ad. Another recent trade regulation rule required that light bulb containers provide information on the light output of the bulbs (measured in lumens) and on the expected life of the bulbs, as well as the usual information on wattage.

In 1969, Ralph Nader, the well-known consumer spokesman, and his associates issued a comprehensive report on the FTC, criticizing it for spending too much time on trivial matters and ignoring large-scale deception by major firms, especially those that advertise heavily on television. As a result both of these criticisms and of new leadership, the FTC has taken a much more active role in the last few years.

In 1971, the FTC began, on a product-by-product basis, to require advertisers to supply evidence to support certain advertising claims. The automobile manufacturers were the first to be called upon to supply evidence. They were asked to document certain specific claims they had made about safety, quality, efficiency, performance, and comparative prices. Among the claims that the FTC wanted supported was the Ford Motor Company's claim that their LTD was "over 700% quieter" and American Motor Company's claim that their Hornet was "the lowest priced compact made in America." Manufacturers of electric shavers and air-conditioners were the next to be called on to provide backing for the claims in their ads. The evidence supplied to the FTC is to be placed on file for inspection by any interested parties. Because of the volume of evidence required to support claims, the FTC is not attempting to publish any of the information supplied.

In 1971, the FTC for the first time required the publication of *corrective advertising,* which was designed to correct the impressions consumers get from advertising that is judged false or unfair. The first order of this kind involved ITT Continental Baking Company, which was judged to have mispresented the facts when it claimed that its Profile bread had fewer calories than ordinary bread and provided substantial benefits for controlling or reducing weight. The company was required to devote 25 percent of its advertising expenditures for Profile bread for the next year to ads approved by the FTC that indicated that the bread was not, in fact, effective for weight reduction. The FTC believes that corrective ads offer several benefits, since they help to correct false impressions consumers may have received from deceptive advertising and also restore competitive balance in markets where deceptive advertisers may have gained an unfair advantage. The advertising profession has objected vigorously to corrective advertising, and its use by the FTC seems certain to be tested in the courts.

State laws

The laws under which the FTC operates regulate a major portion of all advertising, since they cover all goods and services that are included in interstate commerce. Laws are needed, however, to cover advertising by firms that operate strictly in a local area or within state boundaries. Most state laws regulating deceptive advertising are based on the *Printers' Ink* Model Statute. This model for a state law was first proposed in 1911 by an advertising trade paper that was called *Printers' Ink.* It has been passed in various stronger and weaker forms by almost all the states and also covers the District of Columbia. In some states the law has been weakened by requiring proof that the advertiser intended to deceive. The law deals only with deceptive information included in an ad and does not classify the omission of important facts as deceptive. This is regarded by many as a very serious weakness.

Relatively few offenders have actually been prosecuted under the state laws. The laws do, however, provide severe penalties and are considered useful in deterring wrongdoers.

A few states have adopted various forms of a new model law, the Unfair Trade Practices and Consumer Protection Law, developed by the FTC. The law would give state attorneys general powers to control deceptive advertising much like those of the FTC. Those who back these proposals believe that "little FTCs" at the state level would be better able to give ready assistance to consumers.

Other federal agencies

Although the FTC has the major responsibility for regulating advertising, certain other federal agencies have responsibilities for particular areas. The Federal Communications Commission (FCC) has certain controls over the content of radio and television advertising as well as over the number and length of commercials. As a result of FCC actions, cigarette advertising was removed from both media. The chief concern of the U.S. Postal Service regarding advertising is with ads sent by mail that involve obscenity, lotteries, or fraud. The Food and Drug Administration regulates the labeling of food and drugs and the content of literature that is included with the items, as well as folders and booklets that might be shipped separately. The Securities and Exchange Commission is responsible for regulating deceptive advertising of investment securities.

Self-regulation by business

Businessmen themselves have played an important role in working to control deceptive claims and bad taste in advertising. Associations of professionals in advertising have worked over the years to combat misleading advertising and develop codes of advertising ethics. The local better business bureaus are an outgrowth of early efforts by local advertising men's clubs to control exaggerated ad claims and fraudulent schemes. The vigilance committees organized by the local advertising clubs evolved over time into the present system of better business bureaus.

In 1971, three major advertising associations joined with the Council of Better Business Bureaus, Inc. to undertake a new program of reviewing advertising at the national level by major companies. Under the proposed plan complaints are to be considered by a National Advertising Review Board. The board will consist of 30 representatives of advertisers, 10 advertising agency representatives, and 10 representatives of the general public. Attention will be focussed first on deceptive claims. The board later may broaden its activities to include ads considered to be in bad taste. The board plans to rely chiefly on persuasion to end practices it considers undesirable. However, if persuasion fails, the board plans to refer cases involving deceptive ads to the FTC and other regulatory agencies.

Other business groups also have been active in improving advertising standards. Many individual newspapers, magazines, and radio and television stations screen the advertising they carry both for misleading claims and bad taste. The standards used and the amount of attention given to screening advertising appear, however, to vary greatly. Trade publications have spoken out to help improve advertising. As mentioned earlier, *Printers' Ink* played a key role in the passage of state laws to control deceptive advertising and in the passage of the Federal Trade Commission Act. Another major publication, *Advertising Age,* frequently criticizes ads and practices that it considers misleading or in poor taste. In addition to these efforts, many individual firms have established procedures for reviewing their ads before they appear.

Checking your reading

1. What three major roles does advertising perform in our economy?
2. Describe the modern view of how advertising affects an audience.
3. What is an irrational appeal? Give an example. How would you classify your example—as an internal or an external association?
4. Why do advertisers generally dislike the idea of full disclosure?
5. Why do some spokesmen for advertising argue that it adds value to products?
6. Why do some economists believe that advertising gives an unfair competitive advantage to large companies?
7. What is product differentiation? What devices do manufacturers use to differentiate products?
8. Why is the meaning of such claims as "stronger, longer-lasting suds!" unclear?
9. How does the bait and switch technique work?
10. Why are consumers who participate in referral sales schemes often disappointed?
11. What is meant by fictitious pricing?
12. What four factors are taken into account by the FTC in deciding whether an ad is deceptive?
13. Why does the FTC put so much emphasis on getting the voluntary cooperation of business in controlling advertising claims?
14. Why are some of the state laws on deceptive advertising considered inadequate?
15. What is the purpose of the new National Advertising Review Board?

Consumer problems and projects

1.   Study the ads in publications aimed at purchasing agents (perhaps your principal's office can make some available) and businessmen. (The public library subscribes to such magazines as *Business Week*.) Compare the contents of these ads with the contents of ads in general consumer magazines. What differences do you note? What are the reasons for these differences?

2.   Make a collection of ads that make rational and irrational appeals, and label each. Would you classify the irrational appeals as internal or external associations?

3.   Watch the mass media, and collect examples of claims you consider deceptive. Can you find examples of meaningless claims, vague terms, exaggerated claims that may be false, bait advertising, and referral sales schemes?

4.   Visit nearby drugstores and discount stores. What examples of preticketing of merchandise can you find? Are the items being offered for sale at the preticketed price? If not, do you feel deception is involved? Why?

5.   Study the advertising in a recent magazine or newspaper. What ad claims can you find that you believe should be supported with scientific evidence? What kind of evidence or tests would be necessary to supply satisfactory proof?

6.   Watch the mass media for advertising supported by the Advertising Council. It can be identified by a small letter "a" in a circle surrounded by the words "Advertising Council." What are the subjects of the ads you noted? Do you feel these are important public issues? What other issues do you believe should be covered?

7.   Study the ads for a product in which you are interested. What information do they provide? How helpful do you find them? What other information would you like to see provided?

Chapter 7

Buying clothing

Although most of us seldom think of our clothes in this way, clothes are really a kind of portable environment with which we surround ourselves. One of their key functions is to provide us with a shelter within which we can be comfortable—protected from sun, wind, and cold. Providing a portable shelter is not, however, their only function. If all we wanted from our clothes was shelter from the elements, we might all go around in pup tents with a hole cut out for our heads.

Our interest in clothes goes far beyond their function as a shelter. For most of us, clothes are an expression of our uniqueness and our individuality. We express ourselves in the styles and colors we pick and the combinations of clothes we put together. In this country we are so devoted to this idea of self-expression in dress that one of the things that seems strangest about life in modern China under communism is the uniformity of dress—with people in all walks of life and of all ages and both sexes in the same kind of baggy blue suits.

At the same time we use clothes to express our individuality, we also use them to demonstrate our membership in particular groups. Although high school students pride themselves in the individuality of their clothes, they actually limit their choices to particular types of clothes. Even the most individualistic students are not likely to choose clothes that will lead them to be mistaken for businessmen or housewives. Clothes can be used to demonstrate group membership in even more direct ways. The athlete shows his team membership when he wears his letter jacket. Other students demonstrate their school pride when they wear clothes in the school colors.

From this discussion you can see that clothes serve several important purposes. This is why, in choosing clothes, we need to keep both functional considerations such as durability, comfort, and ease of care in mind and aesthetic considerations such as style, pattern, and color.

PLANNING YOUR PURCHASES

Some people act as if they think about nothing but what they wear while others hardly seem to think about it at all. Some balance between these two extremes is needed. No one can really afford to neglect his appearance. Just as we use clothes to express ourselves, other people use them as a way to find out what kind of people we are. If someone looked at the clothes you have on now, how would he judge you? Would he think you are sloppy, dull, lively, sporty, or sociable? Whether we think it is fair or not, others do judge us by our dress and our appearance. With effort most of us can make a good appearance. While not everyone can afford to be expensively dressed, there are few people in this country who cannot afford to be neatly dressed.

Determining your needs

To be well dressed, we need something more than a miscellaneous collection of slacks, sweaters, skirts, and shoes. To really meet our needs, a wardrobe must be planned in relation to the kinds of things we do and the kinds of places we go. Only in this way can it truly meet our needs.

To begin with, we must consider all our different activities and the kinds of clothes we need for each. For example, this might be our list:

- School
- Sports
- Informal social events; school events
- Dress-up social events
- Church
- After-school job
- Home chores—cleaning, working on car, yard work

Clothes for one of the categories may also serve another category. Clothes suitable for school usually are also suitable for informal parties. Clothes for dress-up social occasions may be suitable for church.

Our needs vary with the season and changes in the climate. Those people who live in the Midwest and Northeast will need a more varied wardrobe than those who live on the West Coast and in the South.

Taking an inventory

Once you have some idea about your clothing needs, you will need to evaluate your present situation. In Chapter 4 we discussed the best way to determine one's situation—taking an inventory. Inventory taking is a good time to review the condition of one's clothes and a good time to get rid of items that are no longer used, outgrown, or beyond repair. You probably will want to get rid of things that you have not worn in the last year. Try on all the items you plan to keep to be certain they still fit—some may be outgrown, and others may need alterations. Once you have sorted things out, you can begin to determine the additional things you need—and the things of which you have enough.

Inventory time is also a good time to study your wardrobe to see what it can tell you about your tastes and preferences. Which items do you like best? Which items have been most useful? Which ones do you feel you look best in? Which ones do you feel most comfortable in? The reasons behind your answers will help you learn why some of your past clothing choices were successful while others fell short.

One of the best ways to get an overview of what you have and what you need is to fill out a table such as the following one, which reflects needs for both different activities and different seasons.

	Activities		
	---	---	---
Seasons	School and Informal Social Events	Dress-up Occasions and Church	Home Chores

Deciding on additional items

When you have your inventory completed you will be ready to begin deciding what additional items you need to fill out your wardrobe. These decisions will, of course, have to be governed by how much you can spend. You may not have much to spend right away, so you will need a long-range plan toward which you can work.

Most of us can afford to buy relatively few new items in a given year. This is why it is important to make every choice count. A boy from a typical middle-income family might, for example, buy the following items in a year:

- 3–4 pairs of slacks
- 4–5 sport shirts
-   1 jacket or sport coat
- 3–4 pairs of shoes

We can see that this does not allow much margin for errors and poor choices. There are, however, some buying strategies that can help you stretch a limited clothing budget.

CHOOSE VERSATILE ITEMS One strategy in buying that can help to stretch a clothing budget is to choose versatile items. Versatile items are ones that have several different functions. They may be suitable for more than one season of the year—an example is a raincoat with a zip-in lining for cold weather. Or they may be versatile because they can be worn for different types of occasions—an example would be a basic dress whose appearance can be changed by wearing different accessories.

If you have more funds available, you can afford to develop a more specialized wardrobe. You can choose items that are well suited for a particular purpose but are not well suited for others. You could, for example, choose a tie that looks great with a particular shirt or a scarf that goes only with one particular blouse without worrying that they do not go well with other items in your wardrobe.

COORDINATE COLORS AND STYLES If your funds are limited you will also want to give some thought to another kind of versatility—the ability of wardrobe items to look good in different combinations. An example would be a sweater that looks good with several different skirts or pairs of slacks. This kind of versatility comes from concentrating your clothing choices on a particular group of colors and styles that go well together. This might mean concentrating your choices on clothes in shades of blue that go well together, plus some clothes in colors that go well with blue—perhaps yellow or red. These items plus some in neutral colors such as white, off-white, and tan will go together well in all sorts of combinations. Such a variety of possible combinations in a wardrobe will make it seem larger than it really is.

STICK TO BASIC STYLES Many clothing items are discarded long before they are worn out because they are no longer in style. If your clothing funds are limited you will want to choose styles that remain in fashion for several years, especially for more expensive items such as a sport jacket or a good dress. Longer-lasting styles typically are simpler, less extreme designs. They are never "the latest thing" but can be counted on to be in good taste and attractive for several years.

If you like the latest styles and have little money to spend, your best bet is to limit yourself to less expensive items such as sportswear and casual wear. These items usually are expected to give only one or two years' wear, anyway.

SELECTING CLOTHING

A number of considerations need to be taken into account in choosing clothing—color, style, fiber and fabrics, durability, and ease of care. Different people weigh these considerations differently. Those who are especially concerned about their personal appearance are likely to give particular attention to color and style. Others, with limited clothing budgets, may feel they have to sacrifice color and style for durability and ease of care. In this section on selecting clothing we will give some attention to them all.

Color and style

We all know that some combinations of colors are more pleasing than others. Yet we often forget about our own natural coloring in choosing clothing items. The fact is that each of us has several natural coloring features—the color of our hair, of our skin, and of our eyes. These colors need to be taken into account in choosing clothing colors if the total combination is to be a pleasing one.

Even when we do think about our natural coloring we often group hair, eye, and skin colors in broad categories without taking full account of all the variations within each category. We classify people with brown-green, brown-gold, light-brown, and dark-brown eyes as having "brown" eyes. We do the same with skin color—we classify people as either white, black, or yellow. Yet if we look around we can see that skin colors vary widely within these three categories.

Among white people, skin tones may vary from very fair, with a hint of blue, to pink. Redheads' skins have orange tones, and those with olive complexions have yellow skin tones. The skins of black people show a similar range of tones. Some are more yellow or orange in tone, while darker skins may have underlying tones of red or blue. Orientals' skin tones also vary widely.

Clothing specialists have developed a number of suggestions about the most pleasing combinations of clothing colors with skin coloring, and you may want to read what they have to say. But once you are aware of your skin coloring you can begin to do some thinking about clothing colors for yourself. You can study color pictures in magazines to see what colors look best on people with coloring similar to yours. You can note what colors other people with coloring similar to yours seem to look best in. You can also note the colors of the clothes that seem to bring you the most compliments. We all have our own unique natural coloring, and picking clothing colors that go well with it is one way we can emphasize our individuality.

Clothing experts have developed a number of suggestions about clothing styles that best suit different body types. They suggest, for example, that shorter people choose styles that emphasize vertical lines. This might be done by choosing patterns with vertical stripes or avoiding colors that contrast too sharply above and below the waist. For example, a medium-blue sweater instead of a white one to go with a medium-blue skirt or slacks would be a good choice for a short person. There are other suggestions for heavy people, thin people, and so on.

The teacher who teaches clothing in home economics in your school probably can make helpful suggestions, or, if you ask your librarian, she will be able to help you find a useful reference book on making style choices.

Fibers and fabrics

Consumer product-testing information can be a useful guide in selecting many products. There is, however, relatively little test information available on clothing. Only a few items are tested regularly—men's dress shirts, T-shirts, and raincoats; women's hosiery; and children's jeans, shoes, and sneakers. Because of the large number of fabrics and fiber combinations used, the large number of manufacturers involved in producing fabrics and clothing, and the use of store brands by many retailers, the number of clothing products to be tested is too large to handle. As a result, testing efforts have been concentrated on products produced by large manufacturers that can be readily identified by their brand names. This leaves the consumer without any product-testing information to guide important purchases of wool coats, sport jackets, good dresses, and so on. For these items, then, the consumer must develop criteria for judging quality.

Consumers must learn to judge clothing quality for themselves. They can be guided in judging quality by the textile fibers and fabric used in a garment and also by the garment's construction. Once consumers have some general information about the characteristics of particular fibers, such as cotton, nylon, and acrylic, they are more able to judge how a fabric made from them is likely to perform, and whether they will be satisfied with their purchases.

FIBER CHARACTERISTICS The two most familiar natural fibers used in clothing are cotton and wool. Cotton is popular because it is absorbent, comfortable, easy to wash, and easy to care for when treated with permanent-press finishes. It also has the advantage of being inexpensive. Wool is popular because of its warmth, its relatively good resistance to wrinkles, and its ability to absorb a good deal of moisture without feeling damp.

Rayon and acetate are the two oldest man-made fibers. Both are made from cellulose (usually obtained from wood pulp), and both are relatively inexpensive, but the two have somewhat different characteristics. Because of its luster and silky feel, acetate is often used as a substitute for silk. Rayon dyes well and can be made to imitate a variety of fibers; unlike acetate, it is relatively absorbent. Thus, for certain garments this difference can be an important factor.

Nylon is the first of the truly synthetic fibers. One of its main assets is its versatility. It can be used in sheer hosiery or to give strength and durability to work clothes. Polyester, in combination with cotton, made modern permanent-press clothing possible. Polyester contributed the important advantages of resistance to shrinking and resistance to wrinkles, and because it is not absorbent, it is fast-drying. Acrylic is popular because it offers wool-like qualities but is easy to care for and is washable. Triacetate is chemically similar to acetate and has some of the same qualities. It is popular because pleats and creases can be permanently set with heat, and it is easy to care for. The characteristics of these textile fibers are set forth in more detail in the table on pages 116–117. In considering the characteristics of individual fibers, the reader should bear in mind that these can be changed in the course of the manufacturing process, and some limitations can be overcome with special finishes and treatments.

CHARACTERISTICS OF TEXTILE FIBERS USED IN CLOTHING

Fibers and Selected Trade Names	Wearing Quality		Appearance Factors			Ease of Care		Uses
	Strength	Resistance to Abrasion	Resistance to Wrinkling	Resistance to Stains	Wash-and-Wear Characteristics	Care Recommendations		
Cotton	Good to excellent	Medium	Fair to poor (unless treated)	Fair to poor (unless treated)	Fair to poor (unless treated)	Machine-wash and tumble dry, or dry-clean	Undergarments, work clothes; in blends with polyester	
Wool	Fair to poor	Medium	Good to excellent	Fair to poor	Fair to poor	Dry-clean, or wash by hand with extreme care	Outerwear, suits, dresses, knit goods	
Rayon Avisco Bemberg Celanese	Fair to poor	Fair to poor	Fair to poor	Fair to poor	Fair to poor	Wash by hand (unless otherwise indicated)	Slacks and suits, women's wear, linings	
New Rayons Avril Avron Zantrel	Improved in new rayons	Improved in new rayons		Improved in new rayons		Machine-wash and tumble dry, or dry-clean		
Acetate Acele Avisco Celanese Chromspun	Fair to poor	Fair to poor	Fair to poor	Medium	Fair to poor	Hand-launder, if indicated, or dry-clean	Lingerie, dresses; as a substitute for silk	

Fiber							Uses
Triacetate *Arnel*	Fair to poor	Fair to poor	Good to excellent	Medium	Good to excellent	Machine-wash and tumble dry	Tricot lingerie and outer-wear, knits, permanently pleated garments
Nylon *Antron* *Cantrece* *Caprolan* *Qiana*	Good to excellent	Good to excellent	Fair to poor	Good to excellent	Good to excellent	Machine-wash and tumble dry at low temperature	Hosiery, socks, windproof jackets, work clothes; new Qiana has silklike qualities
Acrylic *Acrilan* *Creslan* *Orlon* *Zefran*	Fair to poor	Fair to poor	Good to excellent	Good to excellent	Good to excellent	Machine-wash and tumble dry at low temperature, or dry-clean	Sweaters, knit goods, fake furs; as a substitute for wool
Polyester *Dacron* *Fortrel* *Kodel* *Trevira*	Good to excellent	Good to excellent (some types subject to pilling)	Good to excellent	Good to excellent, but low resistance to oily stains	Good to excellent	Machine-wash and tumble dry, or dry-clean	In blends with cotton for shirts, dresses, sportswear, slacks

Source: Josephine M. Blandford and Lois M. Gurel, *Fibers and Fabrics*, U.S. National Bureau of Standards Consumer Information Series No. 1, 1970.

Blends and combinations of two or more fibers often are used in order to get the best characteristics of each. For example, the popular combination of cotton and polyester provides the comfort and absorbency of cotton and the strength and wash-and-wear qualities of polyester. Many combinations use an absorbent fiber (cotton, wool, or rayon) along with a nonabsorbent one (polyester or acetate)—a garment made entirely of a nonabsorbent synthetic fiber seems too warm to many people. Polyester is also useful in combination with cotton for permanent-press fabrics because the special finish used to get easy-care characteristics seriously weakens cotton. Polyester is used to add needed strength. Experts do not agree on how much of a fiber is needed for it to have a significant effect on a fabric's performance. Some say 25 percent; others say 50 percent. There are some exceptions to this, however. As little as 15 percent nylon in a fabric contributes significantly to its strength. This is why small amounts of nylon frequently are added to work clothes and jeans. Also, 10 percent or less of such elastic fibers as rubber or spandex can add stretch qualities to a fabric.

FIBER LABELING   In the years just after World War II a number of new man-made fibers appeared on the market. Each was marketed under its own trade name, and consumers had little way of knowing which had similar characteristics and which differed. To simplify this problem, family names were developed for man-made fibers with similar chemical compositions. In 1960, when the Textile Fiber Products Identification Act took effect, manufacturers were required to label fabrics with the family (or generic) names of the fibers used. Trade names also may be listed; for example, the label on a polyester-cotton blend fabric might list "65% Dacron [the trade name of a polyester fiber made by E. I. du Pont de Nemours & Co.] polyester [the family name], 35% cotton [also a family name]." Under the terms of the act all textile products must be labeled, and the labels must list fibers in order by weight and indicate the percent by weight for each fiber for which the weight is 5 percent or more. Fibers that make up less than 5 percent by weight can be listed only if they have some specific function. This is to control attempts to confuse consumers by listing small amounts of expensive fibers. A listing such as "4% spandex for elasticity" is permitted because it states the function of the fiber. In addition, the label must indicate the name or identification number of the firm marketing the product and the country of origin, if the item is imported.

The other major law governing textile labeling is the Wool Products Labeling Act, which became effective in 1941. This act requires that every article of wool clothing must be labeled to indicate the kind of wool used in its manufacture. The label must indicate the amount of wool fiber in the fabric and the percent by weight of new or virgin wool fibers, of reprocessed fibers (wool remanufactured from scraps of wool cloth), and of reused fibers (wool from used clothing). Experts point out that the use of reprocessed wool is not necessarily the sign of an inferior product if the wool is of good quality.

The consumer should bear in mind that while fibers with the same family or generic name perform in a similar fashion, they are not identical. There are, for example, several different types of nylons. Some newer types have antistatic properties; another new type has a silklike appearance. Consumers' problems in learning about these differences in characteristics point up the need for more informative fabric labeling.

The most useful kind of information would be ratings of a fabric on such key characteristics as shrinkage, durability, and colorfastness. This would involve the development of generally accepted *standards* or methods of measuring and rating a fabric on each of these characteristics. Once standards are developed for a characteristic such as shrinkage, fabrics can be rated by how well they resist shrinkage. Fabrics might, for example, be classified into four categories or grades according to how much they shrink. Those with the least shrinkage would fall in the top grade and be labeled "excellent"; the next group could be labeled "good," the next "fair," and the lowest "poor." Although grading of textile fabrics has been suggested many times, businessmen have resisted the idea. Businessmen fear that once product-grading information is available, consumers will rely less on brand names. This would weaken the position of large firms that have built up a special reputation for their brand names by heavy advertising. No firm with a well-known brand name wants to lose the special advantages that the brand name gives it.

FABRIC CONSTRUCTION   There are several different methods of making cloth. The most familiar is weaving. In woven fabrics durability is determined by (1) the closeness and evenness of the weave, (2) the thread count (the number of yarns in both directions in a square inch of fabric), and (3) the thickness of the yarn. Close, tightly woven fabrics are less subject to wear and abrasion, while ones with loose, "floating" yarns may snag.

Another familiar method of fabric construction is knitting. In regular knit fabrics a single yarn is formed into loops that are interlocked.

Doubleknits, which became very popular in the early 1970s, are made somewhat differently. Doubleknits are made by interlocking loops in two strands of yarn with a double stitch. The result is a fabric with loops on both sides instead of on just one, as in regular knits, and a fabric that is stronger than regular knits. Polyester and polyester-wool combinations have been especially popular for double-knits. The garments produced have been comfortably light and resistant to wrinkling. There have been some problems, however. Double-knits are subject to snags, and some people have found them too warm for summer wear. They are also more difficult to alter than garments made of woven fabric, since needle holes remain visible when a garment is let out. This problem can be avoided by buying a larger size and taking it in rather than letting out a smaller size.

FABRIC FINISHES   A variety of special finishes has been developed to improve fabric performance. The most familiar is the *permanent-press finish,* which helps garments retain their initial shape and pressed-in creases and resist wrinkling when laundered or dry-cleaned. This finish is produced by applying a resin compound to the fabric and then following with a heat treatment that permanently sets the fabric in the desired shape. This finish is now used on a wide variety of clothing and is frequently used with polyester-cotton blends. As we noted earlier, the use of polyester helps overcome the finish's weakening effect on cotton fibers. Well-known trade names for permanent-press finishes include Coneprest, Dan-Press, Koratron, Penn-Prest, and Perma-Prest. If the manufacturer's instructions for care are not given on a hang-tag, it is suggested that for best results permanent-press items be machine-washed, tumbled dry, and removed from the dryer as soon as they are dry and then placed on hangers. Permanent-press finishes are softened by heat. Clothes can pick up wrinkles if they are washed in water that is too hot or dried at too high a temperature without a "cool-down" period at the end. It should be noted that several man-made fibers have permanent heat-set characteristics and resist wrinkling without special finishes; these include nylon, triacetate, polyester, and acrylic.

Stains tend to be a particular problem in cotton-polyester permanent-press fabrics because both polyester fiber and the permanent-press finish have a tendency to attract oily stains. This problem shows up in dark rings around collars and cuffs that cannot be washed out. The problem is eased by the use of *soil-release finishes* that permit soil to be released from the fabric more easily during

The trousers at the left of the photograph have a permanent-press finish, which helps garments retain their initial shape and pressed-in creases even after washing or dry cleaning.

Courtesy J. P. Stevens & Co., Inc.

washing. Such a finish is Scotchgard Dual-Action Fabric Protector, which provides both stain resistance and soil-release properties.

Water-repellent finishes also are available. Fabrics treated with *water-repellent* finishes resist the absorption and penetration of water for a time, but are not fully waterproof. There is a variety of water-repellent finishes, including the Cravenette finishes and Syl-mer. These finishes vary in how well they resist the effects of laundering and dry cleaning. Another group of finishes repels water and resists water- and oil-borne stains. These finishes are based on fluorocarbon compounds and include Scotchgard and Zepel. It should be noted that some fibers such as nylon and polyester have water-repellent qualities without special finishes because they absorb relatively little water.

Shrinkage in fabrics can be controlled by special manufacturing processes, such as the Sanforized process, or by chemical finishes. Shrinkage-control finishes include:

- Sanforized, Rigmel: cotton fabrics
- Sanforset: rayon
- Pak-Nit, Redmanized: cotton-knit goods
- Lanaset, Wurlan: wool

When shrinkage-control finishes are used, tags should indicate the amount of shrinkage remaining.

Liquids "bead up" on the surface of fabrics treated with Scotchgard Fabric Protector, a water- and oil-repellent fabric finish.

Courtesy 3M Co.

In addition to the special finishes mentioned, other finishes provide fire-retardant properties, mothproofing, mildewproofing, and antibacterial properties.

Garment construction

While the fabric used in making a garment is important, the way this fabric is put together to form the garment is important, too. In making clothes the basic problem is to shape a two-dimensional piece of cloth to cover a three-dimensional form that, like a landscape, has contours, hills, and valleys.

SHAPE Garments get their basic shape from the way the pieces of fabric used in making them are cut. As these pieces of fabric are sewn together they may be further shaped by pressing. Other methods of adjusting to the contours of the body are needed, however, to make a garment fuller in some places and narrower in others. This is done with darts, tucks, and pleats that remove excess fabric in some places and provide extra room at others.

Garments are kept in shape by the resistance of the fabric to stretching and shrinking. A garment made of a fabric that shrinks or stretches quickly loses its original shape. *Interfacings,* the extra pieces of fabric sewn inside the garment at such places as lapels and collars, also help hold a garment in shape. Interfacings give body to lapels and collars and help them lie flat; they prevent stretching at armholes and reinforce areas where buttons are sewn. Garments also get their shape from the padding used in shoulders and from linings used in jackets and skirts that help them to hang smoothly. Although we cannot see the interfacings and padding used, we can see how well they do their job. When lifted out of place or crushed, lapels should snap quickly back into place. Padding should give a smooth contour to the shoulders and should not be lumpy.

SIGNS OF QUALITY   There are other signs of quality in clothing construction that the shopper can use in judging garments. The garment should be cut on the grain (the yarns in the fabric should run perpendicular and parallel to the floor). If the fabric is cut off the grain, the garment will sag and hang unevenly. The fabric pieces should be securely joined with neat, short stitches that are neither too tight nor too loose. If fabric is sewn too loosely you will be able to see a gap between two pieces when they are pulled apart. Fabric patterns will be matched at the seams in higher-quality garments. Seams should be generous to resist strain and in case the garment needs to be let out. Hems should lie flat and be inconspicuous from the outside of the garment. Edges of seams should be finished to prevent raveling.

In the finishing of the garment, points of strain should be reinforced with extra stitching or bar tacks (stitching back and forth in the same place, such as on the corners of jean pockets). Buttonholes should be neatly made, with the buttons securely sewn. Zippers should be neatly placed to lie flat and should work easily. The fittings on a garment should be appropriate to the way it will be cleaned. Plastic straps and nonremovable belts are not likely to stand up well in either washing or dry cleaning. Nylon lace or trim on a cotton garment is apt to be melted by the usual ironing temperatures for cotton.

SIZE AND FIT   Although standards have been developed for the sizes of children's clothing and women's clothing and for youth sizes, these standards are voluntary. Many manufacturers make adjustments that they believe are necessary for their particular operation and clientele. As a result, the fit of a particular size will vary among manufacturers and, over time, for the same manufacturer.

Poor fits may be the result of the choice of the wrong size or of a garment that is badly proportioned for the build of the wearer. Examples of badly proportioned garments are ones that are too narrow in the hips or too large in the shoulders for the wearer. A well-fitted garment should provide an appropriate amount of *ease*. This is the extra fabric needed to allow for body movements. If there is too little ease there will be strain marks in the fabric, such as the strain marks seen across the front of skirts and trousers that are too narrow across the hips. If there is too much ease, the garment will seem baggy and too loose.

A well-fitted garment will lie close to the body around the neck, without gaps in front or in back. Shoulder seams should lie in the center of the shoulder. Sleeves should be the correct length, and the garment should be cut so that the wearer can raise his arms without the garment pulling up excessively. The waistline of the garment should fall at the wearer's natural waistline, except in special designs.

CARING FOR CLOTHES

We spend a good deal of money on clothes, and they deserve to be treated like any other valuable investment—with care. Clothes that are treated with care will last longer, and, probably even more important, they will look good for a long time. Good care involves taking care of clothes on a day-to-day basis and using proper cleaning procedures.

Everyday care for clothes

Clothes should be hung up at once when you take them off. Wrinkles hang out quickly when clothes are still warm from body heat and slightly damp from body moisture. Use padded or shaped hangers for coats and jackets, not the wire ones that dry cleaners use. This will help these items keep their shape. Clothes should not be crowded too closely in the closet; they should be allowed room to air. Wool, in particular, tends to absorb odors if not allowed to air.

Both clothes and shoes will last longer if you can rotate them instead of wearing the same clothes or pair of shoes several days in a row. Rotating clothes gives them the "rest" they need in order to dry out and resume their original shape. To protect good clothes from spills and stains, change to work clothes before you do chores around the house, work on the car, or help in the kitchen.

Mend clothes promptly. This will keep tears and rips from getting bigger and will keep loose buttons from getting lost. Boys as well as girls should learn how to make simple clothing repairs. Out-of-season clothes should be stored to protect them from dust and moths.

Rainwear should be used when needed to protect clothes. Its use will help save on extra cleaning and pressing bills. Wet shoes should be stuffed with paper (shoe trees might stretch them too much) and allowed to dry slowly away from radiators and hot-air vents.

Cleaning procedures

Stains should be treated before a garment is washed, otherwise they may be set by the heat of the cleaning process. You probably will need a guide on stain removal to help you deal with the variety of stain problems that arise. Techniques differ depending on the type of stain (greasy, nongreasy, or a combination of the two such as gravy or chocolate) and the fabric (washable and nonwashable). One useful guide is *Removing Stains from Fabrics—Home Methods,* U.S. Department of Agriculture Home and Garden Bulletin No. 62, available from the U.S. Government Printing Office, 20 cents postpaid. For clothes that are dry-cleaned, identify stains for the cleaners, if possible. This will help them choose the best stain-removal procedures.

You can see from the table on the characteristics of textile fibers on pages 116–117 that the care requirements of different fibers vary a good deal. Some fibers, such as cotton, can be machine-washed and tumble-dried without difficulty. Others such as wool require dry cleaning or special care in washing. Confusion often arises because of the different care requirements of similar fabrics. Machine washing and drying is not recommended for acetate fabrics but is for triacetate fabrics. The variety of fabrics and their special care requirements have created a number of problems for consumers. Many people have ruined articles of clothing by mistakenly machine-washing them when they should have been dry-cleaned. Even experienced cleaners cannot always identify a fabric by just looking at it, and they sometimes make mistakes.

These problems led to pressure for the use of permanent care labels that provide necessary care instructions. The use of permanent care labels was ordered by the FTC, beginning in 1972, for many types of garments—with a few exceptions: (1) articles of clothing that sell for $3 or less at retail and are completely washable under normal conditions—for example, men's cotton T-shirts or handkerchiefs; (2) hats, gloves, and footwear other than hosiery; (3) items whose usefulness or appearance might be impaired by a label—for example, a lacy blouse. The instructions on the labels indicate appropriate cleaning procedures for regular care and maintenance. They do not provide any information on spot-removal procedures. The instructions provided are meant to cover all component parts of a garment, unless exceptions are noted.

The law now requires that permanent labels be attached to textile products to provide instructions for proper care.

Courtesy Londontown Manufacturing Co.

The FTC regulations indicate that labels should tell both what to do and what not to do with a particular garment. Both kinds of instructions can be seen in these examples of labels that conform to the FTC rules:

- Machine-wash warm. Gentle cycle. Do not use chlorine bleach.
- Hand-wash cold. Do not twist or wring. Reshape. Dry flat. Do not dry-clean.
- Dry-clean only. Do not use petroleum solvents or the coin-operated method of dry cleaning.

Checking your reading

1. How can high school students' clothes express both individuality and group membership at the same time?

2. When taking an inventory of the articles of clothing you own, what else should you do besides simply making a list of the things you have?

3. Why is it useful to choose versatile items when selecting clothes?

4. Why is polyester used in combination with cotton in many permanent-press items?

5. What label information does the Textile Fiber Products Identification Act require?

6. What are fabric standards?

7. What three factors influence the durability of a woven fabric?

8. What can happen if permanent-press items are washed in very hot water or dried at too high a temperature? Why does this problem occur?

9. How do water-repellent finishes work?
10. How is fabric shaped to fit body contours during the construction of a garment?
11. What is the function of interfacings?
12. What two key factors can guide consumers in judging the quality of clothing?
13. What two general problems may result in a poorly fitting garment?
14. Why is it best to hang clothes up at once after taking them off?
15. What problems led to the requirement that garments carry permanent care labels?

Consumer problems and projects

1. Take an inventory of the items you have in your wardrobe for the coming season (do not forget to try on every item and to check its condition). What other items will you need? Can you develop a program to get these items?

2. Study some recent issues of men's or women's fashion and clothing magazines, and identify pictures in which the models have hair, skin, and eye coloring similar to yours. Record (1) your own coloring, (2) the colors of the articles of clothing in the pictures you selected, and (3) the colors that you thought were most attractive in combination with the models' coloring.

3. Look ahead for a year or two to a new job or role you are likely to have that will require you to have special clothing. This might be a secretarial job, a sales job, or the role of a student at college, business, or technical school. Make a list of the wardrobe items that you will need for your first season on the job or in school. What items do you already have that would be suitable, and what will you need to buy? Use a mail-order catalog or visit local stores to obtain estimates of the prices of items you will need to buy. What program can you develop to get the things you will need?

4. Study some recent issues of *Consumer Bulletin* and *Consumer Reports* that report tests made on articles of clothing. Select a particular item in which you are interested. What tests were used in developing the ratings? What brands were given top ratings? Why? If you were to buy this item, which brand would you choose? Why?

5. Charley Rogers was considering buying a new coat and was having trouble deciding whether to buy a regular top coat or a raincoat with a zip-out lining. What are the advantages and disadvantages of each alternative?

6. Suzie Samuelson complained that her permanent-press dresses and blouses always need ironing when they come out of the wash. If you were advising Suzie, what questions would you want to ask her about how she was handling her permanent-press clothes?

7. Identify an article of clothing that is available at several different price levels. Check the prices of this item in local stores or in a mail-order catalog. How do the construction, styling, and fabrics used differ among price levels? If you were to buy the item, at which price level would you buy? Why?

Chapter 8

Buying food

Food is a major budget item and accounts for about 20 to 25 percent of the typical urban family's income after taxes. There is, however, little question that for most of us food is partly a luxury and partly a necessity. We all could survive on much less expensive, but much less interesting, diets. The U.S. Department of Agriculture has estimated that an adult man could get a balanced diet for 40 cents a day. Few of us, however, would find this low-cost diet of enriched white bread, margarine, nonfat dry milk, potatoes, and cooked dry beans very appealing.

A family's food spending is affected both by its income and by its size and composition. A family with two teen-agers may spend twice as much as a young couple just starting married life. Food costs also vary because families differ in the emphasis they place on the pleasures of eating. Some families place a great deal of importance on having good food and lots of it. On Sundays, holidays, and special occasions the table is loaded with special treats. Other families may prefer to spend less in order to have money for travel, outings, or other interests. Family income and family size explain part of the differences among families in food expenditures. However, by far the greatest part of the differences among families in food expenditures is due to differences in taste.

OUR CHANGING EATING HABITS

Rising incomes, changes in the prices of foods in relation to each other, the shift of population from farms to cities, new foods and food-processing techniques, and the pressure of advertising all have played a part in changing our eating habits.

Until a few years ago, food experts were certain that as family incomes rose, eating habits would improve and diets would get better and better. A recent nationwide dietary study showed that this was not happening. The U.S. Department of Agriculture researchers found, instead, that more families had inadequate diets, measured in terms of vitamins and minerals, than ten years earlier.

What had happened? The causes became clearer when changes in the use of particular foods were studied. Consumption of meat, bakery products, and snack foods had risen, but the quantities of essential foods used such as fruits, vegetables, and dairy products had declined.

HOW IMPORTANT IS GOOD NUTRITION?

Good nutrition is closely linked to some of the things we want the most—a good build, physical fitness, and vitality. The payoff for good eating habits does not come right away, however. An extra glass of milk on Thursday is not likely to produce a winning performance on the football field on Friday. Because the payoff for good nutrition develops over time, some people think good nutrition is not important or can be ignored without harm. A good supply of nutrients is essential to keep our bodies functioning, to provide us with the energy we need, and to provide materials for the continuous job of rebuilding bones and body tissues.

A guide for good nutrition

To help us in knowing what we need to eat, nutritionists have developed what they call the "Basic Four." Although the name sounds like a new music group, the *Basic Four* really is a list of essential food groups and the number of servings from each that we need every day.

- Vegetable and Fruit Group—includes all vegetables and fruits; especially useful ones are oranges and orange juices, grapefruit, tomatoes, carrots, spinach, potatoes and sweet potatoes cooked in their jackets, green beans and winter squash—four or more servings each day.

- Meat Group—includes beef, pork, chicken, eggs, fish, and shell-fish; as alternates, dry peas and beans, peanuts, and peanut butter—two or more servings each day.
- Milk Group—includes whole and skim milk, cottage and cheddar-type cheese, and ice cream—four or more servings each day for teen-agers, two or more for adults, two to three or more for children.
- Bread and Cereal Group—includes bread, cooked and ready-to-eat cereals, cornmeal, and spaghetti—four or more servings each day. Use enriched products when possible.
- Other Foods—some other foods will be needed to round out meals. These include margarine, butter, jelly, seasonings, and salad dressings.

Although it is easier to be well fed if you have a lot of money to spend, it is possible to make good menu plans using the Basic Four at different cost levels. The menu plans shown on page 131 illustrate how an adequate diet can be provided at different levels of spending. The high-cost plan is more expensive, while the low-cost plan is simplified for the sake of economy.

A guide for improving our eating habits

Most people are reluctant to make major changes in the way they eat, even for the sake of good nutrition. There are some relatively easy changes we all could make, however. Here are a few suggestions:

- Avoid skipping breakfast. Even taking just a glass of milk, some orange juice, and a piece of toast is better than skipping breakfast; these foods provide some of the energy we need to start the day. Skipping meals is a poor way to diet. When meals are skipped, it is hard to get a balanced diet. Dieters may end up so hungry that they eat too many high-calorie snacks between meals.
- Get more exercise. The energy requirements of modern life are so low that it is hard to get the vitamins and minerals we need while holding calories down. With more exercise we can eat the foods we need without gaining weight.
- Diet intelligently. One way to diet is to choose well-balanced meals and form the habit of eating smaller portions. Substituting skim milk or low-fat milk for whole milk is another way to cut down on calories without losing needed nutrients.

A DAY'S MENU AT DIFFERENT COSTS FOR A FAMILY OF FOUR (The high-cost menu is more than 2½ times as expensive as the low-cost menu.)		
	Low-Cost Menu	**High-Cost Menu**
Breakfast	Orange juice (canned) Oatmeal with milk Cinnamon toast Milk (nonfat dry) or coffee	Strawberries (fresh) Bacon and eggs Biscuits (frozen) Milk (fresh) or coffee

Lunch	Hard-cooked egg or peanut butter
	  and jelly sandwich
	Celery sticks or a banana
	Milk (nonfat dry)
		Baked ham on seeded roll with
		  lettuce and tomato
		Asparagus in cheese sauce
		  (frozen)
		Milk (fresh)

Snack	Cookies Fruit punch	Pear Chocolate milk (fresh)
Dinner	Fried chicken Carrots (fresh) Mashed potatoes Bread (white enriched) Apple pie (homemade) Milk (nonfat dry) or coffee	Beef rib roast Broccoli with butter sauce Corn on the cob (fresh) Dinner rolls (bakery) German chocolate cake (frozen) Milk (fresh) or coffee

Source: *Your Money's Worth in Foods*, U.S. Department of Agriculture Home and Garden Bulletin No. 183, 1970, p. 7.

■ Choose better snacks. Snacks are a part of our way of life, and few of us would give them up. We can make our snacks do a better job for us by substituting more nutritious foods for typical snack foods that are long on calories and short on the vitamins and minerals we need. A cheeseburger or a hamburger, especially with a slice of tomato, and a glass of milk would be a good snack choice.

SMART MENU PLANNING

Shoppers who are concerned about getting good value for the money they spend on food must make a two-pronged attack on the problem. First, they must plan their menus wisely, including items that are good sources of nutrients at a reasonable cost. Second, they must shop wisely for the items they need to make up the menus they have planned.

Making a menu plan

The first step in smart menu planning is to plan ahead. You begin by making a list of menus for the days ahead. The list may be put down on paper, or it may just be a mental note. A menu plan can only be a general guideline and must be flexible. Changes may be necessary because of unexpected guests or family activities. Changes may also be necessary because items included in the plan are not available. The plan should be flexible so that special bargains can be substituted for more costly items.

Using seasonal bargains and plentiful foods

Prices of fresh food change throughout the year, depending on the season. Many fresh fruits and vegetables are available throughout the year but are especially expensive in the off season. During the off

AVABILITY OF FRESH FRUIT												
G = Good Supply, F = Fair Supply, S = Small Supply												
	January	February	March	April	May	June	July	August	September	October	November	December
Apples	G	G	G	G	F	S	S	S	G	G	G	G
Bananas	G	G	G	G	G	G	G	G	G	G	G	G
Blueberries					S	G	G	G	S			
Cantaloupes		S	S	S	F	G	G	G	G	S	S	
Cherries					S	G	G	S	S			
Cranberries	S									F	F	G	G
Grapefruit	G	G	G	G	G	F	S	S	S	G	G	G
Grapes	S	S	S	S	S	F	G	G	G	G	G	F
Oranges	G	G	G	G	G	F	S	S	S	F	G	G
Peaches					S	G	G	G	G	S		
Strawberries	S	S	F	G	G	G	G	S	S	S	S	S
Watermelons	S	S	S	S	F	G	G	G	S	S	S	S

Source: *Food for Us All,* The Yearbook of Agriculture, U.S. Department of Agriculture, 1969, p. 161.

season and when the first of the new crop comes in, prices are high. As supplies increase, prices become more reasonable. Prices are at their lowest when the produce from nearby sources becomes available. These supply cycles follow a similar pattern each year and can be charted to help consumers plan their purchases (see the table on page 132). Apples, for example, are available all year round but are most abundant in the fall and winter just after the new crop is picked.

One way to keep track of which foods are in plentiful supply and attractively priced is to watch the food pages of the newspapers. Home economists and marketing specialists in the Cooperative Extension Service provide newspapers with new information about plentiful foods every week.

Using the food ads to find specials

Grocers know that meat quality and prices play an important part in determining the shopper's image of a particular store. Because of this, advertised weekend meat specials are an important part of their effort to win new customers and hold their present ones. Meat specials and other specials offer smart shoppers a chance both to fill out the week's menu at lower cost and stock up for the future.

After checking on supermarket beef specials in Washington and Baltimore, Consumers Union concluded that specials "are likely to yield substantial savings over the same cuts at regular price, and at no loss

Agricultural Extension Service, University of California Photo

By checking the newspaper ads for meat and grocery specials, shoppers can sometimes save up to 33 percent of their regular food bills.

of quality." They found savings of 18 to 33 percent on the cuts they checked. They also found, however, that it was difficult to make meaningful price comparisons among stores because trimming practices differed so much. In one case, they found a chain offering sirloin steak at $1.45 a pound, while a major competitor was charging $1.39. The higher-priced special actually was the better buy—its cost was $2.66 per edible pound compared to $4.10 per edible pound for the low-priced special. Consumers Union found also that quality differed among supermarket chains. Some chains consistently offered a better-quality meat than others. Experience with eating quality and trimming practices has to be considered when evaluating a store's meat specials.[1]

Shoppers need to remember that not everything in a store's ad is a special. Some items are advertised because the store wants to emphasize their everyday low prices; other items are advertised because the processor has paid part of the advertising cost.

Economizing wisely

Menu planners can cut family food costs and still serve well-balanced meals if they follow some simple tips.

- Meat accounts for about one-third of the food budget. Economize by using less expensive substitutes for meat as a source of animal protein. Some economical sources of protein are cheese, canned fish, and eggs. Other possibilities are vegetable protein such as dried peas and beans and peanut butter.
- Combine meat, fish, or other high-protein foods with extenders such as noodles, spaghetti, macaroni, rice, or potatoes.
- Cut down on snack items. Soft drinks, potato chips, and candy are high in calories but contribute few needed vitamins and minerals to the diet.
- Think twice and then think again before cutting down on fruits and vegetables or on dairy products. Many families' diets already are too low in these foods. If it is necessary to cut costs, find substitutes; for example, use canned instead of frozen fruit.

Deciding what you really need

An important step in smart menu planning is deciding what you really need—the kind of quality desired for particular uses and the right quantities. It is not always necessary to buy the best quality. Less

---

[1]"Meats on Sale!" *Consumer Reports*, pp. 472–476, August, 1970.

Shoppers need to know the number of servings in a pound of meat before they can determine the right amount to buy.

Courtesy E. I. du Pont de Nemours & Co., Inc.

expensive grades and cuts of beef are fine for making stews. Lower-quality fruits and vegetables can be used when appearance is not important. For example, slightly blemished tomatoes can always be cut up and used in stews.

The smart shopper will learn how to judge the quantity of food that is needed for a serving. The number of servings in a pound of meat differs according to the amount of bone, fat, and inedible portions. For example, if we regard 3 ounces of cooked lean meat, poultry, or fish as a serving, then:

■ Cuts with little or no fat provide three to four servings per pound—ground meat, lean stew meat, liver, center slice of ham, fish steaks, and fillets.

■ Cuts with a medium amount of bone provide two to three servings per pound—most roasts, some chops and steaks, ham, and poultry.

■ Cuts with much bone, gristle, or fat provide one to two servings per pound—spare ribs, short ribs, porterhouse and T-bone steaks, and chicken wings and backs.

We can see from the first column of the table on page 136 that 1 pound of ground beef provides 4 servings, while 1 pound of sirloin steak that includes the bone provides only $2\frac{1}{2}$ servings. We can also use this table to determine the cost per serving of different meat items. For example, if ground beef costs 80 cents a pound, a single serving costs 21 cents, while sirloin steak at $1.30 a pound costs 55 cents a serving.

COST OF A 3-OUNCE SERVING OF COOKED LEAN MEAT

Retail Cut	Approx. Number Servings Per Pound	Price Per Pound of Retail Cuts														
		40¢	50¢	60¢	70¢	80¢	90¢	100¢	110¢	120¢	130¢	140¢	150¢	160¢	170¢	180¢
		Cost of a 3-Ounce Serving (cents)														
Beef																
Sirloin steak—bone in	2½	17	21	26	30	34	38	43	47	51	55	60	64	68	72	77
Ground beef—lean	4	10	13	16	18	21	23	26	29	31	34	36	39	42	44	47
Chuck roast—bone in	2	18	22	27	31	36	40	45	49	54	58	62	67	71	76	80
Short ribs	1½	23	29	35	41	47	53	58	64	70	76	82	88	94	99	105
Pork																
Loin roast—bone in	2	20	25	30	36	41	46	51	56	61	66	71	76	81	86	91
Loin chops	2	18	22	27	31	36	40	45	49	54	58	62	67	71	76	80
Ham slices	3	12	16	19	22	25	28	31	34	38	41	44	47	50	53	56
Ham roast—bone in	3	14	17	21	24	28	31	35	38	42	45	49	52	56	59	62
Lamb																
Leg roast—bone in	2½	17	21	25	29	33	38	42	46	50	54	58	62	67	71	75
Loin chops	2	18	23	27	32	37	41	46	50	55	59	64	68	73	78	82

Source: *Your Money's Worth in Foods*, U.S. Department of Agriculture Home and Garden Bulletin No 183, 1970, p. 12.

Deciding how much to pay for convenience

A wide variety of food products that save preparation time is available, and dozens of new convenience foods appear on the market each year. Some of these foods save both preparation time and money, while others save preparation time but are more expensive than the same items prepared from "scratch."

Convenience foods that are cheaper than the fresh forms of the products usually are the result of processing that reduces the cost of moving them to the market. This is the case for frozen orange juice concentrate. The frozen concentrate eliminates the cost of shipping the rinds and water content of fresh oranges and reduces perishability problems. Canned orange juice offers similar savings. Savings are also possible on other vegetables that include inedible parts, such as pods, or that are highly perishable. Cake mixes are cheaper than buying the separate ingredients, and they save time as well.

Next consider the group of convenience foods that provides important savings in preparation time but does cost extra. The extra cost may range from a few cents for every hour of preparation time saved, as in the case of frozen French fries, to several dollars per hour saved, as in the case of frozen baked goods. Even the housewife interested in economy considers her time worth more than a few cents an hour. But most housewives might think twice before they spent several dollars to save an hour of preparation time. Although the most widely used convenience foods save both time and money, many others do cost extra, so it is worth considering whether their extra cost offsets the savings in preparation time that they offer.

SMART FOOD SHOPPING

When the menu plan is finished, the problem of purchasing needed items at the lowest possible cost still remains. Smart food shopping, like smart menu planning, depends on good information and workable plans. The ability to make and use a shopping list, the ability to choose a place to shop, and the ability to use label information all are important skills for smart food shoppers.

Using a shopping list

The first step in smart food shopping is to prepare a shopping list of the items needed to complete the meals planned. This shopping list will also include staple items such as salt, sugar, and paper towels.

With a shopping list, shoppers can avoid several costly mistakes. They are more certain to get everything they need and avoid extra trips to the store, which are costly in terms of both time and car-operating expenses. A shopping list also helps the shopper avoid impulse pur chases that increase the grocery bill. A shopping list can help the shopper avoid overbuying perishables and consequently helps eliminate wasteful spoilage.

Choosing a place to shop

An important part of smart shopping is the choice of a place to shop, for prices and quality do differ among stores.

Price competition among supermarkets tends to keep prices from differing too greatly among different companies. Price differences are larger between supermarkets and small neighborhood and convenience stores. These smaller stores are open long hours, and their average sales are small. This raises their operating costs. Since the stores' total sales are small, extra operating costs result in higher prices. Smart shoppers will try to hold their purchases from these higher-priced stores to a minimum. One of the problems faced by city dwellers is that supermarket-type stores may not be conveniently located. The extra savings to be had from supermarket shopping may make some extra effort worthwhile, especially for large orders.

Choosing a supermarket may be difficult. Some stores try to attract shoppers by offering attractive specials. These stores have to make up for their specials by charging higher prices for other items. Other stores advertise "everyday low prices" or "discount prices." To make up for their lower average prices, these stores may not offer good specials.

Understanding the information on the label

Information included on the labels of food products is strictly controlled by law. Food shoppers will find labels to be one of their most useful and reliable sources of information, once they learn how to interpret the information presented. Labels can provide such important facts as the ingredients and the relative amounts of each that were used, the net weight of the package contents, the name of the processor or distributor, and federal inspection information.

NAME OF THE PRODUCT   The idea of reading the product name on a package label seems so obvious that the casual shopper may ignore the information that the name can provide. This information is important for mixtures, especially those that include meat. For these products the wording of the name can be an important indication of the contents. For example, a product called "Turkey with Noodles" contains more turkey than one labeled "Noodles with Turkey."

Along with the name of the product, other useful information about the product may be indicated on the label. Here are some examples:

- Meat: "All Beef"—the product contains beef only, no other types of meat. "All Meat"—the product may include various types of meats, including beef, pork, and mutton, but no cereal or other extenders have been added. "Cereal Added"—indicates that cereal has been added to extend the meat.
- Fruit: The packing liquid, either syrup, juice, or water, is indicated. Syrups used may be light, heavy, or extra-heavy. Fruit packed in light syrup is the least expensive.
- Vegetables: Maturity of the product—younger varieties—baby beets and early peas, for example—suggest tenderness. Style of cut—sliced, diced, or fancy cuts such as French-style green beans or julienne carrots (both of which are cut lengthwise).

For many products there is a *standard of identity* that sets down the characteristics and ingredients that the food product must have before it can be labeled with a specific product name, such as "macaroni." Over 250 foods have standards of identity developed by the federal government. These standards cover many everyday food products, including bread, jam, peanut butter, and margarine.

A standard of identity is something like a recipe. It specifies the key ingredients and the minimum amount of each that must be included in a product. Strawberry jam, for example, must include 45 percent strawberries by weight. A strawberry jam that fails to meet this standard would have to be labeled "Imitation Strawberry Jam" even though it did contain some strawberries. Standards of identity also specify optional ingredients, which processors may include in their products if they choose. These optional ingredients are chiefly preservatives, colors, spices, and flavorings.

Products for which standards of identity have been set do not have to indicate required ingredients on their labels. However, the optional ingredients used, such as preservatives and artificial flavorings and colors, do have to be included on the label. Processors who use ingredients of special quality sometimes choose to list those ingredients even though this is not required.

Standards of identity for most processed foods are administered by the Food and Drug Administration in the U.S. Department of Health,

Education, and Welfare. Standards for meat products are administered by the U.S. Department of Agriculture.

LIST OF INGREDIENTS   Foods that are not covered by a federal standard of identity must have their ingredients listed on the label. Some foods covered by a standard also have their ingredients listed, as we have seen. Ingredients are listed beginning with the one that weighs the most. If we saw two different brands of beef stew, and one label read "water, beef, potatoes" while the other read "water, potatoes, beef," we would know that the first brand contained more beef. Spices, flavoring, and coloring do not have to be listed individually, but the label must indicate if they have been used. The use of preservatives must be indicated.

NET WEIGHT OF THE CONTENTS   The label, by federal law, must indicate the actual weight of the contents of the package, not including the weight of the package itself. The net weight stated on the container represents the combined weight of the food and the packing liquids or syrups used, except in a very few cases. In a few special cases, such as mushrooms and olives, the weight reported is a weight for the drained product only.

NAME OF THE PACKER OR DISTRIBUTOR   The label will include the name of the food processor who packages the item or the name of the firm that distributes it. Store brands typically list the retailer's name. The address and zip code is listed to assist the customer who wishes to send comments or complaints.

INSPECTION INFORMATION   Assurance that meat, poultry, and fish and their processed products are produced under sanitary conditions is provided by federal inspection stamps and seals (see the illustrations on page 142). Federal inspectors go to processing plants and keep a careful watch to ensure that processed meat, poultry, and fish are wholesome and that they are produced under sanitary conditions. All meat and poultry and processed products must conform to federal standards, regardless of whether the products are moving within or between states. However, only a small fraction of the fish and fish products consumed in this country is covered by federal inspection. New legislation is badly needed to extend inspection coverage to all domestically processed and imported fish.

PRODUCTION AND EXPIRATION DATES Some perishable products are labeled with the date on which they were produced or with a "pull date" after which they should no longer be sold. Refrigerated dough for biscuits and rolls, for example, carries an expiration date. Store employees use this information to rotate stock so that older items are sold first; they "pull" items that have become too old. On some products the date information is coded so that the store employees, but not the consumers, will know how old a product is. Consumer spokesmen have argued that all dating should be "open" to help assure consumers that the products they buy are fresh and to force store personnel to do a better job of rotating stock.

OTHER LABEL INFORMATION Other useful information may be included on the label, such as cooking directions or recipes. Information on the number and size of servings may be included. For foods sold for diet purposes, the label must provide information on calorie content. When artificial sweeteners are used, the label must indicate the type of sweetener.

Understanding the use of grades as guides to quality

Standards of quality have been developed to provide a basis for assigning grades to food products. These standards of quality are something like the grading system for a report card. They set down the characteristics on which a product will be judged and how well it must do to be placed in a particular grade category. Each grade category has a name attached to it in just the same way different levels of school performance are classified A, B, C, D, or F.

U.S. GRADE NAMES The food grades used by the federal government are generally letters or adjectives. The system for naming grades unfortunately differs among products, and this confuses many consumers. The top grade of beef is USDA Prime, and the top grade of butter is U.S. Grade AA, while the top grade of poultry is U.S. Grade A. To make the best use of grades, the shopper will have to learn the meanings of the grades commonly seen in the supermarket. Some states and some processors also use grading systems and assign grade names to their products. These should not be confused with U.S. grades. U.S. grade labels always include a shield and the letters U.S. or USDA.

Most of the federal grading program, including grading for beef, chicken, eggs, dairy products, fruits, and vegetables, is administered by the U.S. Department of Agriculture. Fish grading is administered by the U.S. Department of the Interior. Participation in these grading programs is voluntary. Many of the processors who choose to participate have high quality products and wish to use the U.S. grade as a selling point to emphasize the quality of their products. All plants producing U.S.-graded products are inspected for sanitation, so a U.S. grade provides assurance both of quality and wholesomeness.

BEEF GRADES   Of the eight U.S. grades for beef, only the three top grades are usually seen in grocery stores. These three grades in order of quality are Prime, Choice, and Good. "Choice" is the grade seen most frequently. Beef of "Prime" grade goes chiefly to exclusive restaurants and fancy grocery stores in larger cities. Meat of a quality that would be graded "Good" typically is sold ungraded or may be marked with a store's or meat packer's own brand.

USDA inspection stamps and grade labels provide the consumer with valuable information needed to make effective food buying decisions.

USDA Photos

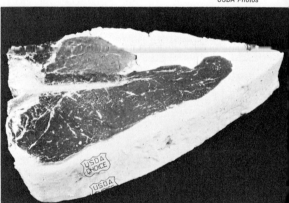

While grades are not perfect predictors of the tenderness and flavor of beef, they are one of the best guides consumers have. Key factors used in the grading of beef are as follows:

- The age of the animal. Prime, Choice, and Good beef all must be from young animals.
- The color and texture of the lean meat. A fine, velvety-looking texture and a bright red color are considered most desirable. In general, the older the animal the darker the meat.
- The amount, color, and texture of the fat. Higher-grade cuts include more marbling (the small flecks of fat scattered through the lean portion of the cut) and a good covering of firm, white fat around the edge of the cut.

From this discussion, it should be clear that beef is judged by its appearance rather than by mechanical or chemical tests. While grades are fairly good predictors of eating quality, they have no relation to nutritional value because vitamin and mineral content differs little among grades.

VIEWPOINTS ON COMPULSORY GRADE LABELING Grading standards have been developed and are in use for many fresh and processed fruits and vegetables, for dairy products, and for chicken, as well as for beef and eggs. Most of these grades are seldom seen by consumers, although they are widely used by processors, wholesalers, and grocery chains. Some consumer spokesmen have argued that grade labeling should be required by law for common food products in order to help consumers in judging quality. Opponents of this view have argued that different consumers have different ideas of what makes a product "good." Another argument against compulsory grade labeling is that no reliable method exists for measuring the key factor of "flavor." Consumer spokesmen have responded to these arguments by asking why, if grades are so unreliable, they are so widely used by processors, wholesalers, and retailers in their dealings with one another.

Choosing manufacturers' brands or store brands

Grocers offer shoppers a variety of items in the hope that at least one item will suit them. They do this by offering several brands of each product at different prices and quality levels. For example, a store may offer three choices of canned peaches, including both manufacturers' brands and store brands (see the discussion in Chapter 4 of manufacturers' brands and store brands). The top-priced item typically is a widely advertised and well-known manufacturer's brand of high quality. Next in price will be a store brand of perhaps equal or slightly lower quality. Often this brand carries the store name. The lowest-priced item usually will be another store brand of somewhat lower quality; the fruit may be broken or blemished and the syrup lighter.

A major reason why store brands are cheaper than manufacturers' brands of similar quality is that their price does not have to cover any separate advertising costs. Advertising and sales promotion costs are a substantial part of the cost of some foods. Producers of peanut butter, crackers, and cookies spend about 4 percent of their sales revenue on advertising and sales promotion; cake mix producers spend about 7 percent; and producers of ready-to-eat cereals spend about 20 percent.

Checking the appearance of the package

Before an individual package is selected it should be examined carefully. Do not buy or use cans that are bulging or leaking. The contents are likely to be spoiled and may be dangerous. The contents of a dented can are safe as long as the can has not been pierced. In buying frozen foods, choose only firm, solidly frozen packages. Wet, limp, or sweating packages are signs that the contents have thawed or are in the process of thawing. Stained and frost-covered packages also should be avoided. They may have thawed and been refrozen. When packages are partly thawed or have thawed and then been refrozen, there is danger of spoilage, and the quality of the contents is certain to have suffered. When buying food in jars, avoid jars that show evidence of having been opened.

Checking your reading

1. Why is a good supply of nutrients essential?
2. What four categories make up the Basic Four? How many servings from each group should someone your age eat each day?
3. Name four ways in which we can improve our eating habits.
4. When are the prices of fresh fruits and vegetables highest and lowest?
5. Is everything listed in a grocery store ad a special?
6. How can families reduce their spending on meat and still obtain needed protein?

7.   Why should most families think carefully before cutting their spending on fruits, vegetables, and dairy products?

8.   Why do some cuts of meat provide more servings per pound than others? What kind of cuts provide the most servings per pound? The least?

9.   What are convenience foods? Are all convenience foods more expensive than the same items prepared from "scratch"? Why?

10.   Why is a shopping list useful?

11.   Why are prices usually higher in small neighborhood grocery stores and convenience stores than in supermarkets?

12.   What is a standard of identity?

13.   What can the consumer learn from the order in which ingredients are listed on a food package?

14.   What assurance do federal inspection seals on meat, poultry, and fish products provide consumers?

15.   Why should consumers check the appearance of cans, packages of frozen food, and jars when buying food?

Consumer problems and projects

1.   Using the table on page 132 in this chapter, determine the months when prices are apt to be highest and lowest for the following fresh fruits: apples, cantaloupes, strawberries, watermelons.

2.   How good was your diet yesterday? Write down everything you ate yesterday. Rule a table like the one below, and place each item you ate in the correct category of the Basic Four. Did you get the recommended number of servings in each category?

	Basic Four			
Your Meals	Vegetables and Fruits	Meat	Milk	Bread and Cereals

3.   How can you improve your diet? Review the categories in the exercise above in which your diet fell short. What food items are needed to meet the Basic Four recommendations? Are there any foods you ate yesterday that you might have been better off without?

4.   Make a list of 10 menu items a family could use to reduce spending on meat. Your list should include some menu items in each of the following categories:

     a. Less expensive sources of animal protein such as cheese and canned fish

b. Sources of vegetable protein such as dried peas and beans and peanut butter

c. Dishes that combine meat, fish, and other high-protein foods with extenders such as noodles, macaroni, rice, and potatoes

5. Using the table on page 136, answer the following questions:

a. If sirloin steak is $1.50 per pound, what is the cost of an individual serving?

b. If lean ground beef is $1.10 per pound, what is the cost per serving?

c. How many 3-ounce cooked servings could we expect to get from a 1-pound slice of ham?

d. If the price of all meats was $1 per pound, which meat would cost the least per serving? Which would cost the most per serving?

e. Which cut of meat is cheaper per serving—ground beef at $1 per pound or short ribs at 50 cents per pound?

6. Make a list of five processed food items that your family frequently uses and that provide a list of ingredients on their labels. Choose as wide a variety of products as possible; for example, canned soup, frozen dinners or chicken pot pie, canned spaghetti and meat balls, and frozen or canned fruit drinks. What are the three leading ingredients in each product?

7. Check the food pages of your local newspapers for information on foods that currently are in plentiful supply and are good buys.

a. Make a list of the products suggested.

b. Prepare a menu plan for one day that includes as many of these items as possible. Be sure your plan meets the Basic Four requirements.

8. How economical is the "large economy size"? Identify five grocery items that are offered in several sizes; for example, laundry detergent, breakfast cereal, toothpaste, and soft drinks. Select a particular brand of each item, and record the various sizes offered and the price of each size. Calculate the price per ounce (or per unit) for each size. Which size is the most economical buy?

Chapter

Recreation and vacations

A recent national survey of vacation habits showed that 55 percent of the families questioned spent more than $400 while they were on vacation. Some families spend much more. One family in ten indicated that they spend more than $1,000 while on their vacation. Americans are spending more money for recreation and vacations, and many consumers now must face the fact that vacations take a substantial chunk of the money they have available for spending. If vacation spending represents a major expenditure, then the wise consumer plans his vacation carefully so he gets the biggest return for his money.

WHY RECREATION AND VACATIONS?

Countless writers have indicated in magazine articles and essays that we are now experiencing a major leisure upheaval. Some business firms and even certain government agencies are switching from the five-day week to the four-day week. Some offices have experimented with having employees work three ten-hour days each week. The office is divided into two shifts: one shift works on Mondays, Tuesdays, and Thursdays, and the other shift works on Wednesdays, Fridays, and Saturdays. The employees have reported that they like the arrangement because it gives them plenty of time for recreation and leisure. What a change from just a few decades ago! Before World War II, many

Courtesy Crestliner Division, North American Rockwell

The unprecedented increase in the amount of leisure time most people have has led to the growth of "leisure" industries.

people worked six-day weeks, and often they could count on working a ten- or twelve-hour day.

Because of this leisure upheaval, people have changed their life styles. According to a recent issue of *Business Week,* such an unprecedented number of people have such an unprecedented amount of nonworking time at their disposal that "leisure" is becoming a major industry in our country.

In addition to the fact that we have more leisure time, there is another important reason for the interest people have in recreation and vacations. Our economy is complex, and our society is undergoing many changes. Jobs are more technical in nature and exert certain pressures on workers. All this strain upon people increases the need for escapism and personal renewal. Vacations can satisfy this need.

TYPES OF VACATIONS

Because Americans are spending more time and money on their vacations, it is important that their expenditures are made wisely so that they reap rewarding experiences. According to a national survey, almost half of all American families resolve the problem of where to go on their vacations by returning to a place they have been to before. In some cases, such a decision is probably a wise one, but in other cases it may mean that the family members are depriving themselves of an opportunity to visit different places, to do different things, and to expand their interests. With more leisure time now available, many people think that vacation time should not be filled merely with hectic amusement but rather should be used to develop new forms of leisure that will contribute to one's self-fulfillment.

Creative vacations

To enjoy a rewarding, refreshing vacation, consumers should usually do some careful planning. For example, a family might get together during an afternoon or evening in January or February to discuss when they should take their vacation and what they should do. Some families mark on a calendar all holidays, long weekends, and the dates for their full-length vacations. Then they engage in some "brainstorming" concerning the possibilities for vacation trips or projects. Some general ideas for vacations are discussed in the following paragraphs.

VACATIONS THAT PROVIDE NEW INTERESTS Some persons have developed new interests because of discoveries they have made on vacations. While hiking through a state park in Indiana or climbing a mountain in Colorado, you might discover an interesting fossil that could ignite a spark of interest in the earth sciences. Or you might become interested in the history of certain parts of the country because of a vacation trip that included visits to historic sites. Then, during the following year you could continue your exploration through reading and study.

Some families have become interested in regional history, have read about the interesting historical events in a certain area, and then have spent part of their vacation time visiting the places they have read about. They find the experience stimulating and much more rewarding than simply traveling to a certain location where they may spend five or six unplanned days yawning on a hammock or reading newspapers and magazines on a cabin porch.

Some persons have discovered new hobbies while on vacations. A few lessons in oil painting, taken while at a family vacation camp or resort, have caused some persons to become enthusiastic painters. They came away from their vacations with an enjoyable leisure-time pursuit that they can engage in throughout the year.

VACATIONS THAT HELP OTHERS Some people have discovered the joy of using their vacation time to help others. For example, we read increasingly of physicians, dentists, nurses, and other medical personnel who spend their entire vacations giving medical aid to people living in back-country regions in various parts of the world.

Photograph by Wendy Holmes, Wave Hill Center   Editorial Photocolor Archives, Inc.

Vacation activities can spark new interests and lead to new year-round hobbies.

One does not have to be a professional worker to help others, nor is it necessary to travel far from home to find people who need help. Some people volunteer their time during their scheduled vacations to work at settlement houses, at city recreation areas, at church camps and scout camps, and at many other places and at many other tasks where the help of volunteers is needed and appreciated. Part of a vacation could be devoted to taking underprivileged children to parks, fairs, concerts, and other places where they would not otherwise be able to go. People who have spent vacations helping others usually say they return to work refreshed mentally and physically.

VACATIONS THAT LEAD TO VOCATIONS In some cases a vacation can be used to help one decide on a vocation or a profession. A young person who is interested in mechanical engineering might take tours of manufacturing plants in various locations. Another young person interested in health occupations could visit hospitals and clinics. Some families have used their vacation time to travel to several college and university campuses so that a teen-age son or daughter would have the opportunity to look at campus facilities and talk with school officials and students before making a decision about where to attend college.

A few years ago, a popular magazine featured a story about several men who actually changed careers because they had become so deeply absorbed in new interests. In some cases the interests were discovered during vacation trips. In other cases vacation time was used to cultivate an interest that already existed.

Vacations at home

Everyone needs a vacation, a chance to get away from routine duties. We think of a vacation as a chance to rest and relax, but then sometimes we analyze what we did during our vacation and discover that we did not really rest physically or mentally. We might have driven for long hours on crowded freeways. We may have put forth so much physical effort at recreational activities that our muscles ached for several days after our vacation was over. We realize, of course, that we have done something different and that change of pace is what we really needed.

On the other hand, perhaps there are times when we should consider spending our vacation at home. For one thing, we could save the money we would otherwise spend for travel. We could still change our pace of living considerably. To get the most from a vacation at home, we should plan the vacation just as seriously as for a vacation that requires travel. The vacation should be planned for the whole family, and that might well mean eating at least some meals away from the home. Or, it could mean sharing cooking duties so that the mother is not responsible for all meals. Some of the money that would have been spent on a traveling vacation for gasoline, tolls, motels, and so on can be used for activities such as those that follow.

- Visit places in the vicinity of your home that you never seem to have time to visit during the regular year. For example, a day might be set aside to visit a zoo, an amusement park, a lake, a state park, or a museum. A local tourist bureau or the chamber of commerce will usually be happy to supply information about historic buildings, monuments, and other interesting places to visit.
- Discover the cultural activities available at nearby colleges. College campuses often have an abundance of activities during the summer that the public is welcome to participate in—often free, or for a reasonable admission price. Included in these activities are plays, concerts, art exhibits, and lectures. Public community colleges, especially, have programs tailored for persons of all ages in the community.
- Do something that you would not ordinarily plan to do at any other time. For example, on one afternoon you could visit the local airport just to watch the giant jets take off and land, and on another afternoon you could tour a manufacturing plant. One day could be spent visiting a television studio.

- Take a short, one-day trip to a place that you have not visited before or that you do not visit frequently. If you drive from one part of a big city to another or from a rural area to a big city, browse through stores, take in a movie, a sports event, or a concert, or pack a picnic lunch and drive to a rural area outside the city.

The preceding suggestions should give you ideas for a vacation at home. Most of us, with a little thought and planning, can think of a number of things that we would like to do at or near home if we had more time. A vacation at home would give us that time.

Camping vacations

A popular guide to camp grounds in the United States and Canada recently listed 15,000 camp grounds in these two countries. Some estimates indicate that more than 40 million Americans go camping each year.

One reason for the increase in camping is its low cost. A family with an interest in traveling may not be able to pay for the cost of motels and meals in restaurants. By taking a camping vacation, families can prepare their own meals, and the cost of owning or renting camping equipment may be much cheaper in the long run than paying for lodging at a motel. There are, of course, other things that make camping attractive. For example, psychologists say that camping makes people feel needed and important. Every member of the family is often counted on for help at the camp site. Children may help set up and break camp. This takes time and effort but also helps them to know that their contribution is needed. Parents may share the responsibilities of gathering and cutting wood for the fire and food preparation.

Most camp grounds charge a fee—typically about $2 or $3 for spending the night in your own tent or trailer. The amount of money spent on food varies considerably among families, but it would certainly be less than the cost of meals in restaurants. One of the big expenses for campers is camping equipment. Some people prefer the rugged experience of using a tent, and that is probably the cheapest way to camp. In addition to tents, a variety of camping trailers are available. They range from small trailer tents to large, luxurious trailers complete with cooking and bathroom facilities. Truck campers and bus campers have increased in popularity during recent years, and they add to the large assortment of equipment available to campers.

If a vacation requires traveling, should it be done by car, plane, train, bus, or ship? If air transportation is decided upon, is it possible to fly cheaply by taking advantage of special fares? How attractive are tour packages? In the following pages we will discuss answers to questions such as these.

By car

Vacation travel for most families is done by car because in most cases it is the least expensive and most convenient means of transportation. A car represents a major investment of money, so if the family owns one, it makes sense to use it for travel whenever possible. Then, of course, car travelers are not bound to arrival and departure schedules, and the fact that they have the car available for transportation when they reach their destination will probably enable them to reduce some of the costs of touring. These factors make vacation travel by car quite popular.

The cost of driving a car depends on many factors, such as the size of the car, the age of the car, and the condition of the car. Also, the price of gasoline and oil may vary substantially from region to region in the United States and Canada. At the present time, and according to most estimates, the typical car costs about 12 cents per mile to operate. That figure includes such items as car insurance, registration fees, and depreciation. Because these standard costs go on even if the car is not used, the 12-cents-per-mile figure is inappropriate for calculating the cost of using the car on a vacation. The cost of just gasoline and oil is probably about 3 cents per mile for most cars and to cover other running expenses, such as tires, a figure of about $4\frac{1}{2}$ cents per mile would be a reasonable estimate.

If a family drives 700 miles to a lake where they have reserved a cabin for five days, their travel expenses would include, in addition to the cost of running their car, such things as meals, motel rooms, and perhaps tolls for the use of highways. Let us say a family consisting of a father and mother and two children decide to spend two days covering the 700-mile distance. They will leave after breakfast on one day and arrive before the evening meal on the second day. Thus, they will count on eating two meals in restaurants each day while traveling. They know from experience that they spend an average of about $10 per meal while traveling, so that means spending $40 on food on the way to the lake and another $40 on food on their return trip. Their estimate of their round-trip travel expenses might look as follows:

Running expenses for car (1,400 miles at 4½ cents per mile)	$ 63
Motel (2 nights at $28 per night)	56
Meals while traveling	80
Tolls	11
	$210

If the same family were to travel between two cities about 700 miles apart, would air travel cost a great deal more than driving their own car? It depends; they would save the cost of the motel rooms and the meals, of course, and those two items add up to quite a sum. In addition to the cost of the plane fares, they would probably have to pay for airport limousine service or taxi transportation to and from the airports. Many special fares are offered by airlines to promote business, and consumers should ask about discount plans in existence at the time they wish to fly. If we assume that the family could get rides from neighbors or friends to and from the airports, the cost of their trip between two cities about 700 miles apart might be as follows:

Father's ticket	$104
Mother's ticket	78
Two children's tickets	70
	$252

In the illustration above, the family has taken advantage of a family-plan fare that some airlines have made available if the family flies at certain times and on certain days of the week. The father's ticket is issued at full fare, the mother's ticket is issued at a discount of 25 percent, and the children, who are both under 12 years of age, are issued tickets at one-third fare.

The longer the trip, the more important it is for families to compare plane fares with the cost of traveling by car. When the trip takes several days by car, the cost of motels and meals may offset the higher cost of traveling by airplane. Of course, other factors must be considered when deciding whether to drive one's car or travel by commercial airlines. The opportunity to see the country and to stop and visit interesting places along the way when the mood strikes makes car travel especially attractive. For some persons, a combination of air travel and car travel might be the best idea. Air travel can be used for long cross-country trips, and a car can be rented at the destination.

By plane

Travel by airplane has become exceedingly popular in our country. Except, of course, for short trips, modern jet planes speed passengers to their destinations faster than other means of transportation. Just a few decades ago, when businessmen and others had to go to different cities or states, they traveled by train. Now, passenger trains have been discontinued between many cities, so the traveler must go by car, bus, or plane.

Although most consumers use cars for their vacation travel, air transportation offers many possibilities. In some cases, consumers should check the cost of plane tickets when considering vacation travel.

DISCOUNTS   When slightly more than half the seats on their flights have been filled for the year, the airlines consider the year to be a good one. If you have traveled by air a few times you may have noticed that on certain days, Saturdays and Sundays, for example, the plane was loaded with people; on other days, your plane may have been only one-third filled. The airlines make no money on empty seats on their flights, of course, so they offer cheaper rates under certain circumstances to attract more customers.

In the past, airlines have offered an excursion plan, a plan under which the passenger bought his ticket at a discount of about 25 percent off the standard round-trip fare. The plan's two restrictions were that the traveler had to depart during one week and return the following week and that he could not travel on weekends. Other special fares are offered by the airlines. For example, some airlines have a night-coach plan. If the traveler is willing to fly at night, usually after midnight, he can get a 25 percent discount off the regular fare. Youth fares have been popular recently. A young person can get a reduction on his plane fare if he purchases an identification card and is willing to be a "standby" passenger, which means he can board the plane only if all the seats are not sold to customers who pay the regular fare.

Other discount plans exist, of course. Not all discount plans are available from all airlines, and those that do exist can be canceled at any time. The consumer has to investigate the possibility of special fares. If his times of departure and arrival are not of great consequence, it makes sense to check all discount plans. Airlines are glad to explain their discounts, and travel agents should be helpful in arranging the lowest-cost means of travel for their customers. The work done by travel agents will be discussed later in this chapter.

OVERSEAS TRAVEL   The cost of an overseas vacation is still too expensive for many of us, but the difference in cost between a vacation trip within the country and a trip overseas is not as great as it once was. More people than ever are traveling to Europe during their vacations, and even college students without big bankrolls are traveling overseas.

For one thing, a shrewd consumer can look for and find some excellent bargains when scheduling a trip overseas. Probably the best advice is to use the services of a reliable travel agent. A travel agent can arrange a complete package, including air transportation, hotel accommodations, meals, transportation in the countries visited, and even entertainment, and he can offer this package for less money than you would spend if you arranged these things yourself.

If you look at a table of air fares, you will discover that air fares overseas vary with the seasons. For example, fares to Europe are highest during spring and summer rush periods, when flights to and from Europe are especially crowded. Late autumn and winter are normally considered off season, when popular low-cost fares prevail.

Another way to save money on air fares overseas is to take advantage of excursion plans. To be eligible for excursion-plan fares, a passenger must plan his trip to be between a certain minimum and maximum number of days. On some plans, the minimum stay in Europe has been 14 days and the maximum stay 28 days. Other factors, too, determine the air fare for overseas flights. A midweek fare may be different from a weekend fare, for example. The fares change, and the discount plans

Editorial Photocolor Archives, Inc.

An overseas vacation is no longer beyond the reach of many consumers.

vary, so the consumer must do some investigating when he is ready to take his trip. As mentioned earlier, a reputable travel agent can be a big help to consumers going on overseas trips.

By train

Although passenger service offered by the railroads has decreased in recent years, some good train service still exists. Because of the increasingly crowded airways, some social planners have indicated that in the future our nation will have to work out a transportation system other than air travel to take care of trips shorter than, say, 300 miles. Perhaps fast rail transportation, or a monorail system of some type, will be the transportation of the future for travel between cities within a few hundred miles of each other.

By bus

The bus companies offer attractive rates for vacation trips. By traveling on a bus, the passenger has the opportunity to see the countryside without having to do the driving. Buses provide express service between many cities; that is, they travel from one city to another without stopping to pick up or drop off passengers. For the convenience of their passengers, the buses schedule rest and meal stops.

By ship

Steamships represent still another means of transportation for consumers. In most cases people who go by steamship do so for more than just transportation. The opportunity to relax on the ship and enjoy excellent meals and service appeals to some persons. For example, some ships based in Florida cruise the Bahamas. A ship might leave Miami late in the afternoon and arrive at a port in Nassau early the next morning. The ship might stay at the Nassau harbor for two or three days while the passengers enjoy swimming, sightseeing, golf, parties, and shopping. Then the ship might travel to other ports in the Bahamas before returning to Miami. Vacation cruises of this type are popular during the winter months.

TRAVEL AGENTS

Many travelers think that using a travel agent means that the trip will cost more, but that usually is not true. A travel agent earns commissions from airlines, hotels, and other travel operators whose services he sells to you. In most cases, you pay nothing for the extra services that a travel agent provides. And in many cases, a good travel agent will save the consumer money by finding a vacation package to suit his budget.

A travel agent is not merely a ticket seller. He is a specialist who can give you valuable advice and information about a vacation that can fit your budget. A travel agent can arrange a type of package tour, for example. A package tour is a prearranged tour designed to fit the requirements of a wide variety of travelers. The tour may be either escorted or unescorted. In most cases, the travel agent will have brochures that describe various tours. If you should want to visit a big city, such as New York, you might discover that through a travel agent you can buy a package trip for a weekend that might include air fare, two nights in a hotel with breakfast, a theater ticket for one evening, and perhaps a meal in a fine restaurant. The cost should be considerably below what you would have to pay if you purchased the items separately. The reason, of course, is that the agent is able to get the tickets at vastly reduced prices.

Anybody can set up shop as a travel agent. Although most agents are honest and try to give clients good, reliable service, some of them are ill-informed, and a few of them are downright dishonest. An established travel agency that has given good service to people you know should be reliable. If you are in doubt, you should check the reputation of the agency with your local better business bureau. The following points should be helpful in dealing with a travel agent.

- Be specific when telling the agent what your requirements are and how much money you are able to spend.
- Make certain you understand the terms and conditions of the agreement. In particular, make certain you know the cancellation provisions.
- Determine exactly what charges are involved. If the service given by the travel agent is simply that of procuring transportation tickets and making hotel reservations, there is ordinarily no charge because the agent gets his commission from the carrier or the hotel. If complicated travel arrangements are needed, however, the agent will charge his client a fee.

PAYING FOR THE VACATION

Some people no doubt save money periodically during the year so that they can afford the kind of vacation they want. Another way to finance a vacation is to pay for it later. Many consumers buy such things as television sets, refrigerators, and sewing machines and pay for them over a period of several months, so why not borrow $400 or $500 for a vacation and pay it back with monthly installments?

When one borrows money for a vacation, the cost of the vacation is increased by the amount of the finance charge, so there is a good argument for saving the money ahead of time for vacations. An item such as a television set has a useful life that is longer than the duration of the payments. In the case of a vacation, however, we would be making payments long after we returned from the vacation. But perhaps in some cases the memory of an unusual vacation is worth so much that we would not mind paying for it over a long period of time.

Credit cards may be used to charge most things that one needs money for on trips. Of course, the full payment will become due in several weeks, unless the consumer elects to pay the charges in installments, in which case a finance charge of about 18 percent annually is added.

Checking your reading

1. Give two reasons why people in our nation are more interested now in recreation and vacations.
2. According to a national survey, how do almost half of all American families resolve the problem of where to go on their vacations?
3. By taking a vacation at a place they have been to before, the family may often deprive themselves of three things. What are they?
4. Discuss three different types of creative vacations.
5. List four things that might be done on a vacation at home.
6. What are some of the costs of camping?
7. Why is vacation travel for most families done by car?
8. What items are included in the cost of driving a car?
9. Discuss the factors to be considered when deciding whether vacation travel should be by car or commercial airline.
10. Why do airline companies offer special rates, such as excursion fares?
11. What were the two restrictions to excursion-plan fares?
12. To take advantage of youth fares, young people must travel "standby." What does standby mean?
13. When are air fares to Europe highest?
14. How can a passenger be eligible for excursion-plan fares to Europe?
15. What is meant by the express service used by some bus companies?
16. List three suggestions that might be helpful when dealing with a travel agent.

Consumer problems and projects

1.   From a travel agency get information on the cost of several "package" tours currently available for vacations to places such as Hawaii and the Bahamas or to places in Mexico, Europe, and the Far East. The agency should have available brochures with detailed information pertaining to dates, modes of transportation, types of hotels, meal arrangements, and cost. For each trip construct a careful comparison of the costs of the package tours and the costs of approximately the same vacation trips arranged independently. The travel agency should be helpful in supplying information for individually arranged vacation trips. Present your findings, and indicate the pros and cons of package tours.

2.   Locate information about vacation homes. The homes can range from small cabins near mountain streams to larger structures on exclusive lake-front property. Certain real estate agencies will have information available concerning vacation homes. Prepare a report listing the advantages and disadvantages of vacation homes. Be certain to examine costs. Use library reference sources to find information about the desirability of owning or leasing vacation homes.

3.   Use the technique of brainstorming to compile a list of things a family can do if they spend their vacation at home. When the list has been completed, organize the ideas by type of activity.

4.   Construct a table to show comparative costs of traveling by car, train, bus, and airplane. Choose a place to travel to that is at least 200 or 300 miles from your home. For example, you might determine the cost of traveling round trip from Chicago to San Francisco. Decide how many people will be traveling—one person or a family of three or four. Include the round-trip fare or cost in the case of traveling by car, the daily cost of meals, and the daily cost of lodging. For car transportation assume your total running expenses are $4\frac{1}{2}$ cents per mile.

5.   Because traveling vacationers often assume unusual risks, insurance companies offer a variety of lesser-known, special-risk policies that provide coverage for a certain number of days. Ask an insurance agent in your community to give you information about a typical trip policy. Get information about the maximum amount that will be paid for medical bills resulting from accident or illness, the maximum death benefit, and the amount per day that will be paid for hospital expenses.

6.   Make a list of tips for travelers. Include such things as advice for persons who will be staying in motels, advice for motorists, and advice for persons who make reservations through airlines or travel agents. Consider everything a traveler does, and offer advice that will be helpful.

Chapter

Buying cars

Owning a car is now much more than a practical necessity. A car is often a status symbol—an indication to others that the owner has climbed a number of rungs on the ladder of success. For some people a glistening new car is very high on their list of goals. Our cars, whether new or old, affect our families, our jobs, our vacations, our social lives, and many other areas of life.

Cars have a considerable affect on our pocketbooks, too. The U.S. Department of Transportation reports that a typical standard-size, one-year-old car costs its owner $1,467 during the year. To put it another way, cars and their expenses rank third, next to housing and food, in typical family budgets. Suburban families owning two cars often report spending from 15 to 20 percent of their income on cars.

BUYING A NEW CAR

Unless he is acquiring his first car, the prospective buyer usually faces the problem of determining when he should trade in his old car for a new one. Should he trade it in in the fall just before the new models come out? Should he wait until the new models are available and then trade in his car for one of the previous year's models (a leftover)? Should he trade in his car for a new model when the new models first come out? Or, should he wait until, say, December or January? How many years should he drive a car before trading it in for a new model?

We are becoming a nation on wheels. Many consumer decisions and problems involve automobiles.

Courtesy The Houston Chronicle

To begin with, the consumer should know that the biggest single cost in owning and operating a car is depreciation. As the car grows older, its market value decreases. Age, in fact, is usually more important than mileage in determining a car's worth.

How much does depreciation cost? Some authorities estimate depreciation for the first year alone to be as high as one-third of the original cost of the car. In each succeeding year, the car depreciates 25 percent of its current value. More typical of depreciation estimates, however, are the following:

Year 1 . . . . . . 25% to 30%

Year 2 . . . . . . 18%

Year 3 . . . . . . 14%

Year 4 . . . . . . 11%

Year 5 . . . . . . 9%

Year 6 . . . . . . 6%

Year 7 . . . . . . 2%

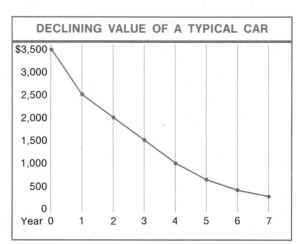

DECLINING VALUE OF A TYPICAL CAR

Thus, a car costing $3,500 would depreciate about $875 the first year (25 percent of $3,500). During the second year, the car would decline in market value another $630 (18 percent of $3,500). By the end of the third year, the market value of the car could be expected to be about $1,505, or less than half the original cost of the car.

Some people say that the most expensive drive you will ever take is when you drive that new car home from the dealer's showroom. The statement is true, at least on the basis of cost per mile. Once it is sold by the dealer to the customer, the car is "used," and its market value has decreased several hundred dollars.

You have noticed that depreciation costs become less each succeeding year, so that by the end of the sixth year depreciation becomes almost negligible. Why, then, does it not make sense to keep a car for many years so that depreciation costs will be minimized? One catch to this line of thinking is that while depreciation costs decrease as a car grows older, maintenance costs tend to increase.

A study by the U.S. Department of Transportation indicates that repairs and maintenance costs begin to exceed depreciation costs during the car's fourth year. Many other reasons could be given for wanting to trade in a car for a new one after two, three, or four years. For example, an older car generally requires more repair work, and most of us do not like the inconvenience of being without a car while it is being repaired. Furthermore, a newer car may be safer. Then, of course, many of us suffer from an affliction known as new-car fever. We have many personal reasons for wanting a new car—some logical, some not so logical—and we sometimes succeed in convincing ourselves that we should make the purchase.

An accounting firm specializing in consulting work for car-fleet operators says that the most economical trade-in time is at the end of three years or 60,000 miles, whichever comes first. The car should, according to this firm, deliver its maximum economy during that time. For a family, however, the best time to trade in a car depends upon so many variables (for example, how many miles it is driven per month, whether the driving is on rural roads or modern freeways, the climate in which the owner lives) that it is just not possible to say at exactly what time an old car should be traded in for a new car.

Where should you begin?

The place to start shopping for a new car is at home. Prepare a careful buying plan by gathering facts from as many sources as possible. The booklet *Performance Data for New Passenger Cars and Motorcycles* is available from the Superintendent of Documents, Government Printing Office, Washington, D.C. The "Auto Buying Guide" issue of *Consumer Reports* gives detailed data on new cars, and performance information on various models of cars is featured in various monthly issues of the magazine. *Changing Times* magazine also gives performance data on new cars, including the results of the Union 76 Performance Trials held annually. Automotive magazines and other periodicals available in libraries also give information about cars that may be helpful in deciding what kind of car to buy.

Before embarking on a tour of dealers, the prospective car buyer should know a great deal about what kind of car he needs, how much he can afford to pay, how much he will need to finance, where he can obtain financing, and where he can obtain insurance.

More specifically, the prospective car buyer should decide as rationally as possible whether he should buy a big luxury car with a big engine, for example, or an intermediate-size car with a medium-size engine. A luxury car not only costs more to buy but also costs more

77 Locust Valley Road
Coy, Alabama 36435

July 2, 19--

Locust Valley Motors, Inc.
1234 Main Street
Coy, Alabama 36435

Gentlemen:

Please make ,to the undersigned a firm offer to sell one Chevrolet Nova, four-door sedan, 200-hp V8 engine, Biscayne blue, 19-- model. This automobile is to have the standard equipment plus the following accessories:

ZJ 1	Custom Interior Group
ZJ 2	Custom Exterior Group
ZJ 5	Exterior Decor Package
M 35	Powerglide Transmission
J 50	Power Brakes (drum type)
N 40	Power Steering
C 60	Air Conditioning
U 63	AM Radio
D 33	Left Mirror (outside remote control)

To be considered, your offer must be received by me personally by July 24, 19--, at the address shown above.

Yours truly,

Fred G. Wiggins

Fred G. Wiggins

Some consumers approach buying a new car as a business does with a request for offers (left) or by making a firm offer (top of next page). Consumers who use this approach should first consult an attorney to avoid possible legal problems.

```
                                          77 Locust Valley Road
                                          Coy, Alabama 36435

                                          July 2, 19--


Locust Valley Motors, Inc.
1234 Main Street
Coy, Alabama 36435

Gentlemen:

The undersigned hereby makes to you a firm offer to purchase
one Chevrolet Nova, four-door sedan, 200-hp V8 engine, 19--
model, Biscayne blue, for the cash price of $3,150.00, with
delivery thereof within 60 days after acceptance.  This auto-
mobile is to have the standard equipment plus the following
accessories:

        ZJ 1      Custom Interior Group
        ZJ 2      Custom Exterior Group
        ZJ 5      Exterior Decor Package
        M 35      Powerglide Transmission
        J 50      Power Brakes (drum type)
        N 40      Power Steering
        C 60      Air Conditioning
        U 63      AM Radio
        D 33      Left Mirror (outside remote control)

This offer will remain open until 5 p.m. on July 24, 19--.
It must be accepted in writing within that time by delivery
of acceptance to the undersigned personally at the address
shown above.

                                  Yours truly,

                                  Fred G. Wiggins

                                  Fred G. Wiggins
```

to operate. Should the family buy a station wagon? Why? If hauling
things a few times a year is the reason for wanting a station wagon,
would it be cheaper to rent a trailer or pay someone to haul the items?
Currently, American-made compacts and subcompacts are increasing
in popularity. If one of the functions of the car will be extensive
highway driving, the compact car may not be a wise choice. The
National Highway Safety Bureau has shown that compacts are involved
in a higher percentage of accidents resulting in deaths or severe injuries
than are standard-size cars.

Some consumers follow the lead of company purchasing agents.
They duplicate a bid form that spells out in detail exactly the car they
want to buy. These forms are taken to as many dealers as possible
with the instruction that the dealer make an offer within a certain
period. When the dealer refuses to offer a price on a car that he does
not have in stock, he may be a dealer to avoid. Another technique used
by some consumers is to make the dealer an offer in writing for a
specific car with the provision that the dealer must accept the offer
within a certain period, say 24 or 48 hours.

How much should you pay?

Fortunately, the consumer can get some approximate information on how much a car should cost. By federal law, all cars now sold must have price information posted on them. The *sticker,* as it is called, includes the manufacturer's suggested retail price for the car with standard equipment, the price of each item of optional equipment, transportation charges, and taxes. Few cars, however, are sold at the sticker price. In fact, according to the Federal Trade Commission, less than 2 percent of domestic cars and about 19 percent of foreign cars are sold at the price indicated on the sticker. Discounts of at least $200 off the sticker price are given in nearly nine out of ten cases. Persons willing to pay the sticker price are known as "barefoot pilgrims" by car dealers.

To estimate how much the dealer paid for the car, take the sticker price and deduct the freight charges. Then deduct from 17 to 25 percent, depending upon the size of the car. For a compact car without accessories, for example, deduct about 17 percent; for an intermediate-size car, deduct 20 percent; for a full-size car, deduct 25 percent.

Let us say the sticker price on a full-size car is $3,415, and the freight charge is $95. Subtracting the freight charge leaves $3,320. The cost to the dealer is $3,320 minus 25 percent, or about $2,500. To determine about how much you should be charged, add to the dealer's cost the freight charge plus from $200 to $250 to cover the dealer's expenses and profit. Thus, you would expect to pay between $2,795 and $2,845.

A more exact way of determining the dealer's cost is to consult one of several books available that give precise data concerning what a dealer pays the manufacturer for a current make and model. Cost information on accessories is also available in these books. Two examples of books available are *Price Buying Directory,* published by Consumers Digest, 6316 North Lincoln Avenue, Chicago, Illinois 60645, and *Car Fax,* published by Fax Publications, Inc., 220 Madison Avenue, New York, New York 10016.

Of course, complicating the matter of determining a fair price is the trade-in that most persons have. The car dealer may offer an extremely attractive price on the new car and then make up the difference by knocking down the trade-in offer on the old car. Conversely, the dealer may begin by making a high trade-in offer on the old car and then not give as big a discount on the new car.

Knowing how much the old car is worth is, then, just as important as knowing what is a fair price for the new car. It is possible for consumers to get information on the approximate value of used cars. A banker or a credit union can give information on the values of various makes, models, and years of cars. The banker consults the *National Automobile Dealers Association Official Used Car Guide*. The guide is an up-to-date book with figures showing the average prices paid for all types of used cars sold at wholesale auctions. With information about the true wholesale value of your used car, and with an idea of the cost of the new car to the dealer, it is possible to estimate the amount of cash needed to make the transaction (the difference between the price of the new car and the trade-in value of the old car).

Should you buy a leftover car?

Some people save money on new-car purchases by waiting until the new models appear and then buying an old model that the dealer still has on hand. The dealer may be given factory rebates on leftovers, so it is possible to pass this saving on to the customer. Then, too, the dealer has his capital invested in these cars, and he should want to clear his inventory of old-model cars as rapidly as possible after the new models come out. Some reports have indicated that discounts offered range from $500 on compact cars to $800 on full-size medium-priced models. One must remember, however, that discounts are also common on current models, so the entire amount of the discount on a leftover car is not due to the fact that it is a leftover car.

Whether or not buying a leftover car is a wise choice depends upon many factors. Remember that a leftover is a year-old car (even though it is brand new), and the first year's depreciation is from 25 to 30 percent. So if the buyer intends to sell the car within a year or two, buying a leftover may not be wise, unless the unlikely situation exists where the dealer's discount is large enough to cover the first year's depreciation. If the car will be kept for a number of years, and if the consumer is not especially concerned about the model year, then buying a leftover may make sense.

How should you deal with dealers?

Some car dealers use reprehensible tricks to induce people to buy cars. One popular technique, known as "low-balling," is to suggest that the car can be bought for a certain price that the prospective customer recognizes as a rather low one and that is therefore attractive to him. The price is so attractive that the customer often stops shopping at other dealers. Furthermore, the prospective buyer becomes more and more eager to get the car and get it soon. He has made the decision to buy.

Now he wants to enjoy the car. When he discovers that the car cannot be bought for the initial price, he is disappointed, but often he will buy anyway because he has his mind set on owning the car.

Even careful shoppers are often taken in by low-balling. A family may shop carefully at many different places for a particular type of car. A price is agreed on at one of the dealers, and the family then waits for several weeks while the car is being obtained by the dealer. When the car arrives, the dealer "discovers" that the price quoted originally is in error. Not only has the family wasted time, it has also stopped shopping around. Often the car is bought at a much higher price.

What can be done about low-balling? For one thing, be certain that the price quoted is approved in writing by an authorized representative of the firm, and be certain that the deal is binding. Another thing, if you are the victim of a low-ball scheme, do not buy from the dealer. The better business bureaus and the automobile industry consider low-balling reprehensible and suggests that dealers using such a tactic be avoided.

Most new-car transactions involve trading in an old car, and a technique known as "high-balling" is sometimes used by unscrupulous dealers. The scheme in this case is to offer more for the old car than it is really worth.

Consider the case of a man who owns a five-year-old car that sold for about $3,000 when it was new. He knows that the car depreciates each year, and using the percentages given on page 162, he calculates that the total depreciation on his car to date may be about $2,310. He hopes, however, that his car will bring much more than $690 ($3,000 less $2,310) because he has taken good care of the car, and it is a fairly popular model. Actually, he is hoping to get about $1,000 on a trade-in. The salesman might say something like, "How would you like to get $1,300 for that old station wagon of yours? I think that I may have a buyer for it."

The prospective customer might be so overwhelmed at this unexpected generosity that he wants to close the deal quickly before the salesman changes his mind or discovers that he has made a mistake. Later he discovers that the high price is subject to reappraisal when he picks up his new car and turns over his old car to the dealer. By this time he wants the new car and may accept the deal, even though the cash he must now pay (the difference between the price of the new car and the trade-in value of his old car) may represent an increase of $200 or $300.

Other schemes are used by some car dealers to get people to pay more money for cars. For example, in a prearranged setup, a salesman may say some rather harsh words to a prospective customer who has turned down the salesman's proposal. The sales manager just "happens" to hear the insult, and he rushes out to stop the customer, who will be in the process of leaving the premises in anger by that time. After begging the customer to wait a few moments so he can apologize, the sales manager takes the salesman to task for his indiscretion. The sales manager may even indicate to the salesman that he may be fired. All this is done, of course, in the presence of the prospective customer. Then, the customer is invited to the sales manager's office, offered a soft drink or coffee, and given a profuse apology. To make up for the unkind words of the salesman, the sales manager then offers to make a "special" deal on the car under consideration. The price may be just a few dollars ($25 to $75) under that offered by the salesman and refused previously by the prospective customer. Although the scheme seems rather far-fetched, it is used and often works.

Some dealers have even gone so far as to bug their small sales offices. The salesman uses some pretense to leave the husband and wife for a few moments. While the husband and wife discuss privately what they think of the latest offer that has been made, the salesman listens through an intercom and thus has the advantage of knowing the private thoughts of the buyer.

Choosing a dealer is considered especially important by some people who place high value on service. In fact, some dealers in certain cities are now advertising the fact that they charge slightly more for their cars because they expect their customers to want good service, and the dealers expect to give good service. A dealer in or near your neighborhood may give you the full benefit of a new-car warranty. A dealer farther from your home may offer a bargain price, but the cost and inconvenience of taking the car to this dealer for service may offset the savings in the price of the car. Of course, a dealer can claim to give good service and thus charge more, but in fact the buyer has no real assurance that the service will be any better.

BUYING A USED CAR

Modern cars have what is called a "100,000-mile engine." With reasonably careful upkeep, most cars should last long enough to travel 100,000 miles or more. The average car is owned by one person for about three years, so good values should be available in the used-car market.

Community Series, University Films/McGraw-Hill

A consumer buying a used car should seek the help of a qualified mechanic.

The starting point in searching for a used car is often newspaper want ads, but these ads can be extremely misleading. For example, an astonishingly low price may be quoted on a popular model that purportedly is in excellent shape. When you arrive at the used-car lot you are told that the car has already been sold, but many other fantastic buys are still available. The ad may have been just a come-on to induce you to visit the lot. An ad may read: "Repossessions—take over payments." Most readers of the ad would conclude that the offer means a buyer can take over the payments left by a former owner who could not keep them up. In fact, this ad, too, may be simply a way to induce people to visit the lot. Some of the cars may have been repossessed at one time, but they are now selling at the regular price.

Probably in most cases the best source for a used car is the used-car lot of an established dealer. The dealer has the shop facilities and the mechanics to put a used car in good shape, and he will more likely stand behind a warranty. Often an established dealer will keep on his own lot only the cars that he thinks can give reasonably good service. He may sell the worst lemons at a used-car auction. Buying a used car from such a dealer may mean paying a few dollars more for the car, but it may be well worth the money.

Following are a few pointers that a prospective used-car buyer should bear in mind.

- Have an impartial mechanic check the car over thoroughly to determine whether or not it will be a reasonably reliable car. A mechanic can, for example, look under the car for indications of frame straightening that show that the car has been in a major accident. Some localities now have diagnostic clinics (see page 173) where mechanics specialize in applying elaborate tests to determine the condition of a car. The cost of a checkup might be as high as $20 or $25, but that could be money well spent if it reveals a car that is in poor condition.

- Take the car for a road test. Over a rough stretch of road, check for any looseness in the steering mechanism. Check for bounce that may reveal worn shock absorbers. Listen for odd noises. Accelerate rapidly to 60 miles per hour to determine whether the car gains speed smoothly without sputtering. Check the brakes. Brakes should hold equally on all four wheels without causing the car to veer to one side. While the car is stopped, race the engine, and check the exhaust. Blue smoke means the engine is burning oil.
- Do not take a salesman's word for the fact that the car is in good condition. In most cases, he does not know that much about the car. Especially in large lots, used cars are cleaned thoroughly (even the engines) and often painted.
- Check the frequency-of-repair record of the make and model you are interested in buying. *Consumer Reports,* for example, features such information in certain issues. In addition, automotive magazines available in libraries can be a good source of information about the dependability of various models.

FINANCING A CAR

Many car purchases, especially new-car purchases, involve borrowing money for part of the cost. Typically, a customer hands over his old car as the down payment on a new car and then signs an installment agreement with the dealer. No cash changes hands.

Often the customer can save money by arranging the financing himself through a bank or a credit union. The car dealer in most instances has an arrangement with a finance company for an installment contract. The dealer customarily gets a rebate from the finance company he recommends.

A dealer may offer financing on a 3-year $2,500 loan for a total interest charge of $600. In contrast, a bank might offer a 3-year $2,500 loan for a total interest charge of $525. The difference between finance charges in this case may not seem especially large, but consider how important $75 seems when the salesman and the customer are trying to agree on the price of the car. Furthermore, the difference in finance charges between the dealer's arrangement and a bank or credit union may be much larger than the illustration given here. For used cars, particularly, finance companies operating through dealers often charge considerably more than the customer would have to pay if he shopped around for lower interest rates.

In summary, the wise consumer shops around carefully not only for his car but also for credit.

CAR REPAIRS

Mrs. Zedelak drove one of her family's two cars to a women's association meeting in a city about 150 miles from her home. On her return home, Mrs. Zedelak stopped at a service station for gasoline. One of the attendants lifted the car's hood to make the usual service checks. After several minutes, he explained to Mrs. Zedelak that the car's oil level was fine, but he had spotted a bad alternator—a very serious situation. The attendant showed Mrs. Zedelak the problem and explained that the alternator was about to malfunction. He suggested that she not attempt to drive any great distance before having the part replaced. In answer to her question, the attendant said they did happen to have one on hand. Mrs. Zedelak bought a new alternator.

The service station attendant had sprayed oil on the car's alternator, causing it to appear to be malfunctioning. Thus, a new alternator seemed necessary. Such reprehensible tactics are not resorted to by the majority of service stations, of course, but schemes such as the fictitious one described are being used by some unscrupulous people.

Modern cars have so many different parts with overlapping functions that most owners find it difficult, if not impossible, to have a good understanding of their cars. Dual ignition systems, submersible fuel pumps, and the host of other new parts and systems on rapidly changing and improving models mean that more and more the average car owner is at the mercy of dishonest or incompetent mechanics. Dishonest shops have countless ways of extracting money from car owners. A mechanic can show the customer metal filings taken from the bottom of the automatic transmission case. Such particles may come from the normal meshing of gears, but because the car owner does not know this he can easily be convinced that he needs a several-hundred-dollar transmission overhaul. What the customer may get is a single change of transmission fluid. The better business bureaus report that they receive many complaints from travelers far from home who fall prey to unscrupulous mechanics and service station attendants who have found "something wrong" under the hood.

The shortage of mechanics

The shortage of mechanics, the shoddiness of repair work, and the increasing costs of repair work have been so serious that they have received special attention from the Senate Anti-Trust and Monopoly Subcommittee. The automobile manufacturers themselves acknowledge the seriousness of the problems and note that they reflect on the success of their product. The problems include the rising costs of parts, the serious shortage of mechanics, and frauds perpetrated on customers who are uninitiated in the mysteries of modern cars.

The late 1950s saw the beginning of the explosion of car models and options. At the same time, more and more families became owners of more than one car. Unfortunately, the number of trained auto mechanics has not kept pace with the increase in cars. In 1950, there was one mechanic for every 73 cars; the estimate for 1975 is one mechanic for every 154 cars. One effect of the shortage of mechanics is that shop operators hire mediocre repairmen. Repair bills obviously increase when unskilled men diagnose car malfunctions by trial and error. Then, too, an untrained and unskilled mechanic is more likely to install a new part than to attempt to save the customer money by repairing the old one.

Obviously, new ways must be found to attract and train mechanics in our country. Vocational and technical schools are now doing their part, and auto manufacturers annually train mechanics in an effort to keep them abreast of new technical developments. But informed opinion suggests that these efforts must be increased.

The importance of a good mechanic

Many car owners attest to the wisdom of finding a mechanic who can be trusted and then sticking with him. He will get to know the car and can be on the lookout for potential weak points. Sometimes the service department of an automobile agency that handles your particular make of car may prove to be convenient. If the agency wishes to build goodwill for future car sales, the service may be good.

Diagnostic centers are becoming popular in certain parts of the country. Several hundred such centers now exist, and they range from relatively small slots in service stations to long lanes in special buildings that can handle a dozen cars at the same time. The expensive electronic equipment in these larger centers probably offer the best means now available to discover defective, worn-out, and maladjusted items on a car.

A diagnostic center with complete equipment and trained diagnosticians can check the performance of an amazingly large number of items. Such things as the horns, lights, and windshield wipers are examined as part of a general inspection. Then the car is lifted for an examination of such things as the steering mechanism, wheel bearings, tires, springs, exhaust system, and the front suspension. Leaks from the engine, transmission, and differential are investigated.

An oscilloscope and related electronic gear are used to test the engine. The car may be put on a dynamometer and given a simulated road test as the wheels turn against huge rollers in the floor. Break testing can also be an integral function of the dynamometer.

The cost of sending a car through a diagnostic clinic may vary from as little as $5 to as much as $25 or more, depending on the completeness of the equipment and the thoroughness of the checkup. In any case, the car owner should remember that even sophisticated equipment properly maintained requires a human being to interpret the results of testing. Thus, the competence and honesty of the diagnosticians are extremely important.

Courtesy Ford Customer Service Division

An automobile diagnostic center uses sophisticated equipment to determine the condition of a car.

Some diagnostic centers operate independently of a repair shop, but thus far not many of these centers exist. If the interpretation of the results of testing is given by a mechanic who wants your business, the interpretation may point out defects that are not really there. When a diagnostic center is a part of a new-car dealer's operation, the possibility exists that in some cases the repair estimates could be inflated enough to make buying a new car seem attractive to the customer.

SAVING MONEY ON UPKEEP

Car owners should pay attention to proper maintenance in order to keep the costs of operation as low as possible. The owner's manual should be studied carefully because, in addition to the maintenance schedule the owner is required to follow to keep his warranty in effect, it has a wealth of information that can help keep the car in good condition for a long time.

Information on starting the car, for example, is given in the owner's manual. Although the method of starting engines has changed over the years, many drivers still pump the accelerator pedal and permit the starter to grind away for long periods of time, thus overheating the starter and damaging it. Air conditioning systems on cars should be operated periodically even in cold weather so that the seal is lubricated adequately to prevent loss of the gas charge.

Driving tips, too, are given in owner's manuals. The car will get better gasoline mileage and have a longer engine life if the manufacturer's advice is taken. It is possible to cut your gas bill by 10 percent or more by acquiring good driving habits. Quick starts, for example, may be exhilarating, but they use up a great deal of gasoline. The accelerator should not be slammed to the floor; instead, the gas should be fed slowly and evenly to the engine as speed is picked up. Gas consumption at speeds in excess of 50 miles per hour increases at a rapid rate. The faster you drive, the more fuel you burn.

SAFETY ON THE HIGHWAYS

According to the National Safety Council, 56,400 persons were killed in auto accidents in a recent year in the United States. By 1980, the Secretary of Transportation foresees perhaps only 41,000 deaths. The phrase "only 41,000 deaths" sounds horrible, but unless all the combined safety efforts cut the upward trend, the number of deaths resulting from car accidents could be as high as 75,000 in 1980.

The 1970 cars had some 80 safety improvements that did not exist in the 1965 models. These safety improvements varied from seat belts and shoulder harnesses to such things as a new type of windshield glass, side-impact bars inside doors, and controlled-crush chassis frames. The energy-absorbing steering assembly, which became standard in 1967, has prevented many fatalities. The new door latches and seat belts and shoulder harnesses have reduced the number of ejections (a prime cause of fatal injuries). Currently, new safety devices and refinements of existing safety features are being tested and evaluated.

Safer cars must be a concern of all people, and the prospects for safer cars in the future seem bright. But the most crucial determinant of safety in any car is the driver. Driver education courses in schools have contributed immeasurably to safety on our highways. Although the contribution of driver education is difficult to measure, insurance companies have taken note of it and offer special rates to young drivers who have completed such training. A large part of safe driving is the driver's attitude. A genuine concern for the welfare of others goes far in contributing to safety on our roads.

THE BASIC PRINCIPLE OF INSURANCE

Let us assume that exactly 1,000 students in your school have formed a camera club and have each purchased a camera costing $100. The students recognize that their cameras could be lost or stolen.

Although there is no way of knowing how many cameras will be missing at the end of the school year, assume that the students estimate that during the first year five will disappear. If they are right, five students will suffer $100 losses. So the students decide that if each of them (1,000 students) contributes 50 cents to a fund, they would have $500 that they could use to give to the unlucky persons whose cameras were stolen. The students are spreading the loss—insurance people would say that they are "sharing the risk." The club might have collected $1 from each student, just in case the losses are more in the neighborhood of $1,000 a year.

Risk sharing is the basic principle of insurance. An insurance company collects money (called a "premium") from each person who wishes to be a part of the plan. Because insurance companies insure so many people, they can rely on past experience to estimate quite accurately how much they will pay out in claims each year. They set premium rates by estimating the amount of money they will pay out in claims and then add to that their administrative expenses and the profit they must earn. The discussion following pertains to automobile insurance. When you read about life insurance and health insurance in later chapters, you will recognize that these kinds of insurance, too, are based on the principle of risk sharing.

Car insurance

A major expense resulting from owning a car is insurance. Although the cost of car insurance has been increasing considerably during recent years, the need for such insurance is so great that nobody should operate a car unless he is adequately covered by insurance. An automobile insurance reform plan known as "no-fault" insurance is being instituted in the United States, and its backers hope it will eliminate long court fights and give motorists a greater return for their insurance dollar. The plan provides that insurance companies promptly pay their clients' claims for actual losses regardless of who was at fault in the accident. A modified no-fault plan began operating in Massachusetts in 1971, and by 1972 a few other states had their own versions of no-fault insurance. But before examining no-fault insurance more completely, we will look at the traditional five types of protection that offer car owners complete insurance coverage: (1) liability insurance, (2) collision coverage, (3) medical payments coverage, (4) uninsured motorist coverage, and (5) fire, theft, and comprehensive insurance.

LIABILITY INSURANCE Liability insurance protects the insured against claims for personal injuries or claims for property damage caused by his car or by someone else's car when it is driven by him. The insured gets nothing for his own losses from this provision; the payments go to others for their injuries, property damages, lost wages, or other similar losses. Most states require all car owners to carry both personal and property liability insurance. Liability insurance is by far the most important insurance a car owner buys because at today's high speeds cars can cause fantastic damage.

Liability is referred to in a three-part series describing its coverage. For example, a policy referred to as "100/300/10" means that the insurance company's liability is limited to $100,000 for injury to one person, $300,000 for two or more persons injured in one accident, and $10,000 for property damage. A policy as large as 100/300/10 is becoming more common, but less coverage is possible, of course. The premium for liability insurance does not increase in proportion to the coverage. One company, for example, charges a driver over age twenty-five an annual premium of $117 for personal liability coverage of $5,000 for injury to one person and $10,000 for injury to two or more in a single accident. By increasing the protection to $100,000 for one injury and $300,000 for multiple injuries, the premium is increased to $189.54. Thus, the protection is increased 30 times at less than twice the price. Liability policies are important, and it does not make sense to try to skimp on the coverage. Some people with considerable assets carry million-dollar liability policies to protect them from damage suits.

COLLISION COVERAGE Collision insurance covers the repair or replacement of the insured's own car after an accident, unless the accident was caused by another car and he collects from the negligent driver (or the negligent driver's insurance company). Money can be saved on collision coverage by agreeing to pay more of the repair bill out of your own pocket. Most collision coverage plans include a deductible clause. On a $50-deductible policy, for example, the car owner pays the first $50 of repair, and the insurance company pays the remainder. By agreeing to a $100-deductible clause, you can save a good deal of money on the premium. The insurance company obviously does not pay out as much money, nor do they pay out as often (thus saving on paperwork). Because some drivers believe they can absorb a loss even as high as $250 without undue financial strain, they save money on premiums by purchasing $250-deductible policies.

Courtesy Consumers Union

Automobile design has a significant influence on insurance rates. For example, a five-mile-per-hour collision caused $128.30 worth of damage to this car.

As a car gets older, of course, the need for collision insurance decreases. When a car's value decreases to about $500, the need for collision insurance should probably be questioned seriously.

MEDICAL PAYMENTS COVERAGE   Medical payments coverage takes care of medical, hospital, and funeral costs for the insured, his family, and his passengers, whether or not the insured is at fault, and for the insured and his family, no matter whose car the victim was in. This type of coverage also compensates the insured and his family for certain medical expenses that result from being hit while a pedestrian.

UNINSURED MOTORIST COVERAGE   The purpose of uninsured motorist coverage is to protect the car owner who is unable to collect from a negligent driver who does not have liability insurance. The car owner's own insurance company makes liability payments, but usually up to a limit such as $10,000 per person or $20,000 per accident. The policy also pays off if the negligent driver's insurance company is insolvent or if the guilty person cannot be found (a hit-and-run driver).

FIRE, THEFT, AND COMPREHENSIVE INSURANCE   Fire insurance compensates for fire or lightning damage to the car, but it does not cover damage to the owner's clothes or to other articles that happen to be in the car. Theft insurance compensates the owner for a stolen car, but it does not cover the contents of the car. (Special fire or theft policies may be taken out on the contents.) Fire insurance alone may be obtained, but theft insurance is never written without fire insurance.

Most people now buy what is known as comprehensive coverage. Comprehensive automobile insurance combines fire and theft coverage with coverage for many other kinds of damage to the car, including damage resulting from tornadoes, windstorms, hail, water, riots, falling objects, and many other causes listed in the policy. The cost of this type of policy is slightly higher than the standard fire and theft policy.

GROUP PLANS FOR CAR INSURANCE   Although group life and health insurance has been available for quite some time, group car insurance has just recently become available through employers. The insurance company sells the insurance to the employees of a firm. Each employee who participates in the plan decides on the extent of coverage he wants and pays rates tailored to the coverage. The employer withholds each employee's premium from his paycheck and periodically sends a single check to the insurance company.

Fewer agents are needed to bring in customers, and the insurance company has fewer expenses because the employer takes on the burden of collecting the premiums from the insured persons. Therefore, the insurance company can usually afford to offer a discount. This type of insurance may become increasingly popular in the years ahead.

No-fault car insurance

The principle that a man must pay for the results of his negligence underlies our automobile insurance system. For that reason, of course, liability insurance is so extremely important. If we cause the accident, we need protection against the claims of other people involved in the accident.

But how easy is it to determine who is at fault in automobile accidents? According to some studies, a driver makes more than 200 observations and 20 decisions for almost every mile he drives. Even a careful driver, according to some experts, makes one driving error every 2 miles. Is fault then sometimes a matter of bad timing rather than negligence? In some cases, of course, determining who is at fault in the accident is quite easy. If a car darts past a stop sign and smashes a car at the intersection, there is little doubt about who was negligent. If a drunken driver weaves his car into the wrong lane and collides head-on with another car, placing blame is easy. But most accidents are not so easily resolved.

A *no-fault* insurance plan would eliminate the need to prove that someone was at fault in an accident before any claims are paid. Determining who is at fault is often a long, costly process involving legal action. In some cities such as New York and Chicago, the process can take as long as 5 years in court; nationwide, in 1970, the average time required to settle claims was 16 months. When both parties to an accident are at fault, usually neither insurance company is legally required to pay. In many cases seriously injured persons settle out of court for far less than their actual loss simply because they cannot afford to wait for a court settlement.

The no-fault insurance idea would eliminate the problem of long waits while courts determine guilt. Furthermore, it would put an end to out-of-court settlements for amounts of money far less than the losses suffered. Studies conducted by the Department of Transportation reveal that the higher the loss, the lower the percentage of recovery from insurance companies. Accident victims usually are reimbursed for less than half their out-of-pocket losses when the losses are over

$5,000. When the loss is more than $25,000, the average settlement is about one-third the loss. On the other hand, when the accidents involve losses of less than $500, the settlement is generally more than the loss because the company prefers to avoid expensive suits.

When fault does not have to be determined, insurance companies save money that would otherwise go to lawyers and claims investigators. In a New York study, an average of 23 cents out of every premium dollar was used for this purpose. A study for the Department of Transportation showed that, in 1968, parties to automobile accident litigation paid legal fees totaling $600 million—one-fifth of the total income of the legal profession that year.

Basically, no-fault automobile insurance would work as follows:

- A driver would be paid for accident expenses by his own insurance company, regardless of who was to blame for the accident.
- The insurance policy would cover the driver and occupants of his car, and pedestrians.
- Medical bills and wage losses would be paid as they were incurred.
- Persons in other cars involved in the accident would be covered by each driver's insurance policy.

The principal argument used by people who oppose no-fault insurance plans is that drivers will be encouraged to drive recklessly if they know they cannot be sued. Persons who favor no-fault plans answer the argument by pointing out that an accident is not a premeditated thing. People have a natural instinct for self-preservation, and any person who would deliberately cause an accident would probably do so without any thought about negligence suits. Puerto Rico has had a no-fault insurance plan since 1969, and at the end of 1971 it could report that the number of deaths resulting from traffic accidents had actually dropped and that the rise in the accident rate had been halved from 10 percent to 5 percent since no-fault insurance began.

After Massachusetts began its no-fault insurance plan at the beginning of 1971, several other states (Florida, Illinois, Delaware, and Oregon) approved their own versions within the year. At the beginning of 1972, many other states were considering no-fault insurance plans. Drivers living in states that have no-fault insurance need liability insurance if they drive in other states.

Checking your reading

1. What is the biggest single cost in owning and operating a car? Give an indication of this cost during the car's first year.
2. When should a family car be traded in for a new car?
3. Discuss how a consumer should begin his shopping for a new car before he actually visits new-car dealers.
4. Although, because of federal law, new cars must have price information posted on them, few cars are sold at their sticker price. How can one determine about how much is a reasonable price to pay for the car?
5. How can one get an estimate of the value of an old car that is to be traded in for a new car?
6. Explain when buying a "leftover car" (one that is a year-old model, even though it is brand new) may be a good buy and when it may not be a good buy.
7. Explain what is meant by the car-selling techniques known as low-balling and high-balling.
8. Explain two schemes (in addition to low-balling and high-balling) used by unscrupulous dealers to sell cars.
9. List four pointers that a prospective buyer of a used car should follow.
10. What is an automobile diagnostic center?
11. In what ways can an owner's manual be valuable to the car owner?
12. Discuss the safety improvements that have been added to cars since 1965.
13. Explain how car insurance is a matter of "sharing the risk."
14. List the five traditional types of car insurance.
15. Which of the five traditional types of car insurance is the most important type to have? Why?
16. Explain what collision insurance covers.
17. Explain what comprehensive insurance covers.
18. What is no-fault car insurance?
19. Give some reasons for the introduction of no-fault car insurance.
20. What is the principal argument used by persons who oppose no-fault insurance?

Consumer problems and projects

1. Because so many car owners complain about the high price of repairs, manufacturers have made available manuals and kits to help car owners do some of their own repair work. From car dealers in your community, or from the manufacturers, collect two or three of these do-it-yourself manuals. Make a list of the jobs for which each manual gives directions.

2.   Assume that a tune-up for a car will require the following parts: spark plugs, points, condenser, distributor cap, rotor, spark plug wire set, and coil. Compare the cost of a tune-up done at home by the car owner and the cost of one done at a garage. Obtain prices for the parts at auto supply stores. Get estimates for a tune-up requiring these parts at as many garages as possible. Estimate as realistically as possible the amount of time an average car owner would spend on the tune-up job. Draw conclusions as to the desirability of doing one's own tune-up work.

3.   As a buying project, assume that you will buy a new car. Follow the advice in this chapter by beginning your shopping "at home." First, decide what type of car you should buy (consider such things as size, price range, and style). Write a brief justification of your decisions. Then, arm yourself with as many facts as you can find in consumer magazines and automotive magazines. Finally, visit new-car dealers, and get as much price information as you can.

4.   By consulting library indexes, such as the *Reader's Guide to Periodical Literature,* locate articles about highway safety. The National Safety Council has been active in publicizing statistics pertaining to car accidents and fatalities, and popular magazines have featured articles about traffic accidents and what is being done about the problem. Note particularly the trend in the statistics. (Have fatalities been increasing or decreasing in recent years?) Also, note predictions for future years. To what extent are solutions being sought by improving the cars? To what extent are drivers considered the problem? Report your findings to the class.

5.   Investigate the kinds of car tires being sold. For example, cord materials in general use are nylon, rayon, polyester, fiber glass, and steel wire. Three common types of construction in use are bias ply, belted bias ply, and radial ply. How important are the cord materials? Is one type of construction superior to other types? What are the differences in price? Is it possible for consumers to know what type of tire they are buying? Can one compare the quality of tires of different manufacturers? Are guarantees of any value?

6.   Construct a bulletin board display with the heading "What Consumers Should Know About No-Fault Auto Insurance." Include the latest statistics about the cost savings for auto insurers in Massachusetts since the passage of the state's no-fault insurance plan. If your state now has a no-fault plan, include information about that plan. Daily newspapers and news magazines often feature stories about no-fault plans. From these sources, and from the information in this chapter, indicate the advantages of no-fault plans and the questions raised by those who are opposed to them.

7.   A news story indicated that a new model of a certain American car had a list price of $3,500. If all the parts of the car were bought individually, their total cost would be $7,500. Labor to assemble the parts would cost another $7,500. Thus, the total cost of this car would be $15,000 if one bought the parts separately and paid to have the car assembled. Discuss the implications of this fact for car insurance premium rates. What recommendations can you make to car manufacturers?

Buying shelter, furniture, and appliances

Part **3**

Chapter 1

Deciding on
a place to live

Practically everyone wants to have an attractive and comfortable home. For some people, this means finding a suitable apartment or house to rent. For others, it means fulfilling dreams of owning a home. When we consider the fact that housing is the second largest item in most family budgets (the largest is food), we get a better understanding of the importance of deciding on a place to live.

Whether to rent or buy housing, however, is a decision that deserves more than just financial consideration. Many people decide to buy because owning a home gives them a sense of independence and security that cannot be obtained through renting. Other people rent because they do not want to invest their savings in real estate or because they want to be free to move about without too much difficulty. Housing decisions are often governed, too, by the facilities that are available. But whether you decide to rent or buy, the satisfaction gained from the right home is one of the great joys of family life.

HOUSING NEEDS VARY

An important factor influencing a family's needs is the stage in the family life cycle. The *family life cycle* includes the successive stages of development through which a family moves, beginning with the formation of an independent household, followed by the formation of a family at marriage, and ending with the death of the surviving spouse. Most people progress through all these stages:

1. Young singles
2. Newlyweds
3. Young family—consisting of parents and young children (Experts on family life sometimes refer to this as the "nest-building stage.")
4. Older family—parents and older children, sometimes labeled "the full-nest stage"
5. Older couples with no children at home—sometimes labeled "the empty-nest stage"
6. Single adult living alone—the surviving spouse living in separate quarters

Most single people prefer living in a rented apartment. Their housing needs do not warrant the investment and responsibility of home ownership. Apartment living usually enables them to enjoy the maximum in convenience and comfort with a minimum of effort and investment.

The majority of young couples begin their life together in a rented apartment or house. Because income and savings at this stage of life are usually not adequate to make a substantial down payment on a home, their housing needs can usually best be met by renting. Renting gives new families a chance to decide what type of home they want and where they want it before they invest in a home of their own.

Families with growing children or with youngsters in school often find that their housing needs can best be met by buying rather than renting. Income is usually higher at this stage of life than it is in earlier years, and the family may be ready to make a long-term investment. And owning a house usually offers the advantage of additional space, an important consideration for families with growing children.

An older couple whose children no longer live at home may find it convenient to sell their house and rent or buy a smaller house or an apartment. Their need for space has decreased, and their income is sometimes lower. Thus, they often find that smaller and more convenient living quarters are more practical and desirable.

DETERMINING YOUR RESOURCES

Many families find that they cannot obtain the kind of housing they need and want because of the restrictions that their resources place on them. These resources include their financial resources, the spare

Bonnie D. Unsworth

Renting an apartment is often the first choice of single people.

time and energy they have available for home care, and their special home-care skills.

Two kinds of financial resources affect housing decisions. Monthly or weekly income influences how much a family can afford to commit to rental or mortgage payments and other housing costs. The amount of savings available determines whether the family is in a position to consider purchasing a home. If the family has sufficient funds for a down payment, plus the extra money required for moving and for the other costs involved in purchasing a home, it can consider buying a home. Young families and single people usually have few savings accumulated; as a result, they have little choice but to rent.

The spare time and energy that family members have available for home care also influence housing choices. Young single people usually do not want to spend their spare time mowing grass and raking leaves. Obviously, an apartment is better suited to their wants. Individuals' special skills in home repair and care also may have a bearing on their choice. Those who are skilled at painting, repairs, and decorating may choose to rent an apartment or buy a house that is in poor condition but costs less. Thus they can use their special skills to cut housing costs.

EVALUATING THE ALTERNATIVES

The choices for the housing shopper fall into three general categories: buying an apartment or house, renting a house or apartment, and buying a mobile home. The first two categories, renting and buying a house or apartment, are familiar. The third, buying a mobile home, is less familiar and requires special examination since it involves aspects of both buying and renting. This is because the typical mobile home owner rents the lot on which his home stands. The advantages of each of these three categories will be carefully examined in the sections that follow.

The advantages of buying a home

Many people dream of the day when they will have a home of their own—a home with sufficient bedrooms, ample closet space, and plenty of play area for their children.

For millions of American families, buying a home involves making the decision to undertake a long-term credit purchase. Because this purchase is the largest single investment that most families ever make, it deserves careful consideration. Some of the advantages of owning a home are listed below.

- Making payments on a home is one method of saving automatically. As the owner pays for his home, he is building up an equity—that is, ownership—in real estate, instead of merely collecting rent receipts. Furthermore, owning a home is a form of investment that provides a considerable amount of security for a wife and children.
- Buying a home stabilizes the long-range cost of a family's housing. The homeowner knows what the loan payments will be, and he knows that the amounts of these payments will not be increased. With some degree of certainty, he can also ascertain the amounts that he will pay in taxes, insurance, and maintenance. The renter has less assurance of what the long-range cost of his housing will be.
- A homeowner has a feeling of security and independence. As long as he continues his payments, he need not worry about where he is going to live. A renter, on the other hand, is not always sure of getting a place to live; nor is he always sure how long he can remain in his rented home.
- There are some tax advantages in owning a home. Property taxes and interest charges on a mortgage are both valid income tax deductions. A person can pay rent of $1,800 a year, and none of it will count as an income tax deduction. A homeowner, on the other hand, can pay the same $1,800 a year, but $340

might represent property taxes, and $660 might represent interest on the mortgage. Thus, the homeowner would have a $1,000 income tax deduction that the renter does not have.

- The homeowner is often accorded a better credit rating. In addition, the equity in the home investment can be used as security to borrow money for an emergency.
- The homeowner can arrange his home to suit his own taste. He can change room dimensions by adding partitions. He can add closet space. He can landscape the lawn any way he likes. There is great satisfaction in arranging a home just the way you like it.
- The homeowner experiences pride of ownership and a feeling of security that helps to give him peace of mind.

The advantages of renting a home

Renting a home has many advantages. It gives a family the chance to analyze a neighborhood or a community and decide whether or not they want to live there permanently. They are better prepared to judge a house if they later decide to buy. Those who prefer to rent offer the following arguments in favor of their position.

- There is a definite limit to the financial risks involved in renting. If a family's income decreases, they can leave a rented apartment or house with little sacrifice of savings or investment.
- People who rent are not tied down to one spot. They are free to move to bigger or smaller quarters, to leave a deteriorating neighborhood, or to accept a better position in another city. In the lifetime of a family, there are many reasons for moving.
- Renters seldom have the responsibility of maintaining property. They are not faced with unforeseen repair bills that may upset their budget; the landlord carries this burden.
- A tenant who has a lease can easily budget for housing, since rent payments are the same each month. Unusual expenses or price increases are of no immediate concern to him. Rising property taxes and operating costs do, of course, eventually affect rents.
- Renting is frequently cheaper than buying, at least on a short-term basis. This is because the renter avoids the real-estate commissions, property transfer taxes, and closing costs that buyers must pay.

The advantages of buying a mobile home

As pointed out earlier, the typical mobile home buyer is both a buyer and a renter. While he buys the mobile home, he usually rents the space on which it is located. New mobile homes provide clean, newly built quarters for a relatively low monthly outlay. They can be purchased complete with furniture if desired. Mobile homes have several appeals.

- Financing is easy to arrange. Although interest rates usually are higher than for house purchases, there are no large closing costs at the time of purchase.
- Because of their compact size, the low-upkeep materials used, and small lots, mobile homes are easy to maintain.
- Although most mobile homes are not moved after they are placed in a park, they can be moved if this proves necessary.
- The mobile home owner, like the house owner, is free to modify and redecorate to suit his own preferences.

FACTORS TO CONSIDER IN SELECTING A PLACE TO LIVE

Once housing shoppers have some general idea of their needs, their resources, and the kinds of alternatives available they are in a position to begin making a more detailed investigation of the choices that are available to them. In evaluating each particular choice a number of factors will have to be taken into account, including the distance from jobs and urban centers, governmental jurisdiction, the quality of the neighborhood, the interior spaces, the exterior spaces, and the types of facilities provided.

Distance from jobs and shopping

A key consideration that influences housing choices is the distance to be traveled to jobs and shopping. Most people would like to live close to work and shopping areas because of the savings in time and transportation costs. Rents and house prices reflect this preference. Quarters close to urban centers are more expensive than similar ones in outlying areas. Many people are attracted by the lower prices in outlying areas and decide the extra travel time and transportation costs involved are worth it.

Not all home buyers and renters recognize the extra transportation costs involved when they settle in outlying areas. The extra costs involved may not become clear until they discover that the family badly needs a second car and that their auto operating and repair expenses are far higher than they had expected.

Governmental jurisdiction

Housing shoppers in most urban areas may find that it is possible for them to choose among several different municipalities, each with its own separate government. To the inexperienced shopper the choice of community may not seem very important. Attention may be focussed on the house or apartment under consideration, and the importance of the governmental jurisdiction neglected. The municipality you choose can, in fact, prove quite important. It influences the amount of taxes you will pay and the kind and quality of community services you get for your money.

Your choice of community may also influence your enjoyment of your home, for communities differ in control of air pollution, noise, and heavy traffic. Municipalities also differ in zoning laws and practices. In some communities zoning laws are inadequate or subject to change because of pressure from big developers and commercial interests. A home buyer in such a community may find the value of his home and his privacy destroyed when a seven-story apartment house goes up in the vacant lot next door.

Choosing a community is very important, because the local government often determines the kind of services the consumer gets for his local tax dollars.

Reprinted courtesy of Penney News, © 1972, J. C. Penney Co., Inc.

Neighborhood

The immediate surroundings of your home, its neighborhood, will have an important effect on your satisfaction. Are the streets clean, well lighted, and well patrolled? Is there noisy through traffic, or is the street quiet, with only local traffic?

Does the neighborhood look attractive and stable? Are the buildings kept in good condition, or does the area show signs of becoming run-down? Is there an interesting variety of design and architecture, or do the buildings look like they were cut out with a cooky cutter? Are there enough trees and landscaping to soften the appearance of the buildings and the streets?

Do the other residents seem like the kind of people you want to have as neighbors? Young people often prefer to live near others of the same age, and many young families place great importance on there being nearby playmates for their children.

Interior and exterior space

In looking at empty apartments and houses it often is difficult to visualize how usable the space provided will prove to be. One consideration is how well the usual furniture pieces will fit into the plan. Is the space laid out so that large pieces such as sofas and beds can be arranged easily? Or, are the wall spaces so cut up with doors and windows that there is little room for furniture along the walls?

Another consideration is how well the plan and the room sizes fit your life style and your usual activities. In a study of young families, researchers identified four different family life styles.[1] The housing preferences associated with these life styles reflect basic differences in values. Where would you place yourself among these groups?

- "Economy" Value Group—concerned about good practical housing that gives good value for the money spent. This group puts more emphasis on space and durabilty than on special design features or other extras. Family life is informal. Meals are usually eaten in the kitchen, and as a result these families put little importance on a separate dining area. Watching television is a favorite recreation, and this needs to be taken into account in living-room planning.
- "Family" Value Group—concerned about the well-being and development of family members, with much emphasis placed

[1] Glenn H. Beyer, Thomas W. Mackesey, and James E. Montgomery, *Houses Are for People,* Research Publication No. 3, Cornell University Housing Research Center, 1955, 58 pp.

on common family activities and interests. Space is desired for joint family activities and children's play. A separate dining area in the living room or a family room big enough to entertain large numbers of relatives at meals is considered desirable.

- "Personal" Value Group—concerned about self-expression and space for family members to pursue their individual interests. Good design is especially valued. Space is desired in bedrooms for individual activities such as reading and listening to records. Yard space should offer privacy.
- "Prestige" Value Group—concerned about the relationship between a home and social standing. The families are striving to advance economically and socially and are concerned about good taste and current styles. They prefer to entertain formally and desire a separate dining area. They are willing to make sacrifices in some areas to obtain impressive features such as a formal exterior design and a fireplace in the living room.

There are certain housing design concepts that have had an important influence on house and apartment planning in recent years. Knowing something about these concepts will help you to judge housing plans and to think about your own design preferences.

Recent designs have aimed for a feeling of openness and spaciousness—walls and doors have been eliminated wherever possible. Separate dining rooms have been eliminated in favor of dining alcoves or els in the living room or family room. Large windows and sliding glass doors with views to the outside also have been used to give the feeling of spaciousness. This emphasis on spaciousness has made the problem of *zoning,* the separation of different family activities, more difficult. This kind of separation is needed when one activity can interfere with another. For example, a plan with good zoning will provide separate, quiet areas for family members who need to study while the rest of the family watches television. Modern plans also emphasize easy indoor-outdoor movement. Outdoor living areas are regarded as extensions of interior spaces and are connected to them with sliding glass doors. To really be useful for family activities, outdoor spaces must have both shade and privacy.

Facilities

Although space and its arrangement are important in determining how livable a home will be, housing is not just a series of rooms. The facilities in a home also determine how livable it will be.

Satisfaction with living quarters depends to a great extent on the occupants' ability to control the amount of light, heat, and air. These factors are key parts of our environment and are crucial to our comfort. Otherwise satisfactory quarters may make us miserable if we can never get the heat above 65 degrees in the winter or if the air conditioning always seems too cold in the summer.

The number of appliances and pieces of household equipment provided typically increases with price level. At every price level, such eye-catching features as intercoms, dishwashers, and fancy chandeliers are used to give extra sales appeal. In lower-quality housing these items often are stripped-down models without desirable extra features or the durability provided in middle-of-the-line models. The housing shopper should look beyond the fancy extra features to check carefully the quality of such essential facilities as the plumbing, wiring, and heating equipment provided.

THE HOUSING CRISIS

In recent years, housing has been in short supply, and prices have risen rapidly. As a result, many people have not been able to find or afford the kind of housing they want and need. The trends in the supply and price of housing suggest that the widely held dream of home ownership may be becoming less attainable for many groups in our population—especially for low- and lower-middle-income families.

What is the problem?

The basic problem is the shortage of new-housing construction in the low- and medium-price ranges. High interest rates and shortages of loan money in the late 1960s and early 1970s discouraged both home builders and home buyers. Home builders found it difficult to borrow the money they needed to finance their operations, and prospective home buyers found interest rates high and loans difficult to obtain. These problems were a direct result of the high rate of inflation prevailing at that time. Inflation made investors reluctant to commit their funds to long-term fixed-dollar investments such as mortgages. In order to attract depositors, banks and savings and loan associations offered higher interest rates and, in turn, were forced to charge higher rates of interest for the mortgage loans they made. At the same time, government policies designed to stop the inflationary trend have raised interest rates and have also held down the supply of money available to make loans.

The resulting shortage of new homes along with rising labor, land, and materials costs all worked to raise the prices of new homes. Prices for typical new homes being built today place them beyond the reach of many families. In the early 1970s, the typical new home cost around $25,000. To meet the payments on such a house, purchasers would need an annual income of $10,000 or more. It is obvious that new homes at this price are beyond the reach of large groups in the population.

Although the shortage of new medium-priced homes most directly affects middle-income families, it also has an indirect effect on low-income families. Because of the shortage of new homes in the medium-price range, many middle-income families that ordinarily would have moved to better quarters have been unable to do so. This has slowed the "filter-down" process by which older homes vacated by middle-income families become available to low-income families.

What can be done?

New programs have been aimed at two key parts of the housing problem—building costs and land costs. A number of attempts have been made to utilize mass-production techniques in housing construction. Parts and entire sections of homes are being built in factories with assembly-line techniques. The parts may include wall, floor, and roof panels that are erected at the building site, where wiring, plumbing, and heating are installed. Larger sections or *modules* completely assembled with walls, floors, ceilings, and roofs and including utilities also are being factory-built. At the building site, two or more of these modules are joined together on a permanent foundation to form a completed house.

Modular-home construction and the use of other new construction materials and techniques have been restricted by local building codes. New efforts are being made by federal and state governments to encourage the modernization of these codes and, at the same time, provide adequate protection for home buyers. In the past, housing codes were written in terms of descriptive standards. *Descriptive standards* specified, in detail, the kinds of lumber, electrical wire, and other materials to be used. Newer codes specify performance standards. Instead of requiring the use of a particular material, *performance standards* specify the level of performance that must be provided. Any material that can provide the specified level of performance is considered acceptable. This makes the use of new, less expensive labor-saving materials possible. One such material that has been developed is an inexpensive panel for use in walls, ceilings, and floors. The panel

Courtesy Inland Steel Co.

Modular housing is one answer to the rising costs of housing. The lower costs of factory-built houses can result in lower prices for the consumer.

includes interior and exterior surfaces sandwiched together with an insulating core and fire-resistant layers between them.

Rising construction costs have increased the demand for mobile homes. Over 400,000 units are now being produced each year. This is double the number produced in 1965. Mobile homes are available in a variety of sizes, in widths from 8 to 14 feet, and in lengths up to 70 feet, with 12 by 65 feet currently the most popular size. Mobile homes are designed to be towed on their own chassis, which includes both frame and wheels, but in contrast to travel trailers and motorized homes, they are designed for year-round living. Since mobile homes are factory-built, savings due to mass production are possible. In addition, mobile homes do not require a permanent foundation, and this further reduces costs.

The price of construction sites has been one of the most rapidly increasing components of housing costs. This has created pressures for methods of reducing the cost of land used in providing housing. One new concept that has attracted wide attention is the idea of *new towns,* which are completely new towns, with a full range of services, built on cheap, vacant land away from existing urban centers. Other attempts to reduce land costs have focussed on ways of placing more housing units on each acre of land. Some developers have economized on land by constructing houses side-by-side in town-house or row-house style, rather than separately. New designs with front and back patios prove that this type of construction can be attractive and provide as much privacy as a separate house. Other developers have employed the *cluster development* concept. Housing units are grouped together closely to leave as much open space as possible for recreation. In such developments individual yards usually are small, but they open onto more spacious recreation areas owned jointly with other residents.

The development of new systems of housing construction, financing, and land use has been a major emphasis of the Department of Housing and Urban Development (HUD). In recent years, HUD's Operation Breakthrough program has financed the development of demonstration housing, using the most modern materials and technology. At the same time, it is developing experience in specifying performance requirements for fire safety, room size, insulation, and so on. It is clear that these and other new approaches to providing housing must be encouraged if we are to be able to provide sound, safe, durable, and satisfying housing for people in all walks of life—rich and poor, city and country dweller alike.

The cluster arrangement of houses reduces both the total amount of land needed for all the houses and the cost of each housing unit.

Courtesy The Rouse Co.

Checking your reading

1.   Why do some people prefer to rent rather than buy housing? Why do some people prefer to buy rather than rent?
2.   Trace the needs for renting and buying housing in the typical life cycle of persons in the United States.
3.   What two kinds of financial resources can affect one's housing decision?
4.   List seven advantages of buying a home rather than renting.
5.   Explain the income tax advantages that a person owning a home may have.
6.   List six advantages of renting a home.
7.   List five advantages of buying a mobile home.
8.   Assume that in a certain community rents and buying prices for housing are high because the community is close to an urban center. In outlying areas, housing prices are lower. Explain what factors the consumer should consider when deciding in which area to live.
9.   Why is the municipal government important when considering a place to live?
10.   Explain the four different family life styles identified in the study of young families.
11.   Explain how a high rate of inflation affects interest rates.
12.   What is meant by modular-home construction?
13.   Explain the difference between descriptive standards and performance standards in housing codes.
14.   What are some solutions to the rising costs of land needed for housing?

Consumer problems and projects

1.   In 1970, the Department of Housing and Urban Development indicated that more than 22,000,000 housing units would be needed over the following 8 years to provide shelter for our population. A housing unit consists of living quarters in a single-family home, apartment house, or mobile home. The homes are needed to shelter new families and replace buildings that are demolished or become uninhabitable. At the beginning of the decade, housing construction had not been keeping pace with our needs. Use library indexes to locate current information about what is being done to alleviate the situation and what planners are recommending should be done to provide sufficient housing. Write a report based on your findings.
2.   Would it be more advantageous for the following people to rent or own housing? Give reasons for your decisions.

   a. A young man just out of college, working full time in a town some distance from his parents' home

b. A young couple with two children and a modest savings account

c. An older couple whose children are married and living away from home

3.   Mr. and Mrs. Whitestone and their two children are planning to move to a different community and are looking for a house there. They found two similar three-bedroom houses in the same neighborhood. One rents for $250 a month; the other is for sale. If the Whitestones bought the house, they would have to make a down payment of $6,000. Their monthly mortgage payments on a 20-year loan at $8\frac{1}{2}$ percent would be $250. Mrs. Whitestone says that because the monthly payments are the same, common sense dictates that they buy the house that is for sale. She reasons that $250 paid for rent would simply be "money down the drain," while the $250 mortgage payments eventually would enable them to own their own home. Why is her reasoning not completely sound?

4.   Inspect the housing in your community to determine what kinds of homes are available at the following price levels: $12,000; $15,000; $18,000; $22,000; $30,000; $40,000. Begin by examining advertisements for housing in your local newspaper. What special features do the various homes have?

5.   The Caruso family made a cash down payment of $6,000 on a house and lot that cost $26,000. Their monthly payments will total $1,860 each year. During the first year, $680 of the total payments will be applied to reducing the principal (the amount owed on the mortgage). The remaining $1,180 represents interest. Taxes on this house are $510 a year. The insurance premium is $115 a year, and the maintenance costs are estimated at $225 a year.

    a. Excluding the down payment, what is the total amount of money that the family will pay out during the first year? Of this amount, how much represents an investment?

    b. If the $6,000 down payment had been invested at 5 percent interest, what return would the Caruso family have received on their investment during the first year?

    c. Do you think the Caruso family should have considered the interest that could have been earned on this down payment when they were deciding whether or not to buy the house?

Chapter 12

Choosing an apartment or a mobile home

Most young people make their first home in a rented apartment. In recent years, mobile homes also have provided first homes for many new families. Both apartments and mobile homes provide young people with limited funds with an opportunity to set up housekeeping on their own, independent of their families. Arrangements to rent an apartment or purchase a mobile home involve such legal complexities as rental agreements, leases, and purchase contracts. Although such commitments may seem a good deal less complicated than buying a house, they still deserve careful attention. Apartment leases and mobile home purchases are commitments to pay out hundreds and thousands of dollars. The wise consumer needs to consider such a step carefully before he makes that commitment.

With the establishment of their own homes, young people begin to accumulate many new possessions, such as sofas, rugs, stereo equipment, and television sets. They need to know how to protect themselves from financial loss if these items are destroyed in a fire or are stolen. The use of property insurance to protect against such financial losses will be discussed in the final portion of this chapter. Having your own home also creates new responsibilities for injuries to others who are visiting or making deliveries. The use of personal liability insurance to provide protection against such risks also will be discussed.

FACTORS TO CONSIDER IN SELECTING AN APARTMENT

A wide variety of rental quarters is available, ranging from rented rooms to one-room efficiency apartments on up to apartments with two or three bedrooms. The prices for these different types of apartments also vary a good deal, but the considerations involved in selecting an apartment are much the same, regardless of the size of the apartment.

In the previous chapter we examined the factors that need to be considered in any choice of housing. These include the distance to jobs and shopping, governmental jurisdiction, the neighborhood, the interior and exterior spaces, and the facilities provided. In this section, we will consider some additional factors that are of particular concern for prospective apartment dwellers.

Security and safety

Since most apartments are in urban areas where crime and theft are a problem, personal security and safety are important considerations for apartment dwellers. Well-lighted and uncluttered entrances, hallways, and stairways contribute to security, as do locked outside entrances. Apartment doors should be of sturdy construction, strong enough so that they cannot be kicked in, and equipped with secure locks. Many apartment doors are equipped with only cheap key-in-the-knob locks that an intruder can open easily with a strip of plastic. Key-in-the-knob locks with an extra trigger bolt separate from the main latch provide security against this means of entry. Even the best key-in-the-knob locks can be opened easily if the knob is broken off or damaged. Mortise locks, ones in which the keyhole is above the doorknob, provide more security, especially when the dead bolt as well as the latch is engaged. Locks with long latches and doors that fit the doorjamb are more difficult to jimmy open. If the available locks on an apartment are inadequate and cannot be changed, the use of an auxiliary lock can provide some extra security.

Another factor that affects security is the location of the apartment in the building. Basement and first-floor apartments are easily entered unless special window grilles and locks are provided.

Space

Since apartment dwellers live close together, privacy may be a problem. Buildings should be sufficiently soundproof to muffle the sounds of talking, plumbing, and music between apartments and between hallways and apartments. Apartment dwellers usually are bothered

To ensure the safety of residents, many apartment buildings employ doormen and closed-circuit TV systems. Consumers should expect to pay for this added security.

Editorial Photocolor Archives, Inc.

more by sounds from the floor above than the floor below. Upper-floor apartments usually are quieter for this reason, and also because they are further removed from street and parking-lot noises.

Storage may be a particular problem in small-size apartments, so special attention should be given to the amount of closet space provided. Some apartment buildings provide storage lockers in the basement. This space seldom is secure enough to provide safe storage for valuable items, but it can be useful for storing empty packing boxes and crates.

Control of air movement and the temperature should be checked carefully. Do the windows open? Do they provide good ventilation? Are screens provided? If air conditioning is provided, can the temperature be controlled adequately? Does the equipment provided have enough capacity to adequately cool the whole apartment? Although top-floor apartments have advantages, they may be uncomfortably hot in the summer because of the heat absorbed by the building's roof, unless particular attention has been given to insulation. Control of outside light also may be a problem. If draperies or blinds are provided, do they provide adequate control of outside daylight so that you will be able to sleep late when you want to?

Equipment and utilities

The appliances and equipment furnished should all be checked to ensure that they are in good working order. If not, repairs should be agreed on. The prospective renter should also be certain that he understands which utilities are included in the rent and which will be billed separately by the utility company. If an important utility such as gas or electricity is not provided, get an estimate of typical costs from the landlord or tenants. Comparisons of rents among different buildings should take differences in the utilities provided into account.

Management

The renter is dependent on the building's management for many important services. For this reason, it is important to have some representative of the management, such as a resident manager, readily available at all times. You may want to ask building tenants about the reputation of the management. Are they fair and honest? Do they respond quickly to requests for repairs? Are they concerned about security and safety in the building?

Provisions of a lease

Although many rooms and apartments are rented without formal signed leases, most landlords want the protection that a lease gives them. Rentals may be arranged with only an oral agreement on such details as the amount of the rent and when it is to be paid. This type of agreement is called *tenancy-at-will.* It can be terminated at any time by giving notice one rent period in advance—a month in advance if rent is paid monthly or one week in advance if rent is paid weekly.

Most rentals, especially those in larger buildings, require a lease. The *lease* is a written contract between the landlord and the tenant setting the terms under which a specified piece of property is rented. Prospective renters should be aware that a lease is a legal contract that commits them to the payment of hundreds of dollars, in return for which they are provided with the use of an apartment. Such contracts are binding except under special circumstances. Because of the amount of money involved and the difficulty of voiding lease contracts, leases obviously should be entered into with caution. The following items in the lease should be given particular attention:

- Identification of premises. The apartment rented should be clearly identified by address and number.
- Term of the lease. The beginning and ending dates of tenancy should be specified.
- Rent. The amount of rent and where and when it is to be paid should be included. Attention should be given to provisions that permit increases in the rent during the term of the lease. Some leases provide for rent increases if property taxes are increased.

- Number and kinds of occupants. Limits on the number, kinds, and ages of occupants, such as prohibitions against children, should be spelled out clearly. Restrictions on pets, if any, should be made clear.
- Security deposit. Most leases require a security deposit to protect the landlord against damages to the property or non-payment of rent. The renter should be certain that he gets a separate receipt that specifically states that the amount paid is for the security deposit. Landlords' practices in returning security deposits have been a continuing source of problems for tenants. Some landlords refuse to return deposits; they claim abnormal wear and tear or extra cleaning costs regardless of the condition in which an apartment is left. Others are fairer in adjusting their charges to the situation. Renters have little protection against unfair withholding of security deposits short of legal action. One way of protecting oneself is to avoid buildings where the landlords are known to be unfair—present tenants often can tell you what the landlord's practices are. Another way to protect yourself is to insist that the landlord go through the apartment with you before you leave and point out the specific reasons for his deductions from your security deposit.
- Repairs. The lease should clearly state who is responsible for repairs. The renter can expect to be held responsible for any damages made willfully (such as those resulting from a wild party) or because of negligence.
- Furnishings. If an apartment is rented furnished it is a good idea to get attached to the lease a detailed inventory of the contents and notes on the condition of each item.
- Right to sublet. The lease should permit you to sublet the apartment to others, in case you need to move before the period of the lease is up. Most leases provide that the landlord has the right to approve or disapprove prospective tenants who wish to sublease.
- Utilities and services. The lease should specify what public utilities are provided as part of the rent and those for which the tenant is personally responsible.
- Landlord's right of access. The conditions under which the landlord can enter the apartment should be spelled out. He will, of course, need to enter in case of emergencies and to show the

apartment to prospective tenants after notification from the present tenant that the lease is to be terminated. Some leases give the landlord the right to enter the premises at "any reasonable time," while others let the tenant insist on advance notice.

■ Termination procedure. The lease should specify the procedure to be followed when the tenant wishes to terminate the lease. Some leases contain *automatic renewal clauses* that specify the date before which the landlord must be notified if the lease is to be terminated. If he is not notified by this date, the lease is renewed automatically. Some annual leases require that the landlord be notified as much as 90 days before the lease expires. The wise tenant will keep careful track of these notification dates. Letters notifying the landlord about plans to terminate a lease should be sent by registered or certified mail so that there will be official records that they were received.

Any special arrangements or agreements between a landlord and a tenant should be written into a lease, since verbal promises are not binding if the lease specifies some other arrangement. In signing a lease, the tenant can request that objectionable portions of it be crossed out or changed and that these changes be initialed by the landlord to indicate his acceptance.

The tenant should ask for a signed copy of the lease at once or receive a written promise specifying the date when a copy will be delivered. While leases are designed chiefly for the protection of landlords, it is important for tenants to know and understand their provisions in order to protect themselves.

Under the terms of a lease, a tenant is obligated to pay his rent on time and not cause disturbances. He is also obligated to keep his apartment clean, place refuse in the proper containers, and obey other regulations set forth in the lease. In turn, landlords are obligated to maintain the premises in a good state of repair, provide the utilities promised, and maintain adequate supervision over the conduct of other tenants. Historically, tenants have had few defenses against landlords who do not live up to their obligations. Poor maintenance is a frequent complaint; inadequate heat also is a common complaint, as is inadequate control over the behavior of other tenants.

There are, however, some tactics available to tenants whose landlords do not live up to their obligations. One is direct legal pressure and the threat of lawsuits—this, of course, could be expensive unless legal aid or a small claims court is available. If local safety and sanitary

LEASE made __MARCH 28. 19--_____ whereby WE, MICHAEL ALLAN ARMS, INCORPORATED,

the landlord, lease and YOU, __ROBERT HERBERTS__ the tenant, take Apartment _____7A_____ in building

(Print your name here)

_____ at _79 CHESTNUT ST._, Liberty, New York, for a period of two years from the date the

apartment is ready for occupancy, at a rent of $ 220_____ a month, payable in advance, without demand, on the first day of each month.

SECURITY AGREEMENT
We have received $ 220_____ security for your performance of this lease.

1. Which we will return if
   a. you cancel BEFORE notice of occupancy date is mailed, or
   b. we cancel because the Government takes the building or any part of it, or
   c. we cancel because the building is damaged and we decide not to repair it or
   d. this lease remains in effect for the full two-year period.
2. Which we will keep if
   a. you cancel AFTER notice of occupancy date is mailed and before the lease begins or
   b. we cancel because YOU DO NOT OBSERVE this lease and the regulations which are a part of this lease, or
   c. you do not leave the apartment in good condition, regardless of how or when the lease ends or is cancelled

If you cancel after the lease begins, we will return $10.00_____ for each full month's rent paid, and keep the balance.

WE AGREE TO:
3. Give you thirty days notice by registered mail of the date the apartment will be ready for occupancy;
4. Deliver the apartment in good condition;

5. Supply at no extra charge the following:

Gas	Window screens
Electricity	
Heat as re-	Use of:
quired by law	Washing machines
Hot water	Drying machines
Cold water	Television antenna
A refrigerator	Incinerators
A gas range	Parking areas
A sink and	Playgrounds
laundry tub	Storage &
Kitchen floor	Carriage rooms
linoleum	
Venetian blinds	

YOU AGREE TO:
6. Pay all RENT at our office or other place we specify;
7. Observe the regulations which are part of this lease;
8. Leave the apartment in good condition when you move out.

BOTH OF US AGREE:
9. We may repair any damage caused by you and charge the cost to you as ADDITIONAL RENT;
10. You will receive no rent reduction or compensation for inconvenience due to repairs or interruption of service unless caused by our negligence.

17. If you do not leave the apartment in good condition when you move out
    a. we will keep your security, and
    b. you will pay on demand as damages all costs of cleaning and repairing the apartment;

on the property.

MICHAEL ALLAN ARMS, INCORPORATED
BY:
(X)*Robert Herberts*_____ (YOU)

(Sign your name here)

REGULATIONS
YOU AGREE TO COOPERATE WITH US BY OBSERVING THE FOLLOWING REGULATIONS:

An apartment lease must be read carefully, because it is a contract between the landlord and tenant that spells out the terms of the rental.

regulations are being violated, complaints can be made to your local health department. In some areas, tenants' associations have been formed to negotiate with landlords; they use the threat of a rent strike to force attention to their demands. A number of city and state governments recently have given more attention to the problems of tenants and have passed laws that permit tenants to withhold rent when they feel the landlord is not fulfilling his obligations. These laws usually provide for the payment of rents into a special account that is held until needed repairs are made or promised utilities are supplied.

CHOOSING A MOBILE HOME

Mobile homes constitute an increasing proportion of the new housing units being built each year. This relatively new form of housing has helped fill the need of large numbers of families for a moderately priced place to live. Mobile homes have been especially popular with those who need only a limited amount of living space—young married couples and retired people.

Factors to consider in selecting a mobile home

There are three different types of mobile homes. The most familiar is the single-wide type. The most common width for *single-wide* homes is 12 feet. In recent years, more and more models 14 feet wide have been built, since about half of the states now permit these extra-wide models to move over their highways. Most single-wide mobile homes are from 54 to 65 feet long. The length measurements quoted for mobile homes customarily include the 3-foot towing hitch. As a result, the popular 12- by 65-foot model provides usable living space 12 by 62 feet (744 square feet). Prices for single-wide homes range from $4,000 to $10,000; the average price in recent years has been around $6,000. The popular 12- by 65-foot single-wide model can provide three bedrooms, one full bath, one half bath (toilet and wash basin only), and a living room with adjoining kitchen.

The second type, the *expandable* mobile home, has a pull-out addition or wing that can be telescoped into the home when it is being moved. This feature is used to provide more living space and at the same time stay within highway width limitations. This extra section can add 60 to 100 additional square feet of living space to a room. Prices for expandable models recently have been in the $8,000 to $12,000 range. A typical floor plan for an expandable mobile home includes three bedrooms, one of which is a pull-out room, one full bath, one half bath, a living room with a pull-out section, and a kitchen with an adjoining pull-out dining room. In addition there are two porches in the pull-out portion of the home.

The third type of mobile home, the *double-wide*, consists of two separate units that are moved separately and joined together at their final destination to make a single living unit. The prices of double-wide models range upward from $10,000. The floor plan of a typical double-wide home includes three bedrooms, two baths, a kitchen, a living room, and a separate dining room.

Most mobile homes are sold completely equipped and furnished—

Courtesy of the Mobile Homes Manufacturers Association

The three most common types of mobile homes are expandable (top), single-wide (left), and double-wide (right).

with furniture, carpeting, draperies, and kitchen appliances. Equipment such as central air conditioning, laundry appliances, and dishwashers is available as optional equipment.

There are other extras usually needed that add to the cost of a mobile home. These include:

- Entry steps. These will be needed for each door. They should be well built, and for safety reasons, they should be equipped with hand rails.
- Skirting. Panels are placed around the bottom of the mobile home to conceal the wheels. They should be designed to permit easy access and storage as well as air circulation. Skirting is required in many mobile home parks.
- Supports or piers. These are required to provide a temporary foundation.
- Over-the-roof ties or anchors. These are needed in areas with high winds.

■ Other extras. Many owners equip their homes with patio awnings to provide additional outdoor living space and a sheltered front-door entry. Storage sheds also are often added to provide a place for tools, lawn furniture, and auto equipment.

The increasing number of mobile homes being built has brought increased concern about the quality of their construction and equipment. Inadequate insulation that results in heavy condensation on inside walls in cold weather has been a particular problem in some mobile homes. In order to assure purchasers of good quality and performance, a set of standards for mobile homes was developed by the American National Standards Institute (ANSI). These standards, which have been designated ANSI Standard A119.1, set requirements for the construction, plumbing, heating, and electrical systems of mobile homes. More than half the states now require that homes sold within the state meet these standards. Conformity with these standards is also required for Federal Housing Administration (FHA) and Veterans Administration (VA) guaranteed mortgage loans.

Manufacturers who certify that their homes conform to the A119.1 Standard must meet the minimum requirements set by the standard. These requirements differ among regions of the country to account for differences in the prevailing temperatures and wind velocity. The three separate regions are the North zone, the Middle zone, and the Hurricane zone (coastal areas of Southeastern and Gulf states). As part of the requirements for meeting Standard A119.1, the manufacturer must provide a map to indicate the area for which the mobile home was built. He must also post a certificate inside each home with information on the ability of the heating system to maintain a comfortable inside temperature under cold-weather conditions.

Factors to consider in selecting a site

Before buying a mobile home, it is important to check carefully where you will be able to put it. The available locations usually are limited to mobile home parks, except in some small towns and rural areas in which mobile homes can be placed on separate lots.

Mobile home parks vary a great deal in design and in the facilities provided. Newer parks typically are less crowded and provide larger lots that are better suited to the larger-size mobile homes now being built. Many parks have provided recreation facilities, and some even have swimming pools. The utilities provided also differ among parks. In some cases, water, sewer facilities, and garbage collection are provided as part of the lot rental.

Monthly rents for spaces differ with the services provided and the area of the country. They range from as low as $15 to over $200 in parks with luxury features and choice locations. Rentals ranging from $40 to $65 a month are more typical. In comparing rents among parks, it is important to take account of differences in the utilities provided. The prospective renter should also be aware that differences in park design may affect insurance rates. Rates are higher for mobile homes located in parks in which the units are crowded close together and water-main facilities are limited.

Parks cater to different groups of people. Many welcome families with children—and people of all ages. Others cater chiefly to older adults and retired persons. Some parks are open only to those who have bought their mobile home from a particular dealer or particular group of dealers. Dealers with such arrangements use their ability to place the homes they sell in attractive parks as one of their major sales appeals.

It is clear that the basic quality of the construction of a mobile home, its floor plan, and the park in which it is located all play important roles in determining consumer satisfaction. Each of these aspects of the choice of a mobile home deserves careful attention.

PROPERTY INSURANCE

Many renters believe that they do not need any insurance protection against property losses from fire. They reason that since they do not own the premises in which they live, they have little to lose in a fire. Those who reason in this way completely neglect the value of the clothing, books, stereo equipment, appliances, and furniture that they own. The value of these things is likely to total hundreds and even thousands of dollars. Few of us would want to run the risk of a loss of this size. Renters also tend to forget their financial liability for injuries suffered by visitors to their apartment or by delivery men or repairmen. Everyone with his own household—renter, mobile home owner, and house owner alike—needs both property insurance and personal liability insurance to protect against such losses and risks.

Fire insurance

A fire insurance policy is a personal contract, covering a person's insurable interest in his property—not the property itself. *Insurable interest* is the extent to which the person would suffer a financial loss if the property were destroyed. You could not insure your neighbor's house unless you would experience a financial loss because of its destruction. Why do you suppose our laws require an insurable interest in order for an insurance policy to be valid?

The insurance company's maximum liability when a loss occurs is the actual cash value of the property at the time of the fire. If you carry $20,000 worth of insurance on your house, but it is worth only $12,000, usually you are paid only $12,000 if the house burns to the ground—an unlikely event. In some states, the value of the property is agreed upon in advance at the time the policy is written. This amount, which is written on the face of the policy, is the maximum amount that can be collected as a result of a fire.

EXTENDED COVERAGE   For a small additional premium, one can buy, along with fire insurance, protection that covers various hazards, such as windstorms, tornadoes, cyclones, hail, explosions, riots, smoke, and damage by motor vehicles or falling aircraft. This additional protection is known as *extended coverage*. In most cases, since the added cost is not much, extended coverage is a sensible addition to make to a fire insurance policy. In fact, straight fire insurance policies are rarely issued today.

Going one step further, insurance companies have made available even more protection than extended coverage provides. This extra protection, which is usually called additional extended coverage, compensates the insured for damage to his property due to such things as falling trees, glass breakage, vandalism and malicious mischief, and other hazards not included in normal extended coverage.

Most extended coverage and additional extended coverage protection is sold only with a deductible clause—usually a $50 deductible. Thus, the company would pay nothing for damages under $50. If the damages total $225, the company pays $175 ($225 minus $50).

COST OF FIRE INSURANCE   Fire insurance policies are usually written for terms of one, three, or five years. The longer the term of insurance, the less the annual cost, so it is usually wise to get at least a three-year policy. If for any reason the policy holder wants to cancel the policy, he may do so at any time; part of the premium he paid for the insurance coverage will be returned to him.

The amount of the premium depends on the many factors that affect the risk of fire, such as location, type of construction, safety devices, the contents of the building, and the quality of fire protection available in the community. In general, fire insurance, even with extended

Reprinted courtesy of Penney News, © *1972, J. C. Penney Co., Inc.*

In addition to providing the consumer with a sense of security, an effective fire department influences the cost of insurance.

coverage, is so low in cost—and the potential losses due to fire so serious—that wise property owners carry it on all important property almost automatically.

Real estate values have increased rapidly in recent years. Property owners who have not increased their fire insurance coverage are likely to be inadequately protected. The value of your property should be carefully reviewed each time a policy is renewed. To help keep coverage up to date during the life of a policy, many companies now offer an *inflation guard endorsement*. This addition to a basic policy increases the coverage provided by 1 percent every 3 months. During the lifetime of a 3-year policy, for example, the coverage provided is increased by 12 percent.

Personal liability insurance

A painter may slip while painting the exterior of your house and break his leg; the milkman may fall on your icy walk; a neighbor's little boy may trip over your garden tools and injure himself; your dog may bite someone, either on or away from your premises; or you may hit a ball on the golf course and injure another golfer. All these instances—and many others—might cause legal action to be brought against you and cost you a great deal of money. Liability insurance offers protection against such risk.

The probability of loss from public liability of this type may be small, but the maximum possible loss is staggering. Most policies contain medical payment provisions under which up to $500 in medical expenses will be paid to anyone injured while on the insured person's premises. This provides protection for guests or for others who may not have a legal claim against the insured. The portion of comprehensive personal liability policies that covers responsibility for bodily injuries usually provides a minimum protection of $25,000. This amount can be increased for a small additional premium.

Homeowners policies

Many insurance companies have issued a new type of policy, called a *homeowners policy,* that covers in one package all the usual property and liability insurance needs of the homeowner. Life insurance, health insurance, and car insurance are not, of course, covered in a homeowners policy, but all other normal insurance needs are covered. Thus, the policy may include fire insurance and extended coverage and additional extended coverage on the insured's home. Personal property, too, may be covered. A typical policy might include theft and unusual-damage coverage of up to 50 percent of the value of the dwelling for items stolen or damaged on or off the premises—for example, golf clubs stolen from the trunk of a car. Sometimes the coverage for items stolen while off the premises is lower than 50 percent of the value of the dwelling, for the chances are rather remote that so much personal property could be lost in this way. Personal liability would also be included in a homeowners policy, along with coverage for physical damage to the property of others. Similar package policies tailored to the needs of renters and mobile home owners are also available. The renter's policy, for example, provides protection against the loss of personal property and comprehensive personal liability coverage.

A homeowners policy is, of course, more expensive than an individual fire insurance policy or a separate theft policy. But it may be considerably less expensive than purchasing all this coverage in separate policies. Your insurance agent should help you decide which plan of coverage is most advantageous for you.

Checking your reading

1. Discuss the construction factors that contribute to safety in apartment buildings.
2. Give two reasons why upper-floor apartments might be more desirable than basement or first-floor apartments.
3. List several important questions that a prospective tenant should seek answers to when he considers the air movement and temperature in an apartment.

4.   What is meant by a tenancy-at-will agreement?

5.   Explain the meaning of an automatic renewal clause. How can the tenant make certain that he will not have his lease renewed automatically when he does not want it to be renewed?

6.   What recourse is available to tenants when landlords do not live up to the obligations of the lease?

7.   For what types of people have mobile homes been popular recently?

8.   List and explain the three types of mobile homes. Which type is most familiar? Which type is usually the most expensive?

9.   What is skirting for a mobile home?

10. Explain the meaning of ANSI Standard A119.1, and state why the standard was developed.

11. Why do the ANSI Standard requirements differ among regions of the country?

12. Since renters do not own the premises where they live, why do they need fire insurance protection?

13. What is meant by insurable interest?

14. What is meant by extended coverage?

15. Explain the type of protection given by personal liability insurance.

16. What is a homeowners policy?

Consumer problems and projects

1.   Is location more important to a family renting an apartment or to a family buying housing?

2.   Name two sources where you might find listings of housing to rent or buy.

3.   Construct a checklist to help families choose sensibly and systematically a neighborhood in which to buy or rent a home. Begin by deciding on a number of factors that are important for someone to consider when choosing a neighborhood. For example, you will probably want to include the following in your list of items: shopping (What types of stores and services are available? Do you need a car to get to the stores?); public safety (Is the police and fire protection adequate? How far away is the nearest fire station?); streets (Are they wide enough? Are they in good repair? Do sidewalks exist?); schools (Where are they located? How good are they?). You should be able to construct a list of from 10 to 20 important factors. Then, provide a place on the list to evaluate each of the factors. Your scale might include these ratings: excellent, good, fair, and poor.

4.   Use the checklist you constructed for the previous problem to evaluate as fairly as possible a neighborhood in your community other than the one in which you live.

5.   George Weems is thirty-one years old, has been married for nine years, and has two children, aged six and three. For the first three years of their marriage, the Weems

family lived in a one-bedroom apartment in an old house. Then they moved into a two-bedroom apartment in a relatively new building. Now Mrs. Weems would like to buy a house, but Mr. Weems says that he prefers to stay in an apartment because he does not want to be tied down to one job or to one locality all his life. He wants to be able to grasp any opportunity for advancement that may arise. Mr. Weems is an automobile mechanic, and during the past twelve years he has worked for two different employers. Is Mr. Weem's argument sound? Should the Weems family continue to live in an apartment? Should they buy a house? Give reasons for your answers.

6. Discuss at least three considerations that might determine whether you would buy a new or a used mobile home.

7. What are the recent trends in the apartment and mobile home markets? Prepare a report on either apartments or mobile homes discussing such topics as (a) trends in number and types being constructed, (b) factors influencing consumers' demand for this type of housing, (c) the effects of government programs on the supply of and demand for this type of housing, (d) design features which are currently popular or sought after, and (e) trends in prices. Consult *Reader's Guide to Periodical Literature* for useful references.

8. Shortly after Jack Barnes sold his stationery store, It was seriously damaged by fire. Can Jack collect insurance on the loss? Why?

9. Albert Williams intends to buy a house in the near future. He says that he has just examined statistics regarding the number of fires in homes in your community, and he has decided that the chances of suffering a financial loss due to fire are so low that he doubts that he will buy fire insurance. Discuss the soundness of Mr. Williams's reasoning.

Chapter 13

Buying a house

Most families hope to someday own their own home. In recent years, rapid increases in the prices of houses has made this goal more difficult to attain. Owning a home, nevertheless, remains an important goal for most families.

In the early 1970s, the typical new one-family house was a one-story ranch style and cost around $25,000. It had 3 bedrooms, $1\frac{1}{2}$ or 2 baths, plus a garage—in many cases a 2-car garage. The appliances provided included a stove and frequently a dishwasher, but central air conditioning was not usually provided. The typical house was built without a basement. It was built either on a concrete slab or with a crawl space. While the house had warm-air central heating, it did not have a fireplace. Only a small fraction of the families who bought such homes were able to pay cash for them. Most families instead made a cash down payment and then borrowed the difference needed to cover the cost of the house. This mortgage loan provided for monthly payments over a period of many years.

In this chapter we will examine some of the things to look for when buying a house, such as the condition of the site, the quality of construction, the efficiency of the facilities, and the general condition of the house. We will also examine the preliminary costs involved; mortgage loan arrangements; and the legal aspects of buying a home.

THINGS TO CHECK BEFORE BUYING

There are many points prospective home buyers will want to check before they settle on a particular house. These include the site of the house, the quality of construction, the facilities provided, and the general condition of the house. Few houses will get top marks in all these categories. Some sort of compromise is always necessary. One house you like may be more expensive but in good condition, while another may need paint and a new roof but costs a good deal less. In situations like this you will need to decide whether the condition of the first house justifies the extra cost or whether the second house, even with the expense of extra repairs, is a better bargain.

Site

One of the first things to check is the site of the house in which you are interested. Is the site well drained and safe from flooding? Many homes are built in valleys or low-lying areas where there is danger of flooding in rainy weather. Although such areas are poorly suited for houses, developers use them for homes because they are cheap. Only recently have communities begun to develop zoning plans that prohibit building in areas that are subject to flooding or are poorly drained. A check for watermarks on basement walls will provide some indication of whether the house in which you are interested has flooding problems.

The prospective home buyer should also check to see if the ground on which the house is built is firm and stable. When homes are built on filled land or in swampy areas, foundations and walls may crack as the house settles. Serious settling problems may eventually break

A prospective home buyer should always check to see if the site is well drained and safe from flooding.

SCS-USDA Photo by S. Cook

water lines and cause damage to the basic structure of the house. Special attention also needs to be given to the stability of houses built on steep hillsides. Is the area known to be subject to slides?

The relation of the house to its site also deserves attention. How is the house situated in relation to the movement of the sun? Will hot afternoon sun pour into picture windows and make the house uncomfortably hot? How will the movement of the summer sun affect the use of porches and patios? Patios and porches on the west side of the house are likely to be too warm in the afternoon unless there are trees or other means of providing shade. Another question is the placement of the house in relation to the prevailing wind. While the house should be positioned to take advantage of summer breezes, it should also be positioned so that the front entry is sheltered from driving rain and blowing snow.

The landscaping provided also merits some attention. Are there trees that will shade the house from the heat of the summer sun? This will make the house more comfortable and reduce the need for air conditioning. Are the shrubs around the house slow-growing varieties, or are they likely to tower over the house in a few years? Builders often landscape with inexpensive shrubs such as arborvitae that look attractive when young but soon grow much too tall and need to be replaced.

Construction

It is difficult for the average home buyer to judge the quality of the construction in a house. Local building codes provide buyers with some protection. They ensure that new houses being constructed meet minimum strength, safety, and health requirements. Conformity to Federal Housing Administration (FHA) standards also provides some protection. However, the FHA standards are also minimum requirements—a house built in such a way that it meets only these minimum requirements may provide a lower level of performance than many buyers would desire.

Since the foundation of the house is its basic underpinning, it is essential that it be of strong construction and in good condition. Signs of settling and cracks are evidence of potential problems. Basements should be dry. Wet walls may be the result of condensation—this can be cured with better ventilation or a dehumidifier. Wet walls can also be the result of seepage from the outside—a more serious problem. Seepage sometimes can be controlled with better rain gutters and drains. If the problem is serious it may require excavation around the foundation, the application of waterproofing to the exterior walls, and the installation of drainage tile to collect moisture. If the house is in a wet, low-lying area, even these measures may be insufficient.

To prevent squeaking and swaying, floors should be built with *cross bridging,* that is, cross braces nailed in an X shape between floor joists. These braces can be seen when you look up at the floor from the basement. You can judge the sturdiness of a wooden floor by jumping up and down in the middle of a large room. The floor should not give or sway noticeably.

The interior walls of most newer homes are plasterboard rather than plaster. The use of plasterboard, or drywall as it is often called, can involve several problems. Drywall is relatively thin and weak—holes can easily be punched through it by accident. When green lumber is used for the studding inside the wall, the nails used to install the drywall tend to pop out, creating unsightly bumps. The joints between panels of drywall may show when the installation has been poorly finished. When buying a new house you should inquire what steps the builder has taken to guard against these problems. In older houses, problems with drywall, if present, will be obvious.

Peeling paint on outside walls can be a sign of a serious construction problem. Peeling paint often is a result of moisture condensing inside exterior walls in cold weather. This condensation occurs when warm, moist air from the interior of the house hits the cold surfaces inside the exterior wall. Condensation inside exterior walls can be controlled

Courtesy National Paint and Coatings Association

Peeling paint on exterior walls is a sign that in cold weather moisture is condensing inside the walls.

by the installation of *vapor barriers* (materials that prevent the movement of water vapor) when a house is built. Vapor barriers may be a layer of vapor-impermeable paper or foil on one side of the insulation installed or a separate sheet of plastic. If vapor barriers have not been used, or are inadequate, it may be necessary to install vents to the outside in the roof and outside walls. The installation of these vents can be expensive and complicated. If ignored, condensation not only will make it necessary to repaint every year or two but also can lead to structural damage from woodrot and decay.

Facilities

The cost of heat is a major operating expense for households in most parts of the country. Operating costs are affected both by the efficiency of the heating system and by the soundness of a house's construction and insulation. In older homes you can get some idea of the costs involved by asking to see the previous year's fuel bills. You may wish to double-check them with the fuel company's records.

In new houses the length of the guarantee provided with the furnace provides some clues to its quality. For warm-air furnaces (the most common type of furnace) a 10-year guarantee indicates a good-quality furnace. To cut costs, many builders use lower-quality furnaces that carry only a 1-year guarantee.

Gas and oil are the two most widely used heating fuels. In recent years, electric heat has been promoted heavily by electric companies in many parts of the country, increasing the interest of home buyers and homeowners in this type of heat. Electric heat is popular with builders because installation costs are lower than for gas or oil heat. Operating costs for electric heat may be high unless houses are specially insulated and local electric rates are low. Before considering a house with electric heat it may be wise to check the experiences other local families have had with it.

In the chapter on appliances, we note the substantial increase in recent years in the number of appliances typical families own and use. The wiring of many houses, both old and new, is not fully adequate to handle this increased load. Both the total amount of current available for distribution within the house and the number of circuits available to distribute current are important. The total current available is determined by the electrical service entrance. Today minimum service is considered to be 100 amperes with both 120-volt circuits (for lighting and small appliances) and 240-volt circuits (for electric ranges, water heaters, large air-conditioners, and electric heat). An entrance of 150 or 200 amperes is needed for houses with an electric range and electric heat or air conditioning. Some older houses have only 60-amp entrances. The electric-entrance capacity is usually indicated on the fuse box.

Most houses have only six separate electrical circuits but need at least eight to ten. The number of separate circuits can be determined by counting the number of fuses (or circuit breakers) in the fuse box. There will be one fuse for each 120-volt circuit and two for each 240-volt circuit. If the total number of circuits is inadequate, individual circuits will become overloaded, fuses will blow frequently, appliances may not work properly, and wiring may become dangerously over-heated. A typical house should have three to four circuits for lights and wall outlets plus a separate circuit for each of the following appli-ances: electric range, air-conditioner, washer, dryer, water heater, and furnace.

Inadequate water pressure is a frequent and annoying problem in many houses. When water pressure is low, shower temperatures can become too hot or too cold without warning when faucets are turned on or toilets flushed in another part of the house. To check for low water pressure, turn all the tub and sink faucets on fully and then flush the toilet. If the water pressure is good, the flow of water should not vary too much.

Condition

Houses in good condition, with fresh paint and attractive lawns and shrubs, usually command top prices and are in short supply. The typical home buyer is likely to find that the available choices require some repairs or redecoration to be put in good condition. The costs involved for repairs and refurbishing need to be considered carefully. Interior and exterior painting can be done on a do-it-yourself basis for a few hundred dollars. Refinishing floors probably will require expert help and will be more expensive. Replacing carpeting and vinyl flooring is a major expense. Some estimate of the cost involved would be a good idea.

In looking over the condition of the interior, you should check for signs of paint discolored and plaster damaged by water leakage. Such damage may be a result of a leaky roof or leaky plumbing—in either case, it is a sign of a serious problem.

Before agreement is reached on a purchase, the house should be inspected to ensure that it is termite-free. Termites are a particular

When buying a house, consumers should distinguish between conditions that require the costly work of experts and conditions that can be remedied on a do-it-yourself basis.

Charles Moore from Black Star

problem in the Southeast and in California but are also a serious concern in the Middle Atlantic states, the Middle West, and Southwest. The inspection should be made by experts (this is required by many mortgage lenders). Termites can move through cracks in concrete foundations and slabs and are a potential problem in all types of houses.

THE PRELIMINARY COSTS INVOLVED

The first step in buying your own home is to decide how expensive a house you can afford. Begin by figuring out how much of your monthly income you can afford to allocate for mortgage payments and other monthly housing expenses. Then determine how much of your cash savings you can safely use for a down payment and for the preliminary costs of buying or building a home. Some experts estimate that families can usually afford to spend from 2 to $2\frac{1}{2}$ times the amount of the annual family income on a home. However, this is only a rough guide. The amount you can afford to invest in a home will depend on your other financial commitments, your average living expenses, your future earning power, your savings, and possibly also on other factors.

A future homeowner has to plan for the initial costs of buying or building as well as for his mortgage payments. Preliminary costs vary with the type of home, the area, and the financing arrangement. The table on page 224 lists some of the preliminary costs that may be involved in buying, building, and moving into a home. You will probably not have to pay all these expenses, but you should be prepared to pay preliminary costs not covered in your mortgage loan.

PRELIMINARY COSTS OF BUYING, BUILDING, AND MOVING INTO A HOME		
Buying May Include Preliminary Costs of	**Building Includes Additional Costs of**	**Moving into the Home May Include the Costs of**
A land survey House inspection A title search and insurance Mortgage service charges and credit reports Recording fees for the deed and mortgage A notary fee Real estate transfer taxes Advance payments on taxes, fire insurance, and special assessments An attorney's fees	The lot House plans The fees of the architect or contractor The building permit The inspection fee The permit to connect utilities The margin for extra expenses during building	Extra furniture Draperies and curtains Carpeting Maintenance equipment Outdoor furniture Landscaping Movers Decorating Necessary repairs and improvements for older houses

THE MORTGAGE

After you decide how much you can pay for your home, the next step is to shop for a mortgage. A home mortgage is a loan contract in which the lender agrees to lend to the borrower a specified amount of money at a specified interest rate to be repaid according to the terms of the contract. If the borrower, called the *mortgagor,* fails to repay the loan, the lender, called the *mortgagee,* has the legal right to *foreclose;* that is, to obtain possession of the property. Mortgage loans are usually repaid on the *amortization plan,* a plan that provides for repayment in uniform monthly installments of interest and principal combined. As the loan is paid off, the amount of each payment that is applied to the principal increases; since the amount owed keeps decreasing as payments are made, the amount applied to interest decreases. The loan is paid in full when the last scheduled payment is made. The size of the monthly payments is determined by the amount borrowed, the length of the loan, and the interest rate.

When shopping for a home mortgage, you may encounter one or more of the following features:

■ The package mortgage covers, along with the house itself, the cost of such items as home appliances, furniture, and carpeting. It permits the borrower to pay for these items as he pays the mortgage on the home.

- The open-end mortgage permits the borrower to obtain more money at a later date under the terms of the original mortgage. It is especially helpful in obtaining money for future repairs, modernization, or expansion.
- The escrow agreement provides that insurance and real estate taxes be paid by the lender. The monthly payment is increased by the necessary amount to pay these costs and is adjusted if the amount of taxes or insurance changes.
- The prepayment privilege permits the borrower to make larger payments at any payment date during the mortgage. It may be necessary to pay extra for this, but the borrower can save interest charges if he pays the mortgage before the time specified.

The amount of money you can borrow through a home mortgage loan will depend on your credit rating and income and on the value of the home you are mortgaging. Before you can obtain a mortgage loan of any size, the mortgagee will want to be sure that title to the property is clear, that the property is covered by insurance, that the taxes are paid promptly, and that the mortgagor will keep the property in good condition.

The mortage bond is an important legal document that ensures repayment of the mortage loan.

THIS MORTGAGE, made the 15th day of JANUARY , nineteen hundred and -- ,

BETWEEN JOHN MERTEN, THE MORTGAGOR, AND LEONARD SPRUCE, THE MORTGAGEE

WITNESSETH, that to secure the payment of an indebtedness in the sum of dollars,
. TWELVE THOUSAND ($12,000.00)
lawful money of the United States, to be paid ON THE FIFTEENTH DAY OF JANUARY , 19 --,
with interest thereon to be computed from 15th day of JANUARY , 19 --, at
the rate of SEVEN per centum per annum, and to be paid according to a certain bond, note or obligation
bearing even date herewith, the mortgagor hereby mortgages to the mortgagee

ALL THE TWO-STORY AND BASEMENT DWELLING, LOCATED AT NO. 732
WESTFIELD AVENUE, IN THE CITY OF ELIZABETH, IN THE STATE OF NEW JERSEY.

AND the mortgagor covenants with the mortgagee as follows:
1. That the mortgagor will pay the indebtedness as hereinbefore provided.
2. That the mortgagor will keep the buildings on the premises insured against loss by fire for the benefit of the mortgagee.
3. That no building on the premises shall be removed or demolished without the consent of the mortgagee.
4. That the whole of said principal sum and interest shall become due at the option of the mortgagee: after default in the payment of any instalment of principal or of interest for twenty days; or after default in the payment of any tax, water rate, sewer rent or assessment for thirty days after notice and demand.
5. That the holder of this mortgage, in any action to foreclose it, shall be entitled to the appointment of a receiver.
6. That the mortgagor will pay all taxes, assessments, sewer rents or water rates, and in default thereof, the mortgagee may pay the same.
7. That the mortgagor within six days upon request in person or within fifteen days upon request by mail will furnish a written statement duly acknowledged of the amount due on this mortgage.
8. That notice and demand or request may be in writing and may be served in person or by mail.
9. That the mortgagor warrants the title to the premises.

IN WITNESS WHEREOF, this mortgage has been duly executed by the mortgagor.

IN PRESENCE OF:

Henry Smith.
George Rose

John Merten

STATE OF NEW JERSEY
COUNTY OF UNION } ss.:

On the 15th day of JANUARY 19 --,
before me came JOHN MERTEN

to me known to be the individual described in, and who executed the foregoing instrument, and acknowledged that he executed the same.

Frederick Mann
Notary Public

Types of home mortgage loans

There are three basic types of home mortgage loans available—Federal Housing Administration (FHA) loans, conventional loans, and Veterans Administration (VA) loans. FHA and VA loans differ from conventional loans in that the two government agencies involved provide lenders with guarantees against loss. The three types of loans vary in the amount of down payment required, the length of the repayment period, and the interest charges. Prospective home buyers should compare the terms of these types of loans to find the type that best meets their needs.

FHA GUARANTEED LOANS   A substantial portion of all home mortgage loans are insured by the FHA, which protects banks, savings and loan associations, and other private lenders against bad-debt losses. FHA loan insurance was developed to make it possible for people to purchase homes with only a small down payment and low monthly payments. Because lenders are protected against loss by the FHA, they are willing to accept low down payments, charge a somewhat lower interest rate, and permit long repayment periods (up to 30 or 35 years). In order to get an FHA guaranteed loan, the borrower must meet the requirements of the FHA as well as those of the lender. The cost of the mortgage insurance is covered by a charge (one-half of one percent of the unpaid balance of the loan) that is paid monthly along with the payments on the principal and interest charges of the loan. The FHA plan provides for inspection of the property by appraisal experts.

CONVENTIONAL LOANS   Conventional loans are the other major type of home mortgage loan. Such loans involve only two parties, the lender and the borrower. They are made on the basis of the borrower's credit rating and the value of the house he pledges as security. Because of the risks involved to the lender, the down payments required for conventional loans are larger than those required for FHA and VA loans. The repayment periods for conventional loans usually are shorter than those for FHA and VA loans, the usual repayment period being 20 to 25 years.

VA GUARANTEED LOANS   Loans guaranteed by the Veterans Administration make up only a small proportion of all home mortgage loans. These loans, often called *GI loans,* were developed to make it possible for veterans to purchase homes for little or no down payment and low monthly payments. By insuring private lenders against loss, VA loans permit low interest rates, long repayment periods, and lower down payments. Under the terms of GI loans, the government guarantees private lenders against loss for up to 60 percent of an approved loan, with a maximum guarantee of $12,500. VA loans are available only to qualified veterans. Details on such loans are available through local VA offices.

Terms of home mortgage loans

Home buyers need to shop for mortgage loans for the same reasons other borrowers need to shop for credit. Shopping for mortgage loans is, however, somewhat more complicated. Different lenders offer different interest rates and lengths of loan periods and have differing down payment requirements.

INTEREST RATES   Because of the length of the period for which mortgage loans are made, even small differences in interest rates among lenders can have a substantial effect on the total interest paid over the life of a loan. In the table shown below you can see, for example, that a difference of one-half of one percent results in a difference of several thousand dollars in the total interest paid on a typical mortgage loan.

EFFECT OF DIFFERING INTEREST RATES ON THE COST OF A $20,000 LOAN OVER A 25-YEAR PERIOD		
Interest Rate (percent)	Monthly Payment (including principal and interest)*	Total Interest Paid Over 25-Year Loan Period†
5½	$123	$16,840
6	129	18,600
6½	135	20,440
7	141	22,390
7½	148	24,330
8	154	26,280
8½	161	28,200
9	168	30,220
9½	175	32,370
10	182	34,460

* Rounded to nearest $1
† Rounded to nearest $10

The interest rates charged for conventional mortgage loans are governed by the state of the loan market. If funds for long-term loans such as home mortgage loans are in short supply, interest rates will be high. This was the case in the early 1970s when interest rates of 8 and 9 percent were not uncommon, in contrast to rates of 5 and 6 percent just a few years before.

The maximum interest rates on conventional mortgage loans are set by law in most states. The VA and FHA also set maximum interest rates on the mortgage loans they guarantee. When money is scarce, lenders may consider these rates too low, and since maximum interest rates are set by law, lenders charge a premium or "points" to make a loan and thus increase their effective return without violating the law. A *point* is a one-time charge made at the time a loan is arranged; it is equivalent to 1 percent of the total mortgage loan. A two-point charge on a $20,000 mortgage loan would be $400. Points affect the lender's return from the loan in much the same way charging a higher interest rate would. To avoid violating the law, the lender requires the seller to pay the extra charge. Even though the seller pays the extra charge, it affects the buyer too because the seller will probably increase the price that he asks for his house.

LENGTH OF LOAN PERIOD Longer loan periods reduce the size of the monthly payments required and may, at first glance, seem desirable to borrowers. Borrowers need to keep in mind, however, that the total interest paid on a loan increases rapidly as the loan period is lengthened. As can be seen in the table shown below, lengthening the period of a typical loan from 20 to 25 years increases the total interest that must be paid by about 30 percent. Borrowers should also note that the total interest paid over 25 years on this loan will actually exceed the amount of the loan itself.

Increasing the monthly payment by just a few dollars can cut the length of a mortgage substantially. As can be seen in the table, by

EFFECT OF LOAN PERIOD ON THE COST OF A LOAN AT 7 PERCENT		
Length of Loan Period (years)	Monthly Payment (including principal and interest)*	Total Interest Paid Over Loan Period†
5	$396	$ 3,760
10	232	7,870
15	180	12,360
20	155	17,210
25	141	22,410
30	133	27,910

*Rounded to nearest $1
†Rounded to nearest $10

increasing the monthly payments from $133 to $141, the length of this typical mortgage is cut by 5 years. By increasing the payments by $22, from $133 to $155, the mortgage term is reduced from 30 to 20 years.

DOWN PAYMENT The larger the down payment made, the less a home buyer needs to borrow. Since the amount borrowed is smaller, total interest costs will be less. A larger down payment may also be useful in obtaining a more favorable interest rate, since the risk involved in making the loan will be reduced. Although large down payments have important advantages, home buyers need to retain sufficient funds to cover the preliminary costs discussed earlier in the chapter; in addition, they should have a reserve for emergencies.

Sources of credit for home mortgage loans

There are several sources of credit for home mortgage loans. Although all lending institutions generally make the same types of loans, they do have different lending practices and policies. You should be familiar with a few basic characteristics of each lender. The lending institutions that offer home mortgage loans include the following:

- Savings Banks. Savings banks are licensed to operate in a number of states, chiefly in the Northeast, and are an important source of credit for home mortgage loans. State laws vary, but usually savings banks can lend from 60 to 90 percent of the purchase price of the property and can offer the borrower up to 30 years to repay. They handle conventional, FHA, and VA loans.
- Savings and Loan Associations. Savings and loan associations are permitted to lend a relatively large proportion of the appraised value of a property. The repayment periods usually are a maximum of 30 years. They handle FHA and VA loans as well as conventional loans.
- Life Insurance Companies. For conventional loans, life insurance companies generally require relatively large down payments but permit long repayment periods. They also make FHA and VA loans.
- Commercial Banks. For conventional loans, commercial banks generally require relatively large down payments and typically limit the repayment period to 20 to 25 years. When banks make FHA insured loans, they will generally lend a higher percentage of the property value.

- Mortgage Bankers. Mortgage bankers are a relatively new source of credit for mortgage loans. They have connections with many other sources of credit including banks, insurance companies, and pension funds. Mortgage bankers lend the money initially but usually sell their interest within a month or so to another lender.
- Mortgage Brokers. Mortgage brokers are firms or individuals who, like mortgage bankers, assist the prospective borrower in locating a lender. But unlike mortgage bankers, they lend no money. They merely act as a go-between to help a prospective borrower and a lender get together.

HANDLING THE LEGAL ASPECTS OF BUYING

There are certain legal aspects connected with buying real estate. Your lawyer can take the major responsibility for these matters; nevertheless, you should be familiar with the legal documents discussed in the following paragraphs. These documents include the contract for sale; title protection, which may be in the form of an abstract, a certificate of title, a Torrens certificate, or title insurance; and the deed.

The contract for sale

The contract for sale is a written agreement between the buyer and the seller that states the terms and conditions of the sale. It is often contingent on the buyer's obtaining a mortgage loan. The contract for sale should include the following items:

- The purchase price
- When and how payment is to be made
- A legal description of the real estate and any additional property included in the sale
- The date the buyer may take possession
- The seller's promise to provide the deed and a marketable title
- Provisions for payment of any taxes, insurance, utility bills, or other costs owed by the seller but not yet due
- Any additional agreements between the buyer and the seller in connection with the sale

Title protection

Title protection may be in the form of an abstract, a certificate of title, a Torrens certificate, or title insurance.

An *abstract* is a formal legal document prepared by a lawyer or a title guarantee company. It is a condensed history of the ownership of the property that determines whether there are any outstanding claims or liens on the property. While an abstract does not guarantee that the title is free, it does reveal any unsettled claims on the property on record.

A *certificate of title* is used in some areas rather than an abstract. It is a certificate signed by a lawyer indicating that he has examined all records related to the property and that, to the best of his knowledge, there are no unsettled claims against the property.

A *Torrens certificate* is used in some states. It is issued by an official recorder after an official notice has been placed in the newspaper inviting anyone who has a claim against the property to file suit. If there is no suit within a given time, the title is recorded in the new owner's name. The new owner is then issued a Torrens certificate as proof of ownership.

Title insurance is issued by an insurance company. It protects, according to the terms of the policy, against any loss from title defects. Before the insurance company issues a title policy, the records are searched to be sure that the title is clear.

The deed

The deed is a formal paper that transfers the title from seller to buyer. It is usually drawn up by a lawyer at the seller's expense. A *warranty deed* is preferred to any other type. It guarantees that the seller will defend the title against any outside claims. Other deeds merely transfer the seller's interests in the property to the buyer.

BUYING AN APARTMENT

Some people who want to combine the financial advantages and security of ownership with the conveniences of apartment living buy either a cooperative apartment or a condominium.

A person who buys a *cooperative apartment* is actually purchasing stock in a corporation that is the legal owner of a piece of property. Through buying stock, the buyer becomes a part owner of the property. Each stockholder pays a monthly fee to cover his share of the taxes, mortgage payments, and operating and maintenance costs. Stockholders are responsible for the corporation as a whole—to the extent of their interest—and if one or more of the owners fails to meet financial obligations to the corporation, the other owners must temporarily assume this additional obligation. In addition, each stockholder enters into a lease with the corporation, which sets out his rights and obligations as a tenant.

The *condominium* is a form of home ownership that combines the individual ownership of a single family unit in a multifamily building with joint ownership of that part of the property common to other occupants—such as hallways, yards, central heating and air conditioning, electric wiring, plumbing, elevators, lobbies, and the land itself. The owner pays his share of maintenance and operating expenses for that part of the condominium that is common to all occupants. He also agrees to maintain his individual property and to avoid any remodeling or alterations that change the outward appearance of the building. Each dwelling in a condominium is separately owned, taxed, and mortgaged.

Checking your reading

1. Discuss four things about the site of a house that should be considered when judging its value.
2. What should one look for when examining the basement or foundation of a house. Why?
3. What is meant by cross bridging? Why is cross bridging important?
4. Discuss the problems that can arise because of the use of plasterboard in houses.
5. Why are vapor barriers installed in houses? If vapor barriers are not installed, or if they are inadequate, what can be done?
6. Explain what is considered to be minimum electrical service in homes today. When a house has an electric range and electric heat or air conditioning, what electrical service entrance is needed?
7. Generally, how many separate electrical circuits are needed in houses today? What is the consequence of having too few electrical circuits?
8. Describe an easy way to check for low water pressure in a house.
9. Under most amortization plans, the amount of money that goes to pay off the mortgage loan increases and the amount paid for interest decreases as payments are made. Why is this true?
10. What is a package mortgage? What is an open-end mortgage?
11. How do FHA and VA loans differ from conventional loans?
12. Explain why FHA loans may involve lower down payments, lower interest rates, and longer repayment periods.
13. Lenders at certain times charge "points" to make a loan. Explain what is meant by points, and give an example.
14. What is the difference between mortgage bankers and mortgage brokers?

15. What are the various forms that title protection may take?
16. Explain what is meant by a warranty deed.
17. Who owns a cooperative apartment? With whom do the tenants have a lease agreement?
18. What is a condominium?

Consumer problems and projects

1. Make a comparison of the interest rates on home mortgage loans that are offered by various lending agencies—banks, savings and loan associations, etc. What arrangements does each agency offer for repayment of the loan?

2. Obtain literature on housing from the Federal Housing Administration. The literature should include information about how the FHA works, how the FHA determines the amount that families can borrow safely, and how the FHA estimates the effective income of customers.

3. Simon Anderson decided to buy a house and applied at a savings bank for a $20,000 home mortgage loan. The loan officer recommended a 15-year loan on which the interest charge would be 7 percent. The monthly payments for such a loan would be $179.77. Mr. Anderson thought that this amount might be more than he could afford. The loan officer then gave him the monthly payment figures for a $20,000 loan at 7 percent for longer periods. The amounts were as follows: 20 years, $155.06; 25 years, $141.36. Mr. Anderson thinks he should take a 25-year loan. What possible advantages and disadvantages would a 25-year loan have for Mr. Anderson?

4. The Penna family is moving to another city. Eight years ago they bought a house for $22,500. During the eight years that they lived in the house, they maintained it well and made normal repairs to keep it in good condition, but they did not add any improvements to the house. The house is now seventeen years old. The Pennas have just sold their house for $24,900. How can you explain the fact that although the house is eight years older than when they bought it, it is apparently worth only $2,400 more?

5. Mr. Wichansky, Mr. Hodges, and Mr. Rodriguez have all bought $18,000 homes, and all are borrowing money at 7 percent interest. However, their down payments and the length of their loans vary as follows:

    Mr. Wichansky made no down payment at all. He has 25 years to repay the loan, and his monthly payment for principal and interest is $127.23.

    Mr. Hodges made a down payment of $1,000. He has to repay the balance in 20 years, and his monthly payment for principal and interest is $131.81.

    Mr. Rodriguez paid $2,000 down and plans to repay the loan in 15 years. His monthly payment for principal and interest is $143.82.

    a. What is the total interest bill for each of the men?

    b. Which man has the most attractive plan?

Chapter 14

Choosing furniture

When we set out to buy furnishings for our homes we need to consider the functions we want our home to serve—what do we want it to be like, and what do we want it to do for us? Is our home to be a center of family life with a place for the hobbies and activities of all family members? Do we prefer a casual life style, or a more formal one? How much importance do we place on impressing others with our home?

Sometimes the opinions of family members conflict. Recently one teen-ager complained that her family had an all-white living room and that family members were never permitted to enter except when there was company. The daughter complained that the mother even went so far as to keep a rope across the door and take it down only when the doorbell rang. The daughter summed up her views by adding, "It was like living in a kennel." Do you think it was worth it?

In addition to judging furnishings on how well they meet family needs, we also need to judge them on three other criteria:

1. Do they look attractive in themselves and look well together?
2. Do they fit into the family's quarters, whether the family lives in a house or an apartment?
3. Do they fit the family budget? Will they give good service and value for the price paid?

In this chapter, we will consider how to judge furniture on all four of these counts.

In Chapter 11 we introduced the concept of the *family life cycle,* the stages in the development of a family beginning with the formation of an independent household by young singles followed by the formation of a family at marriage. The same changes in the size and composition of the family that affect housing also have important effects on furniture needs. Because of the differences in the makeup of families at these different stages, there are important differences in their needs and wants.

In the first two family life cycle stages, young singles and newlyweds need to assemble basic home furnishings for their new home. Because they usually have both enough time and money available for leisure activities, they often purchase televisions, stereo sets, and equipment for entertaining guests. With the arrival of children the family moves to the third life cycle stage. Families with young children need to provide equipment and play space for them. Laundry equipment frequently is purchased to help with heavy wash loads. Because of the need for increased play space, many families buy houses at this stage and need additional furnishings for them. These needs of young families often outrun incomes, and families at this stage typically are heavy users of consumer credit.

Older families with children often are concerned about making their home an attractive place for their children to bring friends and entertain. They may find they need to replace furniture that they bought earlier. Special family interests often bring about the purchase of such items as pianos, ping-pong and billiard tables, and sports equipment that must be accommodated in the home.

Setting up housekeeping

Just how much money does it take for a young person or a young couple to set up housekeeping independently? An estimate developed a few years ago by *Changing Times* magazine provides some clues. *Changing Times* estimated that providing "moderately comfortable" furnishings for a one-bedroom apartment would cost $1,600. This estimate included all-new items for the living room and bedroom and for dining and cooking. The items included were not the lowest-priced ones available but were of durable quality, since it was felt that the lowest-priced items would not be most economical in the long run. The furnishings in the $1,600 estimate did not include all the items many young people might want. The living room furnishings were a sofa, one upholstered

Even with simple furnishings, most consumers find that setting up housekeeping is a major expense.

Robert Goldstein, Home Decoration Series, University Films/McGraw-Hill

chair, two end tables and two lamps, one bookcase, one 9- by 12-foot area rug, and draperies (unlined). No entertainment equipment such as a television or stereo set was included in the estimate. It was figured that for another $400 many desirable extras could be added. For the living room these included a coffee table, a second upholstered chair, a floor lamp, a table-model AM-FM radio, and lined draperies instead of unlined. We can see from this estimate that even setting up a small apartment can be an expensive proposition. Many people, including low-income families and students, of course, spend less. To cut costs they rely on second-hand purchases, gifts, and makeshift pieces.

Few young people are likely to be able to afford all the furnishings they want right away. This makes it especially important for them to decide which things they need first and plan a program of purchases. Such a plan has several advantages. It will help them move toward their goals easily and quickly. It may also help them decide that they do not need to buy everything right away on credit and perhaps run the risk of becoming overcommitted to installment payments. A plan will also help in evaluating whether the overall goal is realistic.

In recent years the furniture industry has begun to give more attention to the special needs of young adults and has begun to design more furniture suited to their limited budgets and small quarters. Multipurpose furniture, fold-up and nesting tables, and tall, vertical storage pieces all have been designed to save floor space. Inflatable furniture and paper furniture have been developed to reduce costs.

Some young families save money by filling out their needs with used furniture. Pieces that are still sturdy can be made usable with new slipcovers or a coat or two of paint. Family attics, used-furniture stores, classified ads, and neighborhood bulletin boards all are good sources for used items. Unfinished furniture also may provide an opportunity for savings. Other young families may prefer to make their own furniture from low-cost materials. Some examples are bookcases made with bricks and boards, desks made from doors placed on top of pairs of two-drawer file cabinets, and coffee tables and end tables made with electrical cable spools. In evaluating the cost of used and unfinished pieces, the cost of finishing materials and the value of one's time should be taken into account as well as the prices of the items themselves.

Learning about good design

An understanding of good design can help consumers choose furnishings that are attractive and look well when combined. Two general goals guide the best designs, whether they are of individual furniture pieces, entire rooms, or individual appliances.

The first goal is that the form or shape of an item should follow or grow out of its functions. In evaluating furniture against this goal, we must realize that most items have several functions. Chairs are not just for sitting; they should also be pleasing in appearance and should, in addition, provide durable, economical service. There are many different ways these different functions can be provided. Finding a solution that satisfactorily serves them all is where creativity comes into design.

The second goal of good design is providing variety within a unified whole. This means that a total design should include interesting and varied features, such as varied colors, textures, and shapes, and that this variety should be chosen so that all the features make up a unified, total design. Drawer pulls on chests and dressers, for example, should be attractively related to the design of the piece and should not look as if they were stuck on as an afterthought. Color schemes and repeating colors and textures throughout a room are techniques designers use to help "tie" a room together.

CHOOSING A FURNITURE STYLE One of the first things furniture shoppers are likely to think about is choosing a furniture style. The decision is complicated by the wide variety of styles available, ranging from reproductions of furniture dating back hundreds of years to the newest modern styles. To make the problem even more difficult, there are good and bad designs in every style. Furniture styles can be grouped into two broad categories: traditional and modern. Traditional styles are reproductions or, more often, adaptations of designs of the past. This category includes such styles as Early American and Spanish-Mediterranean. Modern styles are simple, straightforward designs with a minimum of ornamentation.

There are formal and informal styles in both these categories. The informal styles typically look heavier and sturdier and have cruder lines; their finishes are duller and sometimes antiqued or distressed; and the upholstery fabrics used are rough or nubby. Oak, pine, and maple are among the woods often used for informal styles.

The formal styles are lighter-looking and have refined lines; their finishes are smooth and polished; and the upholstery fabrics are delicate-looking velvets, silks, and damasks. Mahogany, walnut, and highly polished metal are often used in formal styles.

Courtesy Ethan Allen Inc.

Courtesy Pennsylvania House Furniture

Both formal and informal styles are available in furniture of all periods. Both the rooms at left are furnished in traditional styles. However, the room at top is furnished with informal Early American furniture, and the room at bottom is furnished with formal Queen Anne and Chippendale styles.

Among the traditional styles Early American furniture is relatively informal. While most Spanish-Mediterranean and French Provincial furniture is relatively informal, some designs with refined lines and polished finishes are formal. Traditional English styles such as Queen Anne and Chippendale are rather formal. Among the modern styles, Danish Modern is somewhat informal, while designs using highly polished chrome and glass tend to be formal.

In choosing a furniture style, the family life style should be kept in mind. Families that prefer a more casual, relaxed life style probably will feel more comfortable with furniture in an informal style. The sturdier lines and fabrics of informal styles are also well suited for active families and families with young children. Furniture styles can be mixed—this is one interesting way to add variety. One style should, however, be dominant, with only one or two pieces of the other added. In general, informal styles look better with other informal styles, and formal styles look better with other formal styles. A formal modern piece such as a chrome and glass coffee table would look better with formal traditional English styles than with informal Early American maple pieces.

APPLYING THE RULES OF DESIGN The rules of design apply both to choosing individual pieces of furniture and to the way they are combined to furnish a room. Furniture should serve its intended functions well. Upholstered furniture should be comfortable. Storage pieces should have designs that emphasize useful storage space, not ornamentation.

Furnishings should "go together" well. A room can be unified by repeating colors, upholstery fabrics, and furniture styles. Most designers think the typical home interior is too varied with too many unrelated colors, patterns, and textures. Each room should have a center of interest on which principal attention is focussed. This can be a fireplace, an interesting picture, or perhaps a colorful rug or bedspread. Often the item chosen as the center of interest provides the basis for the color scheme used in the room. When the other design elements in the room are well related to the center of interest, this helps pull the whole room together.

Furnishings must also be adapted to the size and scale of rooms in which they will be used. Most young people have small quarters with small rooms. They also move frequently. These considerations make smaller-size pieces especially appropriate. Triple dressers, king-size beds, large stereo-television consoles, and extra-long sofas are likely to be hard to get through the doorway and up the stairs and will prove even more of a problem when a place has to be found for them in a small room.

There are a number of sources of design help to which furniture shoppers can turn. In deciding on a furniture style and color choices, the interior design books available in most libraries and the home furnishings magazines are helpful. Many larger stores have interior designers who will give free advice on simple problems; they will also develop designs for entire rooms when all the purchases are made through their store. Independent interior designers, not associated with stores, typically specialize in large and costly decorating jobs. Furniture manufacturers also have tried to simplify the shopper's problems by developing color-coordinated upholstery fabrics that look attractive in combination.

FURNITURE CONSTRUCTION

In judging any piece of furniture, the shopper should first begin with a general inspection of the piece. Does it stand evenly on the floor without wobbling? When moved or lifted, does it feel rigid and well made, or does it sway slightly? Is the finish of the exposed wood parts smooth and evenly applied? Are the seams of the upholstery neatly made and even? Are the patterns of the upholstery matched well at the seams? These exterior appearances provide some clues to the overall quality of the piece. However, to fully judge furniture quality we need to learn how to look beneath the surface.

In the furniture trade, furniture pieces are grouped into two general categories, case goods and upholstered pieces. *Case goods* are all-wood items such as chests, dressers, and desks, while the upholstered category includes sofas and upholstered chairs.

Case goods

We can get a look at the basic construction of case goods by removing a drawer and looking at the interior. Case goods, we can see from the interior, are made of flat sheets, or panels, that are fastened together and to a supporting frame. The frame is the skeleton of a piece and gives it strength and support. The frame should be made of knot-free and kiln-dried hardwood. Strongly made interlocking joints are essential to keep the frame rigid. Mortise-and-tenon joints and double-dowel joints are the strongest. Joints should be reinforced with *corner blocks*, wedge-shaped pieces of wood that are glued into the angle of the joint

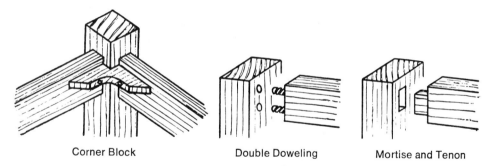

| Corner Block | Double Doweling | Mortise and Tenon |

between the members of the frame. Large corner blocks should be screwed in place as well as glued.

In earlier times the panels or flat surfaces of furniture were made of solid wood. Currently, very little furniture is made of solid wood; most instead is veneered. Veneered panels are built up with thin plies of wood glued together under pressure with special adhesives over a core material. Four plies plus the core are usually used, but some panels are made of two plies plus the core or six plies plus the core. In recent years solid lumber and particle board (small chips of wood glued together under pressure) frequently have been used as cores. Hardwood veneer sheets also are used for cores.

Veneered panels have advantages over solid wood in that they are less likely to crack, swell, or warp and are, in addition, less costly. Terms such as "solid walnut" can be used only when all the exposed surfaces are made of solid pieces of the wood named. In contrast, furniture labeled "genuine walnut" must have all exposed surfaces covered with the wood named, but it usually is made with veneer sheets. Terms such as "walnut finish" mean only that the wood used has been finished to look like walnut; these terms do not mean that the piece is actually made of the wood named.

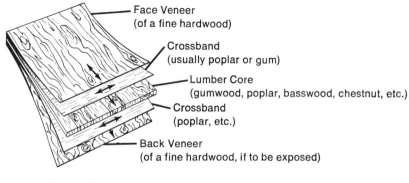

Face Veneer
(of a fine hardwood)

Crossband
(usually poplar or gum)

Lumber Core
(gumwood, poplar, basswood, chestnut, etc.)

Crossband
(poplar, etc.)

Back Veneer
(of a fine hardwood, if to be exposed)

Veneer Sheet

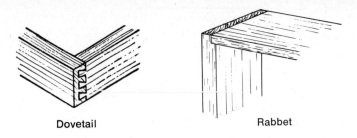

Dovetail   Rabbet

The construction of drawers often provides useful indications of quality. Drawers should pull out smoothly and close easily and should fit closely without being either too loose or too tight. High-quality furniture has glued dovetail joints joining all four drawer sides. The bottom panel of the drawer should be fitted tightly in grooves and held rigidly in place with small glued corner blocks. Some lower-quality furniture is made without interlocking joints on the drawer sides. In such pieces, rabbet joints are used and sometimes are secured with nails or staples rather than glue. Drawers made in this way are not as rigid as those with glued dovetail joints and are more likely to jam or pull out less smoothly and evenly. Drawers should have center or side guides of hardwood; softwood is too likely to wear over time. Durable drawer guides can also be made of metal or plastic. The interior surfaces of drawers should be smoothly finished; in better-quality furniture they are waxed or lacquered. In better-quality case goods the spaces between drawers are separated by dust panels.

The final finish on wood surfaces should be smooth and evenly applied with no runs or drips. The wood tones should be uniform over the entire piece rather than spotty or varied. Most interior designers prefer finishes through which the grain is clearly visible rather than opaque finishes that hide the grain. High-quality pieces have a smooth, almost silky finish, while low-quality pieces have rougher surfaces.

Upholstered pieces

Judging quality in upholstered furniture is more difficult than in case goods since the outer covering hides the basic construction of the piece. As in case goods, the basic frame of an upholstered piece should be made of knot-free and kiln-dried hardwood. Interlocking glued joints, either mortise-and-tenon or doweled, should be used in the frame, and these should be reinforced with glued corner blocks or metal plates.

SEAT AND BACK CONSTRUCTION Once the frame is constructed, the seat and back bases are attached to it to provide a foundation for the springs and padding materials that make the piece comfortable.

The type of base used depends upon the kind of springs to be used. When coil springs are used the base for them is made from (1) a sheet of canvas or burlap or (2) a webbing woven with 3- to 4-inch strips of jute, rubber, or plastic. When S-shaped springs are used, they serve as both base and springs. These springs are used in chair seats, sofa backs, less-expensive furniture, and contemporary pieces in which slim lines are desired.

Once the springs are in place, a sheet of insulation material is placed over them to keep the padding material in place and separated from the springs. Materials used as insulation include sheets of rubberized animal hair and sisal (a leaf fiber). Padding is then added on. Cellulose and cotton are used for padding in relatively inexpensive furniture, while urethane foam and polyester fiberfill are used in somewhat higher-priced furniture. Some furniture is made with combinations of these materials, such as a thick sheet of urethane foam over cotton padding. Padding should be applied evenly and smoothly over the entire piece and should be thick enough on chair arms so that the sharp edges of the frame cannot be felt. In high-quality pieces, muslin is applied over the padding before the piece is upholstered. This holds the padding in place and gives the upholstery a smoother appearance.

Loose cushions may be stuffed with urethane foam or latex foam. In some cases spring units wrapped in foam or covered with cotton or other types of padding are used. Wrapped foam cushions are relatively new and have the advantage of a softer "feel" and a plump,

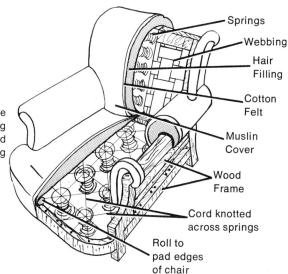

Upholstered furniture is made by building a frame, attaching seat and back bases, and adding springs and padding materials.

Springs

Webbing

Hair Filling

Cotton Felt

Muslin Cover

Wood Frame

Cord knotted across springs

Roll to pad edges of chair

comfortable appearance. They consist of a latex or urethane core wrapped in polyester fibers. The polyester fibers used (such as Dacron, Fortrel, Kodel, and Vycron) are given a two-dimensional crimp to prevent packing and compressing. In more expensive furniture, fibers with a three-dimensional crimp now are being used. Down filling for cushions is very expensive and now is rarely used. According to the information now available, urethane foam and latex foam are about equally durable. Latex foam, however, is considered more resilient; that is, better able to recover its shape after being compressed.

By law, in most states, the material used in cushioning and padding furniture must be stated in a label attached to the piece. These labels can provide some useful information for judging the quality of upholstered pieces and should be examined carefully. They may be removed after the piece is purchased.

SIZE AND COMFORT   A single piece of upholstered furniture is not likely to be comfortable for all the members of a family. Tall people will be more comfortable in seats that are higher from the floor and have deeper cushions from front to back. Shorter people will prefer lower seats and shallower cushions. The seat back should be high enough to provide comfortable support for the upper portion of the shoulders. Seating pieces for the living room and family room should be chosen so that every family member can have a place to sit comfortably. Before buying, the best way to be certain that a piece will be comfortable is to try it out for a few minutes.

UPHOLSTERY FABRICS   In contrast to the label information provided for padding and cushioning, little information is available on the upholstery fabrics used. The shopper is left without clues to such important considerations as fabric durability, resistance to fading from sunlight, and ease of care.

A fabric's basic fiber content does, however, provide some indications of the kind of performance that can be expected. Each textile fiber (such as cotton, wool, or polyester) has certain general characteristics that usually carry over after these fibers are woven into textiles. Sometimes several fibers are combined in weaving textiles to take advantage of the best characteristics of each. Textile experts say that, in general, a fabric must have at least a 20 percent content of a fiber for the fiber to offer any real advantages.

Cotton, rayon, and acetate are frequently used as upholstery fabrics because they are inexpensive and are easily dyed. They are, however, somewhat less durable than other upholstery fabrics and more subject to staining. Wool is more durable, but it is more expensive and is also subject to staining. The newer synthetics offer important improvements in durability but do have certain disadvantages. Nylon and polyester fabrics may *pill* when friction causes fibers to break and form small balls or "pills" on the fabric surface. The basic characteristics of fibers can be altered in the course of production, and problems such as staining can be overcome with the use of special finishes. The characteristics of the fibers most commonly used in upholstery fabrics are summarized in the table on page 246.

Another factor that influences performance is *fabric construction;* that is, how the fibers are fastened together to form a fabric. Woven fabrics are perhaps most familiar. The closeness of the weave is an important indication of durability. Fabrics with more threads per inch are more resistant to abrasion, stretching, wrinkling, and raveling. Loosely woven fabrics of heavy yarns are popular because of their interesting rough texture. Such fabrics are more durable when acrylic or rubberized backing is applied to help hold fibers in place. Pile fabrics, including velvets and fake furs, have an interesting "feel" but are more likely to stain because of the amount of fiber surface exposed.

Knit fabrics are being used on some modern-style pieces because they conform well to curved lines and rounded shapes. Knit fabrics are wrinkle-resistant but may snag and run. Some knit fabrics are laminated to foam backing to help control stretching and sagging.

Nonwoven fabrics, such as the vinyl plastics, are popular because they are durable and easy to care for. They are nonabsorbent but can pick up some stains. They also tend to feel hot in the summer and cold in the winter. Vinyl fabrics with woven or knitted backs are more flexible and less subject to tearing or ripping than those without such backing. Expanded vinyl has a thin layer of foam between the vinyl face and the backing; this layer helps give it a softer, more comfortable feel. Some new urethane-coated fabrics are now appearing on the market; these are made of urethane foam applied to a knit or woven fabric backing. These fabrics are flexible and soft with the look and feel of leather. Since they are chemically different from the vinyls, they are expected to perform differently. They do have an advantage over vinyl in that they are full of fine pores that help to overcome some of the comfort problems associated with vinyls. Leather is another nonwoven material used in upholstery. It is soft, flexible, and long-wearing but expensive. It is subject to staining but can be treated with stain-resistant finishes.

CHARACTERISTICS OF TEXTILE FIBERS USED IN HOME FURNISHINGS

Fibers and Selected Trade Names	Resistance to Fading From Sunlight	Strength	Resistance to Abrasion	Resistance to Stains	Resilience
Cotton	Good to excellent	Good to excellent	Medium	Fair to poor	Fair to poor
Rayon *Avisco* *Bemberg* *Celanese* *New Rayons* *Avril* *Avron* *Zantrel*	Good to excellent	Fair to poor; improved in new rayons	Fair to poor; improved in new rayons	Fair to poor; improved in new rayons	Fair to poor
Acetate *Avisco* *Celanese* *Chromspun*	Good to excellent for fibers dyed in solution or in spinning; others fair to poor	Fair to poor	Fair to poor	Medium	Fair to poor
Acrylic *Acrilan* *Creslan* *Orlon* *Zefran*	Good to excellent	Fair to poor	Fair to poor; may pill	Good to excellent	Good to excellent
Nylon *Antron* *Cantrece* *Caprolan* *Cumuloft*	Good to excellent	Good to excellent	Good to excellent	Good to excellent	Good to excellent
Olefin *DLP* *Herculon* *Vectra*	Good to excellent	Good to excellent	Good to excellent	Good to excellent	Good to excellent
Polyester *Dacron* *Fortrel* *Kodel* *Vycron*	Good to excellent	Good to excellent	Good to excellent; spun yarns may pill	Good to excellent, but has low resistance to oily stains	Good to excellent
Wool	Good to excellent	Fair to poor	Medium	Fair to poor; should have mothproof finish	Good to excellent

Reference: Josephine M. Blandford and Lois M. Gurel, *Fibers and Fabrics*, U.S. National Bureau of Standards Consumer Information Series No. 1, 1970.

Several special fabric finishes are available that help to control staining. These finishes decrease the rate at which a fabric absorbs moisture so that spills bead up on the surface rather than soak in. Silicone finishes protect fabrics from water-borne stains. Fluorocarbon finishes (such as Scotchgard and Zepel) protect against both water-borne and oil-borne stains.

A variety of upholstery fabrics is available for most pieces of furniture. These fabrics come in different "grades" at varying price levels. The same sofa upholstered with different fabrics may differ in price by as much as several hundred dollars. Upholstery grades indicate price level and do not necessarily indicate quality or durability. Some of the least expensive fabrics, such as cotton and rayon, probably will prove less durable than more expensive ones such as nylon, olefin, and wool. The most expensive grades generally are fancy velvets and elaborately patterned fabrics that do not necessarily provide good wearing quality. Many inexperienced furniture buyers make the mistake of trying to save money by sacrificing upholstery quality. Since both the fabric and labor costs involved in reupholstering are high, it is more economical to buy good-quality upholstery.

Checking your reading

1.   How does the stage of the family life cycle influence a family's furniture needs?
2.   What two general goals guide the best furniture designs?
3.   What are the two broad categories of furniture styles? What is an example of an informal style in each of these two categories?
4.   What two general rules are used in combining furniture styles?
5.   What are case goods?
6.   In evaluating the quality of a piece of furniture, what is a useful first step?
7.   Why are interlocking joints and corner blocks used in constructing case goods?
8.   Why is veneer so often used in making furniture?
9.   How does the wood used in constructing pieces labeled "genuine walnut," "solid walnut," and "walnut finish" differ?
10.   Why is the use of dovetail joints considered desirable for constructing drawers?
11.   How can the shopper determine the cushioning and padding materials used in constructing a piece of upholstered furniture?
12.   What characteristics does an upholstered piece need if it is to be comfortable for a tall person? A short person?

13. What are the good and bad features of cotton, rayon, and acetate when used as upholstery fabrics?

14. What is meant by fabric construction?

15. Are upholstery "grades" a useful guide to wearing quality?

Consumer problems and projects

1. What style of furniture do you prefer? Why do you feel it is a good choice for you?

2. Collect some pictures of furniture pieces from newspapers and magazines that you feel represent examples of good and bad design. In what ways do the good designs meet the two goals of good design discussed in this chapter? In what ways have the bad designs ignored these goals?

3. If you had an apartment of your own, what furniture pieces (not including appliances) would you like to have? Make a list of these. Visit a local furniture store or use a mail-order catalog to obtain prices for the items you would like to have. List these prices along with your choices of furniture. In what order would you buy these pieces if you could not afford them all at once? Why?

4. Check around your house for examples of furniture defects such as cracked joints and worn or stained upholstery. What construction and design features should you and your family look for to avoid these problems in the future?

5. Sally and Jack Bogen are considering buying a new living room sofa. They especially like a 10-foot sofa upholstered in white velvet. When they asked the salesman about how durable the fabric would be he said he was not sure but that the fabric was the finest quality cotton. Sally and Jack are expecting their first child in three months and are hoping to buy a home of their own soon. What are the possible disadvantages of the sofa they are considering?

6. Select an item of furniture in which you are interested. Check the price levels of this item at a local furniture store or in a mail-order catalog. How do the features offered, the construction, and overall quality differ among price levels? If you were to buy, which particular piece would you select? Why?

Chapter 15

Buying appliances

What electrical appliances do you own and use? A radio? A record player? An alarm clock? A study lamp? A hair dryer? An electric shaver? Perhaps a typewriter? Maybe a sewing machine? Your own TV set? What about electric tools, drills, and hobby equipment? These things are just some of the pieces of electrical equipment that young people and their families use every day.

Fifty years ago most American families owned few electrical appliances. Most American families now own a dozen or more electrical applicances of various sizes. These appliances represent a substantial investment, and their care, maintenance, and replacement are a continuing major expense. Clearly, the amount of money spent on appliances makes good buymanship important. Appliance purchases also deserve careful consideration because many appliances offer labor- and time-saving features that help us conserve important personal resources—our own energy and time.

In this chapter we will first discuss how consumers' individual needs and situations influence choices of appliances. Next, we will consider the factors that need to be taken into account in shopping for appliances, in arranging the purchase, and in using them. Finally, we will discuss the replacement of appliances.

EVALUATING YOUR NEEDS AND SITUATION

Choosing appliances is an important part of setting up a new household. Since young people often start out in rented quarters that provide kitchen appliances, their first purchases are likely to be television sets and hi-fi equipment. As they move to later stages in the family life cycle, they buy other pieces of major equipment.

In choosing appliances consumers need to consider both their needs and the factors that may limit their choices. The factors that limit choices include the amount of space available. A small apartment or a mobile home may not have space for a full-size washer and dryer, and choices may have to be limited to small-size ones. Choices are also limited by landlord's rules. Some landlords do not permit tenants to install laundry equipment in their apartments because of the problems created by washing machines running over and because of the amount of water and electricity used. Choices may also be limited by the number and kinds of electrical circuits available. Some major appliances such as electric ranges, clothes dryers, and large air-conditioners require a 240-volt service instead of the regular 120-volt circuit.

In planning the purchase of some equipment, particularly home laundry equipment, consumers need to consider whether they will get enough use out of it to make the purchase worthwhile. The purchase of home laundry equipment represents a major expense, and unless the equipment is used frequently, it may be more costly than using public coin-operated facilities.

Consumer economists with the U.S. Department of Agriculture have estimated the cost of doing laundry at home. These estimates can help families decide whether the purchase of laundry equipment is a good investment. They started by assuming that both the washer and dryer were bought new, on credit, and that the washer would last 10 years and the dryer 14 years. The cost per load for different rates of use was then calculated. The result was 28 cents per load, based on equipment costs, when the machines are used for an average of five loads per week (see the table on page 251). This figure plus the cost of water and electricity (17 cents per load) and the cost of detergent and bleach (10 cents per load) add up to 55 cents, the total cost of doing a load of laundry at home. As you can see in the table, with more frequent use the cost per load is lower, since the cost of the equipment is spread over more loads. The cost per load for water and electricity and for detergent and bleach does not change.

ESTIMATED COST PER LOAD OF LAUNDRY DONE AT HOME, WASHINGTON, D.C., AREA, 1970						
	Number of Loads Done Per Week					
	3	4	5	6	8	10
Equipment Costs	$.46	$.35	$.28	$.23	$.17	$.14
Water and Electricity	.17	.17	.17	.17	.17	.17
Detergent and Bleach	.10	.10	.10	.10	.10	.10
Total Cost Per Load	$.73	$.62	$.55	$.50	$.44	$.41

Source: *Family Economics Review,* Consumer and Food Economics Research Division, U.S. Department of Agriculture, December, 1970, p. 7.

Let us take an individual situation to see how the table can be used. Suppose you had access to coin-operated laundry equipment that requires 25 cents per load for the washer, 20 cents per load for the dryer, and 10 cents per load for detergent and bleach—a total of 55 cents per load. We can see that if you did only three to four loads a week, the coin-operated facilities would be cheaper per load than home equipment. For five loads a week the costs would be the same, but for more than five loads, home facilities would be cheaper. These calculations do not take account of the extra time or travel costs that may be required to get to the coin-operated facilities. From this example you can see that it is not always cheaper to own appliances. Using rentals and coin-operated facilities may be more economical in some cases.

SHOPPING FOR APPLIANCES

After they have done some thinking about their appliance needs, consumers should begin to gather information on the kinds of equipment that are available and then consider how this equipment can meet their needs. In Chapter 5 we discussed some of the sources of product information that consumers can use. The reports of the consumer-supported product-testing organizations are especially helpful. They provide both information on the kinds of features available with different brands and an evaluation of their usefulness. With this information in hand, the consumer is ready to begin looking at different brands and models and collecting price quotations.

Features

One of the biggest problems in shopping for appliances is determining what features are available on a particular model and how useful or important they are. Salesmen are not always as well informed or helpful as they could be, and descriptive sales brochures may be hard to locate. The use of informative labels that provide the same kinds of information about each product would go a long way in solving the problem of making comparisons. Teltag labels that provide basic information on important product features are now in use in Britain and several other European countries. The "Buying Guide Tags" reproduced here were developed for use in an experiment at the F and R Lazarus Department Store in Columbus, Ohio, to test consumers' reactions to this way of providing product information. They illustrate the kinds of product information that tags could provide. The experiment showed that, in general, consumers found the tags helpful in providing information. In addition, salespeople reported finding them helpful in answering customers' questions.

Persistence in asking questions, the consumer product-testing magazines, and an appliance's instruction manual all may have to be used to get needed information about product features. With this information you will have a clearer idea of which features are available on a particular model and how useful they can be to you. Only then can

Teltag labels that provide basic information on important product features help the consumer make intelligent comparisons of products.

Buying Guide

Brand A

Model C-2

Electric Percolator

Makes ____10____ 5-oz. cups

Minimum brew ____4____ cups

Brew time about ____9____ minutes but varies according to brew strength, tap water temperature, number of cups.

Holds serving temperature ____yes____

Immersible ____no____

Material ____stainless steel____

(UL) Approved ____yes____

Lazarus
ESTABLISHED 1851

For best selection, be sure to consider these points:

Performance
Best taste results from cleanest pots, so investigate material of interior for ease of cleaning.

Convenience
Depends on: whether immersible, for cleaning; fit of lid for safe pouring; whether a signal light; visibility of graduated fill markings; special features.

Safety
Need adequate handle clearance or shield to avoid contact with hot metal.

Warranty
Ask sales associate for your Service Policy at time of purchase.

Some manufacturers place informative labels on their appliances. A wise consumer uses the information on the label to help her decide which features are really necessary.

Courtesy The Maytag Co.

you begin to decide whether the top-of-the-line models are worth the extra cost to you or whether a less expensive model with fewer features would be acceptable. In choosing a model it is important to recognize that while most of the features offered on the most expensive models would be desirable, not all are really necessary. In fact, many home economists suggest avoiding models with complicated extra features because of the extra repair problems involved.

Safety

Because of the potential lethal effects of the energy sources used—gas and electricity—safety is a key consideration in choosing appliances. Shock hazards are a possible risk with all electrical equipment. Such hazards can be controlled by good design and good manufacturing practices. Because of the work of Underwriters' Laboratories (UL) in these areas, shoppers should look for the UL seal on electrical appliances (see page 82). They should also look for the star seal of the American Gas Association on gas appliances (see page 82). These seals cannot, however, fully guarantee safety, since production-line errors, wear, and misuse all can make an individual appliance dangerous.

Shock hazards from electrical appliances with short circuits are eliminated when the appliance is grounded—that is, when the appliance is linked to the earth by an electrical conductor such as a cold-water pipe, a drain pipe, or a grounding wire. When an ungrounded appliance contains a short circuit, and the user is in contact with a ground, electricity can pass through his body, and a shock hazard exists. This is why the use of ungrounded appliances is especially dangerous around sinks and bathtubs that are grounded by plumbing pipes, on damp basement floors, on damp garage floors, and on the bare earth itself.

Shock hazards can be prevented by insulating electric equipment to prevent current leakage and by building in a grounding wire or grounding conductor. If there is a short circuit in a piece of equipment, the grounding conductor allows the current to travel safely to the earth rather than through the user's body. Equipment with a built-in grounding conductor can be recognized because it has three wires in the appliance cord instead of the usual two and has a special three-prong plug or a regular two-prong plug plus a "pigtail." Appliances with a grounding conductor are properly grounded only when they are plugged into a grounded outlet box. Individuals can help protect themselves by plugging appliances with grounding conductors into grounded outlet boxes and by taking special care in using appliances in the presence of grounds. Consumers Union has paid particular attention to shock hazards when testing appliances, and an appliance with a design that creates a shock hazard is rated "Not Acceptable."

Using equipment with a ground wire and a properly grounded outlet box provides protection against electric shock.

Courtesy Association of Home Appliance Manufacturers

Appliances that appear to be the same size often vary greatly in their capacity. Note the difference in the sizes of the loads handled by these two washers.

Courtesy Consumers Union

Capacity

Shoppers are likely to find on careful inspection that many models that appear similar vary greatly in their actual capacity. For example, Consumers Union recently found that the loads handled by medium-priced automatic washers varied greatly. Some washers could handle loads twice as large as others. CU has also found that the actual usable storage space in refrigerators is several cubic feet less than the volumes reported by manufacturers. The reported capacities are based on "net refrigerated volume"—the total amount of space inside the refrigerator that is cooled. Not all this space, however, is really usable. Some space is used up by shelves, trays, and trim, and some space is awkward to use effectively.

Service and warranties

Unsatisfactory repair service and disagreements over the terms of guarantees are major headaches for consumers. Consumers can protect themselves, to some extent, by choosing brands and models that have good frequency-of-repair records. Consumers Union test results and the information that it collects on the number and kinds of repairs needed by different models of appliances provide a useful indication of the models that are likely to be the most trouble-free. Many models seem to have the same kind of record year after year—those with good records continue to have them, while those with poor records continue to require more than the average number of repairs.

Guarantees offered by different companies for a particular type of appliance often are similar. One of the chief differences is in who pays for labor costs. This question deserves special attention when you are comparing guarantees. Do the guarantees make clear what is covered and what is not? How well do they conform to the requirements for a good guarantee that we discussed in Chapter 4 (pages 62–63)?

The availability of appliance parts for repairs has been a serious problem in recent years. Some companies are working to improve the situation. Sears, Roebuck and Company now offers a guarantee with their refrigerators that repair parts will be kept available for 15 years. It will pay to check the arrangements that have been made to keep parts available for the appliance in which you are interested. Where is the nearest parts supply center? How long does it take to obtain parts? How long will parts be kept available?

Operating costs

Different brands and models may differ substantially in their operating costs. Operating costs are particularly important for appliances such as refrigerators and air-conditioners that are heavy users of electricity. Consumers Union recently calculated that the cost of operating different brands of no-frost refrigerators of similar size might vary from $2.25 to $4.25 a month. Room air-conditioners also were found to vary in operating costs, but to a lesser extent. Automatic washers vary a good deal in the amount of water they use to do a load of wash. These differences, however, are related to the size of the load they can handle.

Used appliances

Many consumers have learned how to get good value for their money by buying used appliances. Most of the shopping techniques we have discussed can be used in purchasing used appliances as well as new ones. For example, suppose you were considering buying a particular used television set. After checking the picture on different channels, you could check the age of the set by looking at the nameplate on the back or inside. All major appliances have such plates, and all carry a serial number, part of which is a code number for the year the appliance was made. Once you know the serial number you can check

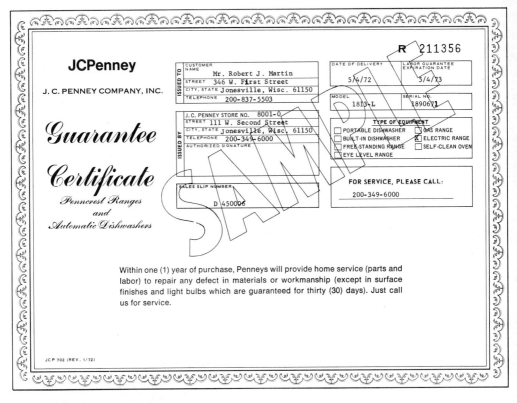

JCPenney

J. C. PENNEY COMPANY, INC.

Guarantee

Certificate

Penncrest Ranges
and
Automatic Dishwashers

JCP 702 (REV. 1/72)

R 211356

ISSUED TO		DATE OF DELIVERY	LABOR GUARANTEE EXPIRATION DATE
CUSTOMER NAME	Mr. Robert J. Martin	5/4/72	5/4/73
STREET	346 W. First Street		
CITY, STATE	Jonesville, Wisc. 61150	MODEL	SERIAL NO.
TELEPHONE	200-837-5503	1813-L	1890671

ISSUED BY

J. C. PENNEY STORE NO. 8001-0
STREET 111 W. Second Street
CITY, STATE Jonesville, Wisc 61150
TELEPHONE 200-349-6000
AUTHORIZED SIGNATURE

TYPE OF EQUIPMENT

☐ PORTABLE DISHWASHER ☐ GAS RANGE
☐ BUILT-IN DISHWASHER ☒ ELECTRIC RANGE
☐ FREE-STANDING RANGE ☐ SELF-CLEAN OVEN
☐ EYE LEVEL RANGE

SALES SLIP NUMBER
D 450006

FOR SERVICE, PLEASE CALL:
200-349-6000

Within one (1) year of purchase, Penneys will provide home service (parts and labor) to repair any defect in materials or workmanship (except in surface finishes and light bulbs which are guaranteed for thirty (30) days). Just call us for service.

In recent years some companies have made an effort to simplify the language of their guarantees so that they can be easily understood.

the age of the set by making a phone call to an authorized repair shop for that brand. At the same time, you could also ask what problems that year's models tend to have and how serious they are. Once you know the model number and year, you can check back in *Consumer Reports* and *Consumer Bulletin* to see how it was rated when new.

PURCHASE, DELIVERY, AND USE

Few appliances are sold only at list price nowadays, so it generally pays to shop around. Even the first price quoted may be subject to bargaining. It pays to find out. Discount stores frequently quote the lowest prices but often make up for this by charging more for installment-plan credit. If you plan to buy from a discount house and plan to use credit, you may wish to borrow elsewhere.

When a final price is quoted, it should be clear whether delivery and installation are included. The extent of the services provided should also be made clear. Does delivery mean delivery to your front door or delivery to the desired place inside your home? What is or is not included in installation also should be clear. This is particularly important for items such as clothes dryers that require venting and also for clothes washers and dishwashers, which require both electrical and plumbing hookups. The sales receipt should clearly indicate the brand and model number purchased and any qualifications or limitations on the guarantee. There sometimes are limitations in the case of "floor models." The receipt should be saved along with the guarantee to provide evidence of the date of purchase in case any work covered by the guarantee is needed.

When a new appliance is delivered it is desirable to check it out fully before the installation men leave. Small appliances should be checked before you leave the store. It is also desirable to get a demonstration on how to operate a complex new piece of equipment such as a color television set or an automatic washer. When it is not possible to check an appliance immediately upon delivery, it should be checked as soon as possible afterward so that complaints and adjustments can be made promptly.

Instruction books should be read carefully. They contain directions on operating appliances and information on what to do when particular operating problems arise. A careful review of the operating instructions may eliminate the need for a service call. It has been estimated that one-third of all appliance service calls are unnecessary. Typical problems are as follows:

- Failure to check to be sure the appliance is plugged in
- Failure to check fuses
- Failure to check control settings
- Failure to ensure that doors that must be fully latched before equipment will operate are tightly shut

When service is needed, call the dealer from whom you purchased the appliance, the service agency he recommends, or an organization franchised by the manufacturer to repair your brand. Repairs covered by the guarantee should, of course, be made without charge. In arranging for service you will want to check the method used in calculating service charges. Many service organizations charge a set fee for home service calls in addition to labor charges for the time required to make the necessary repairs. They may also charge a "bench fee" for diagnosing problems of appliances brought into the shop in addition to a labor charge for the actual repairs.

Appliance manufacturers have set up a special consumer committee to help consumers who have problems with major appliances. Consumers who are unable to get satisfactory solutions to their problems with major appliances (home laundry equipment, refrigerators, ranges, freezers, room air-conditioners, garbage disposals, dishwashers, dehumidifiers, and water heaters) may forward their complaints to this group, the Major Appliance Consumer Action Panel (MACAP). MACAP is a group of independent consumer experts who communicate consumer problems and concerns to appliance industry executives. Complaints may be directed to the Major Appliance Consumer Action Panel, 20 North Wacker Drive, Chicago, Illinois 60606.

PLANNING FOR REPLACEMENT

When buying appliances consumers should be aware of how much useful life they can expect from a new piece of equipment. Studies of the average number of years appliances typically are used before they are replaced provide some clues. As you can see from the table shown below, sewing machines are used longer than other appliances, while television sets and automatic washers are replaced a good deal sooner. With information on the life of individual appliances, you can begin to plan ahead for their replacement in the same way businesses plan the replacement of worn-out machinery. Some family financial experts advise building up a replacement fund as appliances become worn out so that cash will be available to pay for a replacement when it is needed. By building up a replacement fund for appliances, families can avoid costly borrowing on credit when a new appliance is needed.

AVERAGE NUMBER OF YEARS NEW APPLIANCES ARE USED BY THEIR FIRST OWNERS BEFORE REPLACEMENT	
Appliance	**Average Number of Years Used**
Electric Refrigerator	16
Electric Range	16
Gas Range	16
Automatic Washer	10
Electric Clothes Dryer	14
Tank Vacuum Cleaner	15
Electric Sewing Machine	24
Automatic Electric Toaster	15
Television Set	11

Source: Consumer and Food Economics Research Division, U.S. Department of Agriculture.

Checking your reading

1. What kinds of factors may limit consumers in their choice of appliances?
2. Is purchasing an appliance that you need and use always a good investment?
3. What sources of information can be used to find out what features are available on a particular appliance model?
4. Why would the use of Teltags help shoppers?
5. Why do many home economists suggest avoiding appliance models with costly extra features?
6. Do the UL and star seals on electrical and gas appliances fully guarantee their safety? Why?
7. In what situations can an electrical shock hazard exist?
8. Why is it unwise to assume that appliance models that appear similar have the same capacity?
9. How can frequency-of-repair records be useful to appliance shoppers?
10. Why is the promise that repair parts will be kept available a significant recent addition to appliance guarantees?
11. For what particular kinds of appliances are differences in operating costs likely to be especially important?
12. Why is it important to know what services are included in the sale price of an appliance?
13. What kinds of problems often result in unnecessary service calls?
14. Whom should you call for appliance repairs?
15. How can families use a replacement fund to help them avoid credit costs?

Consumer problems and projects

1. If you had an apartment of your own, what appliances would you want to have? Make a list of these items. Visit a local appliance store or use a mail-order catalog to obtain prices of the appliances you would like to have. What is the total cost? If you could not obtain all these items at once, which ones would you want first? Why?
2. Check some recent issues of *Consumer Reports* and *Consumer Bulletin* for reports of tests of electrical and gas appliances. Select an appliance in which you are interested or would like to own. What factors were considered in rating it? What tests were used? What brands and models were given top ratings? If you were to buy the item, which brand and model would you buy? What are the reasons for your choice?
3. Visit local stores to check the availability of the two or three brands and models that you rated highest in activity number two. How do the prices in these different

stores compare? In light of the information you have obtained on product features, on availability, and on prices, which brand and model would you buy? Where would you buy it? Why?

4.   Select an appliance in which you are interested that is available at several different price levels. Some examples are radios, electric typewriters, electric shavers, and electric drills. Visit local stores or use a mail-order catalog to obtain information on differences in construction and features among these price levels. What are the basic differences among the various price levels? If you were to buy the item, at which price level would you buy? Why?

5.   Josie and Bob Hamilton were recently married, and both are working. They are considering buying a washer and dryer. They figure they would use it for only four or five loads a week. The nearest coin laundry charges 45 cents per load and is 3 miles away. If the Hamiltons asked you for your opinion on the purchase, what factors would you advise them to take into consideration?

6.   Joe Dorfman has just washed his car and is standing on the wet grass polishing it with a buffer pad attached to an electric drill. What safety precautions should we hope he has taken?

7.   Lynda Barrios has a chance to buy a three-year-old refrigerator for $75 from a friend who is moving out of town. After checking the classified ads and used-appliance stores she is convinced the price is fair. She wonders, however, if she is likely to have a lot of problems with the refrigerator since it is used. If she asked you for advice, what would you tell her?

Financial security

Part

Chapter 16

Savings programs

Saving money is still a highly valued goal. This fact was revealed by a University of Michigan study of the nation's families. The study also indicated that although most people want to accumulate savings, many believe they are unable to save. Other people have difficulty mustering the will to save because they have never really examined the many reasons why saving money is important. This chapter will examine some of the reasons for saving money and offer several suggestions for making saving easier.

WHY PEOPLE SAVE MONEY

You may have already started a savings program. If you set aside $2 a week from your allowance or your income from a part-time job so that you will have $100 available for a summer vacation, you have established a savings program. If an engaged couple agree to spend less money while on dates and instead accumulate money to buy furniture, they, too, have started a savings program. Again and again throughout a person's lifetime he must decide whether to spend money for something that seems quite important at the moment or save with the goal of spending it sometime in the future.

The key to successful saving is to save with a goal in mind. Only a miser, such as Silas Marner, saves because of a desire to have lots of money. Saving can be fun if you look forward to using the money in the future for some purpose that will give you more happiness than present spending will give. Instead of setting aside $2 each week for a summer vacation, you could, no doubt, find many ways to spend the extra money each week. The question is whether or not spending the extra money each week on perhaps foolish or unnecessary things will bring you as much happiness as the additional $100 will bring you at vacation time.

The first point about saving that should be remembered, then, is that when you save a dollar, you are not forever surrendering your right to spend it. The second point is that as soon as you have savings, you have a silent partner working for you. You work for your money; then you put your money to work for you. But before looking into how your money will work for you, we will check some of the more specific reasons for saving money.

Emergency fund

The most important savings for most individuals and families is an emergency fund. In fact, creating an emergency fund that can be drawn upon when necessary should be the starting point for any savings plan. Once the fund is established, it should be maintained within certain dollar limits. When money is withdrawn from the fund, the amount taken should be replaced as soon as possible.

A savings account can be a source of money for unexpected financial emergencies, such as extensive and costly dental care.

Community Series, University Films/McGraw-Hill

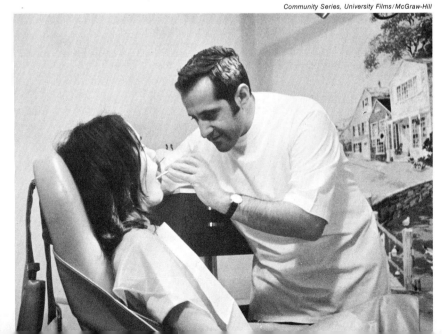

Individuals or families use money saved in an emergency fund for many different reasons. Repair bills on home appliances, for example, might be an important reason for having money on hand. A distant relative might die, and the cost of traveling to the funeral is an expense that would have to be met.

Unfortunately, no family can predict accurately how much money is needed to take care of emergencies. A traditional rule of thumb that had been followed through the years was to have available in a savings account an emergency fund equal to from six months' to a year's income. The savings was to be used only in extreme emergencies; for example, to pay a major medical bill or to pay living expenses during a period of unemployment. The amount of money needed for emergencies has probably changed somewhat in recent years. For example, families can more easily protect themselves against heavy medical bills through medical insurance plans. Government unemployment compensation may help when one loses his job, and there are other financial cushions that breadwinners can fall back on in times of crises. In our present society, many bills can be paid 30 days or even later after a debt is incurred.

So, how much money is now needed in an emergency fund? Probably the best answer to this question is that it depends on the individual or the family. It depends on the security of one's job, the financial needs of the family, the life style of the family, the extent of insurance protection, and many other variable factors. A self-employed worker probably needs a larger emergency fund than a salaried employee. An unskilled worker might need a larger fund than a skilled worker, because an unskilled worker might be more likely to hit job slumps for longer periods of time.

Changing Times magazine reported in the early 1970s that a poll of money management authorities produced guideline figures concerning the size of a family's emergency fund. The figures ranged from two months' to a year's income. The consensus of opinion was that an emergency fund equivalent to three months' income is a realistic goal for many people.

Large recurring expenses

Some people save money systematically so that when large recurring expenses such as income taxes, annual insurance premiums, and real estate taxes are due, money will be available for payment. In this case, the amounts needed are predictable, and the money that must be saved each week or each month can be quite exact. Chapter 3, "Financial

Planning and Budgeting," discusses in greater detail the need for planning for these relatively large expenses.

Expensive purchases

Many times during everyone's lifetime expensive items must be purchased. Buying such items out of current income is usually not possible, so the consumer must decide whether to borrow money for these purchases (or buy the goods on the installment plan, which is a way of borrowing money) or save in advance so that enough cash is available when the purchase is made. Most consumers, of course, do both. Borrowing money means paying an interest charge, of course. Money saved earns interest, so the consumer who saves money in advance to pay for expensive items gains in two ways: he pays less because there is no interest charge, and he earns interest on the money he is saving.

A person's ability to save during his early years is a good indication of the life he will build for himself later on. A nice home, fine books and records, convenient appliances, and other things that enrich our lives can more often be purchased by the person who looks ahead and plans his spending carefully.

Every family experiences times when substantial funds are required: the time when a down payment of several thousand dollars is needed for the purchase of a home; the time when money is needed to help pay for a child's college education. These and many additional needs must be recognized and planned for with a savings program.

Retirement

Some retirement income is provided for most workers through the compulsory old-age, survivors, and disability insurance program (often called the social security program) administered by the federal government. Many workers are also covered by pension plans or retirement-income savings plans provided by their employers. Many people, however, want to supplement the income received from these sources with savings accumulated during their working years. The typical American works for 40 years. If he is to be financially independent after his retirement from active work, he must look ahead to his years of retirement and plan to save money during his productive working years.

Money put away over many, many years in a savings account will grow into a sizeable amount, but such a plan does not take into account inflation. *Inflation* is a rise in prices—or to look at it in another way, it is a decrease in the purchasing value of the dollar. For example, the monthly cost of providing food for a family of four might now be $200. Forty years from now, if inflation continues at its present rate, the cost might be double, or $400. Thus, money put away for retirement purposes might better be invested in some way that closely follows the basic changes in the economy. Inflation and investments will be discussed in Chapter 17.

HOW MONEY GROWS

In the last few pages you have learned that the first point about savings is that when you save a dollar, you are not forever surrendering your right to spend it. The second point is that as soon as you have savings, you have a silent partner working for you. The money works for you by earning interest. A hundred dollars in a savings account that pays 3 percent interest compounded annually will become $180.61 in 20 years. At 4 percent the money will double itself in 18 years. And it is sometimes possible to get a 6 percent return or even more by shrewd investment.

Money deposited in a savings institution grows rapidly because of compound interest. During the first interest period, interest is paid only on the amount deposited, but during the second period, interest is paid also on the interest earned during the first period. Thus, in every succeeding period the amount of money in the bank—called the *principal*—will be greater, growing slowly at first but more rapidly later.

To see how money grows when interest is compounded, let us consider the table illustrated below, which shows the growth of savings of $100 on which interest is compounded annually at 5 percent. During

Year	Principal During Year	Interest Earned (5% of principal)	Principal at End of Year
1	$100.00	$ 5.00	$105.00
2	105.00	5.25	110.25
3	110.25	5.51	115.76
4	115.76	5.79	121.55
5	121.55	6.08	127.63
6	127.63	6.38	134.01
7	134.01	6.70	140.71
8	140.71	7.04	147.75
9	147.75	7.38	155.13
10	155.13	7.76	162.89
15	197.99	9.90	207.89
20	252.70	12.63	265.33

the first year, the principal is $100. The interest earned the first year is $100 multiplied by .05 (5 percent), or $5. The $5 is added to the principal, so the principal during the second year is $105. The interest earned the second year is $105 multiplied by .05, or $5.25. Thus the principal during the third year is $5.25 plus $105, or $110.25. Notice that by the twentieth year, the interest earned exceeds $12, which is more than twice the interest earned the first year. And by the end of the twentieth year, the principal has grown from $100 to $265.33.

Now let us see how regularly invested savings will grow. The table below illustrates how much money will be accumulated if, at the end of each half year, $100 is invested at various annual rates of interest compounded semiannually. If you invest $100 at the end of each 6-month period, and if the annual interest of 6 percent is compounded semiannually, you will have $1,146.39 at the end of 5 years. At the end of 6 years, you will have $1,419.20. At the end of 20 years, your fund will have grown to $7,540.13.

| Period | PRINCIPAL | | |
(years)	At 4 Percent	At 6 Percent	At 8 Percent
5	$1,094.97	$1,146.39	$1,200.61
6	1,341.21	1,419.20	1,502.58
7	1,597.39	1,708.63	1,829.19
8	1,863.93	2,015.69	2,182.45
9	2,141.23	2,341.44	2,564.54
10	2,429.74	2,687.04	2,977.81
12	3,042.17	3,442.65	3,908.26
14	3,705.12	4,293.09	4,996.76
16	4,422.70	5,250.28	6,270.15
18	5,199.44	6,327.59	7,759.83
20	6,040.20	7,540.13	9,502.55

THE DISCIPLINE TO SAVE

Deciding where to put one's savings is a problem that consumers must face, of course; but a far bigger problem for most of us is the act of disciplining ourselves sufficiently so that we do in fact begin to save money systematically. We would like to save some money each week or each month, but we so easily find other uses for our money. Think back about our earlier illustration involving a summer vacation. Even though you know you need about $100 for that vacation, putting aside $2 every week may be quite difficult. One week you may want to spend the $2 for a theater ticket. If you save the $2 you must forgo attending a play that many of your friends are going to see. At another time it might be tempting to use the $2 to help buy an article of clothing that you really would like to have.

Families, too, find saving money difficult because there are so many uses for their money. The high cost of raising a family discourages many young married couples from saving at the very time that many of them should be starting a systematic savings program.

Savings must be started early in life. If you do not form a habit of setting aside some of the money you earn, you will find that money has a way of sliding through your fingers. People who have been successful at saving money often say that they owe their success to their resolve to set aside part of their income for savings first and then live on what is left. As money experts often put it, if you think you will pay all your living expenses and all your bills first each month and then save whatever money remains, you are fooling yourself.

A good way to build savings is to set aside a sizable portion of all pay raises or other increases in income. Some young families split all pay increases: half of the increase goes into a savings account, and the remaining half is added to the funds available for immediate spending. In any case, to be successful at saving, most persons have to divert the money at its source. If you do not have the money, you cannot spend it. Two ways in which money can be saved by making certain that it is not easily available for immediate spending are discussed in the following paragraphs.

Courtesy Jeremiah Beam

It is more important to develop the habit of saving regularly than to try to save large amounts occasionally.

PAYROLL DEDUCTIONS Many business firms encourage employees to save by offering plans that permit payroll deductions. The employer is authorized to transfer a set amount from each paycheck to a savings fund, just as is done for income tax and social security deductions. The deduction may be put in a savings account in a bank or in a savings and loan association. Or the money may be used to buy United States savings bonds. If the company has a credit union, the money may be placed in this type of savings account.

AUTOMATIC DEDUCTIONS FROM CHECKING ACCOUNTS Another way to save systematically is to have your bank transfer each month a stipulated amount from your checking account to a savings account. Some employers will send payroll checks directly to the worker's bank for deposit in his checking account. When this is done, it is easy to take the second step. The only action this step entails is to ask the bank to transfer part of the money to a savings account.

SAVINGS INSTITUTIONS

Savings should be placed in an institution where the money will produce financial returns for the saver and economic growth for society. But how does a person go about choosing such an institution? In making a choice, he should consider four important factors.

1. Safety. The money should be as secure as possible against loss through economic trouble or criminal action. The degree of safety depends on how the savings institutions are regulated and insured and in some cases on how they invest their assets.
2. Liquidity. *Liquidity* is a business term that refers to the ease and speed with which an investor can get his cash when he wants it. In some cases, invested money can be readily liquidated—that is, turned into cash. In other cases, it might be necessary to wait a number of days, or even months, to obtain cash for the amount invested.
3. Earnings. Earnings must be satisfactory. One of the major reasons for placing money in a savings institution is to earn interest. If you want safety and liquidity, however, you have to sacrifice some earnings. Generally, the higher the rate of interest promised, the greater the risk.
4. Purpose. The *purpose* for which a person is saving money should affect his choice of a savings institution. If he were saving to buy a $500 television set in two or three months, there

would not be enough time for his savings to earn much interest. All he would really need would be a safe place to keep his money. On the other hand, if he were saving money to buy a house in three or four years, his money could earn valuable interest for him as it accumulated.

When sizable amounts of money are involved, the wise investor will not want to keep all his savings in the same place or in the same form, for there would always be the danger that the failure of any one person or institution would wreck him financially. Fortunately there is a variety of safe and convenient savings institutions, and the investor can put various funds in various suitable places.

Commercial banks

Most consumers deal regularly with commercial banks. Commercial banks provide checking facilities for individuals and businesses; they grant loans; they offer safe-deposit facilities, student-aid programs, and various types of financial advisory services. Most commercial banks offer savings account facilities as well.

Many consumers find it helpful to maintain a checking account. They find it convenient to pay bills by mail, and their canceled checks are a valuable record of payments made. A checking account also provides a safe place for small funds to accumulate—either for spending or investing. But large sums of money should not be left in a checking account for a long period of time, for the money will earn no interest.

In selecting a bank in which to open a savings account, the safety of your money is, of course, of prime importance. But since all banks are closely supervised by state or federal governments, and since individual deposits are insured up to $20,000 in banks that are members of the Federal Deposit Insurance Corporation (FDIC), one bank is frequently as safe as another. Nearly all commercial banks in the United States (97 percent) are insured by the FDIC. You can choose a bank so insured by looking for a displayed metal plaque that announces the bank's membership in the FDIC. If the bank is not covered by federal insurance, it probably is covered by state insurance. If you do not see the FDIC plaque, ask. There is no point in taking a chance.

In the early 1970s, 4 percent was the typical interest rate on regular accounts—those accounts that you can add to or withdraw from at will. On special time-deposit accounts, commercial banks offer slightly higher interest rates. A time deposit is usually made for six months, one year, or longer. The higher interest rate on time deposits is payable only if the funds are left untouched in the account for the full period. Thus, these accounts are not as liquid as regular ones. If you need money in a hurry, liquidity may cost you part of the return expected. Some of the time accounts require withdrawal notice, so you cannot get your money immediately.

Commercial banks offer a great deal of convenience, especially for consumers who want their savings in the same institution as their checking account. Also, persons who want such services as automatic transfer of funds from checking accounts to savings accounts or automatic payroll savings plans will find commercial banks convenient. You may want the services of a large commercial bank that carries huge business accounts, or you may feel more at home in the friendly atmosphere of a small neighborhood bank that handles chiefly personal accounts (possibly a branch of the larger one).

Mutual savings banks

Mutual savings banks specialize in savings accounts and use the deposits mostly to make home mortgage loans and home improvement loans. These institutions are chartered in only 18 states, mostly in the Northeastern part of the United States.

The interest paid on savings in mutual savings banks is slightly higher than in most commercial banks. Government regulations allow mutuals to pay up to 5 percent interest on passbook accounts, making them an attractive place for setting aside savings to be used for emergency funds.

Almost all mutual savings banks have the same type of FDIC insurance as commercial banks, so the principal considerations in choosing one are generally its convenience and suitability to your purposes. Ordinarily, funds may be withdrawn from mutual savings banks without notice, but in times of crises an advance notice of one to three months could be required. The period varies from state to state.

Savings and loan associations

Savings and loan associations are sometimes known as building and loan associations or as savings associations. These institutions are associations of people who pool funds and lend money to people who wish to buy or build a home. They do not perform the usual banking functions.

Most savings and loan associations operate as mutual associations, and in this respect they are much like mutual savings banks. The money entrusted to these associations earns dividends. The rate of dividend payment tends to be stable in large communities, and competition among savings and loan associations has resulted in fairly uniform dividend payments. A few associations are organized as business corporations, with the owners sharing profits in the form of dividends and the savers receiving their interest at a specified rate. The interest rates depend on overall earnings and vary from one association to another and from time to time. In the early 1970s, the general range of association rates was from 4.75 to 5.25 percent.

Most savings and loan association accounts are insured up to $20,000 by the Federal Savings and Loan Insurance Corporation (FSLIC) in the same manner in which FDIC insures banks. Those not insured by FSLIC may have state agency or private insurance.

As in the case of banks, savings and loan associations can require depositors to give advance notice before withdrawing savings, but there is usually no delay in withdrawing money. For saving money, these institutions are nearly as convenient as commercial banks, although there are not as many of them and they lack commercial bank services. For example, they do not offer checking accounts, so it is not possible to have automatic transfer of funds to savings accounts.

Credit unions

A credit union is a nonprofit organization owned by its members. The membership is limited to people with some common bond or interest, such as employment in the same business firm. Other common bonds might be membership in a church, a club, a fraternal association, or a labor union. By saving collectively and systematically, the members create a source of low-cost credit for themselves and their families.

In the early 1970s, about 24,000 credit unions in the United States claimed more than 24 million members. Credit unions range in size from small ones with fewer than 100 members to large ones such as Navy Federal, an organization with more than 190,000 members and $200 million in assets. More than half of the credit unions are chartered and supervised under federal law. State laws govern the credit unions not federally chartered.

Federally chartered credit unions cannot pay more than 6 percent interest on savings. Actually, the savings are known as "shares," and the interest paid is referred to as a "dividend." In 1971, the typical dividend rate on credit union shares was between 5 and 6 percent. However, some of the large state-chartered credit unions have paid interest rates as high as $8\frac{1}{2}$ percent.

For some time, credit unions were the only savings institutions that did not have insurance on accounts through the federal government. As you read earlier in this chapter, banks have insurance through FDIC, and savings and loan associations have insurance through FSLIC. In 1970, Congress enacted a mandatory share (members' savings) insurance law for credit unions with federal charters. Members' savings are now insured up to $20,000. Some states have enacted laws either making it possible for state-chartered credit unions to get federal insurance or requiring that they have insurance from a state-operated program.

UNITED STATES SAVINGS BONDS

Many families in the nation buy United States savings bonds—at the beginning of the 1970s, more than $50 billion worth of these securities were outstanding. Some persons are attracted to government savings bonds because of appeals to patriotism, but there are other sound reasons for investing money in this way. Some of these reasons are listed below.

1. Savings bonds are considered to be an extremely safe investment because they are backed by the credit of the United States government.
2. Savings bonds can be quickly and easily converted into cash when cash is needed. They can always be redeemed at a stated value on demand two months from the date they are issued. When these bonds are cashed in early, however, the interest earned is less than when they are held to maturity.
3. The interest on savings bonds is not subject to state or local income tax or to personal property taxes. They are subject to federal income tax, however.
4. If savings bonds are lost, stolen, or destroyed, they can be replaced without cost.
5. Savings bonds are easy and convenient to buy. Neighborhood banks sell them, post offices sell them, and many employers make it possible for workers to buy savings bonds through payroll savings plans.

The federal government is an extremely complex organization with complex activities. The money used to finance these activities comes, of course, from various taxes collected from individuals and business institutions. Sometimes, however, the tax receipts are insufficient to finance the programs of the government. When this happens, the

Federal projects such as bridges require a great deal of money. Some of this money is obtained by selling savings bonds.

Courtesy Engineering News-Record / McGraw-Hill

government must borrow money. Much of this money is borrowed from commercial banks and other financial institutions, but a sizable amount is also borrowed directly from individuals by issuing savings bonds. When consumers save money by investing in United States savings bonds, they are also lending money to the federal government.

Currently, only two types of savings bonds are being sold: Series E and Series H.

Series E bonds

Series E bonds are known as "discount bonds." The financial return to the holder is the difference between what he pays for the bond and what he receives when he cashes the bond. The bonds may be redeemed for cash at any time after they are two months old, but unless they are held for more than six months, the holder gets only the amount he paid for the bond. The period of time the bonds must be held before they mature has changed over the years. In the early 1970s, they had to be held five years and ten months from their date of issue. The following table shows the amount the buyer pays and the amount he receives at maturity for various denominations of Series E bonds.

Cost	Maturity Value
$ 18.75	$ 25
37.50	50
75.00	100
150.00	200
375.00	500
750.00	1,000

The difference between the amount paid for the bond and the amount received for it at maturity is, of course, the interest earned. The interest rate for bonds held to maturity is now $5\frac{1}{2}$ percent. Thus, if you purchased a bond for $75 now and held it for 5 years and 10 months, you would receive $100 upon redeeming the bond. If you should redeem the bond before the 5 years and 10 months have elapsed, you would receive less than $5\frac{1}{2}$ percent interest.

No Series E or Series H bonds have yet been retired because of age. The old bonds still being held have had their original maturity extended, and their current interest rate is $5\frac{1}{2}$ percent. In 1971, the first $18.75 Series E bonds were 30 years old and were worth about $50, twice their original face value.

Series H bonds

The other type of United States savings bond now being sold is known as the Series H bond. This series is sold in denominations of $500, $1,000, $5,000, and $10,000. The main difference between the Series H bond and the Series E bond is that the interest on the purchase price of a Series H bond is paid every six months by check, while the interest on a Series E bond accrues and is paid to the purchaser when the bond is redeemed. If you purchased a $500 Series E bond you would pay $375 and then redeem it for $500 after 5 years and 10 months. If you purchased a $500 Series H bond, you would pay $500 and then receive a check for the interest from the government every six months. The maturity date on Series H bonds is ten years from the date of purchase, and the interest checks now vary to provide an investment yield of about $5\frac{1}{2}$ percent per year if the bond is held to maturity. The Series H bond may be redeemed at any time by giving notice one calendar month in advance.

Checking your reading

1. What is meant by these two statements?
   a. When you save a dollar, you do not forever surrender your right to spend it.
   b. As soon as you have savings, you have a silent partner working for you.
2. Why should an individual or a family establish an emergency fund? How much should be in the emergency fund?
3. In what two ways does a consumer gain when he saves money so that he can pay cash for expensive purchases?
4. Define the term "inflation."
5. Explain how compound interest works.
6. Why is it important to start to save money early in life?

7. List and discuss the four factors that a person should investigate when he chooses an institution in which to save his money.

8. How are deposits in most commercial banks insured and for how much?

9. What is the name of the federal organization that insures most savings and loan associations?

10. Who may join a credit union? For what purposes do people join credit unions?

11. Give five reasons for investing money in United States savings bonds.

Consumer problems and projects

1. Assume that you spend $5.75 each week for between-meal snacks. You have decided to reduce this amount to $2 a week and save the difference.

   a. How much will you save in a half year? A whole year?

   b. Discuss whether or not this decision is a wise one.

2. Assume that you have deposited $1,500 in a savings institution that pays interest at the rate of 5 percent compounded annually.

   a. What amount of interest will be earned the first year? The second year? The third year?

   b. What will be the value of the principal at the end of the first year? The second year? The third year?

   c. What is the total amount of interest earned during the 3-year period?

3. If $3,200 is invested at 5 percent compounded annually, how much will the principal be at the end of 20 years? (You may use the table on page 268.)

4. If you invest $1,200 at the end of every six months during a ten-year period, and if the interest is compounded semiannually at 4 percent a year, how much will your fund be worth at the end of ten years? (You may use the table shown on page 269.)

5. Make a comparison chart listing the advantages and disadvantages of the various kinds of institutions in which you can invest your savings. This chart can guide you in making your savings plans for the future.

6. In addition to the commercial banks and savings banks discussed in this chapter, there are other types of banks that serve specific purposes: investment banks, industrial banks, and trust companies. Find out all you can about these types of banks, and report your findings to the class.

7. List as many services as you can that banks offer to their depositors. Find out how many in your class make use of each of these services.

8. Visit your local bank. Plan in advance the things you are going to look for and the questions you would like to have answered, such as: Is the bank safe? How can you tell? What facilities and services are offered to depositors? If there are several types of banks in your community, you may wish to send a committee to each and compare the reports.

Chapter

Investment programs

How much will money saved now be worth in the future? Inflation, the decline in the purchasing value of our dollars, must be considered by any consumer who is saving money for the future. For example, in 1940 a retirement income of $200 a month might have seemed quite adequate. But to live on the same scale in 1971, a monthly income of about $500 would have been necessary. Inflation reduced the value of the 1940 dollar to about 40 cents in 1971.

THE EFFECT OF INFLATION

What will future inflation be? No one can predict the rate of future inflation, of course, but a small increase ($1\frac{1}{2}$ to 3 percent a year) is almost certain. Nearly every advanced, industrial nation of the world experiences some inflation. It is the price paid for continual growth and prosperity. Because of inflation, special care needs to be exercised to protect the purchasing power of long-term savings.

During 1970, prices rose roughly $5\frac{1}{2}$ percent. Thus, interest on savings in 1970 had to be high enough to give a return after taxes of $5\frac{1}{2}$ percent. If interest payments were not that high, investors did not stay even that year. Of course, 1970 was not a typical year. Inflation slowed considerably in 1971 as a result of President Nixon's wage and price freeze policy during the later months of the year. The reason for mentioning inflation at this point is to show why special importance should be placed on protecting long-term savings from shrinkage due to future inflation.

Some savings methods are highly vulnerable to inflation, while others are less so. The savings methods discussed in Chapter 16 are best suited for money set aside for emergency funds, for large recurring expenses, and for purchases of such expensive items as household appliances and automobiles. Money is always needed for these purposes, and it should be placed where it is easily available. When saving money for long-term purposes, such as retirement, the money should be invested with the thought of protecting it from inflation.

INVESTING IN SECURITIES

Buying securities is a way in which some persons invest the cash reserves they have accumulated. An adequate amount of money should be available in an emergency fund, and such important expenses as life insurance premiums should be planned for before one considers investing in securities.

When you are ready to invest, you should investigate the two major kinds of securities: bonds and stocks. Let us consider some of the differences between these types of securities.

Bonds

When you buy bonds issued by a corporation or by a government, you are lending money to that corporation or government. Thus, by buying bonds, you become a creditor. The organization that issues bonds acknowledges that it owes the holders a certain sum of money and pledges to repay the sum on a certain date and under certain conditions; it also pledges to pay a certain amount of interest on specified dates.

Bonds are issued by many different types of corporations and by various political subdivisions, such as school districts, cities, and states. By buying bonds, you are simply lending your money to the issuer of the bonds; but the many different types of bonds, or lending agreements, and the vast difference in the financial soundness of the organizations offering bonds for sale make the wise buying of bonds difficult.

Corporation stock

A stock certificate represents a share in the ownership of a corporation. If you purchase stock issued by the XYZ Corporation, you become a part owner of that corporation. By contrast, if you purchase bonds issued by the XYZ Corporation, you are lending money to the corporation and you become its creditor. Unlike bonds, stocks are not sold by governmental bodies. They are sold only by business firms that are organized as corporations. The corporation issuing stocks may be a huge firm with millions of dollars in assets, or it may be a small firm with only a few hundred dollars in assets.

Since stockholders are the owners of the corporation, they share in its profits and losses. Their stock may rise or fall in value from day to day as the corporation's assets or potentiality for profit increases or decreases. Stockholders share in the profits of the business by receiving dividends.

Courtesy Union Carbide Corp.

Many companies issue stock in order to raise funds for capital investments.

Courtesy Engineering News-Record/McGraw-Hill

There are so many different kinds of stocks in existence that it is often difficult to distinguish between the various grades. An investor should always carefully study the provisions governing a stock in order to determine the rights and obligations of the stockholders.

COMMON STOCK When just one kind of stock is issued by a corporation, it is usually known as *common stock*. The owners of common stock elect the directors of the corporation, who are responsible for formulating company policy and for appointing the officers who will administer the affairs of the firm. Common stock does not carry a fixed dividend; that is, the amount paid periodically to each stockholder is not set in advance. If corporate profits are small, dividend rates decline or are nonexistent. If profits increase, the dividend rates usually increase also. However, even though the directors of a corporation usually declare a dividend for holders of common stock when profits are relatively high, they are not obligated to do so. They may decide instead to hold the money for future use or to invest it in research or capital goods. You can see then that investing in common stocks can be a risky venture. A bondholder can usually count on a fixed interest rate, but a holder of common stock is promised no specific return on his investment. If a company's financial situation becomes poor and dividends are not distributed, the value of the stock (the amount that buyers are willing to pay for it) will decline. In extreme cases, a company can go bankrupt and its common stock become worthless.

PREFERRED STOCK In addition to common stock, many corporations also issue *preferred stock*. The holders of preferred stock do not ordinarily have a right to vote in the election of directors of the corporation, but holding this type of stock has many advantages. The dividend on preferred stock is usually set at a definite amount per share per year, and the owners of preferred stock receive their stipulated and fixed share of the profits before the holders of common stock receive their dividends. In the event that the corporation discontinues business and the assets of the corporation are sold, the holders of preferred stock will be paid before the holders of common stock.

There are several types of preferred stock, and a buyer should always understand the provisions of the particular stock he buys. For example, some preferred stock dividends are *cumulative;* that is, any dividends for previous years that have not been paid must be paid in full before the corporation can pay dividends on its common stock. On the other hand, the preferred stock dividends can be *noncumulative.* In this case, if the corporation fails to earn a profit for a few years, dividends may not be paid. When dividends are again paid, the holders of preferred stock are paid first, but they do not receive dividends for the years during which no dividends were declared.

Some preferred stocks are *participating;* that is, holders of this type of stock share in any earnings that the company makes in excess of the stated rate of dividend. If a corporation still has surplus earnings available to distribute as dividends after paying the holders of preferred stock the regular dividend and the holders of common stock a certain specified dividend, these earnings will be shared by the holders of common stock and participating preferred stock.

OPERATION OF THE STOCK MARKET

Knowing the differences between the various kinds of securities is the first step in understanding the securities market. An investor should also have an understanding of the methods by which stock values are determined and how buyers and sellers make sales transactions.

Companies issue stock in order to raise money for operations. The company sets a specific price on the stock when it is first offered for sale, but once the stock has been sold to the public, the price is no longer fixed by the company. It is then determined by the price the buyers are willing to pay and the price for which the stockholders are willing to sell.

If a particular stock is considered by many people to be overpriced at a certain time, many stockholders may want to sell the stock and invest in other securities. When this happens, the price of the stock usually drops. On the other hand, if a stock is considered to be a good buy (perhaps because it appears that the company will have an especially bright future), the price of the stock will probably rise, for the demand for the stock will enable the owners to ask and to receive higher prices. So the price of a security at any particular time reflects nothing more than the combined opinions of buyers and sellers about the value of that security.

Investors can follow the daily prices of their securities by consulting almost any major newspaper. On the financial pages, they will find listings of the current prices paid for all the more popular stocks traded. Sometimes stock prices fluctuate only slightly, say by an eighth or a quarter of a point, which means an eighth or a quarter of a dollar. At other times, the prices of certain stocks fluctuate sharply during a day—by several points, or by many dollars.

Courtesy Merrill Lynch, Pierce, Fenner & Smith Inc.

The stock of large and small corporations is traded on stock exchanges. The stock exchanges are located in major cities throughout the country.

Stock exchanges

There are thousands of different stocks and bonds, but the ones that are bought and sold most frequently are those traded on the large exchanges. The largest organized exchange in the United States is the New York Stock Exchange. The American Stock Exchange, another large exchange, is also located in New York. In addition, regional exchanges are scattered throughout the country.

Buying and selling stocks on a security exchange is accomplished by means of the auction method. Someone may offer a stock for sale at a certain price; someone else may bid for the same stock at a different price. When a buyer and seller agree on a price, a sale is made. In financial circles, the agents who act as middlemen for investors who want to buy or sell securities are called *brokers*. Brokers negotiate purchases and sales for their clients, and for this service they charge a commission that is based on the amount of the transaction. The actual buying and selling on the New York Stock Exchange is done by brokers who have bought memberships (commonly called "seats"). The members of the New York Stock Exchange represent brokerage firms located throughout the country.

The current prices of the more popular securities traded are listed in most daily newspapers. A section of a stock listing is shown on page 285. Dollar signs are omitted, and the fractions shown represent parts of a dollar.

- The figures immediately following the name of the stock show the amount of the current annual dividend paid per share. For example, Minnesota Mining and Manufacturing Company (abbreviated Minn MM) is expected to pay $1.85 a share to its stockholders during the year.
- The column to the right of the name of the stock shows the number of shares of that stock sold during the day. Amounts are listed in hundreds. The number of shares of Minnesota Mining and Manufacturing stock sold during that day was 21,300.
- The next three columns show the highest price, the lowest price, and the closing price paid for a share of stock during the day. During the day the price of a share of Minnesota Mining and Manufacturing stock fluctuated from a high of $124.75 to a low of $122.50. The last buyer of the day paid $124.75 (the closing price).
- The amount in the column at the extreme right shows the difference between the final price shown and the final price of the preceding day. A plus sign means the stock rose in price by that amount since the preceding day. A minus sign indicates a drop in price. Buyers paid $2.75 more for a share of Minnesota Mining and Manufacturing stock on the day of the quotation than buyers had paid on the preceding day.

	Sales (hds.)	High	Low	Close	Net Chg.
IntIndA pf	46	9 1/8	8 3/8	9 1/8	+ 1/2
IntMiner .05g	99	15 1/4	14 7/8	15 1/4	+ 1/2
Int Mng	30	9 1/8	8 1/2	8 1/2	
IntMultif 1.20	17	23 1/8	22 5/8	22 3/4	+ 1/8
Int Nickel 1	555	29	28 1/2	28 3/4	− 1/8
Int Pap 1.50	182	32 1/2	31 3/8	32 1/8	+ 5/8
Int Pap pf 4	z100	57	57	57	
Int Rectifier	46	7 7/8	7 1/2	7 5/8	+ 1/4
Int T&T 1.15	1335	55 1/2	53 3/4	54 3/4	+1 1/2
IntT&T pfD 4	z200	182 3/4	182 3/4	182 3/4	+15 1/2
IntT&T pfE 4	z80	164 7/8	164 7/8	164 7/8	+2 1/8
IntT&T pfF 4	1	151	151	151	+7 3/4
IntT&T pfH 4	26	101	97	100	+4
IT&T pfI 4.50	41	96	93	96	+3
IntT&T pfJ 4	12	95	92	95	+4
IntT&T pfK4	151	92 1/2	89	92	+3 1/2
InTT pfL 5.50	z30	73	73	73	
IT&TpfN 2.25	220	69 3/8	67	68 1/2	+2 1/4
IntT&T pfO 5	62	91	87 1/2	91	+4 1/2
Int Util 1.40	399	40 3/4	38 3/4	40	+1 3/8
Int Util A	10	46 3/4	45	46 1/2	+1 3/4
Interpace 1	50	30 5/8	29 1/2	30 5/8	+1 3/8
Interpce pf 5	1	89	89	89	+2
IntpbGp .20g	188	19 1/8	18 1/4	19 1/8	+ 3/4
IntsBrand .96	7	18 3/8	17 7/8	18 3/8	+ 3/4
IntersPw 1.28	16	17 7/8	17 5/8	17 5/8	− 1/4
Interst Strs	257	10 1/2	10 1/8	10 3/8	+ 3/8
Iowa Beef	39	19 7/8	19 1/8	19 7/8	+ 3/4
Iowa El 1.30	29	18 3/4	18 1/2	18 5/8	+ 1/8
IowaIlGs 1.38	18	18 3/4	18 1/2	18 3/4	+ 1/4
IowaPow 1.60	51	23	22 5/8	22 7/8	
IowaPSv 1.40	11	21 1/4	20 7/8	21 1/8	+ 3/8
Ipco Hos 34d	122	13 1/2	12 5/8	13	
ITE Imp .60	208	32 3/4	32 1/2	32 3/4	+ 1/4
Itek Corp	316	36 3/4	34 7/8	34 7/8	− 1/8
ITT Sv pf4.50	10	133 1/4	130 1/2	133 1/4	+6 1/4
— J—J —					
Jaeger .15p	5	7	6 7/8	7	..
JamesF .32	10	36 1/2	36	36 1/2	+ 1/2
Jantzen .60	41	16	15 1/2	16	+ 3/8
JapnFd 1.66g	249	10 1/8	9 7/8	10 1/8	+ 3/8
JpnF fn1.66g	20	9	9	9	
JeffnPilot .88	38	47 1/2	46 5/8	47 1/4	+ 1/4

	Sales (hds.)	High	Low	Close	Net Chg.
MGIC Inv .20	121	77 3/8	76 1/4	77 3/8	+1 1/8
Mich Gs Ut 1	8	15	14 3/4	15	...
Mich Tube 1	8	13 1/4	13	13	..
Microdot .40g	49	16 7/8	16 1/4	16 1/4	− 3/8
MidContT .92	154	17	16 1/2	16 3/4	− 1/4
MidSUtil 1.02	40	22 3/4	22 5/8	22 5/8	...
Midld R 1.40	67	16	15 5/8	15 3/4	− 1/4
Midwst Oil 3	3	109 3/4	108	109 3/4	+5 1/4
MilesLbs 1.20	279	41 5/8	38 1/4	41 3/8	+3 3/8
Milt Brad .60	50	41 1/8	39 7/8	41 1/8	+1 1/4
MinnMM 1.85	213	124 3/4	122 1/2	124 3/4	+2 3/4
MinnPLt 1.30	6	21 5/8	21 1/2	21 1/2	− 1/4
MissnCp 2.40	z2500	135	125	128	+3
MissnEqu .20	108	26	24 1/2	25 7/8	+2
MissRiv .20d	48	15	15	15	
MoPac A 5	1	71 3/4	71 3/4	71 3/4	+ 1/4
MP Cem 1.60	13	26 1/4	26	26 1/8	− 3/8
MoPubS .80g	21	18	17 5/8	18	+ 1/4
MobilOil 2.60	304	50 1/2	49 3/4	50	+ 1/8
Mohas 1.10	152	40 1/4	39 1/2	40	+ 5/8
Mohwk Data	367	17 3/4	16 5/8	17 1/8	+ 1/8
Mohk Rub 1b	14	21 1/4	20 3/4	21 1/4	+ 1/2
Molybden	109	11 1/2	10 5/8	11 1/8	...
Molyb pf2.50	5	27 3/4	27 3/8	27 3/8	+ 1/8
Monarch .40	7	17 1/8	17	17	− 1/8
Monogm Ind	106	11 1/4	10 1/2	11 1/8	+ 5/8
Monroe Equp	333	34 1/2	32 3/4	34 1/8	+1 1/8
Monsant 1.80	338	47	45 1/2	46 1/4	+ 7/8
MontDUt 1.88	21	31 3/8	31	31	− 1/8
Mont Pw 1.68	44	28 5/8	27 7/8	28 3/8	+ 1/2
MONY 1.01a	316	13 1/2	13 1/8	13 1/4	
Moor McCor	12	11 5/8	11	11 3/8	+ 3/8
MorganJ 2.72	89	71 7/8	69 5/8	71 7/8	+2 1/4
Morse Sh .75	71	16 1/2	16 1/4	16 3/8	+ 1/4
MtgTrA 2.19a	94	25	24 1/4	24 5/8	+ 1/8
MorNor .80	207	28	27	28	+ 7/8
Motorola .60	163	77 3/4	75 1/2	76 5/8	+ 7/8
MtFuel S 1.80	34	35 7/8	35 5/8	35 5/8	− 1/8
MtStaTT 1.36	21	22 7/8	22 1/4	22 1/4	− 1/2
MSL Ind .40	17	13 1/2	13 1/8	13 1/2	+ 3/8
Munford .24	148	17 7/8	16	17 1/8	+1 1/4
Munfrd pf.40	38	10 1/2	9 3/4	10	+ 1/2
Munsingwr 1	16	30	29 1/4	30	+1

By checking daily newspaper listings, the consumer can keep abreast of stock activity and prices.

Unlisted securities

Some securities are not listed on any exchange. These stocks and bonds, which are known as *unlisted securities*, may be bought and sold through individual brokers or, in some cases, may be traded on an exchange without having been accepted for formal listing. When securities are sold through brokers, the transactions are popularly called "over-the-counter" transactions. Government and municipal bonds are traded in this way, and so are the stocks of most banks and insurance companies. Generally, however, unlisted securities are those of small companies that are likely to be known better locally than nationally. Because unlisted securities are traded less frequently, it is sometimes difficult to determine the price at which they can be sold. Partly for this reason, over-the-counter stocks are considered a less conservative investment than listed stocks.

Investment clubs

During the past couple of decades, investment clubs have become popular throughout the country. An *investment club* is simply a small group of people who band together to learn about the stock market and invest a small amount of money periodically. A typical club might have 15 members who each put $20 a month into a fund that is used to buy stocks. Many brokers are glad to help organize investment clubs and to supply their members with regular reports on companies and market conditions in general. However, the main purpose of an investment club is to have its members learn about stocks by taking an active part in their selection. Members are not supposed to depend on a broker for every decision.

Investment companies

For persons who want to invest in the stock market but have neither the time nor the experience to keep informed about their holdings, investment companies might be the answer. An *investment company* sells its shares to investors and then uses the money received from the sale to buy the securities of other companies. An investment company obtains its income from the dividends paid on the securities it has purchased and from the profit it receives when it sells certain securities that have increased in value. The income thus earned by the investment company is then passed on to people who own shares in the investment company.

By now you realize that investing in the stock market involves many risks. Ideally, the investor guards against these risks by spreading his

The wise investor checks the performance of his investments by regularly reading the financial section of his daily newspaper.

Editorial Photocolor Archives, Inc.

investments among different kinds of industries and geographic areas. If an investor buys a dozen different securities, and one proves to be bad, he will not lose his whole investment. He may even still make a profit. Spreading the risk in this way is known as *diversification*.

It is difficult, however, for persons with relatively small amounts of money to invest to achieve diversification on their own. The investment company offers this type of investor the advantage of diversification. If the securities selected by the investment company increase in value, the stockholders make money; if they decrease in value, the stockholders lose money. Buying shares in an investment company, then, does not eliminate risks. But because the investments are spread over a number of different stocks and bonds carefully selected by investment experts, the risks are greatly reduced. Furthermore, securities purchased by an investment company are reviewed constantly by a team of experts, who buy and sell as changing values and potentials present opportunities for profit. There are two kinds of investment companies: closed-end and open-end (or mutual funds).

CLOSED-END INVESTMENT COMPANIES A closed-end investment company is a corporation that invests in the securities of other companies. *Closed-end* companies issue only a limited number of shares when they are formed and usually no more. It is for this reason that they are called "closed-end" companies. Furthermore, closed-end companies do not agree to buy back their shares. When you want to sell, you have to find a buyer, just as you do when selling shares of Continental Oil or Chrysler. The shares of the most active closed-end companies are traded on the stock exchanges, and you pay a commission computed in the same way that your commission would be figured in buying shares of any industrial corporation. These commissions range from 6 percent of the total amount of money involved down to about 1 percent on larger transactions.

MUTUAL FUNDS An investment company that is organized to issue and sell new shares at any time so that the number of outstanding shares is always changing is an *open-end* company. These companies are known popularly as "mutual funds." In addition to creating and selling new shares in itself whenever there is a market for them, the open-end company also buys back and retires shares whenever a shareholder wants to cash them in.

Mutual funds have experienced phenomenal growth over the past few decades, and especially during the 1960s. At the end of the decade there were more than 600 funds in existence, and their total assets totaled about $55 billion. Mutual funds can be bought through brokerage offices or through selling organizations set up to handle one or more funds. Commission costs vary, from as high as 8½ to 9 percent of the total cost of the shares for small investments to about half that rate or less for especially large purchases. This sales commission is known as a "load charge." The load charge varies with the mutual fund.

Mutual funds that charge commissions are known as "load funds." The few mutual funds that do not charge a sales commission are known as "no-load funds." When a prospective investor is interested in a load fund, a salesman is typically quite available and eager to explain the mutual fund with charts, figures, and other information to assist you in understanding the investment. This is not so with no-load funds. To acquire shares in a no-load fund you have to write to the fund for a *prospectus*, information that government regulations require the fund to supply before an investment can be made. Then, if you decide to buy, you mail your check. The managers of both load funds and no-load funds receive a management fee for handling the investor's money—the fee is commonly one-half of 1 percent a year or less.

No-load funds have become more popular recently. Experience has shown that among both load funds and no-load funds, there has been a great deal of variation in performance. Certainly no one should pick a mutual fund simply because it does not charge a sales commission. A well-managed load fund is a better buy for an investor than a no-load fund with consistently poor performance.

Mutual funds exist for every type of investment objective. Following are the main categories of funds.

- Growth funds. The objective of growth funds is to achieve an increase in the value of the shares and the eventual growth in income. Growth fund assets are usually invested in common stock, especially that of fast-growing industries such as chemicals and electronics. For young people who are more interested in capital gains than immediate income, this type of mutual fund would be attractive.
- Balanced funds. Investments are divided among common stock, preferred stock, and bonds when the purpose of the mutual fund is to provide a balance between growth and income. When prices in the market are rising, balanced funds will not show the increase in value of a growth fund.
- Income funds. The investments of this type of mutual fund are mostly in securities that provide a high yield, such as utilities and rails. The main purpose of these mutual funds is to provide steady dividend income. For people who are approaching retirement and are interested in a steady source of income, this type of fund would be attractive.

Different systems of buying mutual funds also are available. Following are two general methods.

- Open account. Under some of these plans, the investor can buy as many or as few shares as he wishes whenever he wishes. Other plans provide that the investor buy shares at regular intervals, but the number bought can vary. The dividends may be reinvested automatically, and the agreement to make regular purchases can be terminated at any time the investor wishes. No requirement exists that the investor make a fixed number of purchases.
- Contractual plan. A contractual plan requires that the buyer sign a contract that binds him to make an investment regularly for a specified period of time. The investor is committing himself to make regular payments that over time add up to an investment of a sizable amount of money. The investor can, of course, drop out of the plan at any time he wants, but if he stops making payments, he loses money because of the way in

which the loading charge, or sales commission, is figured. The contractual plan may provide for a loading charge of 9 percent of the total investment, and as much as half of the loading charge may be deducted from the money the investor pays in during the first year of the plan. If the investor discontinues the plan during the first few years, he may receive less than he had paid in because of the heavy commission paid during the early part of the period.

Small investors looking for professional management of their money may decide to buy shares of a mutual fund or a closed-end investment company. Such an investment represents a good way to achieve the kind of diversified risk that might be difficult to reproduce in straight purchases of securities. Generally, an investor should look at the record of the fund during the past 10 years. If it is above average, the management has probably done a good job. Some funds show spectacular profits over a period of a few years, but over a longer period of time they might not show up so well. Stockbrokers and many libraries have copies of *Investment Companies,* an annual compilation of comparative data published by Wiesenberger Services, Inc., 5 Hanover Square, New York, New York 10004. This publication gives information about the performances of mutual funds and closed-end investment companies.

Checking your reading

1. What is meant by inflation?
2. Why are persons who buy bonds considered creditors?
3. What are the two main differences between common stock and preferred stock?
4. What does the term "participating" mean when it refers to preferred-stock dividends?
5. Once the stock of a corporation has been sold to the public, how is the price of the stock determined?
6. Where can you find a listing of the current prices paid for popular stocks?
7. What are over-the-counter securities transactions?
8. How do investment clubs operate?
9. What is the main purpose of an investment club?
10. What is meant by the term "diversification" as it is used in this chapter?
11. Explain the difference between closed-end and open-end investment companies.

12. What is the difference between mutual funds known as "load funds" and mutual funds known as "no-load funds"?

13. Explain how an investor can lose money by dropping out of a contractual plan for buying mutual funds.

Consumer problems and projects

1. Describe how stocks are bought and sold on a security exchange.

2. In addition to the financial terms introduced in this chapter, there are many other important terms used in the field of investments. Use the dictionary and books on investments to help you define the following words.

put	rights	arbitrage	book value
call	warrant	hedge	margin

3. Check a newspaper daily for the closing prices of six common stocks. Make a graph showing their closing prices for a four-week period.

4. From a local broker and from outside reading sources, secure the details of the monthly investment plan sponsored by the New York Stock Exchange. Report your findings to the class.

5. James Holmes is twenty-five years old. He has been married for three years and has one child. His income is about average for a person his age. Two years ago, he purchased a house, taking out a mortgage that will be paid up in 23 years. Mr. Holmes's life is insured for $15,000. He has just made his last payment on his two-year-old car. The Holmes's budget shows that they can now save $100 a month. Mr. Holmes is considering investing the $100 in corporate stocks—perhaps using a monthly investment plan. Mrs. Holmes thinks he should place the monthly savings in a savings account. What do you recommend? Why?

6. Imagine that you have $10,000 to invest and that after you investigate several good companies you select one with a very bright future whose earnings are expected to be high for several years. The return on the preferred stock is good, but before you buy this particular stock, your broker advises you to buy common stock in the same company instead. What reasons might your broker have for this position? If the preferred stock were participating, how would this influence his opinion?

7. A common saying in investment circles is "Don't put all your eggs in one basket." This, of course, means to diversify your holdings and thus avoid the risks involved in putting all your money into one investment. In what sense would you be ignoring this saying if you invested in the common stock of three companies: one a producer of fishing rods, another a producer of outboard motors, and the third a producer of lightweight aluminum boats?

Chapter **18**

Introduction to life insurance

At the beginning of the decade of the 1970s, about 90 percent of all husbands in the United States were insured, and the life insurance owned by families averaged more than $24,000 per insured family. Life insurance in force increases yearly as more Americans purchase larger amounts of life insurance.

Why has life insurance become so popular? Mainly because most people in today's society depend so completely on the money income earned by the family breadwinner. If a husband and father should die prematurely, say at the age of 35, the family may have serious financial difficulties unless life insurance supplies money to help them pay their living expenses during the next several years. The problem has not always been so serious. In earlier times, ties among relatives were much stronger, and during those times a family could look to grandparents, cousins, and other relatives for financial help in the event of the husband's death. Today most families cannot look much beyond their immediate household during financial crises.

THE PURPOSE OF LIFE INSURANCE

In a nationwide survey conducted by the life insurance industry, families gave several reasons why they owned life insurance policies. The reasons given fell into one of two major categories. Life insurance

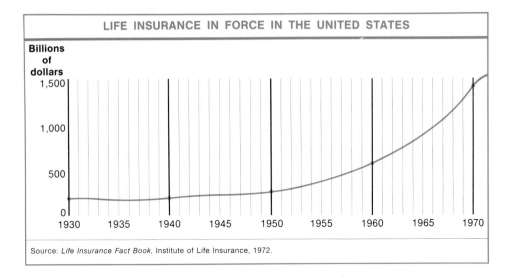

LIFE INSURANCE IN FORCE IN THE UNITED STATES

Billions of dollars

Source: *Life Insurance Fact Book,* Institute of Life Insurance, 1972.

is purchased (1) to provide financial security for dependents after the insured's death and (2) to build up savings.

There are many ways to save money, of course, and saving money through life insurance policies may be a poor way for most people to save. Nevertheless, the life insurance industry advertises savings as a prime purpose of life insurance, and many people believe that saving money by means of life insurance policies is a sound idea.

The main purpose of life insurance is to provide money for persons who are financially dependent on the insured should he die prematurely. Money should be available through life insurance to enable the family to fulfill reasonable financial goals. Viewed in this way, most families are underinsured. The head of a household must face a sobering thought: If he should die, his dependents would be left without their chief source of income. This problem often looms largest during the early years of married life, for at this time children are small and expenses are large. The head of a household, therefore, uses life insurance to create an estate for his family immediately and thereby provide money for them to take care of things such as those discussed in the paragraphs that follow.

Last expenses

Most people want to leave at least enough money to pay for their funeral expenses and for any medical bills resulting from their last illness. Then, too, they should leave enough money to pay other current bills. Possibly many people have sufficient money for this purpose in a savings account, and in that event they need not be concerned about covering this need with life insurance. In any case, needs for immediate cash might be covered by a policy for from $5,000 to $10,000 payable as a lump sum. This amount is not large compared to the total insurance needs of an individual, but it may be an important item to keep in mind when considering life insurance needs.

The home

Families repaying a mortgage on a home can use insurance to cover the amount of the mortgage. Some families may decide that in the event of the breadwinner's death they would move to a smaller house or to rented living quarters. But in the majority of cases, the family would want to continue living in the same house. In this event, an insurance policy large enough to enable the family to pay off the mortgage would be desirable.

Funds for dependents

Most workers are now covered by social security, and the benefits available to widows and children through this government-sponsored program provide a basic family insurance program that is a starting point in figuring life insurance needs. For most families, social security benefits are not sufficient—they provide basic protection that must be supplemented with life insurance.

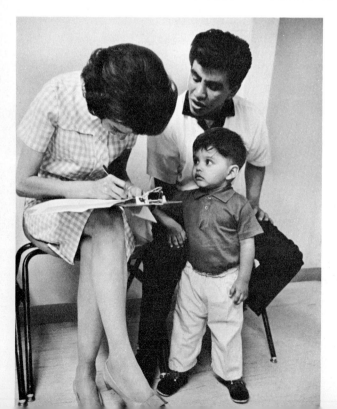

A life insurance agent helps the head of a household select insurance that will provide for his dependents in the event of his death.

If the head of a household dies before his dependents, they will need income during a period of readjustment in which they develop a new way of making a living. In some cases, this income is needed for a relatively long period of time. For example, while children are small, a mother should be able to stay at home or provide good care for her children in some other way and still be able to meet the regular expenses of maintaining a home.

For many persons, especially parents with small children, the long-term support of dependents is the most important purpose of life insurance. Obviously, this type of coverage requires a sizable amount of insurance. In addition to providing for the basic needs of a family, insurance may be wanted for the education of children. If the bread-winner dies prematurely, the remaining family members should expect to fend for themselves to some extent. But many fathers want a fund of money available for the college education of their children.

LIFE INSURANCE NEEDS ARE DIFFICULT TO MEASURE

From what has been said up to this point, you should have concluded that life insurance is extremely important for consumers. Perhaps a few people are wealthy enough to have no real need for life insurance, but most of us who have financial responsibilities to others must assess our life insurance needs and decide what kind of life insurance to buy. Thus, the value of life insurance is indisputable. The important questions are how much and what kind.

When buying insurance to cover property, such as a house or a car, deciding how much to buy is not really very difficult. We can be guided by the replacement value of the house or the car. But life insurance presents a much more complex problem. Nobody has any idea of how long he will live, so nobody knows when his family will need the money from his life insurance. If a father dies at any early age, the period of time during which his dependents will need money for living will be longer, and therefore the total amount of money needed is larger. If the father knew that he would live to the age of 80, he would probably conclude that he really did not need life insurance at all. Later in this chapter, we will examine ways to estimate life insurance needs.

The role of life insurance agents

Most life insurance is sold by salesmen who are usually called agents or field underwriters. The principal task of these agents, according to the life insurance ads, is to help customers or prospective customers estimate the amount of insurance needed. The importance of selecting an agent carefully cannot be overemphasized because of the great importance of life insurance to the security of one's family.

The agent sells a variety of different life insurance packages with a multitude of different names and confusing provisions. The easy thing for a consumer to do is to place implicit trust in the agent and buy the package he recommends. Is this a wise thing for the consumer to do? Or should the consumer become as familiar as possible with the purpose of life insurance and the different forms available so that he is able to do a reasonably good job of judging the merits of agents' suggestions?

Most agents work for commissions, and the commissions vary considerably according to the type of policy. The payments made for insurance policies are called *premiums,* and agents receive as their commission a certain percentage of the premium payments. On some policies the agent may be paid a commission for as long as 10 years, but the percentage declines in the later years, and the first-year commission is far and away the largest that the agent receives. When the agent sells a $10,000 policy that requires large premium payments, he generally earns much more than when he sells a $10,000 policy that requires small premium payments. In fact, the difference in the agent's commission is often four- or fivefold.

Consumers Union reported on a study of life insurance that they conducted in the late 1960s. Consumers Union shoppers approached life insurance agents of five large companies in three different metropolitan areas: one on the East Coast, one on the West Coast, and one in the Midwest. The shoppers did not identify themselves as having a connection with Consumers Union. Thus, 15 agents were asked to recommend a policy for a 38-year-old man with a wife and two children (ages 16 and 8). The shopper (prospective policyholder) indicated that he had a $10,000-a-year income, a $10,000 group life insurance policy through his employer, $3,000 in the bank, and $5,000 ownership in a house; he also indicated that he had mortgage payments and taxes amounting to $1,800 a year. Such a man would be underinsured.

One would think that given the information cited above, the agents would be reasonably uniform in their recommendations for life insurance coverage. The fact is that the agents suggested a variety of policies. According to the report issued by Consumers Union, some agents seemed to base their proposal on the shopper's paycheck rather than on a measurement of his need for protection. The recommendations for additional life insurance coverage given by the 15 agents ranged from $5,000 to $24,145 at annual premiums from $210 to $1,144. Just one of the 15 agents recommended on his own initiative a type of protection that gives the most coverage for the premium dollar.

Selecting just 15 agents at random from among the thousands of agents in the country may not give a completely fair picture of life insurance salesmen, but the experience does indicate the importance of knowing something about life insurance coverage and choosing an agent with care. Considering the great importance of life insurance to the security of a family and the amount of money that will be paid for the insurance protection, consumers should be personally satisfied with the man who will be helping make far-reaching recommendations. You could interview several agents from different companies and ask them to make suggestions for life insurance programs for you. Then you will be able to judge with more discernment both the programs suggested and the agents who present them.

Some life insurance agents use computers to help them recommend insurance programs. Information about a client's needs and obligations is fed into a computer, and within minutes the machine returns an individualized insurance program.

Courtesy Waldron Mahoney, Inc.

DOLLARS FOR FUTURE DELIVERY

$ YOU WANT	$ YOU HAVE	$ YOU NEED	IF YOU DIE BEFORE AGE 65 MONTHLY INCOME – FOR YOUR FAMILY
			a month for the first ___ years and months until your third youngest child is 18. . . . .then
1500.00	1125.72	374.28	1500.00 a month for the next 16 years and 00 months until your second youngest child is 18. . . . .then
1500.00	1125.72	374.28	1500.00 a month for the next 02 years and 00 months until your youngest (or only) child is 18. . . . .
			a month for the next four years until the youngest child is 22.
750.00	375.72	374.28	750.00 a month for the next 11 years and 10 months of the Social Security "blackout" period until your wife is 60 . . . . . .then
			a month for the next ___ years and months of the Social Security "blackout" period until your wife is 60,. . . . .then
750.00	117.00	633.00	117.00 a month for as long thereafter as your wife shall live.
			SPECIAL FUNDS – FOR YOUR FAMILY
			To be immediately available, in cash,
5,000	5,000	0	5,000 to pay the anticipated LAST EXPENSES
24,000	24,000	0	24,000 to pay off the balance of the MORTGAGE.
			To be left on deposit, at interest,
5,000	5,000	0	5,000 subject to withdrawal for EMERGENCIES
20,000	20,000	0	20,000 subject to withdrawal for EDUCATION.
			IF YOU LIVE TO AGE 65 RETIREMENT BENEFITS AVAILABLE TO YOU
1,000.00	302.10	697.90	353.55 a month for as long as you live, plus an additional 78.00 each month, from Social Security to your wife after her age 62

As you probably are quite aware, there are many life insurance agents in most communities. Because the turnover rate among men who go into life insurance sales work is quite high, many life insurance companies are engaged in a continuous program of recruiting agents. Thus, many agents are rank beginners. Other agents, however, may have had years of successful experience. Most agents sell for a single company, but some are brokers for several companies. If an agent adds "C.L.U." after his name, you know he is a Chartered Life Underwriter who has met stringent requirements established by a professional organization known as the American College of Life Underwriters.

THE TWO TYPES OF LIFE INSURANCE

Life insurance is sold under many names. Most companies sell whole life, 20-payment life, life paid up at 65, 20-year endowment, modified life, 10-year renewable term, mortgage protection, and many more. Some companies combine features of various common plans and market the resulting composite plan under their own brand name. There are, however, fundamentally only two types. The policies may be for certain purposes and contain certain complications, but they all fit into one of two categories: term insurance and cash value insurance.

Term insurance is pure protection

A term insurance policy insures your life for a set period of time, such as a year, five years, or ten years, or until you reach a certain age. A *term* insurance policy is pure protection—it has no savings account or cash value feature.

Suppose one thousand 25-year-old men decide to pool their financial resources and insure each life for $1,000. Each man can name a *beneficiary*, the person to whom the $1,000 will be paid if the insured man should die. The first problem facing the men is to decide how much money to collect so they will have enough to pay out the claims that might be made. If they knew exactly how many men would die during the next 12 months, their problem would not be so difficult, but of course they do not know this. They might guess that no more than six should die, so that in order to pay $1,000 to each of the beneficiaries they would need a fund of $6,000 available. By assessing each member of their group $6 they would collect the money they need for claims payments. But, of course, they do not know how many will die; so their calculations could be far off.

Actually, an insurance company begins its calculations of premiums by considering death rates for different age groups. Death rates, or *mortality rates,* are collected over periods of time and then presented in statistical form in mortality tables. Most insurers now use the Commissioners 1958 Standard Ordinary Mortality Table, a table constructed on the basis of mortality statistics in the United States for the years 1950 to 1954. The information given in the table shown below is taken from the Commissioners 1958 Standard Ordinary Mortality Table. The second column shows the number of deaths per 1,000 persons, and the third column shows life expectancy for the various ages given.

EXAMPLE OF MORTALITY RATES		
Age	Deaths per 1,000	Expectation of Life
20	1.79	50.37
25	1.93	45.82
30	2.13	41.25
35	2.51	36.69
40	3.53	32.18
45	5.35	27.81
50	8.32	23.63
55	13.00	19.71
60	20.34	16.12

If the one thousand 25-year-old men discussed earlier were insured by an insurance company, the starting point in computing the premium for the year would be to look at the mortality table. The number of deaths per 1,000 persons at this age is 1.93, so the company would have to collect $1.93 from each man plus an amount to take care of expenses, profit, and the building of a reserve of money to cover contingencies—the possibility that more persons will die than the mortality table indicates. The premium needed in this case would then be considerably more than $1.93.

Persons known as *actuaries* compute premium rates for insurance companies, and their work involves more complicated mathematics than the average laymen can fully understand. The interest earned on the money insurance companies collect, for example, must enter their computations, and, as indicated earlier, the premiums must reflect selling, collection, and administration expenses as well as reasonable margins for contingencies.

The type of insurance just described is term insurance. Term policies are written for various lengths of time, such as five or ten years. The actuaries come up with a *level premium*—a fixed sum of money that is paid for the number of years in the term agreement. In the case of a five-year term policy, for example, one company would charge a 25-year-old man $5.83 per thousand dollars of coverage for a policy guaranteed to be renewable at the end of the five-year term. So for a $10,000 policy, he would pay $58.30 each year for five years. At the end of five years, his insurance agreement would end. If he decided to insure himself for $10,000 for another period of five years, he could renew the contract with the company and pay this time the annual premium for a 30-year-old man: $5.91 per thousand dollars of coverage, or $59.10 for a $10,000 policy.

Cash value insurance is insurance plus savings

A cash value policy combines insurance protection with the gradual building up of a savings account. Such a policy is often called "permanent" because it protects the insured until he dies or discontinues the policy. A term policy, you remember, protects the insured for a set period of time.

Mortality rates increase markedly with age. The mortality table mentioned earlier in this chapter shows the number of deaths per 1,000 for 20-year-old persons to be 1.79. For 65-year-olds, the death rate per thousand is 29.04. The rate increases to 101.19 per thousand at the age of 79, so for these persons the odds are about 1 in 10 for not reaching the age of 80. The mortality rates become larger at an increasing rate until the age of 99, when the rate is 1,000 deaths per 1,000 persons.

How can an insurance company possibly continue to insure the lives of people when they reach older ages? The answer is that each year that the policy is in effect the amount of insurance decreases and the amount of cash value in the savings account increases. Added together, the two elements at any time during the life of the policy equal the death benefit, or *face value,* that will be paid to the beneficiary. The cash value that builds up steadily as premiums are paid is also called the cash surrender value of the policy because the policyholder can surrender his policy with the guarantee that the insurance company will give him this sum of money. The life insurance company asks the insured person to pay larger premiums than would be needed simply to insure his life. The extra amount that he pays is accumulated at a stipulated rate of interest.

A sound life insurance policy may help bring peace of mind to retirement-age people.

Kosti Ruohamaa from Black Star

To illustrate how the idea of decreasing life insurance and increasing cash surrender value works let us assume a man buys a popular type of cash value insurance when he is 25 years old. The face value of his insurance policy (the amount that will be paid his beneficiary when he dies) is $10,000, and he pays an annual premium of $138.50. At the end of 10 years, when the man has reached the age of 35, the cash surrender value of his policy will be $940. If he should die at that time, his beneficiary would receive $10,000. But the $940 is part of that sum, so the "insurance" part of the death benefit is really $9,060. The cash value builds up more rapidly with the passage of time, as illustrated in the table below.

	(1) Cash Surrender Value	(2) Death Protection	(3) Face Value of Policy
After 10 years	$ 940	$9,060	$10,000
After 15 years	1,700	8,300	10,000
After 20 years	2,560	7,440	10,000
At age 60	4,940	5,060	10,000
At age 65	5,730	4,270	10,000

The formula, then, is simple. At any given year, Column 1 plus Column 2 equals Column 3, which is the face value, or death benefit, of the policy. Thus, the insurance company is "on the risk" for the difference between the cash surrender value and the face amount of the policy. Actually, then, cash value (or permanent) insurance is really decreasing insurance. The premium payments remain the same throughout the life of the policy, and the death benefit stays the same. But the amount of actual "insurance" decreases. The premium payment is large enough to make possible the building up of a cash value that is used to help pay the death benefit.

Agents and others in the life insurance industry often extol the value of permanent or cash value life insurance by mentioning the fact that one builds up a savings account while being insured. For example, a 25-year-old man might hear something like this: "By buying this $50,000 policy, you will have a cash value of about $30,000 at age 65—and all this while receiving $50,000 of protection for 40 years."

True, the cash value of $30,000 is available at age 65, but the amount of protection is $50,000 only at the beginning of the long period of time. As the years roll by, the cash value being built up provides some of the death benefit of the policy and during the later years provides most of the death benefit. The fact is that the policyholder can get the money only if he gives up the insurance policy. If a time comes when the policyholder needs the money, he can notify the insurance company, and it will give him the money. But in return, the policyholder must surrender the policy. When this happens, the protection stops.

The policyholder can borrow from the cash surrender value, but he must pay interest on the money borrowed, and the face value of the policy is decreased by the amount of the loan. The important thing for consumers to remember is that in order to get the cash surrender value of an insurance policy, one must discontinue the policy.

One additional point should be clear to consumers. Life insurance agents often urge prospective customers to buy cash value insurance because it is permanent, lifetime insurance. They also point out that the policy has a cash value and can be surrendered after a period of time, say 30 years, for cash. If insurance is to be permanent, if it is to be kept until one dies, then the cash value is really meaningless. One can get the cash only by surrendering the policy, and in that case the coverage is not permanent.

Although cash value insurance and term insurance are the fundamental types of life insurance protection, there are many variations of these two types. Some of these are discussed in the next chapter.

Checking your reading

1. Explain why life insurance coverage has increased so markedly in our society.
2. What are the two main reasons people give for buying life insurance?
3. What is the main purpose of life insurance?
4. Explain why assessing one's need for life insurance is more difficult and complex than assessing one's need for other types of insurance, such as automobile insurance.
5. What is the principal task of life insurance agents?
6. What are the payments made for insurance policies called?
7. What does "C.L.U." after an insurance agent's name mean?
8. What are the two basic types of insurance?
9. What is a term insurance policy?
10. What is a beneficiary?
11. How are mortality rates arrived at?
12. Explain what type of work is done by actuaries.
13. What is a cash value insurance policy?
14. What two elements added together make up the face value of a cash value insurance policy?
15. What must one do in order to get the cash surrender value of an insurance policy?

Consumer problems and projects

1. Sam Wilkins, age 20, died at Good Hope Hospital from injuries sustained when his car was demolished by a hit-and-run driver. Surviving are his parents, two brothers, and a sister. Young Wilkins's father, who earns $135 a week, was faced with the following bills:

Hospital	$ 175
Specialist	310
Doctor	175
Nurse	73
X rays, etc.	108
Ambulance	45
Undertaker	525
Miscellaneous	160
	$1,571

The young man had been earning $90 a week. He had $108 in a savings account, $75 in bonds, no life insurance, and no other assets. Generalize from this case history about the insurance needs of a young single person.

2. To what extent should life insurance be employed as a medium for savings and investment? Some people say that you should simply purchase the protection you need in the cheapest form—in term policies, for example—and put savings into other investments. Other people think of insurance as their major savings for old age. What is your opinion? Could you invest your spare funds to better advantage elsewhere? Will other investments be equally safe? Does the fact that insurance contracts force you to save systematically seem important to you? You might consult several persons who know about insurance and other savings and investment plans.

3. A 40-year-old man has just looked at a mortality table and found an interesting fact: at the age of 40, the expectation of life is 32.18 years. He concludes that he needs no insurance protection because by adding the 32.18 years to his present age, 40 years, he finds he can expect to live to the age of 72. "At age 72," he said, "I will have no one dependent on me, so I would be foolish to buy a life insurance policy." Discuss the fallacy in the man's reasoning.

4. Obtain a copy of *The Consumers Union Report on Life Insurance.* A copy may be available in your school library. If it is not, it may be purchased for $2.00 for nonsubscribers and $1.50 for subscribers from Consumers Union of United States, Inc., 256 Washington Street, Mount Vernon, New York 10550. Find a family that will give you the information you need to fill in the "Life Insurance Planning Worksheet" presented at the rear of the booklet. (Or you may wish to make up financial information for a fictitious family for this purpose.) Arrive at answers to the following questions pertaining to the family.

    a. What are the requirements for a family income fund?

    b. What are the requirements for an education fund?

    c. What are the requirements for a widow's retirement fund and for a widow's income fund for the years between child rearing and retirement?

Chapter

Life insurance programs

In Chapter 18 you read about the importance of life insurance protection for consumers. Although term insurance and cash value insurance are the only two fundamental types of life insurance protection available, insurance companies package their plans in different kinds of policies designed to meet the needs of the people they serve. In this chapter, you will read about the kinds of policies offered to consumers and the ways in which life insurance companies are organized. In addition, you will find answers to such questions as these: Who needs life insurance protection? How much life insurance is needed? How much do various policies cost?

TYPES OF CASH VALUE POLICIES

Three basic types of cash value policies are sold by life insurance companies: ordinary life policies, limited-payment life policies, and endowment policies. In both ordinary life and limited-payment life policies, cash values are built up, and the policies are permanent in that they stay in force until the insured person dies. Endowment policies are primarily savings plans.

Ordinary life policies

The ordinary life policy, most popular of the cash value policies, is also called whole or straight life insurance because it follows life expectancy to the very end. Premiums are payable for life, or until the age of 100 if that should come earlier, but for persons who live much beyond retirement years there would be no point in continuing the policy in force. It usually makes more sense to surrender the policy and take the savings or convert the policy to a lower face value, in which case no additional premiums need be paid. In ordinary life policies the cash surrender value at the age of 65 is approximately 50 percent of the face amount of the policy, regardless of the age at which the policy was begun.

Premium rates for ordinary life policies are the lowest of any cash value policies; in fact, they are not a great deal higher than those for term policies up until the age of 65, especially if the policy is purchased early. For a person who wants a policy that will provide a fixed sum of money for a beneficiary regardless of the age at which he dies, ordinary life will fit the bill. He need not worry about the coverage stopping after a certain number of years or when he reaches a certain age. If he lives to old age, however, he may find it difficult or even impossible to continue paying the premiums after his earning power has ceased. He can, though, at any time he wishes, stop paying on an ordinary life policy and take his choice of withdrawing its accumulated cash value, continuing the protection on a reduced basis, or continuing the full face amount of protection for a specified period of time.

Limited-payment life policies

The principal difference between a limited-payment life policy and an ordinary life policy is that you have the opportunity to pay for the insurance faster. Premium payments are compressed into a shorter time span so that eventually the policy is paid up. Still, the policy does not "mature" until the insured reaches the age of 100. Thus, even though the insured has completed his premium payments, the face value of the policy is not paid until he dies or reaches 100 years of age. Since premiums are paid for a shorter period of time, each premium is somewhat larger than for an ordinary life policy. Cash surrender values build up much faster in limited-payment life policies, of course.

Many limited-payment plans are available. A 20-payment life policy, for example, is fully paid up after 20 years, but it stays in force as long as the insured lives, even though he makes no further payments.

Some limited-payment plans are organized so that they will be paid up by retirement age. For example, a life-paid-up-at-65 policy purchased by a 22-year-old man would require a lower annual premium than a 20-payment life policy, which would be paid up when the man

Black Star

Limited-payment life insurance plans may be attractive to people, such as professional athletes, whose income is high for a relatively short time.

reaches the age of 42. But a life-paid-up-at-65 policy would require a somewhat higher premium than that paid for a straight life policy.

The limited-payment plan should be chosen over an ordinary life plan only in special circumstances. People such as professional athletes whose earnings are high for a brief period of time may be interested in a policy that will be paid up when their high earnings cease. But such high-premium insurance for most young family men could mean that they might not be able to afford the protection their families need.

Endowment policies

Most of the emphasis is on savings rather than on insurance protection in an endowment policy. It resembles a limited-payment policy in that it requires premium payments for a specified period only, say 20 or 30 years, or until a certain age, such as 60 or 65. You will recall that the face value of an ordinary or limited-payment life policy is payable only at the time of the insured's death, or when he reaches the age of 100. An endowment policy provides for payment of the face value to the insured on a certain date called the maturity date. If he dies before this date, the face value is paid, of course, to the beneficiary named in the policy. The maturity date is usually at the end of the premium-paying period. An endowment policy is used, then, mainly as a means of saving money. The cash value must build up much faster than in other types of cash value life insurance, so the "insurance" element of the policy decreases rapidly. In the case of a 20-year policy, the insurance falls to zero in 20 years. Actually, endowment policies represent the most "temporary" kind of insurance available. They are primarily savings plans. Premium payments on endowment policies are quite high for the insurance protection given.

TYPES OF TERM INSURANCE POLICIES

As mentioned in Chapter 18, term insurance policies do not have a savings or investment feature. When an individual purchases term insurance coverage, he is simply providing financial protection for whomever he names as the beneficiary of the policy. Term insurance is often called pure life insurance. The word "term" is derived from the fact that the insured is covered by this type of insurance only if his death occurs within a specified period of time, such as one year, ten years, or fifteen years. Thus, payment is made only if the insured dies within that period of time. If he lives to the end of the term, the policy expires, and the contract is at an end.

Some term policies are renewable. *Renewable* policies guarantee the insured the right to renew the policy for another period of the same length when the original term has expired. But if the policy is renewed, the premium is then increased to the rate applicable to the insured's age at the time of renewal.

Another provision often included in term policies is the *right of conversion,* which enables the policyholder, at any time within a period specified in the policy, to elect to surrender the term policy and receive in exchange a new policy on a permanent plan. The right of conversion is an important provision, for the insured can exercise this right without submitting to a medical examination or meeting other prerequisites that the company may require for a permanent plan of insurance at the time that the conversion is made. The basic kinds of term insurance policies are "level" and "decreasing."

Level term insurance

Level term insurance has a fixed death benefit. If the policy is a nonrenewable policy, the premium is also fixed for the duration of the term. Thus, in the case of a five-year nonrenewable term policy, the annual premium is the same each year for the five-year period. If the policy is a renewable term policy, the annual premium is the same for the five years but increases with each renewal. The new premium is based on the insured's age when the policy is renewed. The size of the death benefit can usually be decreased any year by the term insurance policyholder, but ordinarily the death benefit cannot be increased without a medical examination.

Decreasing term insurance

The death benefit of a decreasing term insurance policy decreases each year, falling to zero at the end of the term. Premiums usually stop a few years before the end of the term, when the policy expires. Because the face value declines as the risk of death rises with age, the premiums are relatively low.

Decreasing term policies have been popular with people who have relatively large mortgages on their homes. A young man with a $30,000 mortgage on his $40,000 home may not want his dependents to be burdened with mortgage payments if he should die. Thus, an insurance policy with a schedule of decreasing death benefits that roughly parallels the decreasing mortgage on his house would enable his beneficiaries to pay off the mortgage. Many insurance companies have designed decreasing term policies precisely for this purpose and call them *mortgage protection policies*.

As a matter of fact, decreasing term insurance has many uses in addition to providing mortgage protection. Once a family's living standard has stabilized somewhat, insurance needs typically go down each year. Furthermore, many families begin a program of systematic saving and investing. As their funds build up, the need for life insurance protection decreases. One of the reasons many decreasing term policies have been sold in recent years is to enable a policyholder's dependents to complete mutual fund accumulation programs in the event that he dies and is unable to do so.

Group term insurance

Group life insurance is a form of term insurance, and the premium rates are usually low. The insurance is written on a group of lives rather than on individual lives, and this fact helps to reduce administrative expenses. A master contract is issued instead of individual policies. Bookkeeping work on the part of the insurance company is simplified because payment for the premium is made in one check, thereby eliminating a multitude of individual entries. This type of insurance is usually written on the employees of a particular business firm, but it may also be written on a group of people with some other common bond—such as members of a fraternal organization or club. Many employers offer group insurance free or for a monthly charge.

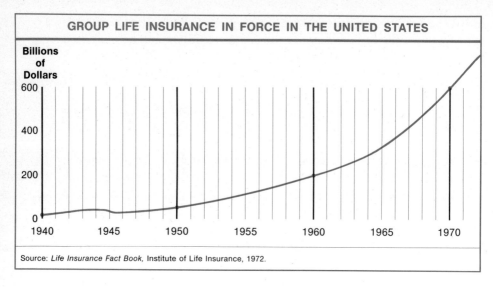

GROUP LIFE INSURANCE IN FORCE IN THE UNITED STATES

Billions of Dollars

600

400

200

0

1940   1945   1950   1955   1960   1965   1970

Source: *Life Insurance Fact Book,* Institute of Life Insurance, 1972.

Although premium rates in group plans are often quite low and represent an excellent insurance buy for consumers, they are rarely guaranteed by the contract. Thus rates may be raised if more deaths occur than the actuaries anticipated or if the average age of the group increases to the point where an increased premium charge is necessary. Where membership is large and the group plan has a history of successful operation, the group life insurance plan should be a good buy. A comparison of the average annual net cost of a group plan for the past several years with the cost of other term policies should reveal whether or not the group plan is a good buy.

COMBINATION POLICIES AND OPTIONAL EXTRAS

In addition to the principal types of cash value policies and term policies discussed in the preceding pages, life insurance companies also offer a number of combination plans and options. Most of these plans involve combining a permanent (or cash value) policy with term insurance. Some of the more popular of these plans are discussed in the following paragraphs.

Modified life

A permanent, or cash value, plan designed to appeal to a young man whose income is low but whose prospects for the future are good is called modified life. For the first few years, typically 5 years, the policyholder pays a lower premium than he would pay for an ordinary life insurance policy. Then, after the initial period of time, the premium becomes higher. A recent college graduate might want a fairly large amount of permanent insurance but feels he cannot afford the premium just now. If he thinks his income will increase sufficiently during the next several years, he may be a good prospect for this type of insurance.

Family plan

The family plan policy provides an insurance package that covers every member of the family. The policy might insure the father's life with $10,000 of permanent insurance. The same package might include $2,000 of insurance on the mother until she is 65 years old and $1,000 insurance coverage on the lives of each dependent child, including those born after the contract is issued.

Family income

A family income policy is usually an ordinary life policy to which a decreasing-term element is added so that in the event the policyholder dies within the term stated in the policy, the beneficiary receives a monthly income. The monthly income is often 1 or 2 percent of the death benefit, but it can be more. Let us say a man bought a $20,000 family income policy on a 20-year plan that calls for a 2 percent monthly income. If he took out the policy on September 1, 1970, and

Group insurance is written on the lives of a group of people, such as the employees of a company.

Chuck Rogers from Black Star

died the month in which it was issued, his beneficiary would receive 240 payments (12 months times 20 years) of $400 (2 percent of $20,000). If he dies on September 1, 1981, his beneficiary will receive 120 payments. Should he die in August 1991, the income payment would be made for only 1 month, since the expiration date is September 1 of that year. After the income-paying term expires, the face value of the policy, in this case $20,000, is collected.

Optional extras

Insurance companies provide an assortment of benefits that can be added to almost any policy for extra payments. For example, by paying a small extra charge it is possible to guarantee the right to purchase additional insurance at standard rates regardless of insurability. Poor health in the future could make a person uninsurable, or insurable only at high rates. The guaranteed insurability option covers this risk.

The waiver of premium clause is another popular option. With this clause in effect, premiums throughout the remaining life of the policy are waived (need not be paid) if the policyholder becomes permanently and totally disabled, as defined in the policy.

PARTICIPATING AND NONPARTICIPATING POLICIES

Life insurance policies are either participating or nonparticipating, and in the life insurance industry they are often referred to as "par" or "nonpar." In a participating policy, the premium payments include what is in effect an overpayment, and at the end of the year the insurance company returns part of the payment as a "dividend."

Stock companies and mutual companies

To understand the origin of participating policies it is necessary to examine the types of life insurance organizations. In our country, state laws require that life insurance organizations be formed as corporations. Actually, there are two different types of life insurance corporations: stock companies and mutual companies. A stock company, like any other corporation, is owned and operated by its stockholders, and the stockholders share in any profits or losses that the company makes. A mutual company, on the other hand, has no stock and no stockholders. It is owned entirely by its policyholders. Each policyholder is a member of the company and has the right to vote in the election of the directors, who control and manage the company. Thus it can be seen that the policyholder's role in a mutual company corresponds in many ways to a stockholder's role in a stock company.

In actual practice, however, there is little difference in the management of stock companies and mutual companies. The average policyholder in a mutual company pays no particular attention to the management of his company. Mutual life insurance companies provided 52 percent of the life insurance in force at the end of 1970. Stock life insurance companies accounted for the other 48 percent.

The idea of dividends

All United States mutual companies, but not all stock companies, pay dividends. Originally, dividends were issued by mutual companies only. The mutual companies reasoned that if the mortality rate among its policyholders was lower than expected during the year, and the company did not use all the money set aside for paying death benefits, the policyholders were entitled, as owners of the company, to receive a refund. A refund could also be made possible by higher returns on premium money invested or lower administrative costs than had been anticipated.

Now most stockholder-owned companies, too, sell participating policies. To meet the competition of mutual companies, it was easy enough for stock companies to issue policies that provided a rebate at the end of each policy year. The premium payments are simply increased enough to make possible a dividend payment at the end of the year.

Some people have criticized the insurance industry for using the term "dividend," stating that a more accurate term such as "refund" should be used. Indeed, the United States Internal Revenue Service says that insurance dividends are not subject to tax because they are not income but simply a refund of an overpayment.

Participating policies accounted for 61 percent of all life insurance in force with United States companies at the end of 1970. Nonparticipating policies made up the remaining 39 percent.

Unfortunately, it is not possible to say whether the net cost of insurance will be less for a participating or a nonparticipating policy. Nor can valid cost generalizations be made for stock versus mutual companies. Every prospective buyer of life insurance should understand that the dividend illustrations used by life insurance agents to arrive at a net annual premium (premium payment minus dividend at the end of each year) is only an estimate. In past years, some companies have paid higher dividends than their estimates. Other companies have paid lower dividends.

How dividends are paid

Most policies offer the policyholder a choice of four different ways in which to receive dividends. The policyholder can take his dividends in cash; he can have each dividend payment applied to his next premium payment; he can use the dividends to buy additional paid-up insurance; or he can leave the money with the insurance company in order to draw interest.

THE CHIEF PROVIDER NEEDS COVERAGE

The primary purpose of life insurance is to provide financial protection for those who are dependent on the person whose life is insured. Life insurance companies have combined the opportunity for saving with many of their policies, but consumers should be concerned first and foremost with insurance when they examine their life insurance needs. Perhaps the term death insurance would be more descriptive, since what is needed is financial security in the event of death.

When does any person need life insurance? The answer is obvious: when his death creates a need for more money than he has left in his estate. When one or more persons must depend on a family member for money on which to live, the need for life insurance is most crucial. Thus, the breadwinner is the key person whose life must be insured. What about other members of the family?

Insurance agents often stress the need for insuring the lives of children, arguing that the premium cost is low and that the death benefit will pay for the cost of a funeral. Usually, the death of a child reduces the financial responsibilities of the father by far more than the cost of a funeral. Another point mentioned in favor of insuring a child's life is the fact that the future insurance costs will be reduced if he is first insured at a young age. The costs are lower, but the payments include money wasted for a number of years when insurance was not needed.

How important is insurance on the life of the wife and mother? If she is a working mother and her income is used to support or to help support others, it is important that her life be adequately insured. If she is a housewife, her life insurance needs usually are not so important. A housewife contributes a great deal of economic value to the family, of course, by her work at home. A sizable economic burden resulting from her death would be the possible need to pay wages to a housekeeper. The death of an adult member of the family, however, decreases the living costs of the family, and this reduction in such things as medical, clothing, and food costs would be sizable. Some insurance on the mother's life might well be important to help the family over the transition period after her death, but the insurance needs of a housewife are not nearly so important in most cases as the insurance needs of the breadwinner.

Thus, the conclusion is that life insurance is most important for the breadwinner of the family. His death causes a stop in family income, and in our society cutting off income for even a short period of time can be quite serious. Most fathers are considerably underinsured. Before spending money to buy life insurance on his children and his wife, a father should make certain that his own life is adequately covered by life insurance. If other members of his family should die, the father (assuming he is the breadwinner) may suffer some economic loss, but his income continues, and he can no doubt weather the storm. If he should die, however, the family might well be in serious financial trouble if he is not adequately insured.

HOW MUCH INSURANCE IS NEEDED?

Once one's life insurance priorities have been established, the next task is to decide how much insurance to buy. A reliable, dependable life insurance agent can be of considerable help at this point, of course.

The first step in figuring life insurance needs is to estimate social security benefits. The life insurance and disability plans of social security are not well known by people in the United States, but they do provide sizable benefits, and these benefits should be considered when beginning the task of deciding how much life insurance is needed.

The insurance needs of a family change as the family progresses from one stage of life to the next. Before children are born, life insurance needs are relatively low if both husband and wife are able to work. When children are small, the needs are quite high. A young mother who is widowed will need money to raise her family, and the number of years during which an income is needed is obviously greater when the children are young. As children grow to be teen-agers, the need for insurance decreases because the length of dependency on the part of the children has now been decreased. Once the children have grown and left home, income protection needs have diminished even more.

After the age of 65, there is really little if any need for insurance to cover the loss of earning power of the husband. For this reason, many people stop paying premiums on permanent life insurance policies when they reach 65 years of age. When premium payments are

A widow with young children needs more income than she would if her children were older.

John Rees from Black Star

stopped, the insured can withdraw the cash value of the insurance if he feels he needs no protection from the policy. Or he can continue the policy at reduced protection without the need for making additional premium payments.

THE COST OF LIFE INSURANCE POLICIES

When buying life insurance, the prospective buyer should consider first the amount of protection needed. Some persons have attempted to reduce life insurance buying to a formula based on the percentage of one's income that should be spent on premiums. A more sensible starting point is to figure one's insurance needs and then attempt to fill those needs with the most sensible type of coverage. The amount of protection one can buy for a given sum of money will be large or small according to the type of policy purchased. The table on page 317 illustrates typical costs of various policies for males at four different ages. The annual premium payments, which are for $1,000 of protection, are the rates charged in 1971 by a large insurance company for nonparticipating policies.

The least expensive policy is the five-year renewable and convertible term policy. The policies with the largest "savings" element require, quite obviously, the largest premium payments. But should one use life insurance as a savings device? The conclusion reached by many persons who have studied family financial planning is that life insurance in most cases should be used as straight protection, and saving

ANNUAL PREMIUM RATES PER $1,000 FOR SELECTED NONPARTICIPATING POLICIES, FOR MALES				
Type of Policy	Age 25	Age 30	Age 35	Age 40
5-Year Renewable and Convertible	$ 5.49	$ 5.73	$ 6.45	$ 8.19
Term to Age 65	8.80	9.97	12.10	14.50
Ordinary Life	13.64	16.01	19.09	23.31
20-Payment Life	22.48	25.40	28.83	32.75
Life Paid Up at Age 65	15.29	18.28	22.40	28.37
Endowment at Age 65	18.49	22.39	27.78	35.41

should be done elsewhere. There are circumstances, however, in which life insurance may serve as a satisfactory method of saving. But the one principal reason for buying life insurance is to gain the protection needed for those persons who depend financially on the life of the insured.

One important thing should be noted when examining the table on this page. If a man buys the five-year term policy at the age of 25, he will have to pay an increased premium at five-year steps as long as he wants the coverage. Let us assume he buys a $20,000 policy at the age of 25. His annual premium payments for the first five years will be $109.80 ($5.49 times 20), but they will increase to $163.80 should he still have the policy and want to renew it at the age of 40. In the case of the other policies, his premium payments would be based on his age at the time he took out the policy, and they would not increase over the years. The premium rates for term insurance policies increase as one gets older. At the age of 45, the annual premium rate for the five-year term policy increases to $11.10 per thousand dollars of coverage. At the age of 50 the rate is $15.85, and at 55 it climbs to $23.40.

The fact is, though, that insurance needs typically decrease as one gets older, so in the case in the above paragraph, the man would no doubt reduce his term insurance coverage as he gets older. The argument against term insurance that points to the fact that it costs more as one gets older is misleading. All life insurance costs more as one gets older and mortality rates increase. Cash value policies have level premiums, but remember that the actual insurance element (the amount for which the company is "on the risk") decreases as the cash value of the policy increases.

Why, then, cannot one buy a decreasing term insurance policy and save one's own money? The argument against such a plan is that few people will save unless forced to do so. This may be true, of course, but it need not be. Many people are able to save regularly. Automatic payroll deductions for United States savings bonds, monthly investment plans, and other means have been developed to help people save systematically. Furthermore, the life insurance lapse rates testify to the fact that life insurance policies are limited in disciplining persons who would not otherwise save.

Checking your reading

1. What three types of cash value policies are sold by insurance companies?
2. For which of the cash value policies are premium rates the lowest?
3. Discuss the main difference between a limited-payment life policy and an ordinary life policy. How are they similar?
4. What kinds of persons might need a limited-payment plan of insurance?
5. Explain why endowment policies represent the most temporary kind of insurance.
6. In what principal way do term insurance policies differ from the other policies issued by insurance companies?
7. What is a renewable term policy?
8. What does the right of conversion enable the term insurance policyholder to do?
9. What are the two basic kinds of term insurance policies? Explain the difference between the two.
10. Discuss the uses for decreasing term insurance.
11. Explain what is meant by group life insurance.
12. What is a family income policy?
13. List two optional extras that may be purchased with an insurance policy.
14. What is the first step for most people in estimating their life insurance needs?
15. Do insurance needs typically decrease or increase as one gets older? Explain.

Consumer problems and projects

1. Steven Carter must meet unexpected bills just when he has been temporarily laid off from work. He does not see how he can possibly pay his next insurance premium. Must he let his policy lapse? What other arrangements can he make through his insurance company? What are the advantages of each? Which arrangements would you recommend?

2. The following premium rates are charged by a certain company for each $1,000 of either ordinary life insurance or 20-year endowment insurance. Study the table, and answer the questions listed below.

Age at Nearest Birthday	Ordinary Life Premium		20-Year Endowment Premium	
	Annual	Monthly	Annual	Monthly
20 years	$13.80	$1.22	$43.65	$3.86
40 years	25.37	2.25	46.54	4.12

a. How do you account for the fact that the annual premium for ordinary life insurance at the age of 40 is almost twice the annual premium for the same plan at the age of 20, while the annual premium for a 20-year endowment policy at 40 years of age is just a few dollars more than it would be at 20?

b. What would be the annual premium for a $20,000 ordinary life policy issued at 20 years of age? at 40?

c. What is the difference in annual cost between making an annual premium payment and a monthly premium payment on a 20-year endowment policy for $10,000 issued at the age of 20?

3. James Green is 25 years old, married, and has a child who is just a few weeks old. Mr. Green's life is currently insured for $1,000 through an ordinary life policy. The Greens wanted to increase the amount of insurance on Mr. Green's life, and after examining their budget, they have decided that they can pay up to $120 a year.

The premium rates listed below are sample annual rates for a 25-year-old man. The rates are for each $1,000 of insurance.

Term Insurance	Ordinary Life	20-Payment Life	20-Year Endowment
$5.17	$15.41	$26.61	$43.84

a. Using the rates above, estimate the amount of each kind of insurance Mr. Green can buy for $120.

b. Discuss the advantages and disadvantages of each of the four plans.

c. Do you think he should consider other plans of insurance? Which ones? Why?

4. Cash value insurance policies combine life insurance and savings. Following are two arguments for combining savings with insurance.

a. The alternative to combining savings with insurance is to buy term insurance, in which case you lose all the money you pay in. If you buy a cash value policy, such as ordinary life, the cash value eventually will be more than all the money you pay in. You will have been insured those years free.

b. If you are like most people, you will not save money for old age unless the insurance company saves it for you.

Point out the fallacies, if any, in these two arguments.

Chapter 20

Social insurance

Suppose that in the year 1971 a young father died. His two small children, both under five years of age, and his wife suddenly were cut off from their source of financial support. What would have happened to this family?

Because of the social security program in the United States, the family would be receiving monthly benefit checks. In fact, if the father's average earnings covered by social security had been $450 a month, the widow and children would be receiving nearly $468 each month, or about $5,616 each year. By the time the older child reaches 18, it is possible that the family will have received $80,000 or more. Then, when the widow reaches the age of 60, she may be eligible to receive additional benefits. The law provides that average monthly earnings covered by social security will increase in years to come, so the benefits in the future will be even greater. In Chapter 19 you read how vitally important it is for a breadwinner to provide financial security for his dependents in the event of his death. Fortunately, most persons in the United States are covered by social security and thus have a foundation on which to build a life insurance program.

The social insurance program in the United States covers old-age, survivors, and disability benefits; and sickness insurance. Why have we adopted such a program of social insurance? How does the social security system operate? The answers to these questions will be covered in this chapter.

WHY SOCIAL INSURANCE PROGRAMS ARE NEEDED

Over the years of our nation's development, both the state and federal governments have recognized that certain risks in an increasingly industrialized economy can best be met with programs of social insurance. The existence of so many successful private insurance companies in the United States has caused some people to question the need for government involvement in social insurance programs, and indeed some critics of private insurance companies attribute at least part of the need for government programs to the default of private insurance companies in this area. But the need for government social insurance plans in industrial nations is well established, and in the United States the development of social insurance has lagged behind other industrial nations.

Social insurance has been shaped by changing economic and social conditions. Some of the principal reasons for establishing social insurance programs are given in the following paragraphs.

■ At one time, we were predominantly an agricultural society. Over the years we have become predominantly a highly mechanized interdependent society, and the conditions of life in such a society have increased our dependence on a money income. In the early history of our country, people did not depend so

In our earlier, largely agricultural society, people produced for themselves much of what they needed and wanted. In today's society, the consumer is dependent on money to obtain the necessities of life.

Editorial Photocolor Archives, Inc.

much on money as we do today. Families then produced for themselves much of the food, clothing, and other things they needed and wanted. Loss of earning power is much more serious now than it once was, because today we must buy with money virtually everything we consume.

■ In an earlier day, the family was an independent unit that took care of old people as well as young people. Many persons never left the home in which they were born and grew up, and few of them migrated to other cities or other states. But our industrialized society has become more complicated. Families now are not so closely knit as they once were. Family members are scattered—sometimes throughout the country or the world. Most parents today want and expect to be financially independent when they retire. They do not want to be supported by their children.

■ Many more people now live to older ages, as insurance mortality tables show us. At the same time, many employers force people to retire at relatively early ages, often at 65. The result is that the number of retired persons in the United States is greater than ever, and the length of time between retirement and death increases.

■ The United States is certainly wealthy enough not to let individuals suffer extremes of misfortune and poverty, and many people believe that the federal government is the agency through which we can best provide a program of social insurance for the American people. Other Americans, however, believe that this program can be handled better through private agencies. For this reason, the United States has not developed social insurance to nearly so great an extent as the highly industrialized countries of Western Europe. For example, Great Britain's so-called "cradle to grave" security program provides many kinds of social insurance that Americans have rejected. In the next few pages, we will look at the social security program provided in our country.

Beginning in colonial times, local towns recognized the need to help impoverished people when adversity became severe. Help was usually available from relatives, friends, and neighbors, but when such assistance was not sufficient, local government was called upon. The aid was given grudgingly, however, and the repressive features of the public relief systems were intended to discourage people from applying

The Bettmann Archive, Inc.

Widespread unemployment of the 1930s resulted in bread lines and led to the passage of the Social Security Act of 1935.

until their circumstances became extremely serious. Progress in giving better relief came steadily, and by the mid-1920s, a number of the states were experimenting with old-age pensions.

The nation experienced a severe depression in the 1930s, and it became apparent that certain economic risks—unemployment, disability, death, and old age—were not being met by previous methods. The answer to the growing need among so many people had to be federal action. In 1932 the federal government made loans and then grants to the states to pay for relief. Congress then passed the Social Security Act, and it was signed into law on August 14, 1935.

THE BEGINNING OF SOCIAL SECURITY

The two social insurance programs established initially by the Social Security Act were a federal system of old-age benefits for retired workers and a federal-state system of unemployment insurance. Many changes and improvements were made in the program in the 1930s and 1940s, such as extending the old-age insurance program to provide monthly benefits for a worker's dependents and survivors (initially the program provided benefits for retired workers only).

Major changes in the social security program came during the decade of the 1950s, when it was broadened to cover many workers who were not covered at the beginning. Amendments during the 1950s extended social security coverage to farm operators, regularly employed farm and household employees, and most persons who work for themselves. Coverage was also made available on a voluntary group basis to employees of state and local governments.

In 1965, self-employed doctors of medicine were included in the program. In fact, nine out of ten working people in the United States are now included in the social security program. Therefore, when they retire or become disabled they can count on a source of income, and when they die their families will have something to fall back on.

SOCIAL SECURITY TODAY

More than 850 social security offices are situated conveniently throughout the country, and these offices send representatives regularly to 3,300 other communities so that the public will be served. If you have worked, you no doubt already have a social security card. If you do not have a card, you need only visit a social security office in your community to apply for one. A social security number is a necessity for us all today. The social security number is used for income tax purposes, and many schools and colleges now use it as the student's identification number.

Social security offices answer questions about social security, supply pamphlets about the various programs and benefits, and help people apply for benefits. To find the address of the office nearest you, look in the telephone directory, or ask at your post office.

Courtesy Social Security Administration

There are more than 850 social security offices located throughout the country.

How is social security financed?

Social security benefits are paid for by a tax, generally referred to as a "contribution," based on covered earnings. Each payday the employer must deduct the contribution from the worker's pay, match it with an equal amount, and send the total monthly or quarterly to the Department of the Treasury. Self-employed persons contribute at about three-fourths the combined employee-employer rate for retirement, survivors, and disability insurance. The hospital insurance contribution rate is identical for employers, employees, and self-employed persons. The self-employed person must pay the tax quarterly along with his income tax.

The government places a maximum on the amount of yearly earnings that can count for social security and on which the social security tax is paid. From 1937 until 1950, the maximum was $3,000 a year. Since that time, the maximum has been increased a number of times, and under the present law, the figure is $10,800 for 1973 and $12,000 for 1974. The amount of yearly earnings on which the social security tax is paid and the benefits paid will be tied to the cost of living.

The table on this page and the table on the next page show the present and future contribution rates as now scheduled in the law.

CONTRIBUTION RATE SCHEDULE FOR EMPLOYEES AND EMPLOYERS (EACH)		
	Percent of Covered Earnings	
Years	For Retirement, Survivors, and Disability Insurance	For Hospital Insurance	Total
1973–77	4.85	1.00	5.85
1978–80	4.80	1.25	6.05
1981–85	4.80	1.35	6.15
1986–92	4.80	1.45	6.25
1993–97	4.80	1.45	6.25

Assume that in 1973 a person earned an annual salary of $7,000. His employer deducted for social security taxes 5.85 percent of the $7,000 (4.85 percent for retirement, survivors, and disability insurance plus 1 percent for hospital insurance). Thus the worker's contribution for the year was $409.50. The employer must also contribute $409.50, so the total amount of money collected for social security takes for this worker was $819. The maximum social security tax paid by a worker in 1973 would have been $631, because $10,800 was the maximum yearly earnings on which the 5.85 percent tax could be applied.

	Percent of Covered Earnings		
Years	**For Retirement, Survivors, and Disability Insurance**	**For Hospital Insurance**	**Total**
1973–77	4.85	1.00	5.85
1978–80	4.80	1.25	6.05
1981–85	4.80	1.35	6.15
1986–92	4.80	1.45	6.25
1993–97	4.80	1.45	6.25

CONTRIBUTION RATE SCHEDULE FOR SELF-EMPLOYED PEOPLE

How are social security benefits earned?

To be eligible for social security payments for himself and his family, a person must work for at least a certain minimum period of time in an occupation covered by social security. The Social Security Administration gives credit to workers for quarters of coverage and divides the year into four calendar quarters:

JANUARY	APRIL
FEBRUARY	MAY
MARCH	JUNE
JULY	OCTOBER
AUGUST	NOVEMBER
SEPTEMBER	DECEMBER

Most workers get credit for one-fourth year of work (called a *quarter of coverage*) if they are paid $50 or more in one calendar quarter. In addition, any worker who earns the maximum wages creditable for social security for a year gets credit for a full year, even though he may work just part of the year.

Social security credit is given for work covered by the social security law no matter how young or how old the worker is. When the work is under social security, the social security tax must be paid regardless of the age of the worker.

What happens if a person stops working on a covered job before he becomes insured? The credits he has built up and which have been reported for him will remain on his record. Later, if he should return to a job covered by social security, he can add to his credits.

In order for a worker or his family to receive benefits based on his earnings, he must have enough credit to become insured. The Social Security Administration classifies a worker as fully insured or currently insured, depending on the total amount of credit he has for work under social security. These types of insured status are explained in the following paragraphs.

FULLY INSURED   When a worker reaches retirement age and is fully insured, he and certain members of his family can receive monthly benefits. If he is fully insured at death, benefits can be paid to certain members of his family.

No one is fully insured with credit for less than $1\frac{1}{2}$ years of work, and no one needs more than 10 years of work to be fully insured. Being fully insured merely means that certain kinds of cash benefits may be payable. The amount of the benefits depends on the worker's average earnings.

The table below shows how much credit for work under social security a worker born after 1929 needs to be fully insured if he dies before retirement age.

If the worker dies when he is	He will be fully insured if he has credit for this much work
28 or younger	1½ years
30	2
32	2½
34	3
36	3½
38	4
40	4½
42	5
46	6
50	7
54	8
58	9
62 or older	10

CURRENTLY INSURED A worker is currently insured if he has social security credit for at least $1\frac{1}{2}$ years of work within the 3 years before he dies. As the table on page 329 shows, the widow of a currently insured worker and her dependent children are entitled to certain benefits under the social security plan.

DISABILITY BENEFITS If a worker becomes disabled before he reaches 65, he and certain members of his family may be eligible for benefits. If disability starts before the age of 24, the worker needs credit for $1\frac{1}{2}$ years of work within the 3 years before he becomes disabled. If he becomes disabled between the ages of 24 and 31, he needs social security credits for half the time after 21 and before he became disabled. At the age of 31 or after, the worker must be fully insured and have credit for 5 years of work in the 10 years just before he became disabled. The amount of the monthly disability payment is generally the same as the retirement benefit a worker would get if he were 65.

A person is considered disabled only if he has a severe physical or mental condition that prevents him from working and that is expected to last (or has lasted) for at least 12 months or is expected to result in death. The Social Security Administration recommends that people who have questions about disability ask for more detailed information at a social security office. The people at the social security office will help a person request the appropriate medical reports from his doctor or from the hospital or clinic where he has been examined.

FAMILY PAYMENTS Social security benefits are payable not only to a worker but also to certain members of a worker's family. Dependents and survivors eligible for benefits include the following:

- Unmarried children under 18 or between 18 and 22 if they are full-time students
- Unmarried sons and daughters 18 or over who were disabled before they reached 22 and who continue to be disabled
- A wife under 65 or widow under 62 if she is caring for a child who is under 18 or disabled and if the child is entitled to payments
- A wife 62 or widow 60 or older, or a disabled widow 50 or over, even if there are no children entitled to payments
- A dependent husband or widower 60 or over, or a disabled dependent widower 50 or over
- A surviving dependent parent 62 or over

In addition to monthly benefits, a lump-sum death benefit of approximately $255.00 may be paid after the worker's death.

The table below illustrates the principal types of family payments and the insured status needed for each.

TYPES OF FAMILY PAYMENTS	
Survivors	
Monthly payments to your	If you are
*Widow 60 or over or disabled widow 50 or over	Fully insured
*Widow (regardless of age) if caring for your child who is under 18 (or disabled) and is entitled to benefits	Either fully or currently insured
Dependent children	Either fully or currently insured
Dependent widower 60 or over or disabled dependent widower 50 or over	Fully insured
Dependent parent 62 or over	Fully insured
(Lump-sum death payment)	Either fully or currently insured
*Note: All types of widow's benefits may be paid to a surviving divorced wife under certain conditions.	
Disability	
Monthly payments to	If
You as a disabled worker and your wife and children	You are fully insured and meet the special work requirements
Your child who became disabled before 22 and continues to be disabled after 22	The parent receives retirement or disability benefits or the parent was fully or currently insured at death

How are benefits estimated?

The exact amount of retirement, disability, and survivors benefits cannot, of course, be figured until there is an application for benefits. This is the case because all earnings up to the time of the application may be considered in figuring the benefit. The exact benefit available at the time of application will be figured by the Social Security Administration. Estimating the amount of retirement, disability, and survivors benefits, is, however, possible, and this information is valuable for consumers who are building an insurance program.

What does the future hold?

Since the social security program began in 1935 it has been repeatedly amended, and the amendments have always been in the direction of greater liberalization. The majority of our congressmen have obviously believed that the financial benefits available to citizens through the social security system needed to be increased.

While many social planners and politicians advocate further liberalization of the social security programs, some critics of the social security system warn that there is a danger in too great an expansion of the system.

These critics point out that the original purpose of social security was to provide a basic floor of protection. This meant keeping the costs of the program low enough to encourage people to maintain private savings and investments. The social security benefits when combined with these private resources would then be high enough to enable most persons to maintain at least an acceptable standard of living during their retirement.

Now, however, some persons are arguing that the social security system alone should provide sufficient income for the elderly to live on. Critics of increased social security expansion point out that every additional benefit that is handed out must be paid for by collecting a tax from the nation's workers. In 1972 more than 96 million persons were making payments into the fund and approximately 28 million persons were receiving social security benefits.

Critics and defenders quarrel over the term "taxes." Defenders claim that payments into the social security system are contributions not taxes. Critics argue that they are not voluntary and are therefore taxes. The principal danger of excessive expansion, according to the critics, will be the difficulty of collecting sufficient taxes to keep up with the payments that must be made.

MEDICARE

Medicare is a popular name for the federal government's system of financing medical care for persons 65 years of age and over and those receiving social security disability benefits for at least two years regardless of their age. This government health insurance plan was established in 1965 when amendments to the Social Security Act added to the law a pair of related contributor health insurance plans for

EXAMPLES OF MONTHLY CASH PAYMENTS

	Average Yearly Earnings After 1950*						
	$923 or Less	$1,800	$3,000	$4,200	$5,400	$6,600	$7,800
Retired worker—65 or older Disabled worker—under 65	$ 84.50	$134.30	$174.80	$213.30	$250.60	$288.40	$331.00
Wife 65 or older	42.30	67.20	87.40	106.70	125.30	144.20	165.50
Retired worker at 62	67.60	107.50	139.90	170.70	200.50	230.80	264.80
Wife at 62, no child	31.80	50.40	65.60	80.10	94.00	108.20	124.20
Widow at 60	73.30	96.10	125.10	152.60	179.30	206.30	236.70
Widow or widower at 62	84.50	110.80	144.30	176.00	206.80	238.00	273.10
Disabled widow at 50	51.30	67.30	87.50	106.80	125.50	144.30	165.60
Wife under 65 and one child	42.30	67.20	92.50	157.40	217.30	233.90	248.30
Widowed mother and one child	126.80	201.50	262.20	320.00	376.60	432.60	496.60
Widowed mother and two children	126.80	201.50	267.30	370.70	467.90	522.30	579.30
One child of retired or disabled worker	42.30	67.20	87.40	106.70	125.30	144.20	165.50
One surviving child	84.50	100.80	131.10	160.00	188.00	216.30	248.30
Maximum family payment	126.80	201.50	267.30	370.70	467.90	522.30	579.30

*The maximum earnings creditable for social security for 1968–1971 is $7,800, and beginning in 1972, the maximum is $9,000, but average earnings usually cannot reach these amounts until later. Because of this, the benefits shown in the last column on the right generally will not be payable until later. When a person is entitled to more than one benefit, the amount actually payable is limited to the larger of the benefits.

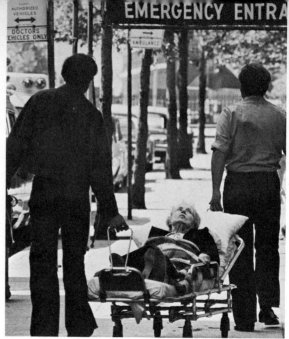

The hospitalization provisions of Medicare help elderly people pay for the care they receive in a hospital.

Editorial Photocolor Archives, Inc.

virtually all people 65 years of age or older. The two plans are these: (1) a basic compulsory program of hospital insurance and (2) a voluntary program of supplementary medical insurance.

Hospital insurance

The first plan, the hospital insurance part of Medicare, helps pay for the care the person receives as a patient in a hospital and for certain follow-up care after he leaves the hospital. Most people 65 and older and those receiving social security benefits for at least two years are eligible for hospital insurance automatically. This protection is financed through contributions paid while the individual is working. The table on page 325 shows the contribution rate schedule.

Medical insurance

The second plan, the medical insurance part of Medicare, helps pay for doctor bills and the cost of many other medical items and services not covered under hospital insurance, including out-patient hospital services. Although coverage is voluntary, persons over 65 and those receiving disability benefits are automatically covered unless they decline. The basic premium paid by most persons is $5.80 each month. The federal government pays an equal amount for each person electing this coverage, so the total monthly premium of $11.60 is shared equally by the insured person and the government. The medical insurance part of Medicare is kept on a pay-as-you-go basis, as required by law.

Additional information about Medicare will be included in Chapter 21—"Health Services and Insurance." The Medicare program is far more complicated than the brief description given on the preceding page suggests, but in broadest outline, you can see that adequate hospital and medical care are now within the reach of most of America's citizens who are 65 years of age or older.

KEEPING SOCIAL SECURITY RECORDS

By now you must realize that social security is an important consideration in the financial planning of modern Americans. Therefore, it is important to maintain reliable social security records. Everyone should observe the following three rules for keeping social security records:

1. Take care of your social security card. Write down the account number that appears on the card, and make a note of the place where the card is usually kept. Your account number keeps your account from being confused with the social security account of anyone else. Both your name and account number are needed to make sure you get full credit for your earnings. If you lose your card, the nearest office of the Social Security Administration will help you get a duplicate. If there is no office near you, write to the Social Security Administration, Baltimore, Maryland 21203. Be sure to give your name, working address, and social security number.

2. Check the official social security record of earnings credited to you. You should check your account at least once every three years, for there is a limit to the period within which certain corrections can be made. If you change employers or have more than one employer during the year, checking the status of your account can be especially important.

   To get a statement of earnings from the Social Security Administration, ask for Form OAR-7004 at the nearest field office. This form is printed on an addressed postal card, which you simply fill in and mail. Or, write to the Social Security Administration, P.O. Box 57, Baltimore, Maryland 21203, and ask them to send you the information. Information about your earnings cannot be given out without a signed request from you.

3. Keep documents that can be used to prove marriage and the date of birth of the members of your family. These proofs are needed when an application is made for social security benefits. Most people keep valuable papers in a safe-deposit box, but wherever you keep them, make a note of their location.

Checking your reading

1. List the specific things (such as unemployment insurance) covered by the social insurance program in the United States.
2. List the four principal reasons for the establishment of social insurance programs.
3. As our economy became more industrialized, people faced certain risks that made social insurance desirable. What kind of social insurance was first made mandatory by state laws?
4. Explain how social security benefits are financed. How does the money reach the government?
5. How much do self-employed persons contribute to social security?
6. What must a person do in order to be eligible for social security payments for himself and his family?
7. Explain the meaning of quarters of coverage as used for credit for social security benefits.
8. Explain the difference between "fully insured" and "currently insured."
9. When is a person considered to be disabled?
10. What dependents and survivors are eligible for social security benefits?
11. What two related contributor health insurance plans were established in 1965 with amendments to the Social Security Act?
12. What three rules should be observed for keeping social security records?

Consumer problems and projects

1. Use the table on page 331 to answer the following questions about persons who are covered by social security.

   a. Mr. Jarko has just retired. He is 65 years old. His wife is 62 years old. Mr. Jarko's average yearly earnings from 1951 were $5,400. What social security benefits will Mr. and Mrs. Jarko receive each month?

b. Janice Menska is a widow. Her husband did not work on a job covered by social security. Mrs. Menska, however, has worked in a covered occupation. She is now 65 and will retire. Her average yearly earnings from 1951 were $4,200. What will be Mrs. Menska's monthly payment?

c. James Pennel has just died, leaving as survivors his wife, who is 39 years old, and four children, ages 6, 9, 11, and 14. Mr. Pennel's average yearly earnings from 1951 were $5,400. What will be the monthly payment to the family? What will be the lump-sum death payment?

2.   From a local office of the Social Security Administration obtain a copy of *Social Security Information for Young Families* (SSI-35b). Using the information contained in this pamphlet, report to the class how social security information can be valuable to young married couples.

3.   Obtain display materials and pamphlets from a local office of the Social Security Administration, and make a bulletin board display of the provisions of the social security program. For example, you could get information about such things as how social security works for nonprofit organizations and their employees, how employees of state and local governments get social security credit, how the self-employed can obtain social security credit, and how social security benefits are financed.

4.   Study the provisions of your state unemployment insurance program. Your school library or your teacher might have this information.

a. What occupational groups are not now covered by the program? What special difficulties, if any, would there be in including them?

b. What persons does the program cover? How much do they contribute to the fund? Under what circumstances do they become eligible to receive benefits? What benefits are paid? For how long?

c. Are the weekly benefits and the maximum period of payment satisfactory? To increase them, it might be necessary to increase the size of the reserve fund. Where does this money come from? Could larger collections be made without harm?

d. Where is your nearest public employment office?

5.   Insurance companies report that it is generally easier to sell life insurance policies and annuity contracts to workers who are covered by old-age, survivors, and disability insurance. How do you account for this?

6.   Report to the class on the changes that have been made in the social security program since 1935. Include in your report current proposals for new legislation that will affect the program. Some of the material for this report can be obtained from a Social Security Administration field office. Encyclopedias and current news magazines will also contain information that will be useful to you.

7.   Prepare a debate—*Resolved:* That social insurance programs are detrimental to our economy.

Chapter 21

Health services and insurance

In a recent issue of a popular news magazine, a writer suggested that in the United States today only the rich can afford to be ill. Medical costs soared during the 1960s, and the situation caused most observers to agree that eventually there will be near revolutionary changes in both how people get medical care and how they pay for it. The average daily cost of hospitalization increased from $56 in 1960 to $144 in 1971.

In a special message to Congress in February, 1971, President Nixon reported that in the previous 12 months alone the nation's medical bill went up 11 percent, from $63 billion to $70 billion. In the previous 10 years, the medical bill climbed 170 percent. In 1960 we spent 5.3 percent of our gross national product[1] on health; in 1970 we spent 7 percent of our gross national product on health. Thus, there exists a general conviction that our nation faces a crisis in health care.

MEDICAL CARE IN THE UNITED STATES

We can well be proud of the achievements of American medicine. Most of the antibiotics now in daily use in the world were developed by our medical researchers, and these medical researchers lead the world in Nobel prizes. Some of our medical centers, such as the Mayo Clinic in Minnesota, are world-renowned. But in the task of preventing and treating routine illness, our achievement is not quite so noteworthy.

[1] Gross national product is the value of all the goods and services produced in a country.

The shortage of professionals

According to medical statisticians, at the beginning of a recent year we were about 50,000 doctors short of the needed amount. Most serious is the shortage of general practitioners, internists, and pediatricians— the doctors we turn to when illness first strikes. The result of this is that many already overworked doctors must work even longer days. People who move to new cities have difficulty finding doctors who are willing to take on new patients. Because some doctors even refuse to schedule office appointments, patients must show up and spend two or three hours in a waiting room in order to receive attention that may take just a few minutes.

The need for registered nurses is great. Hospitals and clinics need trained workers in such areas as X-ray technology and respiratory therapy.

Hospital service

Since World War II the federal government has poured billions of dollars into hospital construction, but 70 percent of the money has gone into hospitals serving small towns and rural areas. In our big metropolitan areas hospitals have become overcrowded to the point that in many communities the situation is quite serious. Some hospitals are so crowded that emergency patients often have to wait for hours on stretchers until beds become available. Patients needing nonemergency surgery may have to schedule their stay at the hospital weeks or even months in advance.

Despite the fact that we spend more money on medical services than any other country, we lag behind in some aspects of health care. The infant mortality rate in the United States is higher than in 13 other

Hospitals in many large metropolitan areas are seriously overcrowded.

Courtesy Medical World News/McGraw-Hill

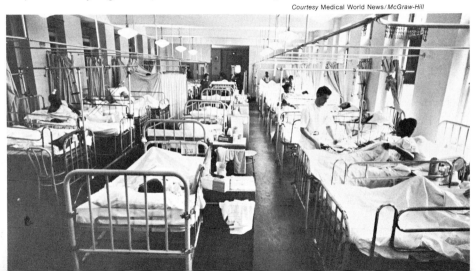

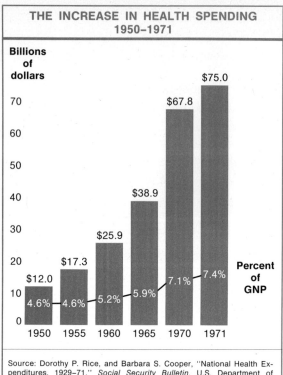

THE INCREASE IN HEALTH SPENDING
1950–1971

Billions of dollars

$75.0

$67.8

$38.9

$25.9

$17.3

$12.0

4.6% 4.6% 5.2% 5.9% 7.1% 7.4%

Percent of GNP

1950 1955 1960 1965 1970 1971

Source: Dorothy P. Rice, and Barbara S. Cooper, "National Health Expenditures, 1929–71," *Social Security Bulletin*, U.S. Department of Health, Education, and Welfare, January, 1972.

countries, and the United States ranks eighteenth in male life expectancy. If we spend so much money on health care, why are we apparently not getting a better return for our dollars? Some critics of our present system point out that health care in the United States is organized and financed in out-of-date ways that are wholly inadequate. They say that hospitals, for instance, have little incentive to reduce costs through efficiencies when they are usually paid on a cost-plus basis by insurance companies or the government, both of which are third parties to the services offered. Such criticisms may not be completely fair but health costs have soared upward, as the graph above shows. The shortage of professional people coupled with crowded hospitals means that from the point of view of many people, the quality of health care has not kept pace with increasing medical costs.

Paying for health services

In this age of soaring health costs and expensive new medical procedures, few people can afford a prolonged illness or a serious injury. Many families would face financial ruin if one member should suddenly require extensive surgery and prolonged hospital care. A severe heart attack requiring heart surgery and months of hospitalization, for example, would cost thousands of dollars. Furthermore, if the stricken member should be the breadwinner, family income might be shut off or vastly curtailed. How do American families pay for such medical care? Health insurance in its many different forms enables many people to protect themselves financially in the event of illness or accident.

Medicare, the federal government's program of health insurance for older people, has aided the portion of our population over 65 years of age. A section of the Medicare law popularly known as *Medicaid* provides federal assistance to states to set up new medical care programs for the needy, regardless of age. Most people, however, have had to rely on private insurance plans to provide health insurance protection. Before looking at the kinds of national health insurance programs considered by Congress in recent years, we will examine the types of coverage offered by nonprofit plans such as Blue Cross–Blue Shield and by private insurance companies.

TYPES OF HEALTH INSURANCE

In a recent year, more than 175 million people in the United States, or about 88 percent of the population, were protected by one or more forms of private health insurance. As the table on page 340 indicates, the number of persons with health insurance protection has increased markedly since 1945, or the period following World War II. Possibly the main reason for the increase in health insurance coverage has been the sharply escalating costs for medical care. Individuals and families have been forced to find a way to protect themselves against the expense. Employers and labor unions have recognized this need for health insurance, and offering group health insurance plans for employees as a fringe benefit has become an important part of labor's bargaining process.

Health insurance policies can be purchased in a variety of forms and combinations, but the available protection can be divided into five types of coverage. The first four types—hospital expense, surgical expense, regular medical expense, and major medical expense—are designed to help persons pay the costs of hospital care, surgery, and medical treatment. The fifth type of health insurance—loss-of-income protection—is designed to help replace income lost during periods of prolonged disability.

NUMBER OF PERSONS WITH HEALTH INSURANCE PROTECTION IN THE UNITED STATES, BY TYPE OF COVERAGE
(000 omitted)

End of Year	Hospital Expense	Surgical Expense	Regular Medical Expense	Major Medical Expense	Disability Income	
					Short-Term	Long-Term
1940	12,312	5,350	3,000	–	n.a.*	n.a.
1945	32,068	12,890	4,713	–	n.a.	n.a.
1950	76,639	54,156	21,589	–	37,793	n.a.
1955	105,452	88,856	54,935	5,241	39,513	n.a.
1960	130,007	117,304	86,889	27,448	42,436	n.a.
1961	134,417	122,951	93,466	34,138	43,055	n.a.
1962	139,176	126,900	97,404	38,250	44,902	n.a.
1963	144,575	131,954	102,302	42,441	43,927	3,029
1964	148,338	135,433	107,686	47,001	44,751	3,420
1965	153,133	140,462	111,696	51,946	46,347	4,457
1966	158,022	144,715	116,462	56,742	49,372	5,002
1967	162,853	150,396	122,570	62,226	51,230	6,682
1968:						
Under 65	159,335	147,252	122,054	65,040	54,955	7,718
65 and over	10,162	8,473	7,051	1,821	–	–
Total, 1968	169,497	155,725	129,105	66,861	54,955	7,718
1969:						
Under 65	164,383	153,304	127,227	70,410	57,004	9,076
65 and over	10,838	8,840	7,703	1,882	–	–
Total, 1969	175,221	162,144	134,930	72,292	57,004	9,076

*n.a. = not available
Source: *Source Book of Health Insurance Data*, 1970, p. 16.

Hospital expense insurance

Hospital expense insurance provides benefits that cover all or part of hospital room-and-board charges as well as an allowance that may be applied toward such things as operating-room charges, laboratory fees, x-ray and fluoroscopic examinations, drugs and dressings, and, occasionally, special nurses' fees. Hospitalization policies typically provide a specified number of dollars a day for a specified number of days— often 100 days or more for each accident or illness, although some plans pay for hospitalization for as many as 365 days. Because hospital charges have increased so sharply in recent years, the cost of hospital insurance has also been forced up. In a recent year, the nationwide average cost of a day in a hospital was $70, but in some New York City and Boston hospitals, the minimum charge for a semiprivate bed was $90. When intensive care is needed for the patient, the cost can be as high as $800 per day.

In a recent year, a total of 175 million persons had hospital expense insurance coverage. More persons are protected by this type of insurance than by any of the other types of health insurance.

Surgical expense insurance

The next most popular type of health insurance coverage is surgical expense insurance. This type of insurance pays benefits according to a schedule of surgical procedures listing the maximum amount of benefits for each type of operation covered. For example, the maximum allowance might be $250 for an appendectomy and $100 for a tonsillectomy. The number of persons having surgical expense insurance reached 162 million in a recent year.

Regular medical expense insurance

Regular medical expense insurance provides benefits toward a physician's fees for nonsurgical care given in the hospital or home or at the doctor's office. Some regular medical expense policies also provide benefits for diagnostic x-ray and laboratory expenses. Most companies usually provide a fixed sum of money for each visit, and the maximum number of calls for each illness or injury is usually specified in the contract.

Recently, a total of 135 million persons were protected by regular medical expense insurance.

Dordy from Black Star

Health insurance often covers the costs of laboratory tests.

Major medical expense insurance

Although few people can afford a medical bill of the size that would pile up should a serious and prolonged illness or injury occur, not even half the people in the nation are covered by the type of health insurance that protects against big bills. Major medical policies could more aptly be called "catastrophe insurance." None of the policies described earlier are designed to meet the needs of persons who require hospitalization for long periods of time and whose surgical bills exceed the maximum amounts set forth in the schedule of benefits paid by surgical expense insurance. Thus, major medical expense insurance serves a real need. A heart attack, a severe case of hepatitis, spinal meningitis, or an accident that might require extensive surgery and months of hospitalization are just a few examples of catastrophes that might hit any family at any time. The chances are not great that such misfortune will strike, but when it strikes a family without insurance coverage, the debt incurred for medical care sometimes takes years to pay.

Major medical expense insurance is growing rapidly, but as indicated earlier, the majority of persons in the nation are not protected by this important type of insurance. From 108,000 persons protected in 1951, the first year the coverage was widely offered, the number grew to 72,000,000 in 1969.

An infinite variety of major medical policies is available, mainly from commercial insurance companies, but also from Blue Cross–Blue Shield plans and through certain independent health insurance plans, such as those operated by labor unions. About 90 percent of the people covered by major medical insurance have group policies, usually made available by their employers. The employer often pays part of or all the premiums.

Major medical expense policies have high maximum benefits. Some plans feature maximums as low as $5,000 per person per illness. But more usual maximums in new policies range from $10,000 to $20,000, and the trend is for even higher maximums. Under group contracts for federal employees, for example, the maximum is $40,000. Costs of all types of medical treatment prescribed, whether in or out of the hospital, are covered, but most major medical policies have a deductible clause and a coinsurance clause.

The *deductible clause*, which is similar in nature to that found in most automobile collision policies, means that the insured must pay a certain amount before the insurer pays anything. For example, if the policy is a $100-deductible policy, the insured pays the first $100. If the expenses do not exceed $100, the insurance company pays nothing.

The deductible clause, which is used to eliminate many small claims for expenses that the policyholder should be able to budget for, enables the insurance company to offer this type of insurance for a lower premium. The deductible amounts commonly range from $50 to $100 for group policies and from $50 to $1,000 for individual policyholders. The higher the deduction, of course, the lower the premium.

The *coinsurance clause* requires the policyholder to pay part of the bill—usually about 20 or 25 percent—that remains after the deductible amount has been subtracted. This provision encourages the person insured to use only reasonable and necessary medical service.

Now let us see how a typical major medical policy with a $100-deductible clause and a 20-percent coinsurance clause works. Suppose a young man underwent surgery, and, in addition to hospitalization, he needed a nurse at home for a few weeks. His total medical charges, including the cost of the home nurse, totaled $6,400. In addition to his major medical expense policy, he was covered by a base plan of hospital expense and surgical expense insurance, which paid $1,800 toward his total expenses. His insurance would be figured as follows:

Total charges	$6,400
Less amount covered by base plan of hospital and surgical expense insurance	−1,800
Amount covered by major medical	$4,600
Less deductible of $100	−100
Balance subject to coinsurance	$4,500
Less coinsurance at 20%	−900
Amount paid by major medical	$3,600

SUMMARY

Paid by base plan	$1,800
Paid by major medical	3,600
Paid by patient	1,000
Total	$6,400

As you can see, of the total bill of $6,400, the young man paid only $1,000. His major medical expense insurance paid $3,600—or more than half the bill.

The major medical expense policy just described is known as a "supplementary" plan. A *supplementary* plan is designed to pick up where a separate basic hospitalization plan stops. Another major medical plan is known as a "comprehensive" plan. *Comprehensive* plans combine the basic and major medical protection in a single policy and typically cover all the hospital, surgical, and medical expenses incurred during an illness or because of an accident. Like the supplementary form of major medical coverage, comprehensive plans have both deductible and coinsurance features, although the deductible provisions do not call for quite so high an amount as those under a supplementary major medical plan.

Loss-of-income insurance

The oldest type of health insurance available is loss-of-income insurance. This type of insurance pays benefits when the insured is unable to work because of illness or injury. At the beginning of this century, medical expenses were not high, and so the financial problem that loomed largest when the wage earner became ill or suffered an accident that prevented him from working was the loss of income during the period of recuperation. Loss-of-income insurance issued by insurance companies may pay as much as 75 percent of the wage earner's normal earnings for a specified period of disability. Usually the payments do not begin until after a certain waiting period has elapsed. There is a good reason for the waiting period and for the pay limit of three-fourths of the regular weekly or monthly income. If a person were able to buy a policy that paid as much or more than he earned while working, he would have an incentive to fake an illness or contrive an accident. The companies would be kept busy trying to prevent fraud.

Loss-of-income policies usually also provide for payment of benefits to a beneficiary in case of the accidental death of the person insured.

Luigi Pellettieri, Medical World News/McGraw-Hill

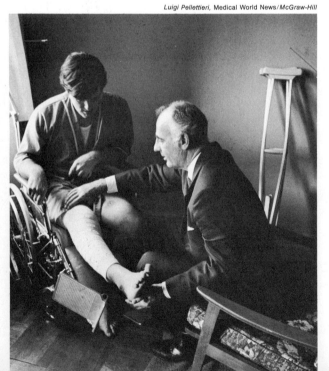

By eliminating financial worry, loss-of-income insurance allows an injured person to concentrate on getting well.

These policies typically also provide for the payment of a stipulated amount to the person insured if he should lose an arm or a leg or some other part of his body.

GROUP HEALTH INSURANCE

Many persons in the United States are included in health insurance plans because it is a fringe benefit offered to them by their employers. Most group policies are written on the employees of business organizations, but they can also be issued to any group of people who have a common bond, such as labor unions, credit unions, churches, and professional associations. The members who make up the group are insured under one policy for an amount determined by a definite formula that applies to all members or to all members in a given classification. Usually a condition of the contract is that the insurance covers the whole group, or a sizable percentage of the group, without discrimination because of age, sex, or physical condition.

The group policy is usually the best health insurance available for the dollar. As is the case in group life insurance, the administrative costs of insuring a number of people under a group plan can be considerably less than insuring the same people under individual plans. Furthermore, by insuring the whole group, the company eliminates the possibility of "adverse selection," the term used in the industry to describe the situation in which people who believe they may collect benefits tend to buy insurance and people who believe they are healthy and will not collect benefits do not buy.

The most common type of group plan is the one in which both employee and employer share costs. In some instances, the employer pays the entire premium, in which case all employees are automatically members of the group plan. Some group plans, on the other hand, require the employee to pay the entire cost. But even when the employee foots the entire premium bill, the kind of coverage is usually superior to an individual policy because of the low cost. Obviously a consumer should check the provisions of his group policy to determine whether he needs to supplement it with an individual policy.

BLUE CROSS AND BLUE SHIELD

Prepaid medical care plans have been organized by medical societies, groups of physicians, consumer cooperatives, fraternal groups, and others. The largest of the nonprofit prepaid medical plans are the Blue

Cross and Blue Shield plans, administered by the American Hospital Association and the American Medical Association. More than 70 million people are insured by Blue Cross–Blue Shield plans. Altogether, 74 autonomous plans exist throughout the country, and they negotiate with hospitals and participating physicians to set benefit rates.

Blue Cross covers hospitalization, and it pays out in benefits about 95 cents on each $1 collected. Although hospitalization plans sold by private insurance companies may charge lower premiums, they may pay out as little as 55 cents on each $1 collected. Blue Shield provides benefits for some of or all the expenses of surgery, medical treatment, and maternity care.

Plans vary. In most areas Blue Cross pays the actual cost of hospitalization, in contrast with most private plans, which pay only a certain agreed upon amount. Thus under Blue Cross, whether the hospital charges are $15 or $45 per day, the insured is covered for the time specified in the contract. Under many private plans there may be an allowance of, say, $20 per day. If the actual cost exceeds $20 per day, the patient is responsible for paying the difference.

NATIONAL HEALTH INSURANCE PROPOSALS

Most American families would face financial ruin if one of their members became seriously ill and required extensive surgery followed by expensive treatments during a long hospital stay. In such countries as Sweden, England, and West Germany the prospect of financial ruin due to prolonged and serious illness has been virtually eliminated because of national health insurance programs. In the United States private medical insurance has expanded greatly during the past several decades, and the amount of money we spend for health purposes represents a large share of our resources. Yet dissatisfaction with what our system provides is widespread.

Although health insurance coverage has increased substantially, the vast system has not tended to encourage efficiency in the use of hospitals. Most families have hospital expense insurance, for example, but no coverage for care outside the hospital. Health care outside the hospital is known as *ambulatory care*. The result of the lack of ambulatory care is that many patients occupy hospital beds for the purpose of gaining insurance benefits to cover the cost of tests and minor surgery that could just as well be taken care of at doctors' offices or clinics at much less cost.

Several proposals for a form of national health insurance have been presented to Congress during recent years, but they have not been acted upon. In February, 1971, President Nixon proposed a health care plan to Congress. The President and the advocates of the other plans proposed recognize that the answer to our health care problem is not just to spend more money. The United States already devotes a larger portion of its gross national product to medical care than other "healthy" countries such as Sweden and Great Britain. The thought is that reform aimed simply at making it easier to pay for medical care could have the effect of boosting medical costs even higher.

The health plan submitted by the President in 1971 was a moderate compromise among the several other health reform proposals that had been submitted to Congress. Senator Edward Kennedy of Massachusetts sponsored a bill that received a great deal of support, and Representative Martha Griffiths of Michigan submitted a bill that had the backing of the AFL-CIO. The American Medical Association backed still another bill, and a number of other organizations formulated their own national health insurance plans. What are the prospects for passing a national health insurance program of the type envisioned by the backers of these bills? Most observers are confident that some form of national health insurance is coming, but some of them say it might take several years. One thing that is probably certain is that no proposal will survive the legislative process intact—compromises will be made. There are certain points of similarity among the bills submitted thus far, and these points will be summarized briefly in the following pages.

An increase in the number of professional workers

The proposed bills recommend an emphasis on increasing the number of doctors and dentists. Funds totaling nearly $100 million were suggested in President Nixon's proposal for encouraging medical schools to train more doctors and other health workers. An emphasis also would be placed on preparing subprofessionals who could perform many time-consuming functions (such as administering tests and injections) that are now performed by doctors. The money could be made available in the form of grants to medical and dental students.

Health-maintenance organizations

A new approach to offering health care to people has become increasingly popular in recent years. It is a plan by which people get all their medical care from the same source, and they pay in advance one fee

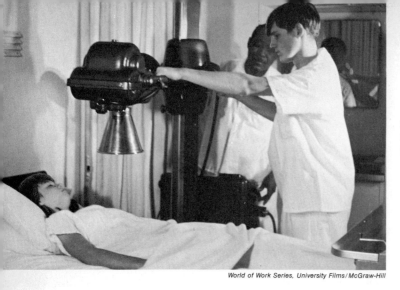

A complete health care system requires the services of skilled medical technicians.

World of Work Series, University Films/McGraw-Hill

for this service. The plans now in existence differ considerably. Some own their own hospitals, clinics, and drugstores. Other plans make arrangements with existing independent facilities. The general term that has been applied to all these plans is "health-maintenance organization" (HMO).

Many of the proposals for a national health insurance program, including the one put forth by President Nixon, place a strong emphasis on developing and enlarging HMOs as a means of providing health services. The two essential features of the plan, remember, are these: (1) It brings together a comprehensive range of medical services in a single organization so that a patient has convenient access to these services. (2) It provides services for a fee paid in advance by all people who join the plan.

Today about 300 HMOs exist in the nation. The largest and perhaps best-known organization is California's Kaiser Plan, which has more than 2 million members served by more than 2,000 full-time physicians in 21 hospitals and 54 medical offices.

One of the most important advantages claimed for HMOs is that they provide a strong financial incentive for better preventive care and for greater efficiency. Under an HMO plan, most of a family's medical costs are paid for in advance under a single monthly fee, and the organization must operate within the revenues generated by these fees. Under the traditional system, the more illnesses doctors and hospitals treat, the more their income rises. Thus, there is no economic incentive for them to concentrate on keeping people healthy. In contrast, health maintenance organizations emphasize preventive medicine.

The patient who does not get good care the first time will return for more medical care. But since he has already paid for his treatment, he will not be bringing in additional money. There is no profit in a sick member. Doctors are paid to keep people healthy.

If a subscriber visited an HMO doctor because of an injured shoulder, he would probably also be given a general examination if he had not had one recently. During the examination the doctor might discover that the patient has high blood pressure, so he is treated for that ailment as well as for his injured shoulder. Under our conventional system of medical care, the man might simply be treated for his shoulder, and his health insurance might pay for the treatment. Later, he might suffer a heart attack because his high blood pressure was overlooked. Of course, the value of preventive medicine to human life is inestimable. Of secondary importance in a case such as this is the high cost of the treatment for the heart attack, but the point being made here is that the insurance company would have to cover some extremely high bills, and such bills help to push up our nation's health costs.

Studies show that HMOs have achieved some dramatic savings. The costs of health care are significantly lower—as much as one-fourth to one-third lower than the costs of traditional care in some areas. Also, the members go to hospitals less often, and they do not stay as long. In fact, they spend from one-fourth to one-half less time in hospitals than nonmembers. Thus people who belong to HMO plans receive high-quality care at lower cost.

Government-sponsored or -supported health insurance is certainly not a new idea in the United States. In 1912 national health insurance was endorsed in the platform of Theodore Roosevelt's Progressive Party, followed by a campaign for enactment of a health program on a statewide basis. The campaign was dropped following the failure of key tests in California and New York. In 1935 a provision for national health insurance was considered for the social security bill, but it was not included.

During the 1940s and 1950s certain legislators worked to obtain health coverage for people in the nation. The first result of their efforts was the passage of Medicare in 1965, a program giving benefits to the aged. Most observers believe that some form of national health insurance for all people will be forthcoming in the near future. Consumers should know, of course, that one way or another they will continue to pay for medical care. The money may be paid in the form of premium payments. Or, some of the money may be paid for by the government from general revenues. General revenues come from taxes, and those taxes will be paid for by people in the nation.

Checking your reading

1. List three undesirable consequences of the shortage of general practitioners, internists, and pediatricians.
2. Why do critics of our present medical services say that hospitals now have little incentive to reduce costs?
3. What is Medicaid?
4. List the five types of coverage into which health insurance is divided.
5. Identify and define the two most popular types of health insurance coverage.
6. Explain what is meant by a deductible clause in a major medical expense policy.
7. Explain how a coinsurance clause works in a major medical expense policy.
8. How does a supplementary major medical plan differ from a comprehensive major medical plan?
9. Give two reasons why a group policy is usually the best health insurance available for the dollar.
10. What type of medical coverage is offered by Blue Cross?
11. What type of medical coverage is offered by Blue Shield?
12. What are the two essential features of a health-maintenance organization (HMO)?
13. Explain one of the most important advantages claimed for HMOs.

Consumer problems and projects

1. Make arrangements to have a representative of an insurance company speak to the class about the risks we all face with regard to health and accidents. Prepare a list of questions to ask the speaker.
2. Mr. Fujita has just recovered from rather extensive surgery. His total medical bill is $9,700. He is covered by a base plan of hospital and surgical expense insurance. In addition, he has a major medical plan that begins to pay only after the benefits of the basic plan have been exhausted. Other provisions of his major medical plan are these: a deductible clause of $100 and a coinsurance clause that specifies that the insured person pays 25 percent of the amount in excess of the deductible. Mr. Fujita's base plan of hospital and surgical expense insurance paid $2,600. How much will the major medical insurance pay? How much will Mr. Fujita have to pay?
3. Examine a group health insurance policy. Make a list of the chief provisions of the policy. Would some families need another health insurance policy to supplement the coverage given by this group policy?
4. Obtain a current copy of *Source Book of Health Insurance Data* from your library or from the Health Insurance Institute, 277 Park Avenue, New York, New York 10017. Find in this book the answers to the following questions:

a. How many persons had hospital expense protection by the end of the most recent year reported? How many had surgical expense coverage? Regular medical expense coverage? Major medical expense coverage? Short-term disability income? Long-term disability income?

b. Summarize the extent of the increase since 1960 in the six types of coverage mentioned above.

c. How much was spent by Americans for medical care in the most recent year reported? Does this represent an increase or a decrease over the amount spent in previous years?

d. Summarize personal consumption expenditures for medical care. For example, how much is spent for hospital services? For physicians' services? For dentists' services?

e. By examining consumer price indexes for medical care items, indicate which medical care items have increased and which have decreased in cost during the past several years.

5.   Obtain a copy of the booklet *Modern Health Insurance* from your library or from the Health Insurance Institute, 277 Park Avenue, New York, New York 10017.

a. From the section of the booklet on major medical expense insurance, summarize the ways in which the program of benefits under major medical insurance may be arranged.

b. From the section of the booklet that discusses principal policy provisions, write statements summarizing the meaning of the following: the insuring clause, benefit provisions, common exclusions, incontestable clause, and grace period.

Consumer credit,
taxes, and services

Chapter

Consumer credit

A hundred years ago, when a man could not pay his debts he was thrown into prison. Before that time, things were even worse for debtors. Getting into debt was considered a moral transgression as well as a money matter, and it was commonplace at one time for a debtor to be sold into slavery. But times have changed, and in today's economy debt is no longer considered sinful. Merchants, banks, and other credit institutions have come to recognize the fact that, when the economy is sound, it is profitable to extend consumer credit.

Stated simply, credit is trust in one's ability to pay later. Consumers find buying on credit to be convenient, and business firms find offering credit to be profitable. In fact, credit is so popular today that some firms would be forced out of business if they did not offer credit service.

WHY CREDIT IS POPULAR TODAY

Borrowing money has become an integral part of the life style in the United States. At the beginning of 1970 more than half of all families in our country were making installment payments of some kind other than mortgages. But "all" families include older families—families who already own most home furnishings they want and who also tend to have higher incomes and thus have less need to borrow money. Some finance counselors estimate that about three-fourths of all young families make installment payments for goods they have purchased.

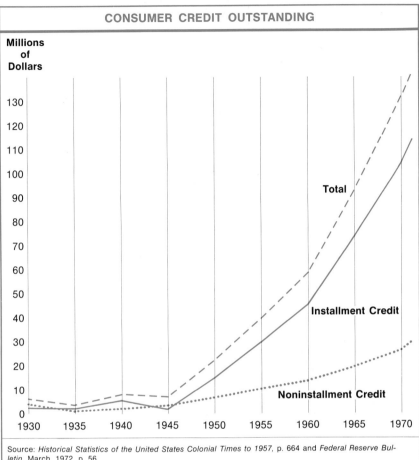

CONSUMER CREDIT OUTSTANDING

Millions
of
Dollars

Total

Installment Credit

Noninstallment Credit

| | 1930 | 1935 | 1940 | 1945 | 1950 | 1955 | 1960 | 1965 | 1970 |

Source: *Historical Statistics of the United States Colonial Times to 1957,* p. 664 and *Federal Reserve Bulletin,* March, 1972, p. 56.

The graph above illustrates the volume of consumer credit outstanding at the end of each of several different years beginning with 1930. Notice that the popularity of consumer credit increased markedly in the two decades following World War II. The volume of total consumer credit outstanding increased about fourfold between 1945 and 1950, and it has been increasing steadily since then.

Why consumers use credit

Several major factors in the economy have made the use of consumer credit popular. First, our economy is now based on the exchange of money. Most people are dependent on a cash income. A continuing flow of money has become as essential to our lives as a supply of oxygen is to an astronaut on the moon. If a person's supply of money is cut off for a short time, he may even find it difficult to get food and shelter and the other necessities of life. When we encounter financial difficulties—as people sometimes do—our need for what lenders call "remedial credit" is imperative.

But present-day consumers do not seek credit in emergencies only. A second development that has influenced the growth in the use of credit is the fact that modern technology has made available to more people than ever before an abundance of "hard goods," such as automobiles, refrigerators, and television sets. These goods are too expensive to be paid for out of one paycheck, so many consumers, counting on future paychecks, borrow money one way or another in order to enjoy the many goods and services that are available.

Another good reason consumers use credit is that it can be more convenient than paying cash. Consumers use gas and electricity in their homes and are billed later for what they use. This is a form of credit. Think of the inconvenience we would be caused if utility companies asked us to pay every day for the gas and electricity we consumed. Many consumers get credit from the dairy that delivers milk, the newsboy who delivers newspapers, and the firm that collects garbage. Consumers often find it convenient to charge purchases at retail stores instead of carrying cash with them while they shop. So you can see that credit in some form is used by just about every consumer in the United States.

Many consumers may not be aware that they are using credit when they pay for fuel oil days or weeks after it has been delivered.

Family Series, University Films / McGraw-Hill

Why merchants offer credit

Because competition is keen, merchants may extend to their customers the privilege of paying for goods at a later date. Many business firms help their customers arrange loans from banks so that expensive items can be bought immediately. The next chapter discusses the use of credit cards for buying merchandise.

Credit enables us to buy now and pay later. Consumers may buy products, such as stereo sets; or services, such as dental work; or money, in the form of a loan. Why is the supplier of the product or service willing to wait for his money? In some cases, of course, because it is convenient to do so. A dairy finds it easier and probably less costly to collect monthly for the milk left at a house. Some business firms may be willing to wait a reasonable time for payments because such a service to customers helps build goodwill. Most business firms extend credit in return for a finance charge. The goods may be purchased with the agreement that payment must be made within a certain period of time, such as 25 days after the bill is mailed, or a finance charge will be added to the cost of the merchandise. Or, a relatively expensive item, such as a sewing machine, may be sold under an agreement in which the consumer makes periodic payments (perhaps monthly) until the price is paid. A finance charge is, of course, added to such install-ment purchases.

IS CREDIT GOOD OR BAD?

From the point of view of consumers, credit has both a good side and a bad side. Consumer credit provides the funds for the purchase of houses, cars, furniture, appliances, and many other goods and services that mark a high standard of living. On the other hand, credit has caused "responsible" families to get into financial trouble by over-extending themselves.

Of course, some people save the money in advance and pay cash for the goods and services they buy. Such a practice is cheaper, but for many persons buying on credit seems to be easier. And if the payments are wisely budgeted and the cost of the credit is not excessive, buying on credit may be perfectly sound. After all, it is a recognized business practice to spread the capital outlay for a new plant over many years. It may be just as sound for a family to spread the cost of its expensive durable goods. At any rate, it is a fact that the possibility of buying on credit has brought people of moderate income into the market for things that were never before available to them. And bringing more consumers into the market has helped to make mass production and its economies possible.

Advantages of buying on credit

Many consumers describe the advantages of using credit in glowing terms. They cite as some of the advantages the convenience of buying, the ease of keeping records, and the satisfaction of using goods while paying for them. Still other consumers consider the use of credit as a form of forced savings. And even the most carefully managed family budget does not always allow for financial emergencies that can be met with the use of credit. These advantages of buying on credit are explained in the following text:

- *Buying on credit is a convenience.* Merchants often allow their customers a certain period, such as a month after billing, in which to pay for their purchases. The consumer who has such credit does not have to carry large amounts of cash with him when he shops. Should he be short of cash during a certain month, he can nevertheless make the purchases he wishes to make and pay for them later. Also, if the credit customer finds that the merchandise he purchased is unsatisfactory, he may find making an adjustment easier if he has not paid for the goods.

- *Credit aids in recordkeeping and budgeting.* Especially in the case where many purchases are made during the month, recordkeeping is easier when one payment is made monthly. A family owning two cars, for example, may buy gasoline as often as 10 or 12 times a month. The monthly bill itemizes the purchases, and the family knows precisely how much they paid for gasoline for the period.

Family Series, University Films/McGraw-Hill

The use of credit enables consumers to meet unexpected expenses, such as furnace repairs.

- *Goods may be used while paying for them.* Relatively expensive items, such as appliances and furniture, are often paid for in installments. The consumer has the use of the goods immediately. The alternative is to wait until enough money can be saved to pay cash for the item. In the latter case, not only does the consumer have to forgo having and using the product for a period of time, but he must also have the discipline to set money aside for the purchase.
- *Credit is a type of forced savings.* A person may never be able to accumulate the money for a big-ticket or expensive item such as a freezer or refrigerator. Without the obligation of regular payments some consumers might fritter away their incomes. If a refrigerator is needed, it can be bought on an installment plan, and the installment payments are, in a sense, a means of savings. For the privilege of buying on an installment plan, a credit charge is added to the cost of the product. But more will be said about that later in this chapter.
- *Credit enables consumers to meet financial emergencies.* Illness, accidents, or death can create unexpected expenses for which credit may be extremely useful to families. Unemployment may reduce or eliminate income for a period of time, and unless the family has built up sufficient reserves, credit may be necessary to have the basic necessities during this period.

Disadvantages of buying on credit

Credit has its bad side, and this side emerges when credit is used unwisely by consumers. Financial disaster can result when people buy more than they can afford or when they pay no attention to finance charges, which can devour a big portion of their incomes. Other disadvantages of buying on credit are as follows:

- *Credit weakens sales resistance.* The development of many new goods and services in our country has intensified selling efforts. In an earlier day, consumers were limited in what they could buy by the amount of cash they had available. One obstacle to high-pressure sales techniques was the inability of the consumer to meet the purchase price. The widespread availability of credit has broken down this defense. It is probably safe to say that in many instances providing money or credit with which to buy goods is as important in marketing goods as creating a desire for the goods.

- *Credit can get out of hand.* Credit can be bad for consumers when they use it to the point where they become so deeply in debt that they experience serious financial problems.
- *Credit encourages impulse buying.* Credit can do harm when consumers buy goods or services on impulse because of the ease of paying for them. The possibility of acquiring a product for only $12 a week makes the purchase price seem inconsequential to some persons, so the item is bought without any real analysis of need and without careful consideration of the other purposes for which the money could be used.
- *Credit costs money.* Finally, credit can be harmful to consumers when they cannot or will not consider the cost of credit. Many consumers will spend considerable time and effort shopping around to save $10 and $15 on the price of an appliance that sells for about $400. Then, having found their bargain they will pay little attention to the finance charge required for the privilege of making installment payments. Yet, the difference in finance charges between a 2-year bank loan for $400 and a 2-year installment plan for a $400 purchase offered by the dealer could be as much as $20 or more.

HOW MUCH DOES CREDIT COST?

The true cost of credit is the total of all the costs that the consumer must pay directly or indirectly for obtaining it. Since the Truth In Lending Act became effective, the total of all credit costs, except in certain cases, must be clearly stated in terms of dollars and cents. The total cost must also be expressed in terms of an annual percentage rate. More information on the scope of the act is given later in this chapter.

In order to arrive at the real cost of a product, the total credit cost must be added to the original purchase price. On some department store charge accounts a typical annual interest rate is 18 percent. That means that nearly $1 out of every $5 paid back on the account goes for interest. In some cases, the true cost of credit will depend on the time taken to repay the loan and the method used in calculating the annual percentage rate.

Time element

Interest charges may seem to be relatively insignificant. For example, a rate of only $1\frac{1}{2}$ percent a month seems rather low—on a $200 purchase it means an interest charge of just $3 a month. If, however, you take a year to pay for the purchase, the interest will amount to $36. In that event, the cost of the product is really $236. Thus, even a seemingly low interest rate becomes costly when you take a long time to repay the loan.

The table below illustrates how much money a bank loan for $2,000 at 12 percent would cost for three different periods, assuming the loan will be repaid in equal monthly payments. Stretching out the repayment time of a loan makes the monthly payments smaller, but increases the total cost.

COST OF A $2,000 LOAN AT 12 PERCENT ANNUAL INTEREST		
Duration of Loan	Monthly Payment	Interest Cost
1 year	$177.50	$130
2 years	93.75	250
3 years	65.83	370

Methods of calculating annual percentage rate

With certain installment loans and sales there are cases in which the annual percentage rate need not be stated. These cases are (1) when the finance charge is $5 or less and applies to credit of $75 or less and (2) when the finance charge is $7.50 or less and applies to credit of more than $75.

When a creditor quotes a low finance charge, in cases such as those described above, the consumer should remember that the annual percentage rate has still to be calculated. The methods of calculating the annual percentage rate have the effect of almost doubling the finance charge. For example, on a 1-year loan for $100 to be paid back monthly a creditor may ask you to pay a $7 finance charge. However, you will pay back a twelfth of the $100 plus a twelfth of the $7 finance charge each month. Because you pay back some of the principal each month, you do not have the use of the $100 for the entire year. Actually, you have the use of only about half the money for the full length of time. Because you are paying $7 for the use of what averages out to about $50 over the full year, you are actually paying interest at an annual rate of nearly 14 percent on the money you use.

Two different ways are used to figure installment interest: the discount method and the add-on method. The *discount* method means that the lender subtracts his interest charge from the amount of the loan and gives you the remainder. For example, on a $1,000 loan for 1 year at 6 percent interest, the lender would deduct 6 percent, or $60, from the principal and give you $940. You would pay back the $1,000 in equal monthly installments. But you do not have the entire amount of money on which the interest charge is figured. The *add-on* method means that the interest is added to the principal, and then the principal plus the interest is repaid in installments. Thus, on a $1,000 loan for 1 year at 6 percent, the lender would give you $1,000 and then ask you to repay $1,060 in equal monthly installments. The discount method of figuring interest is a little more expensive than the add-on method.

A rough rule for determining the actual rate of interest on installment loans is to double the apparent rate. Since the Truth In Lending Act became effective, comparing interest rates is not so difficult as it once was because lenders must now state in the contract the true annual interest rate charged. A simple formula can be used to compute the true interest rate:

$$r = \frac{2\ mi}{p\ (n\ +\ 1)}$$

where r = the true annual rate of interest
  m = the number of payment periods in 1 year
    (usually 12 monthly or 52 weekly or 4 quarterly)
  i = the total cost of the loan in dollars and cents
  p = the amount, or principal, of the loan
  n = the total number of payments to be made
The figures 1 and 2 remain constant.

The formula shown should give the same true annual interest rate as shown in the contract the consumer is asked to sign before credit is extended. The formula can be used in all cases as long as the required payments are always the same amount.

Assume that you are offered a $400 television set for $60 down, with the balance to be repaid in six monthly installments of $58.65 each. You will pay a total of $351.90 (6 times $58.65), so the cost of borrowing $340 is $11.90 ($351.90—the total amount to be repaid—less the amount borrowed, $340).

$$6 \times \$58.65 = \$\ \ \ 351.90 \text{ amount to be repaid}$$
$$-340.00 \text{ amount borrowed}$$
$$\$\ \ \ \ \ 11.90 \text{ cost of borrowing}$$

To apply the formula, use the figures listed above.

r = true annual interest rate

m = 12 (used in all applications of the formula when monthly payments are made, regardless of the actual number of payments required)

i = \$11.90 (the cost of borrowing)

p = \$340 (the amount borrowed)

n = 6 (the number of monthly payments)

The formula using the above figures looks like this:

$$r = \frac{2 \times 12 \times 11.90}{340\,(6 + 1)} = \frac{285.60}{2380}$$

$$r = 2380\overline{)285.60}^{\,.12} \text{ or } 12\%$$

$$r = 12\%$$

TRUTH-IN-LENDING LEGISLATION

Since July 1, 1969, when the Truth In Lending Act, Title I of the Consumer Credit Protection Act, became effective, consumers have been able to do some comparison shopping for credit without a slide rule and an advanced degree in mathematics. The Consumer Credit Protection Act had considerable opposition in Congress but was finally signed into law by President Johnson on May 29, 1968.

Section 102 of the Consumer Credit Protection Act (Public Law 90-321) gives its purpose as follows:

It is the purpose of this title [law] to assure a meaningful disclosure of credit terms so that the consumer will be able to compare more readily the various credit terms available to him and avoid the uninformed use of credit.

The Truth In Lending Act requires the lender or merchant to disclose the finance charge as well as the annual percentage rate. This information helps the consumer compare the credit terms offered by different merchants.

Courtesy J. C. Penney Co., Inc.

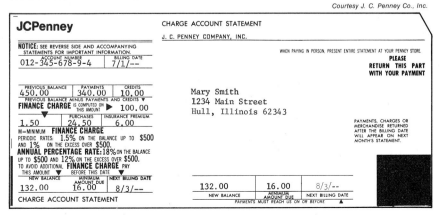

This particular law does not limit the amount of money paid for credit. The intent is to give all borrowers and customers enough information so that they can compare costs and avoid the uninformed use of credit. Almost everyone who extends credit is required by this law to provide a complete and accurate explanation of all the charges and to express the interest rate in a standard, meaningful form.

The scope of the act

Under the Truth In Lending Act, you must be told the total amount of the finance charge in dollars and cents and the true annual percentage rate. On a 1-year loan for $100 to be paid back monthly you may be asked to pay $7 in finance charges. Many borrowers may think this amounts to a charge of 7 percent. But, as you have learned, because the money is being paid back monthly in equal installments, the true annual interest rate in this case is really 12.92 percent. Except in the cases mentioned previously, the lender must indicate the true annual interest rate. The percentage can be rounded to the nearest one-fourth of one percent.

The lender is also required to include almost all fees he requires you to pay as a condition for giving you credit. Before the Truth In Lending Act, the practice had been to separate the interest rate from certain fees and extra charges made as a condition for extending credit. The practice made the cost of credit appear low when the borrower looked solely at the interest rate. Then, too, certain unethical lenders could load up a loan with fees and make the loan appear to be reasonable by showing a lower interest rate. Not any longer. Now, the finance charge or the annual percentage rate must include most fees. Some of these fees include such things as the following: appraisal and credit report fees (except in real estate transactions); any difference between the price of an item sold for cash and an item sold on credit; finder's fees; "points" (extra sums figured as a percentage of the loan amount and charged in a lump sum); service, transaction, and activity charges, and other carrying charges; any charge made because the lender is going to sell the obligation to another lender; the cost of credit; and life, accident, health, or loss-of-income insurance that the lender requires the borrower to buy.

Although most charges must be included in figuring the annual interest rate charged, a few items need not be included. For example, lenders need not include in the finance charge certain government-imposed expenses, such as taxes, or the fees charged for licenses, titles, and registrations.

The forms on pages 366 and 367 are samples distributed by the federal government that show the kinds of information that must be included on the forms used by lenders. In other words, they illustrate the disclosures that must be made by the lender. The form on page 366 is for an installment sale, and the form on page 367 is for a revolving credit account. The list below summarizes some of the important disclosures that are shown on these forms and that must be made by those who grant credit.

- Cash price
- Down payment
- Total amount financed
- Finance charge
- Annual percentage rate
- Late charges
- Total of payments
- Amounts of payments

Kinds of consumer loans covered

Banks, savings and loan associations, department stores, credit card issuers, credit unions, car dealers, consumer finance companies, and many more lenders of money are covered by the Truth In Lending Act. In fact, the law exempts relatively few types of credit transactions involving consumers. Among the main loans that are not covered by the law are the following:

- Loans exceeding $25,000 that do not involve real property (All mortgages, regardless of amount, are covered by the act.)
- Business and commercial credit
- Loans from a registered broker for transactions in securities and commodities

The kinds of loans that are covered by the Truth In Lending Act are installment loans and sales, revolving charge accounts, and real estate mortgages.

INSTALLMENT LOANS AND SALES   The person extending the credit must furnish a full disclosure of loan conditions in writing, and this must be done before the credit is given. It can be done in the contract that is signed to complete the transaction, or it can be made in a separate document that is given to the potential borrower before he signs the contract.

```
Seller's Name: _____                    Contract #_____


            RETAIL INSTALLMENT CONTRACT AND SECURITY AGREEMENT

The undersigned (herein called Purchaser, whether one or     PURCHASER'S NAME_____
more) purchases from _____(seller)
and grants to _____                      PURCHASER'S ADDRESS_____
a security interest in, subject to the terms and conditions   CITY_____STATE_____ZIP_____
hereof, the following described property.
                                                             1. CASH PRICE                        $_____
QUANTITY      DESCRIPTION              AMOUNT                 2. LESS: CASH DOWN PAYMENT $_____
                                                             3.        TRADE-IN          _____
                                                             4.        TOTAL DOWN PAYMENT  _____$_____
                                                             5. UNPAID BALANCE OF CASH PRICE  $_____
                                                             6. OTHER CHARGES:

                                                                                            $_____

Description of Trade-in:
                                                             7. AMOUNT FINANCED             $_____
                                                             8. FINANCE CHARGE              $_____
                                                             9. TOTAL OF PAYMENTS           $_____
                                                             10. DEFERRED PAYMENT PRICE (1+6+8)  $_____
                               Sales Tax                     11. ANNUAL PERCENTAGE RATE     _____%
                               Total
          Insurance Agreement                                Purchaser hereby agrees to pay to_____
The purchase of insurance coverage is voluntary              _____ at their
and not required for credit.   (Type of Ins.)                offices shown above the "TOTAL OF PAYMENTS"
insurance coverage is available at a cost of                 shown above in _____ monthly installments of
$_____ for the term of credit.                             $_____(final payment to be $_____)
                                                             the first installment being payable _____
  I desire insurance coverage                                19____, and all subsequent installments on the
                                                             same day of each consecutive month until paid in
Signed_____ Date_____                                full. The finance charge applies from ___(Date)
  I do not desire insurance coverage

Signed_____ Date_____        Signed_____

Notice to Buyer: You are entitled to a copy of the contract you sign. You have the right to pay in advance the unpaid
balance of this contract and obtain a partial refund of the finance charge based on the "Actuarial Method." [Any other
method of computation may be so identified, for example, "Rule of 78's," "Sum of the Digits," etc.]
```

This form, distributed by the Federal Reserve System, shows how a creditor may comply with the disclosure requirements of the Truth In Lending Act for revolving charge accounts.

REVOLVING CHARGE ACCOUNTS   The consumer opening a new account must receive a statement disclosing certain facts. Some of these facts include the monthly service charge used in computing the finance charge, the time period for paying a balance without incurring a finance charge, and whether the lender will use any of the goods bought as security for the loan.

Any Store U.S.A.

MAIN STREET—ANY CITY, U.S.A.

(Customer's name here)

AMT. PAID $_____

TO INSURE PROPER CREDIT RETURN THIS PORTION WITH YOUR PAYMENT

PREVIOUS BALANCE	FINANCE CHARGE 50 CENT MINIMUM	PAYMENTS	CREDITS	PURCHASES	NEW BALANCE	MINIMUM PAYMENT

FINANCE CHARGE IS COMPUTED BY A "PERIODIC RATE" OF   % PER MONTH (OR A MINIMUM CHARGE OF 50 CENTS FOR BALANCES UNDER $) WHICH IS AN ANNUAL PERCENTAGE RATE OF   % APPLIED TO THE PREVIOUS BALANCE WITHOUT DEDUCTING CURRENT PAYMENTS AND/OR CREDITS APPEARING ON THIS STATEMENT.

NOTICE

PLEASE SEE ACCOMPANYING STATEMENT(S) FOR IMPORTANT INFORMATION.

PAYMENTS, CREDITS OR CHARGES, RECEIVED AFTER THE DATE SHOWN ABOVE THE ARROW, WHICH IS THE CLOSING DATE OF THIS BILLING CYCLE, WILL APPEAR ON YOUR NEXT STATEMENT. TO AVOID ADDITIONAL FINANCE CHARGES PAY THE "NEW BALANCE" BEFORE THIS DATE NEXT MONTH.

ANY STORE, U.S.A.   MAIN STREET, ANY CITY, U.S.A.

This form, distributed by the Federal Reverse System, shows how a creditor may comply with the disclosure requirements of the Truth In Lending Act for installment sales contracts.

In addition, the regular monthly billing statements must contain an itemized account of all the transactions during the billing cycle, a detailed breakdown of the finance charge, and the rates and special fees used to compute the charge. Study carefully the example of the form for a revolving credit account shown above.

At the present time, the law permits different methods of figuring finance charges on revolving charge accounts. A wise consumer should examine carefully the method used by the stores with which he does business because some methods require the consumer to pay more money. Some common methods are listed on the next page.

- The Previous-Balance Method. When there is a balance in the account at the end of the current billing cycle, the interest rate is figured on the balance outstanding at the beginning of the billing cycle. The previous-balance method does not take into account any payments, returns, or purchases during the billing cycle.

  The previous-balance method is the costliest method from the viewpoint of consumers. An example will illustrate how costly the method can be. Assume that one month you buy a product costing $500, and you pay $499 before the next billing date. The store's interest rate is $1\frac{1}{2}$ percent a month. When you receive your bill next month, you find that you owe a total of $8.50—$1 owed on the balance and $7.50 for interest on the previous balance of $500. The previous-balance method is used by many charge account creditors.

- The Average Daily Balance Method. Under this method, the creditor adds up the actual amounts outstanding each day during the billing period and then divides the sum by the number of days in the period. The result is the amount that the interest rate is figured on. Payments are credited on the day they are received. Purchases are excluded in figuring the average daily balance.

- The Adjusted-Balance Method. Of the three methods, the adjusted-balance method is the most advantageous to consumers. The interest charge is figured on the balance in the account after deducting payments and credits. Thus, if you owed $400 at the beginning of the cycle and paid $300 at any time during the cycle period, you would be charged interest on $100. Remember that under the previous-balance method you would pay interest on the entire $400. Some major stores, such as The J. C. Penney Company, use the adjusted-balance method.

When a consumer uses a revolving charge account plan he should, by all means, check on the store's billing method, which the store is now required to explain. There is some concern in Congress about whether the previous-balance method should be banned. Many retailers, of course, are opposed to banning the method, asserting that such a ban would mean that they would have to increase their merchandise prices to make up for the money they would lose by using another method such as the adjusted-balance method. In the meantime, the law does give stores their choice of methods, and the choice of a store is the consumer's business.

REAL ESTATE MORTGAGES Unlike other loans, there is no requirement in the Truth In Lending Act that lenders of money for first mortgages tell the consumer how much the house is going to cost when the
principal and interest are added over the number of years of the loan.
The total amount of interest paid on a long-term mortgage might surprise some consumers, and this is what the real estate people fear, of
course. On second mortgages the lender does have to disclose both
the annual interest rate and the total dollar amount of the interest.

On all mortgages, lenders must state the annual percentage rate of
interest charged. In calculating the annual percentage rate, lenders can
exclude bona fide title examination fees; title insurance premiums; fees
for property surveys; fees for preparing deeds, settlement statements,
and other documents; notary fees; appraisal fees; credit reports;
amounts put in escrow or trustee accounts for payments of taxes,
insurance, and water and sewer fees; and land rents.

When a consumer decides to borrow money using his house as
collateral—that is, security to ensure repayment—and signs a contract
for the loan, he now has the right to cancel the contract without penalty
if he acts in three days. He will get his down payment back in full.
The Truth In Lending Act included this provision to protect homeowners who might be induced by unscrupulous home repair firms to sign
what the homeowners think are ordinary installment loan contracts but
are actually expensive second mortgages. Also, the provision in the
act is designed to protect consumers against lenders who offer their
services to help people solve their financial problems by consolidating
their debts. The consumer may be convinced that he should offer his
home as security. Then he discovers that he has simply exchanged one
headache for another and may be in danger of losing his home. Thus,
now if a consumer finds he has signed a contract that he regrets signing,
he still has three business days in which to change his mind.

The three-day period during which a contract can be canceled also
applies when the homeowner finances repair work on his house and
the contractor intends to place what is called a mechanic's lien on the
home. A mechanic's lien is a kind of interest created by law that
ensures payment to workmen. To get a release from the contract, the
consumer states his wish to cancel on his copy of the contract, signs
and dates it within the three-business-day limit, and mails or delivers
notice to the creditor at the address shown on the contract. Because
of this provision, the contractor must hold up work for three business
days until the cancellation period expires. When the consumer wants
the work done immediately, he must sign a personal statement waiving
his cancellation right.

A summing up

The Truth In Lending Act provides significant protection for consumers. The credit user can now shop around for money and credit terms with information and knowledge that will assist him in finding the most favorable deal and in making the wisest choice. Legislation has made disclosure of credit terms mandatory, and this should help us all do a better job of comparison shopping for money. The law does not limit finance charges or specify which method of computation shall be used on revolving accounts. Our task is to make the right decision about what kind of credit to use in our own unique situations.

Checking your reading

1. What does credit mean?
2. List several major developments in the economy that have made the use of consumer credit more popular.
3. Discuss the advantages of buying on credit.
4. Discuss the disadvantages of buying on credit.
5. Explain why a consumer is really paying interest at a rate of nearly 14 percent when he borrows $100 and repays $107 (the principal plus interest at 7 percent) in 12 equal monthly installments.
6. Describe the "discount" method of figuring installment interest.
7. Describe the "add-on" method of figuring installment interest.
8. What is a rough rule that consumers can use for determining the actual rate of interest on installment loans?
9. What is the intent of the Truth In Lending Act?
10. List eight disclosures that the Truth In Lending Act requires lenders to make.
11. Describe the "previous-balance" method of figuring finance charges on revolving charge accounts.
12. Describe the "average daily balance" method of figuring finance charges on revolving charge accounts.
13. Describe the "adjusted-balance" method of figuring finance charges on revolving charge accounts.

Consumer problems and projects

1. The Smith family's automatic washer is broken and cannot be repaired. The Smiths can save money for six months and pay cash for a new washer, or they can buy a new washer immediately by using credit. If they decide to wait until they have

enough cash, Mrs. Smith will have to use a laundromat for six months. Discuss the advantages and disadvantages of each approach. Which approach would be cheaper?

2.   Apex Department Store sells a variety of home furnishings and appliances. According to the store's advertisements, consumers can pay for their purchases by spreading the cost over a period as long as 18 months with no interest charge. Their cash price and installment price, they say, are identical. Discuss the effect you think such a policy has on the store's cash prices and cash customers.

3.   Obtain a copy of *What You Ought to Know About Federal Reserve Regulation Z*. If your library does not have a copy, you can obtain one free from the Board of Governors, Federal Reserve System, Washington, D.C. 20551. Make a report to the class on the provisions of the Truth In Lending Act that cover real estate. Note particularly the provisions that govern the right of a credit customer to cancel a credit arrangement if his residence is used as collateral for credit.

4.   Report to the class on the legal aspects of installment contracts. Books on business law can be helpful sources of information. You may also refer to later parts of this textbook.

5.   Visit several appliance dealers in your community, and compare the credit arrangements offered on the purchase of a refrigerator in the $300–$550 price range. Try to get figures on a 12-month plan so that you can readily compare credit. Report to the class on your findings.

6.   Assume you are buying a home entertainment center that will cost $1,100. You plan to make a $200 down payment and pay the remaining $900 over a 24-month period. The interest charge is 6 percent of $900 times 2 (2 years), or $108. Thus, the monthly installments will be $42—$37.50 on the principal ($\frac{1}{24}$ of $900) and $4.50 on the interest ($\frac{1}{24}$ of $108). Compute the true annual interest rate using the formula shown on page 362.

7.   Refer to problem 6, and assume that a service charge of $10 is added to the interest charge of $108. Compute the true annual interest rate using the formula given on page 362.

Chapter

Sources and types
of consumer credit

Consumer credit comes in assorted packages and from different sources. Before buying goods on an installment plan or borrowing money for some other purpose, consumers need to know something about the sources of credit, the kinds of credit available, and how their own credit reputation is established. The purpose of this chapter is to supply this kind of information.

Credit in the form of loans may be obtained from financial institutions, insurance companies, pawnbrokers, and unlicensed lenders (although it is now a federal offense for lenders to practice without a license). Consumer credit also may be obtained from retail stores, credit card companies, oil companies, airlines, and from many other sources. The types of credit cards issued by different companies and their use will be discussed later in this chapter.

WHERE TO BORROW MONEY

There are a half dozen or so different institutions whose business it is to lend money: commercial banks, savings banks, savings and loan associations, sales finance companies, credit unions, and consumer finance companies. In addition, money can be borrowed from the cash value of one's life insurance policies.

Commercial banks

At one time, commercial banks lent money only to commercial organizations. Now, consumer loans make up a good part of their lending business. In fact, at the beginning of the 1970s, these banks held more installment credit than any other type of financial institution. In January, 1970, the total amount of installment credit outstanding in the United States was $97.4 billion, and commercial banks held $40.1 billion of that total.

For most consumers, investigating the possibilities of a bank loan should be the starting point when cash is needed. Personal finance counselors report that often people confess that they did not shop for a loan at a commercial bank because they were slightly awed by the imposing facade on the building and were not quite certain that they would be welcomed at the loan officer's desk. Actually, bankers estimate that they grant about 90 percent of the loans requested by consumers. Indeed, your attitude should be that you are doing the bank a favor by investigating the possibility of being one of its customers. A person who has a job and a record of prompt payment of debts should have no difficulty whatsoever in obtaining a loan from a commercial bank.

Terms and interest rates vary from area to area and from bank to bank, so it is important to visit several banks to find the most favorable deal. Banks offer different types of loans. The loans can be small—a

A commercial bank is a convenient and popular source of consumer credit.

Courtesy Chemical Bank

few hundred dollars to pay for some unexpected expense or to buy Christmas gifts. Or, the loan may be as high as several thousand dollars to buy an expensive car. Interest rates can range from an annual rate of about 9 percent to about 26 percent. The lower rates are for *secured loans,* where the value of the security covers the amount of the loan. For example, some people use stocks or bonds as security, and this permits them to borrow usually 60 to 70 percent of the market value of the stocks or bonds. The bank holds the stocks or bonds until the loan is repaid, and they are then returned to the borrower. If the borrower cannot repay the loan, the bank sells all or part of the security in order to collect the debt.

When loans are made for large amounts, to buy an expensive appliance or a car, for example, the bank may ask for a chattel mortgage as security. A chattel mortgage is recorded at the courthouse and indicates that the borrower has a claim against the goods. State laws are not uniform regarding the use of chattel mortgages.

Most bank loans are made on the installment basis. To some clients, however, banks will offer loans on unsecured, short-term notes. Such a loan means simply that the borrower agrees to pay back a certain sum of money at a prescribed interest rate within a limited period of time, such as 3 months. No installments are made; the principal is paid all at one time. These short-term notes are usually figured on a simple interest basis, and the rates are generally quite favorable. For example, a commercial bank may offer a loan of $1,000 at 7 percent per year for 90 days. The interest charge in dollars for the 90-day period would be computed by multiplying the principal P ($1,000) times the annual rate R (.07) times the loan period or time T ($\frac{90}{365}$). $I = PRT$; $I = 1{,}000 \times .07 \times \frac{90}{365}$.

Thus, $17.26 would be the cost of borrowing $1,000 at 7 percent for 90 days. Banks usually restrict short-term unsecured loans to clients with good to excellent credit ratings, and they give established customers extra consideration. For most people, therefore, the best bank to start with when searching for a loan is the bank with which they have been doing business in the past.

Savings banks and savings and loan associations

Savings banks and savings and loan associations are good sources from which to borrow money for certain purposes. The laws governing these institutions vary from state to state. However, the consumer who wants to borrow money would be wise to check these institutions as a possible source because they do grant several types of loans.

All savings banks and savings and loan associations grant mortgage loans. Many grant home-improvement loans, personal loans, and loans for education. Most also grant passbook loans to their depositors.

A person who takes out a passbook loan is, in a way, borrowing money from himself. This type of loan cannot exceed the amount that the borrower has deposited in his account. But when funds are needed for only a short period of time, it is sometimes to the depositor's advantage to take out a low-cost passbook loan rather than lose the interest on his savings, for the interest that must be paid on the loan is less than the interest that the borrower would lose by taking the money out of his account. For example, this type of loan can sometimes be used profitably to make payments that will later be reimbursed by insurance or to buy goods that would otherwise be purchased on a short-term installment basis.

Sales finance companies

Although sales finance companies do not actually lend a consumer cash in the same way as a bank might, they represent an important source of loans. These lenders supply credit through auto dealers, mail-order outlets, and other retailers. Essentially what happens is that when one buys an item such as an automobile on credit, the signed contract is sold by the retailer to a sales finance company for cash. The sales finance company has a legal interest, known as a "lien," in the item to ensure that complete payment will be made. The consumer must make his payments to the sales finance company. In the early 1970s only commercial banks held more installment credit than sales finance companies. Most of the credit extended by sales finance companies has been for the purchase of automobiles.

Credit unions

A credit union is a consumer cooperative lending agency. It is a voluntary association of individuals with some common bond, such as employment with the same firm or membership in the same union or church. The credit union gives members the opportunity to save money, paying interest to members who do so. From this accumulated savings fund, loans are made to any members who wish to borrow money. A member may be able to borrow up to $2,500 on his signature alone, and he may be able to borrow even more with the proper security pledged.

Often a credit union is one of the best sources from which to borrow money, for it has the advantages of low operating costs and also certain tax advantages. The charge on a credit union loan is generally 1 percent a month, sometimes less. An advantage of borrowing from a credit union is that you are dealing with fellow workers or friends who have a special interest in your financial welfare. On the other hand, you may hesitate to reveal your financial problems to the committee of fellow workers or friends who must approve the request.

Consumer finance companies

Consumer finance companies, also known as small-loan companies and personal finance companies, operate under state laws. In 1916 the Russell Sage Foundation cooperated with the National Federation of Remedial Loan Associations to draft a model law regulating interest rates and practices in the making of small, personal loans. In most states, the laws governing consumer finance companies are modeled after this Uniform Small Loan Law. Originally, the maximum loan permitted by licensed small-loan companies was $300, but legislative action in the various states has increased this figure so that most states permit them to make loans of $1,000 or more.

Consumers may find it easier to walk into a friendly small-loan company and walk out with a $500 or $600 loan than they would to get the same money from a commercial bank. Small-loan companies keep longer hours—some stay open evenings and Saturdays—and they may ask fewer questions. But in return for such service, the borrower will usually pay a higher rate of interest. Consumer finance companies make chiefly small loans, and they are usually more willing than other credit institutions to lend money to someone who may be a poor risk. Consequently, their business expenses are proportionately greater than those of more conservative institutions. These companies generally charge interest rates as high as state laws allow for various loan amounts. The typical charge is from 18 to 42 percent per year, depending on the size and nature of the loan and the state in which the firm is located. Before agreeing to pay these rates, consumers should check with other lenders.

Insurance companies

Most Americans own life insurance policies. Insurance is a source of security and a prime resource of most families in our country.

After a year or two, most insurance policies have a cash surrender value, which may be used as a basis for borrowing money. An insurance company will lend a policyholder any amount up to the cash value of a policy; this value is always shown in tables that are included in the policy. Today, borrowing on life insurance is a bargain, since most credit is comparatively expensive. The interest rate for loans specified in most policies currently being issued is 5 or 6 percent. The interest is charged on the unpaid balance, so this is a true annual interest rate. There is no specified time for repayment. This absence of a time limit may be an advantage for persons who cannot make regular payments, but it can also be a disadvantage. If the borrower does not attempt to hold himself to some schedule of repayment, the cost of the loan will be high, for he must pay interest charges as long as he has the money. It is well to remember, too, that an insurance policy is decreased by the amount of the loan. If, for example, a man who borrowed $1,000 on a $5,000 life insurance policy died before he had repaid the loan, the insurance company would pay only $4,000 to his beneficiary. Of course, the net value of his estate would be the same as if he had any other loan of $1,000.

A loan from an insurance company is obtained easily. The insurance company provides loan forms. After they have been completed and returned the loan will be made.

Other sources

Pawn shops are not a usual source for loans, and their role as lenders is relatively small. Nevertheless, people do borrow from pawnbrokers because they find borrowing a small amount of money is quick and simple. The interest charge is extremely high. You must pledge something valuable, such as jewelry or a musical instrument, to get a loan

United Press International, Inc.

In spite of their high interest charges, pawnshops represent a source of small loans for consumers.

from a pawn shop. The pawn shop keeps the pledged article, and if the borrower pays back the sum borrowed plus interest within the agreed period of time he gets his article back. If he does not pay back at the agreed time, the pawnbroker will sell the pledged item.

Reputable loan companies operate under state license. Lenders who operate without a license are called "loan sharks," and the name is appropriate because they can and often do "devour" their victims. Since the passage of the Consumer Credit Protection Act in 1968, loan sharking is a federal offense, but such lenders will no doubt continue to operate as long as they can find persons who will borrow money from them. They flourish in places with inadequate small-loan laws, but they can also be found in almost any city, preying on the unwary, the timid, and the ignorant.

Why does anyone ever try to do business with an unlicensed lender? Only through ignorance or desperation. Many borrowers have over-extended their credit or want to keep their affairs secret from family and friends. They take what to them seems an easy way out. The lender may make an attractive introductory offer, but the heavy credit charges pile up on the borrower a little at a time. Soon he is in such trouble that he cannot see any way out of his financial difficulties.

The person who has become involved with a loan shark is often afraid to report his situation to the proper authorities because he is afraid of strong-arm tactics that the money lender threatens.

TYPES OF CREDIT PLANS

The Truth In Lending Act requires creditors to tell consumers what they pay for credit and how the charge is computed. Learning who offers what credit terms and which are the most advantageous to him is still the job of the consumer. However, it is possible to identify two basic types of credit plans: open-account and service charge. There are many different variations of the service charge type of account, and some variations incorporate features of open-account credit. The kinds of service charge accounts include revolving credit, optional revolving credit, "easy payment" credit, and installment credit.

Open-account credit

The oldest type of credit for consumers is the open account, sometimes called regular account. The customer can buy in person, by telephone, or by mail, and the store transfers the merchandise—usually with no down payment or interest charge. A statement is mailed to the customer, usually monthly, and the customer typically has 25 or 30 days in which to pay the bill without interest charges. Open-account credit is granted not only by retail stores but also by doctors, dentists, television repair firms, plumbers, other professional people, and other types of service firms.

Other kinds of charge accounts

Service charge types of accounts have become popular over the years, and there are a variety of plans used. Names of accounts vary from store to store, and it is difficult to say which name fits which plan. But the important thing to remember is that the following kinds of accounts involve an additional cost to the consumer.

REVOLVING CREDIT ACCOUNTS   Under a revolving credit plan, the maximum amount that may be owed to the store at any one time is determined at the time the account is opened. For example, if a customer's specified credit level is $350, he may charge goods up to the amount of $350 and pay for purchases over a period of time. The part that must be paid monthly depends on the terms set up by the store— the customer pays either a set amount or a percentage of the amount owed. For example, a store could specify that for a credit limit of $350, the monthly payments shall be $20. Or, the minimum monthly payments could be set at 10 percent of the amount owed each month. The unpaid portion of the bill is subject to an interest charge, of course, and the amount is typically $1\frac{1}{2}$ percent a month, or an 18 percent annual rate. New purchases may be charged to the account at any time as long as the total amount owed does not exceed the established maximum of $350.

OPTIONAL REVOLVING CREDIT   Many stores combine the features of open-account credit with revolving credit. That is, the customer can treat the account as open credit. The store bills him on a regular monthly cycle, and he can elect to pay the entire bill within the agreed number of days after billing—usually 25 or 30 days. In that event, he pays no service charge. If, however, he does not wish to pay the entire bill that month, the account is treated as a revolving credit account, and the customer must make at least the agreed upon monthly payment and be subject to a percentage service charge.

EASY PAYMENT PLANS   Some stores set up installment plans that do not have the optional open-account feature. The customer buys a product and agrees to pay a predetermined amount each week or each month until the item is paid for. Interest rates vary, of course, and so do the time periods that are involved in such agreements.

Consumers should consider carefully the amount of the carrying charge they are paying for charge purchases. The Truth In Lending Act makes comparison shopping for credit much easier than it was before, and armed with the dollar cost of credit from various sources, the consumer can select his source of credit wisely. In some instances, money can be saved by getting a personal loan from a credit union or a bank and then paying cash for the merchandise. A large initial payment may reduce the period of time during which the payments will be made, and this can reduce the charges considerably. An ad reading "No Down Payment—Three Years to Pay" may have appeal, but remember that interest charges mount up because payments are spread out over time. Paying quickly reduces credit costs.

Installment credit

When a person obtains credit from the seller of a relatively expensive or big-ticket item, such as an appliance or an automobile, it is called *installment-sales credit*. If the buyer borrowed the money from a lending agency and then used the cash to pay for his purchase, he would be obtaining an *installment cash loan*. In either case, the buyer may end up making the installment payments to someone other than the seller because retailers often "sell" their interest in installment-sales contracts to a sales finance company or have an open agreement with such a company.

Purchases on credit for products such as cars, refrigerators, television sets, and the like are handled differently from purchases on credit for small appliances, clothing, and relatively inexpensive goods. The bigger item serves as a guarantee for repayment. When you buy a refrigerator, for example, you are asked to sign a contract in which the appliance is pledged as security. If you fail to make the payments, the refrigerator could be recovered or repossessed by the creditor and then sold, with the proceeds used to pay off your debt. How the creditor protects himself is, of course, quite important to those who buy on an installment plan.

Usually, the seller protects himself by asking the buyer to sign one of several types of contracts, of which the most used are the chattel mortgage and the conditional sales contract. The provisions of each vary from state to state and from creditor to creditor. The important thing for buyers is to read the fine print carefully and to question the seller or the finance company on all doubtful areas until they are satisfied that they understand their obligations.

CHATTEL MORTGAGE   When a chattel mortgage contract is used, the seller gives title to the goods to the buyer and then takes the mortgage as security. The seller must make the mortgage a matter of public record. The seller has a proportionate interest in the mortgaged property, which is always movable goods such as furniture and automobiles, and he can ask in court to have the property sold at a sheriff's sale for the seller's benefit if the buyer fails to live up to his obligations under the contract.

CONDITIONAL SALES CONTRACT   When a conditional sales contract is used, the title to the merchandise remains with the seller until he has received full payment. When payments are not made according to the agreement, the merchandise can be repossessed, and, depending on state law, the payments that had been made may be regarded as rent for use of the product, or part of the money may be refunded. Usually, the procedure in states that have laws patterned after the Uniform Conditional Sales Act is to sell the merchandise at an auction. After the creditor takes the unpaid balance and the expenses of repossessing and selling the property, any money remaining is given to the debtor. If the money received from the sale at the auction is not sufficient, the creditor may take legal action against the buyer for the remaining amount owed. In that event, the buyer may find himself paying money for a product he no longer has.

In some instances the auction sale is rigged so that only the creditor's friends or relatives are present to bid on the property. Thus, a $2,000 car on which the debtor still owes $1,800 may be sold at such an auction for $300, and the debtor would still be legally required to pay the difference of $1,500. The creditor ends up with the car and the money. The debtor ends up with nothing.

Installment purchase contracts can be full of booby traps, and the buyer should read the contract with care before signing it. Some of the things to watch for are the following:

- Wage assignment clause. A *wage assignment* clause allows the store or finance company to force the borrower's employer to deduct payments from the borrower's paycheck. This is the legal process known as garnisheeing wages, and the Consumer Credit Protection Act restricts the weekly garnishment to the lesser of (1) 25 percent of a wage earner's take-home pay or (2) take-home pay minus 30 times the federal minimum hourly wage. Some states have garnishment legislation that provides even more protection for borrowers than that provided by the federal Consumer Credit Protection Act. In some states wage assignments are not permitted, but other legal means are available to the lender to recover money owed to him.

- Add-on clause. An *add-on* clause in a contract allows a store to repossess other purchases that have already been paid for if a person misses payments on a present purchase. Thus, if a buyer defaults on his new payments, he may lose not only the new products he has purchased but also other products for which he has completed his payments.
- Acceleration clause. When the contract has an *acceleration* clause all payments are due if one payment is missed. Then, if the buyer is unable to pay the total unpaid balance, his merchandise may be taken and resold.
- Balloon clause. Some contracts provide for a blown-up final payment. For example, a contract may call for 11 monthly payments of $30 and a final payment of $100. If the buyer does not realize he agreed to that big final payment, he can easily end up in trouble with the creditor.

CREDIT CARDS

How far are we from the day when a plastic card will replace cash? We have not yet reached the point where cash is obsolete, but the tremendous growth in the use of credit cards during the past two decades has been nothing short of phenomenal. Many people carry more than one credit card with them. In a recent year there were an estimated 250 million credit cards of one kind or another in circulation, more than one for every person in the United States.

Colleges in many places throughout the country now permit students to pay their tuition with credit cards. In some localities, property taxes and automobile registration fees can be paid with a credit card. In at least one city, bail can be arranged with a credit card from a national company. It seems safe to say that credit cards are here to stay.

Types of credit cards

Credit cards are generally divided into three categories: single-purpose cards, travel and entertainment cards, and bank credit cards. As the companies that offer these cards expand their services, and as new companies enter the field, these categories will become less accurate. For example, many so-called single-purpose cards can now be used

Credit cards have been both a convenient source of credit and a financial trap for many consumers. Thus consumers should use them with care.

Courtesy North American Rockwell

to pay for a variety of goods and services, and one might be able to charge books offered by a book club on a travel and entertainment card. These categories are still helpful, however, since they tell you something about the company that offers the card and give some indication of its usefulness.

SINGLE-PURPOSE CARDS   The major oil companies have issued credit cards for quite some time, and department stores have identified their credit customers by issuing cards. No charge is made for the credit card. The customer simply makes application, and if he is credit-worthy, a card is issued. The purpose of the card, of course, is to encourage the cardholder to buy most of or all his products from the firm issuing the card. Oil company cards have proved to be quite convenient, especially when one is traveling. Throughout the country, at any service station franchised by the company whose credit card you hold, oil, gas, tires, accessories, and repairs can be charged by simply using the card.

In recent years cooperative arrangements have been made between major oil companies and motel chains, airlines, and car rental companies so that motel charges, including meals, airline tickets, and car rental charges can be charged to oil company cards. Still another use for oil company credit cards has developed recently, and that is the purchase of consumer goods sold by direct mail. The holder of an oil credit card might receive an advertising brochure through the mail that offers such merchandise as tools, cameras, radios, and so on. To buy the goods offered to him, the consumer simply returns a card indicating that he accepts the offer and that he agrees to have the selling price added to his account.

Restaurants, hotels, telephone companies, and airlines are among other firms that issue credit cards for their customers. From the consumers' point of view, the card furnishes all the advantages of open-account credit. Many of the firms issuing these cards also provide for revolving credit, which the customer can use if he should not want to pay his bill in full within a certain period of time following the billing date. The credit charge is typically $1\frac{1}{2}$ percent a month, or 18 percent a year.

TRAVEL AND ENTERTAINMENT CARDS   Diners Club issued the first travel and entertainment card shortly after the Second World War. Other companies, such as American Express and Carte Blanche, quickly followed their lead. These cards in effect opened charge accounts for the cardholders at specific businesses throughout the country, particularly hotels and restaurants. The cards, which were designed with travelers and businessmen in mind, proved to be convenient items. People could more easily keep records of their expenditures on business trips, and they did not, of course, have to carry a lot of cash.

The person applying for a travel and entertainment card is given a quite thorough credit investigation. About 90 percent of the holders of these cards earn in excess of $10,000 a year, and half of them earn more than $20,000 a year. The annual fee that the cardholder must pay for the privilege of having this credit available throughout the country, and indeed the world, is $15. An additional credit card for use by others, such as one's spouse, costs an additional $10 a year.

A businessman who has a travel and entertainment card can take a client to lunch or dinner, pay the tab, including the tip, with a credit card, and have a convenient receipt of his expenditure. If he is away from home, he can pay for his hotel room and his airline ticket with the same card. The cards are used in the retail field mainly for travel, but increasingly they are being accepted in all types of retail stores.

The participating restaurants, hotels, and other firms pay a discount fee as high as 7 percent to the credit card companies. That is, if the bill comes to $40, the restaurant collects $37.80 from the card issuer.

BANK CREDIT CARDS   Because of the success of travel and entertainment credit cards, banks decided to get into the business. The real credit card revolution has been due to the rapid expansion of these bank credit card plans. While in 1970 travel and entertainment cards numbered about 6 million, the number of bank cards issued at that time was 50 million. The bank cards began as small, local plans but have grown into large regional systems nationally interlinked by two major networks: BankAmericard and Master Charge. Another major bank credit card is Uni-Card, sponsored by Chase Manhattan Bank.

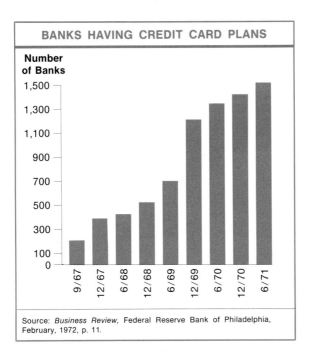

BANKS HAVING CREDIT CARD PLANS

Number
of Banks

Source: *Business Review*, Federal Reserve Bank of Philadelphia,
February, 1972, p. 11.

Under the bank card system, merchants do not have to extend credit in order to permit customers to charge purchases. The bank extends the credit, so the merchant does not have to take the risk of losses due to bad debts. Nor does the merchant have to go through the mechanics of sending out and collecting bills. The bank does this for him.

From the consumers' point of view, one advantage of bank credit cards over travel and entertainment credit cards is that the holder of a bank card pays no fee. The banks charge the stores a discount fee of about 5 percent for handling the transactions.

The bank credit cards, too, enable the customer to treat the charges as open-account credit or as revolving credit. If the bill is paid in full within a specified period of time after the billing date, no service charge is made. If the customer prefers to pay a smaller amount each month, he can pay an amount not less than the minimum payment specified on the monthly bill he receives. The interest charge is usually $1\frac{1}{2}$ percent a month, or 18 percent a year. Thus, banks earn their money from both the merchants and the cardholders.

When a bank credit card is issued, the bank usually assigns to the cardholder a maximum amount of credit, based on his credit reputation, and the card is usually good for one year. The credit available might range from $100 to $1,000 or even more. Also, most banks set a ceiling on the amount that can be charged without having the store check with the bank. Some banks also permit cardholders to borrow cash up to their maximum amount of credit. The amount borrowed is added to the customer's bill, and interest is charged beginning at the time he borrows the money.

Bank cards are designed primarily for retail purchases at stores in one's own community. In many instances, retail stores have discontinued their own credit cards and instead rely on the bank credit cards. As bank cards have become more popular and have become part of major card networks, they have gradually gone into the travel and entertainment business as well. In fact, many hotels and restaurants will accept bank credit cards, so the holders of these cards have many, if not most, of the advantages of holders of travel and entertainment cards. One would think that the increased use of bank cards would reduce the use of travel and entertainment cards, but thus far this has not happened. In a recent year, an official of American Express reported that their business is doubling every $2\frac{1}{2}$ years.

The advantages and drawbacks

One all-purpose credit card, such as a bank card or a travel and entertainment card, has the advantage of enabling consumers to rid their billfold of all but one card. Some of the other advantages of credit cards are listed below:

- Budgeting is made simpler for the consumer because he receives one monthly bill on which his monthly purchases are itemized.
- The consumer makes out one check for many of the purchases he made during the month. In some cases this might reduce his checking account service charge.
- Charge privileges are available at many stores without the necessity of filling out a multitude of credit applications.
- Credit cards are convenient and relatively safe. Travelers do not have to carry large sums of cash with them, and they need not worry about the embarrassment of running out of cash at inopportune times.
- Credit card receipts make good expense account and tax records.
- Even when his bank account may be low, a consumer can take advantage of sales by using his credit card. In the case of an emergency expense, a credit card can be used, and the payment does not have to be made until the bill is received in about a

In some cases, credit cards can be used to obtain cash from banks after regular banking hours.

Courtesy Chemical Bank

month. In effect, the consumer has received a short-term, interest-free loan if he pays his bill within the specified period of time.

- The cash-advance feature of some bank cards gives consumers access to money in emergencies without the red tape of securing a regular bank loan.

Some people have been critical of the increased use of credit cards, citing the fact that merchants increase the cost of their products to compensate for the discount fees they must pay to the credit card issuers. If prices are increased, then people who pay cash will also be paying higher prices for merchandise. But credit card issuers point out that the discount fee is no more, and often less, than the normal costs of extending credit. The merchant who relies on credit cards for his charge sales does not have the bookkeeping expenses that he would have if he handled credit himself. Then, too, losses due to bad debts are suffered by the credit card issuer rather than the merchant. At this time, it is difficult to assess the influence on prices that credit cards have, but the relationship certainly bears watching.

Another major criticism of credit cards relates to the possibility of overextending oneself because of the ease with which credit purchases can be made. This criticism is no doubt well founded, and consumers who have credit cards should learn to use them wisely. Sales slips should be kept, and purchases should be recorded and tallied so that the cardholder knows precisely how much he has spent for various items. Some cardholders limit the use of their cards to certain types of expenditures so that they will not unwittingly buy more than their incomes can bear at the time. Actually, for consumers who overbuy and incur too much debt, any kind of credit can be harmful. It must be acknowledged, though, that credit cards may be especially dangerous because they make credit purchases especially easy.

The problem of fraud

A police official in a medium-size Midwestern city said, "A man can walk into a store armed only with a credit card and walk away with a lot more than he could have taken with a gun." The fraudulent use of credit cards is a growing problem faced by police, merchants, and credit card issuers. A legislative report sponsored by Senator William Proxmire of Wisconsin estimated that in 1969 losses due to the fraudulent use of credit cards exceeded $100 million, while in 1966, losses were estimated to be $20 million. Credit card theft has become an organized crime. Thieves steal credit cards and then use them to acquire services and merchandise. Stolen cards sell for $100 or more on the black market.

The cardholder can be a big loser in the case of fraud, of course, and until a law in 1970 limited the liability of the rightful holder of a credit card, there was special reason for concern. On October 26, 1970, an amendment to the Consumer Credit Protection Act was signed by President Nixon. The law provides that a cardholder shall be liable for no more than $50 of unauthorized charges and not liable at all for unauthorized charges made after he has notified the issuer that the card was lost or stolen. Further, a consumer is not liable for unauthorized charges made on an unsolicited credit card that he has not accepted or used. The law requires that the card issuer give adequate notice to the cardholder of the potential liability and provide him with a self-addressed, prestamped notification that he can mail in the event of loss or theft of the credit card. One other provision of the new credit card law is a stipulation that no credit card shall be issued except in response to a request or an application. Thus, unsolicited credit cards can no longer be mailed to prospective customers.

HOW CREDIT IS ESTABLISHED

A good credit reputation is a valuable asset for a consumer. When you apply for credit, you are asking someone to judge your ability and resolve to make payments on your debt. To enable him to make this judgment, the lender will probably ask you to give a great deal of information about yourself—information about such things as your income, your employer, your education, your home address, your previous address, your bank, and your other credit accounts. If you have used credit before, a local credit bureau no doubt has a file on you, and that file will be used by merchants and lenders. The credit bureau keeps information on your payment record and will watch personal matters that bear on your ability to pay debts. The most important piece of information about you, of course, is your past record of paying off debts. Lenders assume that people who have paid promptly in the past, particularly the recent past, will probably continue to do so.

A credit bureau exists to find out as much as possible about those who request credit and to circulate the information among clients. Some credit bureaus are profit-making business firms; some are mutual organizations supported by a group of merchants. Once you have established a credit record, it will stay in effect for many years. If you move from one city to another, the credit record will follow you as soon as you make a credit application in the new city to which you move. Credit records are maintained mostly for retail merchants, banks, and mortgage lenders, but the information may also be used by prospective employers.

For many consumers, simply filling in a few boxes and answering a few questions is all that is required to obtain credit.

PLEASE PRINT ALL INFORMATION				PLEASE SEND MAIL TO	☒ HOME	☐ BUSINESS	
AMOUNT OF LOAN $2,000	PURPOSE MEDICAL EXPENSES			NO. OF MONTHS 24	CIRCLE DUE DATE 5TH 10TH 15TH (20TH) 25TH 30TH		
FIRST NAME JOSEPH	MIDDLE G.	LAST BOND		DATE OF BIRTH 4-26-40	SPOUSES FIRST NAME/MAIDEN ISABEL WILSON		
HOME ADDRESS (1) 77 MILLER	CITY CLAWSON	STATE MICHIGAN		ZIP 48107	PHONE NO. WA-1-4397	HOW LONG 5 YRS.	NO. OF ROOMS 5
LAST PREVIOUS ADDRESS (2) 2255 BARRINGTON	CITY ROYAL OAK	STATE MICHIGAN	HOW LONG 5 YRS.	YOUR PRESENT LANDLORD, RENTAL AGENT OR (MORTGAGE CO) AND ADDRESS CITIZENS NATIONAL, DETROIT, MICHIGAN			
PREVIOUS ADDRESS (within 5 years) (3)	CITY	STATE	HOW LONG				
MONTHLY RENT OR (MORTGAGE) $195	PURCHASE PRICE $19,500	DOWN PAYMENT $3,000	MARKET VALUE $24,000	MORTGAGE BALANCE $14,800	NO. OF DEPENDENTS. INCLUDE SELF 5	SOCIAL SECURITY NO 366-62-3528	
PARENTS OR NEAREST RELATIVE (Not living with you) HENRY BOND		RELATIONSHIP FATHER	ADDRESS 17565 STONE,	CITY DETROIT	STATE MICHIGAN		
SPOUSE'S PARENTS OR NEAREST RELATIVE (Not living with you) DECEASED	RELATIONSHIP	ADDRESS	CITY	STATE			
EMPLOYER OR BUSINESS NAME (1) ACME MANUFACTURING CO.		ADDRESS 134 PLUM, HAZEL PARK	POSITION FOREMAN	HOW LONG 10 YRS.	TOTAL MO. SAL $1,000		
LAST PREVIOUS EMPLOYER (2)		ADDRESS	POSITION	FROM (DATE)	TO (DATE)		
PREVIOUS EMPLOYER (within 5 years) (3)		ADDRESS	POSITION	FROM (DATE)	TO (DATE)		
SPOUSE'S EMPLOYER (4) NOT EMPLOYED		ADDRESS	POSITION	HOW LONG	TOTAL MO. SAL		
OTHER INCOME NONE	SOURCE		OTHER MONTHLY EXPENSES ALIMONY, SUPPORT, EDUCATION, ETC (LIST TYPE AND AMOUNT)				
IF YOU OWN AN AUTOMOBILE CHEVROLET	MAKE	MODEL BEL AIR	YEAR 1970	FINANCED BY CITY BANK	ADDRESS CLAWSON		BALANCE NONE
SAVINGS BALANCE $400	NAME OF BANK & ADDRESS CITY BANK, CLAWSON			CHECKING BALANCE $50	NAME OF BANK & ADDRESS CITY BANK, CLAWSON		

Fair Credit Reporting Act

The thought of an organization knowing so much about one can be a bit frightening. To make certain that the information is used properly, Congress passed the Fair Credit Reporting Act, and the President signed it into law in October, 1970. The act became effective April 25, 1971. The Fair Credit Reporting Act specifies the purposes for which reports can be used and limits the issuance of them to anyone who intends to use them for evaluating individuals for credit, insurance, or employment or for a legitimate need in connection with a business transaction. It also provides that reports can be issued to an agency of the government if that agency is required by law to consider the consumer's financial status before granting a license or other benefit. Otherwise a report can be issued only in response to a court order or in accordance with the written instructions of the consumer. It is important that consumers be aware of this provision.

Some of the other provisions of the Fair Credit Reporting Act include a requirement that anyone who orders an investigative consumer report (one for insurance company or employment purposes) must notify the consumer a report is being developed within three days after ordering the report. A basic credit report contains only identifying and factual information, as opposed to an investigative consumer report done for insurance or employment purposes. An investigative report contains subjective information with opinions obtained through interviews with various persons who know the person being investigated. The act requires that the reporting agency have reasonable procedures to assure maximum possible accuracy of the information it reports. "Reasonable procedures" can be interpreted to mean that employees must be properly trained before handling information.

An additional provision of the act that is important to consumers is that the credit bureau, upon proper identification, must disclose the following to the consumer:

- The nature and substance of all information in its files concerning the consumer
- The sources of information on file
- The recipient of any credit report furnished within the previous six months

Disclosure shall be made to the consumer in person at the office of the credit bureau or by telephone if the consumer has previously submitted a written request. If the consumer challenges any of the information on file, the act requires the credit bureau to reinvestigate the consumer's record, and if it is still challenged by the consumer, the bureau must accept a statement of any length from the consumer and make the statement a permanent part of his file. Further, if the consumer requests, the credit bureau must send a copy of the consumer's statement to all parties who have received his credit report within the previous six months. This important provision enables the consumer to avoid an unfavorable credit record if he has refused or delayed payment for just cause. It provides the consumer with the opportunity to "tell his side of the story."

What to do when trouble comes

Building and maintaining a record for paying promptly is extremely important for establishing a good credit rating. Credit managers and loan officers constantly stress the importance of good communication between the borrower and the creditor—especially when the borrower has hit upon hard times and may have difficulty for a while making his full payments. Consumers who have overextended themselves financially or who have had their incomes reduced because of sickness, unemployment, or other problems should make a point of speaking with their creditors at once. Often if you have a plan for taking care of the debt, even though it means that you will make smaller payments or will not make payments at scheduled times, the creditors will want to know about it, and usually they will do all they can to help. Silence on the part of a debtor when bills are past due makes creditors uneasy. They understand that any person can experience financial problems, and if they know you are sincere about paying off the obligation, they will usually cooperate fully.

When debt obligations are not met, say on an installment plan for a piece of furniture, the creditor may take legal action and repossess the furniture. Most merchants dislike doing this, however, and they may find that the market for used furniture is not particularly good. They much prefer to work out a plan whereby the debtor can ultimately pay for the goods. The best advice for consumers, of course, is to refrain from getting so deeply in debt. If this advice is followed, a financial crisis will not occur.

Credit bureaus do make mistakes, so whenever a consumer has difficulty getting credit, he should ask the lender which credit bureau supplied information so that the situation can be straightened out before further damage is done to his credit reputation.

Checking your reading

1. List several institutions whose business it is to lend money.
2. Why are rates generally lower on secured loans?
3. Explain what is meant by a chattel mortgage.
4. Why is a credit union often one of the best sources from which to borrow money?
5. When a person borrows money on his life insurance policy, what determines the maximum amount he may borrow?
6. Explain why borrowing money on one's life insurance policy is advantageous.
7. Why do consumers sometimes do business with unlicensed lenders?
8. What is open-account credit?
9. Under a revolving credit plan, when is the maximum amount that may be charged at any time determined?
10. When a conditional sales contract is used, when does title to the merchandise pass on to the buyer?
11. List four things one should examine in installment purchase contracts.
12. How do the issuers of travel and entertainment credit cards earn money?
13. List several advantages of credit cards.
14. Give two criticisms of credit cards.
15. Summarize the important provisions of the 1970 Fair Credit Reporting Act.

Consumer problems and projects

1. Raymond Miller needs $350 to pay certain bills. He has just learned that from the Yen Finance Company he can borrow $350 for 12 months with payments of $34 a month. What is the true annual interest rate being charged by the finance company?
2. Mr. Miller considered borrowing money from the Yen Finance Company. What other lending agencies would Mr. Miller be wise to consider before he borrows the money?
3. Sharon Mancelli has missed five weeks of work because of illness. She is now behind in the payment of certain bills. She owes a department store $85, an oil company $48, and her physician $120. Her monthly rent payment of $130 will be due in one week. What action should Sharon take?
4. Make a comparison chart of the various agencies that lend money to consumers. Compare the amount each agency is generally willing to lend, the true interest rates, and the ease of securing a loan.
5. Using the *Reader's Guide to Periodical Literature*, make a list of recent articles about truth in lending that have appeared in magazines available in your library. Locate the articles, and construct an annotated list of selected readings on the topic of truth in lending.

Chapter

Government services

Throughout most of this book we have considered the problems of the consumer in the marketplace and his relations with business. In this chapter we will consider the problems of the taxpaying consumer's relations with government.

The tax-financed services that government provides are an important factor affecting the way we live. The availability of public services and their quality have a great deal to do with our safety, our health, our education, and our economic security. We can see the importance of public services in our own communities. There can be little argument that life is more pleasant in a community with good fire and police services, adequate recreation facilities, and good schools and hospitals.

WHAT FUNCTIONS DOES GOVERNMENT SERVE?

Expenditures for government, and our taxes, are high because of the wide variety of functions that we have assigned to government. These functions can be classified into three general categories: (1) service functions, (2) income transfer functions, and (3) economic stabilization functions. Let us take a look at these three categories.

Service functions

Service functions of the government include the conservation of natural resources, national defense, and the administration of justice. *Service functions* are the provision of services to individual citizens that

The federal government uses tax dollars to provide many service functions, such as national defense.

Courtesy Aviation Week and Space Technology/*McGraw-Hill*

business enterprises cannot or will not supply effectively. About three-fourths of all government spending goes to pay for the services provided by government. Part of this spending goes for equipment and supplies (for example, missiles, research facilities, and gasoline), and part goes to employees (including servicemen, congressmen, and public health officers). These expenditures are classified as *exhaustive expenditures* by economists because they use up goods and services supplied to government by the private economy. Once these resources have been used by the government they are exhausted and therefore are no longer available for use in other ways.

Income transfer functions

Income transfer functions involve the redistribution of income and other resources to individuals, business enterprises, and state and local governments. Transfer payments are also an important part of government expenditures and account for around 25 percent of total spending. Such *income transfers* are paid on the basis of need rather than as a payment for current services. An example of income transfers to individuals is the welfare payments made to low-income families that include young children. A federal grant-in-aid to a community to assist it in financing a new sewage system is an example of a transfer to a local government. The payments made to farmers who limit the number of acres devoted to specific crops is an example of a transfer made to business. Income transfers to businesses sometimes are also called *subsidies.*

Government expenditures for income transfers differ from government expenditures for services in that they are not exhaustive expenditures. Instead, income transfers are classified as *nonexhaustive expenditures,* since they do not use up any goods or any labor services.

Income transfers are, in effect, a shift in the power to purchase goods and services from the federal government to other decision units—individuals, state and local governments, and business.

Economic stabilization functions

Economic stabilization functions involve government control and regulation of the economic activity of the nation. The goals of this regulation are to maintain full employment of the labor force and to control the rate of inflation. In seeking these goals the federal government relies on its power to regulate governmental spending, taxes, and interest rates.

Many government programs include two functions at the same time. For example, when government builds and operates public housing projects, it is providing a service—housing—and redistributing income—because of the reduced rents charged the tenants. Government spending can also serve both the service function and the economic stabilization function. In times of unemployment, the government may develop new park and recreation facilities, which when finished provide a useful service. By hiring unemployed workers for the project, the government reduces unemployment. Because the workers hired have more money to spend, they contribute to increasing the level of business activity, and in this way the project serves an economic stabilization function.

WHEN SHOULD GOVERNMENT PROVIDE SERVICES?

We rely on business to supply a major part of our consumer wants. Consumer wants usually create a situation in which private sellers can produce and sell goods profitably. Enterprising businessmen, attracted by the chance to make profits, set about supplying these wants. There are, however, certain situations in which the marketplace cannot, or does not, supply the kinds of goods and services the public wants, so if we, as consumers, were to rely on private business to supply these wants, we would find that the goods and services supplied would be inadequate or overpriced.

Recognizing cases in which government activity is appropriate

There are certain kinds of goods and services that cannot be divided up and sold to individual customers. These have been labeled "collective goods." Because of the nature of collective goods we cannot control who uses them in such a way that we can make individual users

Government is often called upon to provide collective goods that are consumed by groups of people.

Courtesy Engineering News-Record/*McGraw-Hill*

pay for them. Suppose, for example, that a private company built a flood-control dam and asked those in the valley below it to pay for the protection they received. Everyone in the valley would be protected whether they paid or not. There would be no way to limit protection only to those who paid.

COLLECTIVE GOODS   Goods and services such as flood-control dams are called *collective goods* because they are consumed by groups of people rather than single individuals and because all the members of the group benefit from them whether they pay or not. The only way such goods and services can effectively be supplied is by government. As we saw in the example of the flood-control dam, there is no way a private company can make a profit supplying such services. A private company cannot force people to pay for flood-control service if they do not want it—and since those who pay and those who do not are all protected, there is no reason for anyone to pay. Because private companies cannot make a profit from providing flood control, we can see that flood-control dams would never be built if government did not step in and build them. When government undertakes such projects, it can finance them by exercising its power to tax the people who receive the service.

Another example of a collective good is national defense. It is not the kind of service that can be provided by a private business and divided up and sold to individual customers. For this reason, it also is best provided by government.

EXTERNAL ECONOMIES   Government activity is also desirable in cases where a service provides benefits to others besides those who use it directly. An example of such a service is education. While it is an important benefit to the student who receives it, education also provides benefits to the entire community. It provides better-educated and more productive workers and more informed citizens and voters.

If the decision about how much to spend on education were left to individual students and their families, their decisions would be guided by how much education would be worth to them. These decisions might ignore the value of education to the community. If the decision were left solely up to individuals we might find them spending less for education than would be desirable from the standpoint of the community as a whole. Because of the value of education to society, it is in the interest of us all to encourage education and provide tax money to finance it. The extra benefits gained by society, or by people other than those who directly use a good or service, have been labeled *external economies* by economists.

EXTERNAL DISECONOMIES Government activity may be necessary in cases where the use of certain goods or services creates harm or damage that affects other members of society. In the previous case of external economies, society benefited from the consumption of the goods and services involved. In the case of *external diseconomies*, society is, instead, harmed.

An example is the situation which occurs in many rural areas. Small towns and individual households along the banks of a river dispose of sewage in the easiest and cheapest way—by dumping it directly into the river without treatment. This creates a costly and dangerous pollution problem for cities downstream. Here we have a situation in which one group's desire to cut sewage disposal expenses involves serious costs for another group.

We can see that government action is needed, since it would be to the advantage of society, as a whole, if the dumping of raw sewage into rivers were stopped. In this case, society, as a whole, would gain if the government helped those living upstream to build sewage treatment plants.

It can also be argued that there are external diseconomies involved in the consumption of alcohol. Consumption of alcohol may harm the individual, and it can also involve costs to society, such as the deaths, injuries, and property damage resulting from accidents caused by drunken drivers. The heavy taxes placed on liquor in most states grow out of a recognition of the social problems and costs involved in its use. A similar attitude is reflected in the heavy taxes on cigarettes in some states.

Utility services are considered natural monopolies, because these services can be provided most efficiently by a single seller.

NATURAL MONOPOLIES Government often is involved in providing or regulating utility services such as telephone, electricity, and water and in providing mass transit. Services such as these, which can be provided most cheaply by a single seller, are called *natural monopolies.* Having a single seller provide a service avoids wasteful duplication of equipment and competition for customers. The single enterprise supplying a market can be operated by the government itself or by a private company. In this country, ultilities most frequently are operated by private companies but are regulated by government to help ensure reasonable prices for customers.

CONVENIENCE In some cases, government may provide services simply because it is more convenient to have it do so. This is the case for highways. Highways could be built by private companies and tolls charged—many roads were built in this way in earlier times. In general, however, it is easier and more convenient to have the government build and maintain roads and finance them out of tax money.

Operating and financing government services

Many government services are paid for out of tax revenues and are provided free to all users. Since our taxes are based in large part on the ability to pay, we can see that our system of taxation and providing free public services has the effect of redistributing income. Those with greater ability to pay are taxed more heavily, while all citizens share, more or less equally, in the benefits provided. Some services, however, are not provided free; instead, users are charged a fee. In certain cases the fee fully covers the cost of the service. This is now the case for the mail, since the reorganization of the postal service. In other cases, the fees charged users may cover only part of the cost of the service. This is the case for tuition charges at public colleges and universities.

We have considered a number of situations where it is necessary or appropriate for government to become involved in supplying services. It is not, however, necessary in these cases for the government itself to actually supply the service. The actual service can be provided by a private firm, with the government involved in financing and regulating the firm's operations.

For example, the government could encourage education in other ways than by providing free public schools. It could, instead, provide each student a grant to be used to attend the private school of his choice. Some people have advocated a shift to such a system. They claim that competition among schools for pupils would improve the quality of the education offered. In addition, because of the desire for profits, operators of privately run schools could be expected to find ways to cut costs. This would help to hold down the cost to government of providing education.

Deciding on government versus private enterprise

There has been a continuing controversy in this country over the proper extent of government activity. Some people feel the government should assume a larger role in providing goods and services, while others feel it already is doing things that would be better left to private enterprise. Some of the greatest disagreements on the proper role of government came during the New Deal administration of Franklin Roosevelt in the 1930s.

During this period the government began a number of new enterprises and activities in order to stimulate the economy and help lift the nation out of the Great Depression. It was during the 1930s that the federal government moved into the social insurance field and instituted the social security program. It also built many dams for electric power and flood control. Many felt the government's activities in producing and distributing electricity should have been left to private enterprise. Others argued that the government had served a useful role by providing electric service to rural areas that the private electric companies had ignored because they had not considered them to be a source of profit.

The Communications Satellite Corporation represents a compromise between government ownership and private ownership.

Courtesy Aviation Week and Space Technology/*McGraw-Hill*

More recently, there was controversy over whether the services of communications satellites should be provided by a government agency or by private enterprise. Some favored a government-controlled corporation. Others favored giving control to the American Telephone and Telegraph Company (The Bell System), since it would be a major user of the satellite services and already had developed the technical skills needed for building and using satellites. Our congressmen instead decided upon a third alternative. In 1962 the Communications Satellite Act provided for the creation of a private corporation owned jointly by the major communications companies and by individual stockholders. The act also ruled that the corporation be operated under strict government control.

The decision about whether a service is to be provided by government or private enterprise is determined, in part, by economic considerations. We have discussed the cases in which government activity is most appropriate—collective goods, goods involving external economies and diseconomies, natural monopolies, and cases of convenience. Only part of the decision about whether government or private enterprise will provide a service is economic, however. Part of the decision is a political one and is determined by citizens and legislators.

ARGUMENTS AGAINST GOVERNMENT PROGRAMS   A number of arguments have been offered against government involvement in providing public services. It is argued that all government activities involve compulsion—people are forced by government to do things they do not wish to do. When services are provided by government, everyone is forced to support the service with his taxes, even though he may object to it. When the government moves into the field of social insurance, for instance, everyone is forced to join the program. This, it is argued, denies people the right to make individual decisions about providing for their own future.

Another argument is that individual citizens seldom have a real opportunity to express support for or objections to a particular program. Many issues are involved in each election—and instead of voting on each issue, we vote for candidates supporting the programs we consider most important. It is also difficult for voters to indicate how much of one service relative to another they would like. It is hard, for example, for voters to indicate that they would like more spending for education and less for highway construction.

Another criticism of government activity is that spending decisions are too much influenced by the actions of pressure groups. It is argued that decisions too often are the result of the relative power of small groups, not of overall public needs. Instead of being judged on their value to society as a whole, projects are judged on their value to a small group with political power.

ARGUMENTS FOR GOVERNMENT PROGRAMS Assigning to government the responsibility for providing certain services does, however, have advantages. The marketplace gives the most attention to those with the most money to spend. Their preferences decide what kinds of goods and services will be produced—even though these may not meet the needs of everyone. The political process, however, differs from the marketplace. Each citizen has one vote and a more equal voice in deciding the kinds of goods and services that will be provided.

In considering the relative merits of having government or private industry supply goods and services, we need to recall that the market does not always operate effectively. Certain kinds of goods and services might never be provided if we had to depend solely on private corporations. We saw that this is the case for collective goods. We also saw the problems in relying solely on the market when external economies and diseconomies are involved. We saw that the activities of more than one firm are wasteful and raise costs to consumers in cases where a service is a natural monopoly.

Government activity may be necessary in certain other special instances, such as cases involving large risks, uncertain outcomes, and high costs. The development of nuclear reactors for electrical power production is one such case. The costs of development were so large and the possibilities of commercial applications so uncertain that no individual private firm could take the risk. Instead, the government took the risk, since the development of peaceful uses of atomic energy was considered to be important for national progress in the long run.

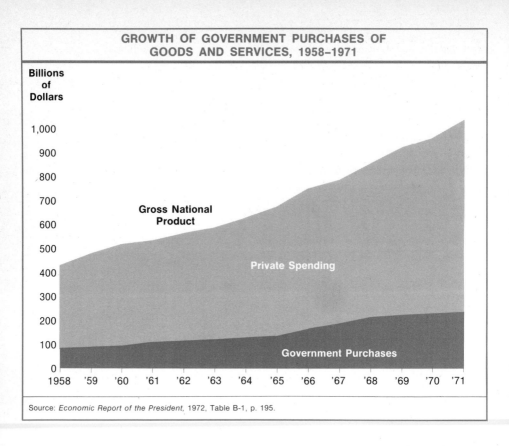

GROWTH OF GOVERNMENT PURCHASES OF
GOODS AND SERVICES, 1958–1971

Billions
of
Dollars

1,000
900
800
700
600
500
400
300
200
100
0

Gross National
Product

Private Spending

Government Purchases

1958 '59 '60 '61 '62 '63 '64 '65 '66 '67 '68 '69 '70 '71

Source: *Economic Report of the President,* 1972, Table B-1, p. 195.

ARE WE SPENDING ENOUGH FOR PUBLIC SERVICES?

Although our taxes already seem high, we can ask whether we really
are spending enough on public services. It is obvious that many problems still exist in this country that can be solved only by increased
government activity. These problems include poverty, pollution, inadequate medical services, and urban decay.

The social balance controversy

Earlier, in the chapter on advertising, we discussed economist John
Kenneth Galbraith's views on the problem of social balance. Galbraith
argues that the heavy expenditures on advertising in this country have
encouraged the consumption of privately owned goods and at the same
time have reduced the emphasis on improving public services. Galbraith and the other advocates of this view argue that private goods
will be enjoyed most fully if there is a proper balance between the
supply of private goods, such as cars, and the supply of public goods,
such as highways. Those concerned about social balance argue that

as a nation we would get more satisfaction for our money if more of it were devoted to public goods rather than private spending.

Social balance is also important because of its relation to long-range economic growth and national progress. Economists concerned about social balance argue that overspending on electric can openers and car air-conditioners may lead to the neglect of medical and technical research, the building of educational facilities, and other public services, which are important in increasing productivity and contributing to economic development.

Other economists have criticized these arguments. They point out that many moderate- and low-income families enjoy few wasteful "frills." They note that higher taxes to finance an increase in public services would constitute a hardship for such families. They also point out that not all public expenditures are wise and not all private expenditures are foolish. They argue that increasing taxes to pay for public football stadiums could be expected to cut into funds individual families are using for medical care, education, and their own recreational activities. Another important criticism is that continued expansion of the role of government as a supplier of services will result in a government that is dangerously large and powerful and a serious threat to democracy.

Why does social imbalance occur?

We may ask why an imbalance between the supply of public goods and private goods occurs. If citizens really want more public services why can't they vote for them? It is, however, difficult to increase the supply of public services as rapidly as the demand for them grows. This is because as incomes increase, our demand for public services increases at a much faster rate than our demand for private goods. As incomes rise we put less priority on spending for food, clothing, and shelter and more on recreation, education, health care, public safety, and sanitation. As a result, the demand for public services grows rapidly.

Although the demands for services have increased, the government has found it difficult to obtain the increased revenues needed to supply them. These difficulties grow out of disagreements about the relative importance of different new services and resistance to the growth of the government. The needed increases in taxes are unpopular, and high taxes are regarded as interference with personal spending. Higher taxes also are resisted because of concern about their effect on the incentive of business to undertake new enterprises that would contribute to economic growth. Still another problem is the disagreement about what kind of taxes should be used to pay for increased public services—sales taxes or income taxes.

CONTROLLING THE QUALITY OF PUBLIC SERVICES

In this chapter we have discussed the important effect of public services on the way we live. Because of their important place in our total consumption of goods and services, and because we are paying for them with our taxes, their quality is of particular concern. As consumers of public services we would like the best quality possible. It is, however, often difficult for the consumer of public services to complain about the quality of services he receives. The dissatisfied consumer may find that the established channel for complaints is through the very official who he believes is responsible for his problems. There is, however, growing recognition of the problem of regulating the quality of public services.

Established sources of assistance

Legislators in this country traditionally have played an important role in obtaining government services for their constituents and in ensuring that they are treated fairly by government. Legislators serve as mediators between citizens and government agencies at all levels of government—local and state, as well as national. Congressmen, for example, handle such matters for their constituents as helping them obtain veteran's and social security benefits and checking into cases of alleged discrimination. Such services are an important part of the legislator's role—the legislator is expected to look after the individual problems of his constituents in their dealings with government. Because of their control over agencies' budgets and their power to conduct hearings and investigations, legislators generally are effective in getting action on constituents' problems. The number of problems coming to the individual legislator is large, especially at the national level, and handling these problems diverts legislators from their other responsibilities. As a result, there has been interest in finding other ways to handle citizens' problems with government agencies.

The courts also have provided a channel for the complaints of citizens who feel they have been treated unfairly by government. The delays and expense of legal action, however, make the courts useful only in the most important cases. The use of the courts is also complicated because of the limitations that are placed on suits against the government. The ancient Anglo-Saxon principle that the government cannot be sued without its consent has been modified over the years. However, it still limits the usefulness of the courts to citizens who feel they have been treated unjustly by government agencies.

New channels for complaints

The need for a better channel for handling citizens' complaints against government has created widespread interest in this country in a new kind of official, the ombudsman. *Ombudsman* is a Swedish word used to designate an official appointed by a legislative body to receive and investigate citizens' complaints about unfairness, dishonesty, and inefficiency in government agencies. The problems handled include consumer problems but also can include problems related to military service, the performance of prison and police officials, and so on. Ombudsmen are not empowered to reverse the decisions of government agencies. They do, however, report to the legislative body they serve and often have the power to publicize the results of their investigations. These pressures usually are sufficient to get government agencies to change their decisions in cases where the ombudsman feels a citizen has been treated unjustly.

The ombudsman serves an important role both in protecting individual rights and in ensuring efficiency in government operations. His examination of complaints about an individual agency gives him a good picture of how well it is serving the public. He can identify situations in which such changes as new rules and procedures and new laws and administrative reorganizations are needed.

The idea of the ombudsman has been adopted by many democratic countries outside Scandinavia, including Great Britain, New Zealand, and several provinces of Canada. The first ombudsman office in the United States was created by the state of Hawaii in 1967, although the office did not go into operation until 1969. In its first year of operation the Hawaii ombudsman office handled a wide variety of complaints. Among the leading categories of complaints were public housing (including problems of getting placement in public housing and difficulties with other tenants), enforcement of pollution laws, highways and highway safety, and public education (including overcrowded school buses and problems in getting schooling for a handicapped child). State ombudsman offices more recently have been created in Oregon, Nebraska, and Iowa. In Iowa, the official is called the citizen's aide rather than ombudsman. The ombudsman plan also has been considered by legislatures in other states and by Congress at the national level.

Consumer advocates in the executive branch

The term "ombudsman" has also been applied to other offices in a number of places in the United States. These offices perform functions similar to the state ombudsman offices in Oregon, Nebraska, and Iowa, described above. For example, the first official of such an office was the public protector appointed by the county executive in Nassau County, Long Island, New York, in 1966. This official was given authority to "protect the public and individual citizens against inefficiency, maladministration, arrogance, abuse and other failures of government." This official, it should be noted, is part of the executive branch rather than an officer of the legislative branch.

Some political scientists have expressed concern about the way the ombudsman concept is developing in the United States. Many of the offices created have been in the executive branch rather than in the legislative branch. It is felt that such offices are less independent and effective than those connected with a legislative body. It seems likely that offices in the executive branch can be effective in resolving citizens' complaints. However, it seems unlikely that they will be effective as ombudsmen in the legislative branch in ensuring government efficiency and in bringing about needed changes in government procedures.

The Consumer Advocate office created in 1971 in the U.S. Postal Service is an important example of an ombudsman in the executive branch at the national level. The office was created to transmit the needs and problems of the individual mail customer to top management in the Postal Service. The Consumer Advocate was also given responsibility for identifying persistent problem areas and trends in complaints and for evaluating progress in solving these problems. In addition, the Consumer Advocate's office considers one of its responsibilities to be educating consumers about the different mail services available and what can be expected of each of them.

Checking your reading

1. What are the three general categories into which government functions can be classified?
2. Why is the money spent by the government to provide services considered an exhaustive expenditure?
3. What are income transfers? Subsidies?
4. Why are income transfers classified as nonexhaustive expenditures?
5. What are collective goods? Why is national defense a collective good?

6.   What are external economies?

7.   Why is pollution considered to create external diseconomies?

8.   Why are such firms as electric companies and city transit lines usually permitted to operate as monopolies?

9.   Why is it argued that providing free public services financed by tax dollars shifts income and benefits to lower-income people?

10.   If the government wants to encourage consumption of a particular good or service, does it necessarily have to produce the good or service itself? Explain.

11.   What is meant by the term "social balance?"

12.   Why do some economists argue that increasing taxes in order to provide more public services may have harmful effects on low- and moderate-income families?

13.   Why has the demand for public services grown so rapidly in recent years?

14.   Why are legislators usually effective in handling problems consumers have in obtaining public services?

15.   What is an ombudsman? What functions does he perform?

 ## Consumer problems and projects

1.   It frequently has been suggested that the federal government should allow educational costs to be deducted from the amount on which families pay income tax. What arguments can you think of for and against this proposal?

2.   Five general situations in which the marketplace does not provide well for consumers' needs were discussed in this chapter. What are these five situations? Why do private enterprise and free competition fail to meet society's needs in each of these situations?

3.   Often when it provides a service, government does not give individuals a choice about whether or not they will use it. Families may be forced to use city water and sewer service even though they do not want it. Families may also be required to send their children to school even though they do not want them to go. Why does government force these kinds of consumption on individuals?

4.   Examine the discussions about a proposed piece of social legislation in newspapers and news magazines. *U.S. News and World Report* is likely to be especially useful. Who will benefit from the proposed service? How is it to be financed? Does the legislation involve the shift of income or benefits from one part of the population to another? From whom and to whom? What are the arguments for and against this shift of income?

5.   List a service provided by government that, in your opinion, private enterprise could provide just as well and a service not now provided by government that you think government should provide. Discuss the reasons for your conclusions, using the considerations you discussed in question 2 above.

Chapter 25

Introduction to taxes

Establishing a fair and reasonable system of taxation is one of the highest goals of good government. It is not an easy thing to achieve. For instance, in every community there are neighborhoods that are wealthier than others. The schools in such neighborhoods tend to be in better condition and are better equipped and staffed, no matter how hard the school authorities try to maintain and foster equal treatment of all neighborhoods. A poor citizen whose children must go to an inferior school may resent the fact that another part of the town gets more of what he thinks should be distributed equally to all citizens.

Furthermore, tax rates vary from town to town, depending upon the other sources of income, the structure of city finances, and other factors. Is it right and fair for Citizen A in one town to have to pay more in taxes than Citizen B in another town for an equivalent home—just because A's town is better governed or more fortunate than B's town? Many families move from one town to another in order to get the benefits from better tax systems and tax rates.

TYPES OF TAXES

Taxes can be classified according to the way they are paid and according to the way they relate to the taxpayer's income. In the first category, taxes may be either direct or indirect. You pay your income taxes and your state car registration and license fees directly to the various levels of government; they are *direct* taxes. On the other hand, you pay the jeweler a tax on luxury items such as rings, and he then pays the tax to the government; for you such taxes are *indirect*.

When taxes are classified according to the way they relate to your income, they are said to be either progressive or regressive.

Progressive taxes vary in rate

Progressive taxes are based upon the taxpayer's income. The more he earns, the larger the percentage of his earnings he is required to pay in taxes. A tax is said to be *progressive* when the applicable tax rate increases with the increase in income. A progressive direct tax would be any income tax or any tax on money inherited by you or given to you. This is because the tax would increase according to the increase in income or in the value of the inheritance or gift and because the tax would be paid directly to the appropriate government agency. There are no progressive indirect taxes because it would be impossible to administer them. The government would have to know the income of a customer, for instance, before the government's agent (the shopkeeper) could decide how much to tax him.

Regressive taxes have fixed rates

The term *regressive* refers to the fact that such taxes take a higher percentage of income from the poor than they do from the rich. They are the reverse of progressive taxes. If a man earns $200 a month, and he buys $50 worth of goods upon which there is a 10 percent excise tax, that tax takes $2\frac{1}{2}$ percent of his income for that month ($50 × 10% ÷ $200). Another man, who earns $1,000 a month, may buy the same goods for the same price of $50. He will be paying only one-half of one percent of his income ($50 × 10% ÷ $1,000) in taxes.

Gasoline taxes are an important source of revenue for state and federal governments. Many highways have been built with the revenue raised from these taxes.

The federal income tax is essentially a progressive direct tax, except that in recent years taxpayers had been required to pay a *surtax,* which is really a tax on the tax. The surtax is a fixed percentage; it amounted to 2½ percent for taxes paid on earnings in 1970. Thus a taxpayer who owed $1,000 in federal income tax was required to pay $25 over and above the $1,000 regardless of his base earnings, the number of persons he supported, his age, or any other qualifications that act to reduce the amount of tax he owed in the first place. The surtax, then, was a direct regressive tax.

Other direct regressive taxes, as you can see in the table shown below, include fees paid to register cars, dogs, or luncheonettes. They also include real estate and property taxes, which are based upon the value of what is owned, not upon ability to pay.

You should remember every tax has two kinds of classification: it may be direct or indirect, and also either progressive or regressive, except that there are no progressive indirect taxes.

All sales taxes, import duties, and excise taxes are indirect and regressive. Corporate income taxes, however, like those paid by individuals, are usually progressive. That is, the more profits a corporation earns, the higher the percentage of its earnings it must pay. This is only partly true. Corporate federal taxes are charged according to ranges: about 20 percent for the first $25,000 of income and about 50 percent for income over $25,000, for instance.

The states tax corporations according to their own laws, which vary from state to state. Some corporation taxes, therefore, are progressive; others are regressive; and many are combinations of both forms.

CHARACTERISTICS OF TAXES*		
	Regressive	
Progressive Direct	**Direct**	**Indirect**
Personal Income Tax	State	Business Taxes
Federal	Property Tax	Federal
State	Motor Vehicle Licenses	Import Duties
Local	Personal Property Tax	Excise Taxes
Estate and Gift Tax	Business Licenses and	State
Federal	Permits	Excise Taxes
State	Local	Sales Taxes
Corporate Income Tax	Property Tax	State
Federal	Business Licenses and	Local
State	Permits	

*The classifications are meant to be general. Different laws and methods of assessment may sometimes modify the progressive or regressive nature of a tax.

Some payments to government may not be taxes

Some government functions are not easy to classify with respect to their financing. The nickel you put into a parking meter can be called direct payment for a service, and it can also be considered a direct, regressive tax. The toll you pay for traveling over a bridge is similar, as is the fee for use of a park or recreational facility.

Social security taxes and unemployment insurance premium payments are unlike other taxes, since they do not benefit the entire population. They are taxes, though, because every wage earner must pay them, because governments collect them, and because they are paid at a flat rate based upon your earnings (and are therefore direct and regressive in nature). However, such funds are not used as other taxes are used—for the purchase of goods and services. Instead, they are paid out again to unemployed persons, the elderly, and widows and dependents of wage earners who have died. In a sense, money collected by governments for social security and unemployment benefits is closer in nature to insurance premiums than it is to taxes.

THE CITIZEN AND HIS TAXES

Aside from the bother of paying for benefits that are hidden or remote in time and place (have you ever seen the Distant Early Warning radar line your tax money built and maintains in northern Canada?), most taxpayers, individual or corporate, dislike turning money over to government. This is a natural feeling and one that grows in intensity every April 15.

However, this country's economy is growing; so is the population. Along with other factors that cause taxes to rise, demand for goods and services supplied by government continues to increase. There is

Family Series, University Films / McGraw-Hill

Few people enjoy paying taxes, yet most people recognize that they must help pay for the services provided by government.

no reason why a citizen who insists upon good police protection, for instance, should balk at paying the taxes necessary to supply salaries and equipment for his police force.

Behind the story of taxation lies a paradox or contradiction that has puzzled citizens and will continue to absorb their interest as long as governments require tax money to carry out their functions. On the one hand we insist that no individual shall be taxed so heavily that he cannot enjoy the use of some of the money he has earned. On the other hand we believe that every citizen has equality under the law— that everybody, therefore, should receive the same benefits from the governments. The first principle limits the amounts of money that are available as tax revenues. The second places unlimited demands upon the tax revenues. Somewhere between the two extremes we must constantly strive to be as fair as possible in order to reduce the injustices that must occur.

WHERE DO THE TAX DOLLARS GO?

In the fiscal year ended June 30, 1970, the federal government collected almost $194 billion and spent almost $197 billion, which resulted in a budget deficit of about $3 billion. (The following year was a different story. In fiscal 1971 the federal government spent $23 billion more than it collected!)

TYPICAL USES OF FUNDS (1970)				
	Federal		State and Local	
Type of Expenditure	Millions		Millions	
Total	$205,121	100%	$132,934	100%
National Defense	78,586	38	510	(a)
Government Operating Expenses	21,239	11	15,212	12
International Affairs and Finance	2,806	2	—	—
Education and Public Health	8,642	4	66,556	50
Social Security and Welfare Services	58,116	28	16,596	13
Civilian Safety	121	(a)	9,583	7
Veterans Services and Benefits	9,808	5	78	(a)
Commerce, Transportation, and Housing	12,708	6	19,107	14
Agriculture, Natural Resources, Other	13,095	6	5,292	4

(a) Less than 0.5%.
Source: Based on U.S. Department of Commerce Survey of Current Business, July, 1971, Table 3.10, p. 30.

Enormous sums of money are raised through taxes to pay for space exploration.

Courtesy Aviation Week and Space Technology/McGraw-Hill

In the fiscal year ended June 30, 1970, state and local governments collected a total of about $131 billion and spent a similar amount. Of the money received by state and local governments in 1970, nearly 17 percent came as aid from the federal government.

While the greater part of these tax expenditures went to pay for goods and services, the federal government was spending $44 billion for social security and similar programs, $7.3 billion for education and manpower development, and $18.3 billion just for interest on its many debts. The table on page 412 lists some other agencies and activities that receive federal tax money, as well as the percentages of total income paid into these accounts by federal, state, and local governments.

Each level of government spends most where its greatest interests lie. The federal government is concerned with the welfare and safety of all the states, so it spends more than half of its income on national defense. The governments of states, on the other hand, are concerned with the welfare and education of their citizens, so they pay more than half of their tax revenues on education and welfare.

FEDERAL TAXES

As a consumer of government goods and services, you are entitled to know how they are paid for and also how the money was raised. As with all matters of taxation, your votes can change the systems. You owe it to yourself to learn about taxation practices and to change them if they do not seem fair or appropriate.

Every year the Internal Revenue Service finds mistakes made by individuals when they are reporting their incomes for tax purposes.

With the use of new computer systems and their accompanying data bases—storehouses of vast amounts of information—the federal government can find such mistakes. Very often they are mistakes that, if corrected, will lead to a refund of overpayments on the part of the taxpayer. In such situations, the citizen is lawfully and correctly avoiding taxes that he should not pay. Lawful tax avoidance is not only a way for you to save money; it is absolutely necessary if the system of taxation is to be fair. You should neither want nor be allowed to pay more taxes than the law requires.

On the other hand, *tax evasion,* which is the conscious attempt to escape paying taxes required by law, is illegal. Just as it is fair for people to pay only what they do owe and no more, it is also fair for people to pay at least what they do owe. As the Internal Revenue Service ties together its data sources and crosschecks the financial information of every American citizen, the chances for successful tax evasion are reduced. Those who would try to receive many benefits without paying for them through taxes are discovered and encouraged to pay their way.

It should be obvious that information systems are a source of great power. There are instances of abuse of that power, where a government agency has used the tax information of individual citizens against them. There are many who claim that as much danger exists from possible government abuse of information as from evasion of tax responsibilities by individuals. The problems suggested by this difference in positions must be the concern of all voters.

Federal income tax

As you have seen, the federal income tax is principally a direct, progressive tax. Because it is progressive, the largest burden of taxation falls upon those who earn most. About one-fifth of the taxpaying population will pay more than half of the total amount collected in most years.

You are familiar with stories about how complicated federal income tax instructions can be. On the contrary, for a complex subject these instructions can be remarkably clear if the taxpayer takes time to read them step by step.

WHO PAYS FEDERAL INCOME TAXES?   All American citizens, including minors, who earn a gross income of $1,700 or more during the year must file federal income tax forms. Those 65 or older on the last day of the tax year are not required to file a return unless they had a gross income of $2,300 or more during the year. However, those with a gross income of less than $1,700 (or less than $2,300 if 65 or older) should file a return to claim the refund of any taxes withheld, even if they are listed as a dependent by another taxpayer.

WITHHOLDING TAXES AND PAYING ESTIMATED TAXES The tax bite can be a big one, and experience has shown that taxpayers may not be entirely careful about setting aside enough money to pay their taxes when they come due. For this reason, and in order to have available a flow of cash, the federal government is empowered to collect and to withhold money from the salaries of individuals.

At the end of each year, every employer sends a record of wages paid and taxes withheld to the Internal Revenue Service. Each employee receives a copy of the same statement, which he then uses to prove his own report of income and tax due.

After computing his income tax, the taxpayer pays the difference if his employer has withheld too little money. If his employer has withheld too much, the taxpayer applies for and obtains a refund. Naturally there are many people who file their returns early to get their refunds as soon as possible, but all citizens must settle their tax accounts before the April 15 deadline or be liable for interest charges on taxes still due.

Students who have summer jobs with earnings totaling less than $1,700 may have had federal income tax withheld from their pay. They are entitled to a refund of the amount withheld, and they should file a tax return form to obtain the refund. If you are such a student, call your nearest Internal Revenue Service office for instructions. You will find it listed under "United States Government" in your local telephone directory.

Those who have very large salaries or income from which the government does not withhold taxes (as would be the case for a professional person who is hired by a number of persons: a doctor, a lawyer, a consultant) must do their own withholding and paying in advance. This is accomplished by the use of the Declaration of Estimated Tax, a system of reporting and paying in advance every three months, which, like withholding, is required by law.

Everybody who is likely to be a taxpayer receives tax forms and detailed instructions for completing them. These documents are mailed by the Internal Revenue Service just after the first of each year. Also, every citizen can get free individual assistance from the IRS, or he can get help in completing his tax forms from a small army of people who

Editorial Photocolor Archives, Inc.

Through a network of offices located throughout the country, the Internal Revenue Service provides taxpayers with help in filing their returns.

specialize in this activity—advertising widely, setting up temporary offices in tax season, and charging either a flat rate or some percentage as a fee.

For those who prefer to work out their tax obligations themselves, there are, in addition to the instructions distributed free with the forms, low-cost comprehensive tax guides published by the Government Printing Office and a number of privately written and published tax guides that are prominently displayed for sale in the first four months of every year. These publications are updated annually to include the latest regulations. You should make a point of reading at least one such tax guide. Keep in touch with taxpayer hints published in newspapers and magazines. Above all, keep careful records of your income and expenditures so that, when tax time comes, you can supply the necessary information with the least amount of confusion and inconvenience.

Federal estate and gift taxes

If you were charged with the responsibility of finding enough tax dollars to cover each year's federal budget, you would look in every direction to find sources of tax revenue. One of the best sources, you would discover, would be the accumulations of wealthy people. In our society, such accumulations often turn out to be the *estates* of the wealthy people: they keep their money in locations or networks of investments so that they can be transferred to their heirs. The federal government takes some of that money from estates, except that it allows payment of "final" expenses, such as medical, legal, and funeral costs, and the estate may keep up to $60,000 tax free. Above that figure, however, the tax, which is progressive and direct, rises from an initial 3 percent to 77 percent (for very large fortunes).

A wealthy man who would rather avoid having his money taken from his estate for tax purposes after his death can give it away during his lifetime—but here, too, the tax collectors get their share. Realizing that gifts are often merely a device to avoid payment of inheritance taxes, and further realizing that such gifts should produce revenue for everybody's welfare, the federal government taxes them if they are larger than $3,000 (paid to any single person during a given year) or if they amount to more than $30,000 over the giver's lifetime.

By setting different tax rates, the government can encourage one course of action and discourage another. The tax rates on gifts are lower than they are on inheritances. In fact, the top tax rate for gifts, which applies to amounts over $10,000,000, is only about 58 percent: nearly 20 percent less than the comparable tax rate for inheritances. You may draw your own conclusions about the government's philosophy in setting such rates. One obvious result of such policies of taxation is that a large amount of money is channeled through charitable contributions and foundations to projects that may benefit all citizens. In that sense the government is enforcing a redistribution of the wealth earned by the very rich.

Excise taxes and customs duties

The consumer can avoid some taxes with no feelings of guilt. Among those most easily avoided are the taxes placed upon goods he may not need to buy: tobacco and liquor, and imported goods and commodities, for instance.

The federal tax on specific commodities and services originating in this country is called an *excise* tax. You pay an excise tax whenever you pay for a long-distance telephone call. Excise taxes do not always apply only to luxury items such as liquor. New tires are sold at prices to which the "federal" (that is, the excise) tax must be added. The government is free to add to or remove from the list of items that bear an excise tax. Among other items in 1970, this list included cars, trucks, buses, motorcycles, jewelry, furs, luggage, and transfers of securities such as stocks and bonds.

In addition to gaining money from excise taxes, the government may use these taxes to help control and direct forces within the economy. For instance, cars were normally subjected to an excise tax in 1971.

In an effort to encourage buyers to make their new-car purchases in that year, the government removed the excise tax. Similarly, serious suggestions have been made from time to time to increase excise taxes on tobacco in an attempt to discourage people from smoking cigarettes.

The excise tax is an indirect tax, which, you will recall, is collected by the merchant and passed on from the buyer to the government. In this sense you will hear excise taxes referred to as "hidden" taxes. There is no deceit or cheating implied by the term; the taxes are not really hidden at all, as a glance at any gasoline pump will show. The gasoline distributors are eager to prove that the price they are charging for gasoline is made up in large part of various excise taxes.

Taxes on imported goods are called *customs duties* or *tariffs*. As a traveler returning from another country, you may bring back up to $100 worth of purchases made abroad without paying any tax on them. Goods over that amount are subject to taxes. Naturally this same scheme applies to importers of great quantities of goods.

When the government wishes to restrict the importing of any goods to protect American jobs or industries, it imposes very high tariffs on imported goods. Since these taxes drive prices up so that the imported items cost more than those made in this country, the tariffs tend to discourage foreign competitors from bringing their products into the American market. Tariffs that do this are called *protective tariffs*. They can cause much disagreement and tension between countries; indeed, protective tariffs on some kinds of textiles proved to be a source of debate between the United States and Japan in 1971. American citizens should keep in mind the need for trade with foreign countries, and therefore the need for using protective tariffs with caution. Exports of farm products and raw materials are very important to the prosperity of our economy, but in order to have money to buy such things from the United States, other countries must be able to sell their own products in this country.

At the same time, American goods often face very high tariffs in countries to which we hope to export them. Consumers have an important interest in free trade—that is, trade with few or no protective tariffs on either side. The competition provided by imported goods helps keep down the prices of goods produced in this country. High tariffs on foreign goods protect the profits of some businesses and the jobs of their workers, but they do so at the cost of higher prices for American consumers.

As a consumer you should know what excise taxes or customs duties you will be required to pay when you make purchases. If you can find goods or services that do not carry these excise taxes or customs duties, you can save money on many of your purchases.

STATE AND LOCAL TAXES

Most local governments, in addition to state-level governments, impose taxes in order to gain revenue to pay for local projects. The taxpayers pay for benefits they can see and experience directly—at least that is the intent. Increasingly, however, governments in financial trouble will borrow from one tax source to finance another, unrelated, project. As a consumer you should be alert to such maneuvers, and you should try, through your elected representatives, to make sure your local tax dollars are not moved from their proper destination.

Property taxes

Although most property taxes are based upon real estate alone, many states and communities charge taxes based upon the value of other kinds of property, such as home furnishings, paintings, sculpture, and jewelry. Property such as money invested in stocks and bonds may also be taxed.

Real estate taxes are based upon the value of the property as that value is decided by professional assessors. The tax rate itself is set by the local government as a percentage of the assessed value. Communities vary widely in their assignment of tax rates and assessments. Some may prefer to charge a low rate based on the actual cash value of the property. Others may charge a higher rate, but apply it to only part of the value of the property. No doubt psychology enters into the setting of tax-rate practices. Here is an example showing how, by juggling the assessment and the tax rate, one community can get more money from a low tax rate than a similar community can get for equally valuable property.

Community A

Tax rate: $35 per $1,000 of
  assessed valuation
Assessment: 50% of market value
The tax on property worth $20,000
  is computed as follows:

$$\$20,000 \times 50\% = \$10,000$$
$$\$10,000 \div \$1,000 = 10$$
$$10 \times \$35 = \$350 \text{ tax}$$

Community B

Tax rate: $30 per $1,000 of
  assessed valuation
Assessment: 70% of market value
The tax on property worth $20,000
  is computed as follows:

$$\$20,000 \times 70\% = \$14,000$$
$$\$14,000 \div \$1,000 = 14$$
$$14 \times \$30 = \$420 \text{ tax}$$

Some states get a large proportion of their tax revenue from property taxes. New Jersey, for instance, did not have either a state income tax or a state sales tax until 1969. State and local services were supported by individual property taxes in most cases. However, as a result of this policy, highway expenditures were among the lowest in the United States, and the lack of higher education facilities was so pronounced that more than half the students from New Jersey had to go elsewhere to get a college education. Realizing the disadvantages the citizens suffered because of the inadequate system of taxation, New Jersey began collecting a sales tax, but still it obtained most of its tax money from individual real estate taxes. By relying chiefly on real estate taxes New Jersey continued to limit itself. While real estate values continued to climb, the tax assessors often were unable to keep up with such increases, and the taxes, therefore, were lower than they could have been.

Sales taxes, license fees, and other taxes

Nearly all states, and many cities, too, charge sales taxes. Combined state and local sales taxes in New York City can raise the price of an item by 7 percent, for instance. Such taxes are regressive, of course, because they hurt the man with little money more than they hurt the man with a lot. However, most sales taxes do not apply to staple items such as food, clothing, and medicines. People with low incomes spend a large proportion of their incomes for these tax-exempt necessities; therefore, such exemptions help somewhat to ease the burden created by a sales tax on other items.

If you want to sell hot dogs or practice medicine; cut hair or drill for oil; tie up a ship at a public dock or sell turnips in a public market; hunt deer or listen to a singer in a nightclub, then you will be taxed or charged fees that in effect are taxes.

About one-sixth of state and local revenues comes from such sources as license fees and entertainment taxes. In this category of taxation there are many different kinds of taxes and ways of taxing. All the taxes are necessary for the state and local governments, and the revenues from them are all used for the people who benefit from the goods and services the tax dollars provide. Hunting license fees, for instance, are used to support state and local game control and the development of recreation facilities. Charging fees only to the users of specific services is a fundamental principle of taxation and one that you as consumer should appreciate. It is up to you to see that governments use their taxing power to give the most benefits to the people.

Checking your reading

1. Explain the differences between direct and indirect taxes.
2. What is meant by a progressive tax? Give two examples.
3. Give an example of how a tax can be regressive.
4. What is the best-known direct-progressive American tax?
5. When consumers demand more goods and services from governments, what effect should they expect their demands to have on taxation?
6. Compare federal and state expenditures. What is the largest spending category for each level of government?
7. What can the citizen do to get and keep fair taxation practices?
8. With more than 200 million people in our country, how can the Internal Revenue Service find mistakes made in individuals' income tax returns?
9. What are the main sources of funds for the federal government?
10. Why does the federal government collect gift taxes?
11. In what way or ways can it be said that the federal estate and gift taxes make for a more even distribution of this country's wealth?
12. What is a customs duty? A protective tariff?

Consumer problems and projects

1. Construct a chart showing for certain selected states (choose at least six) their sources of general revenue (such as money from the federal government, state taxes, and other taxes) and their general expenditures (such as for education, highways, public welfare, and health and hospitals). You can locate information for your chart in almanacs, such as *The American Almanac, The World Almanac,* and the *Economic Almanac.* In addition, the *Statistical Abstract of the United States* is helpful.
2. Excise taxes have sometimes been called "luxury taxes." Do you agree or disagree with this designation? Why?
3. Make a list of the items that you have purchased or used during the past week that were subject to an excise tax.
4. When a tariff is placed on goods imported into the United States, American consumers must pay more for those goods. Do you believe this form of taxation is justified? Why?
5. Even though real estate taxes bring in the most revenue for local governments, many people do not consider the property tax to be the most satisfactory form of taxation. Explain why you agree or disagree with this point of view.
6. What might you suspect about the federal government's attitude toward private borrowing, considering that you deduct interest paid out from your taxable income?

Consumer assistance
and protection

Part **6**

Chapter 26

The development of consumer protection efforts

The present period of concern about consumer protection is not the first. It follows two earlier periods—the early 1900s and the 1930s. In each period, consumer boycotts sprang up as food prices rose, new consumer organizations appeared, and journalistic exposés of the dangers of widely used products created a demand for new protective legislation.

All three eras of concern with consumer protection have occurred in periods of social unrest and economic dislocation. In each era, the social system was under close scrutiny by critics dismayed with the human costs of industrialization and the uneven distribution of income and social benefits. In each of the periods, concern with the apparent failures of the economic system was aggravated by a decline in the purchasing power of a large proportion of the population. These declines made the public sensitive both to the conduct of the business community and to the quality of its products.

ISSUES IN THE EARLY 1900s

The situation of consumers and economic life of the country changed rapidly in the last four decades of the 1800s. Industrial output and employment increased fivefold. The population doubled, and the proportion living in urban areas rose from 20 to 40 percent. During this period, a national network of railroads was completed, creating the possibility of nationwide markets. A few manufacturers of consumer goods recognized the opportunity and began to trademark their wares and to advertise them in the new mass-circulation magazines.

The rapid growth of the cities and industrialization produced a new and unfamiliar set of problems—urban poverty, tenement housing, immigrant ghettos, municipal corruption, hazardous working conditions, sweatshops, child labor, and a variety of consumer problems. About 1900 there emerged from the urban middle and professional classes a new group of political reformers concerned with these problems. These reformers, the Progressives, sought to use the power of government to bring about the social and economic reforms they believed were needed.

The economic situation of the increasing mass of urban workers depended both on their wages and on the prices at which they exchanged their wages for goods. Labor's purchasing power had increased steadily between the end of the Civil War and 1897, due to a long decline in prices. New gold discoveries and refining methods led to an upturn of prices, which, beginning in 1897, turned these gains in purchasing power to losses and began a long chain of increases in the consumer's cost of living. The pressure of rising prices on stable incomes added to the appeal of the growing labor union movement, and it gained membership rapidly. For the most part, the era was one of comfort and prosperity. The pressure of price increases was, however, felt keenly by government employees, clerical workers, ministers, and others on fixed incomes.

The public regarded both the new giant corporations and the expanding union movement as contributors to the price increases. The growth of the corporate trusts had not been viewed as much of a problem, but with the new rise of prices they became a subject of increasing concern. The journalistic exposés of the period both reflected and fed the suspicions of the public.

McClure's Magazine stumbled across the exposé style, which came to be called "muckraking," by accident when it ran a series on Standard Oil, the largest American trust. The series by Ida Tarbell, which began in 1902, documented the unfair and illegal tactics by which Standard Oil had destroyed its competitors and taken almost complete control of the oil industry. The series created a sensation, and *McClure's* and several other new mass-circulation magazines used exposés of corruption in business and government as a device to build circulation. The life insurance companies, railroads, trusts, and politicians were all investigated, and the demand for reform grew.

In the early 1900s the big corporate trusts were a favorite target of journalists and cartoonists.

The Bettmann Archive, Inc.

Antitrust action

The need for government regulation of the business activities and competitive practices of the rapidly growing railroads and industrial corporations was recognized toward the end of the 1800s. The result was the passage of the Interstate Commerce Act of 1887 (creating the Interstate Commerce Commission, with responsibility for regulating the railroads and their rates) and the Sherman Antitrust Act of 1890, which prohibited activities that interfered with competition and were in restraint of trade.

At the turn of the century a series of rapid business mergers created a new group of giant corporations including Standard Oil, United States Steel, General Electric, and American Telephone and Telegraph. These mergers had been encouraged by court interpretations of the Sherman Antitrust Act. In these decisions the courts ruled that agreements between companies to fix the prices charged customers were in restraint of trade and illegal but that control of an industry by a single giant corporation was not. At the same time these mergers were occurring, firms in other industries, including beef packing and sugar refining, had formed combinations, or "trusts," in order to control prices and competition.

During the administrations of Theodore Roosevelt (1901–1909) and William Howard Taft (1909–1913) the government began to take action against the trusts and giant corporations that were seeking monopolistic control of the market. The Supreme Court order to reorganize Standard

Oil into a number of smaller firms, the breakup of the beef trust, and other antitrust action helped halt the trend toward monopoly.

During the administration of Woodrow Wilson (1913–1921), additional government machinery for controlling unfair business practices was created. The Clayton Antitrust Act of 1914 spelled out in more detail the specific practices that were considered in restraint of trade. The Federal Trade Commission Act of 1914 created the FTC and gave it power to investigate unfair trade practices and issue cease-and-desist orders to prohibit unfair practices and violations of antitrust laws. The chief emphasis of the FTC at this time was on maintaining competition by protecting business firms against each other rather than on protecting consumers.

The purity and safety of food and drugs

Attitudes about adulteration and product safety seem to have been more lenient in earlier times. Accounts of food retailing in the 1800s suggest that adulteration was commonplace—inferior ingredients such as ground-up leaves were added to tea, and ground stone was added to flour to increase its weight and volume. The new food-processing industry was, at best, only partly aware of the potential dangers of food preservatives and additives. Formaldehyde, a toxic chemical, was added to canned meats to prevent spoilage, and copper salts were added to canned peas to dye them to the proper fresh green shade.

The development of a nationwide rail network and refrigerated rail cars opened a national market to food processors and meat packers. Unsanitary conditions, unsafe additives and preservatives, and adulteration became less and less tolerable as the public became more dependent on store-bought food and drugs. Attempts to pass a general federal pure food and drugs law began in the early 1890s. In 1902, growing pressure from muckraking journalists, state food chemists, the General Federation of Women's Clubs, and the National Consumers League brought a bill close to passage. These efforts were supported by several major magazines, which ran a succession of exposé stories on food adulteration and the dangers of patent medicines.

A Pure Food and Drugs Act was finally passed in 1906, after a scandal created by Upton Sinclair's book *The Jungle,* a graphic account of working conditions in the Chicago meat-packing houses. This legislation overcame the resistance of business and regional interests that had fought earlier bills and of Southern democrats who were reluctant to grant increased powers to the federal government. The new legislation was a milestone, since it firmly involved the federal government in regulating the safety and purity of consumer products.

Courtesy Food and Drug Administration

In the early 1900s cosmetics such as hair dye contained lead, mercury, and other harmful chemicals. While the 1906 Pure Food and Drugs Act did not prohibit these harmful ingredients, it did require producers to label their products with warning notices.

The Progressives' battle with the trusts, the fight for pure food, rising prices, and an increasing torrent of advertising all helped to make the public increasingly aware of their interests as consumers as opposed to their interests as workers or businessmen. This appearance of a consumer consciousness is perhaps the most important result of the first era of concern with consumer protection. In 1914, journalist Walter Lippmann pointed out the growing political power of consumers as an interest group and noted that "we hear a great deal about the class-consciousness of labor; my own observation is that in America today consumers'-consciousness is growing very much faster." Lippmann predicted that consumer interests would become even more powerful after women were given the right to vote.

ISSUES OF THE 1930s

World War I and the prosperity of the 1920s brought a decline in interest in consumer problems. The prosperity of the 1920s was not without its problems, however. Consumers were faced with the problem of choosing new and unfamiliar durable goods—radios, phonographs, vacuum cleaners, and cars—amidst a growing roar of advertising. In 1927 their problems found expression in a book by Stuart Chase and F. J. Schlink, *Your Money's Worth: A Study in the Waste of the Consumer's Dollar.* This book attacked advertising and high-pressure salesmanship and called for scientific testing and product standards to provide consumers with the information they needed. The idea of a product-testing organization stirred widespread response and led to the founding of the first consumer-oriented product-testing organization, Consumers' Research, Inc., in 1929.

The Depression made the problems of consumers far more immediate and pressing than they had been in the comfortable 1920s. Even those fortunate enough to still have jobs often were forced to adjust to sizable income cuts. Although this adjustment was eased by declining consumer prices, consumers were forced to consider the problem of spending wisely more carefully than ever before. Attention was focussed on the economic system and its operation, and they became the objects of close and continuing scrutiny.

Consumer education

Although consumer problems aroused little interest among the general public in the 1920s, educators began to recognize the need for more and better consumer education. Consumer problems had been a major concern of home economists from the formative years of their association at the turn of the century. In the mid-1920s, spurred by concern about the "scanty amount of economics in our home economics," they began new research into consumer problems to provide the information needed to improve teaching in the area. About the same time, educators began to develop curricula for consumer education based on a comparison of actual consumption patterns and scientifically based studies of consumers' needs.

The Depression gave a new importance to consumer problems, and consumer education topics began to find their way into school curricula for the first time. Emphasis was given to identifying the best buys at the lowest cost and to careful, thrifty management. Consumers were urged: "Wear it out, use it up, make it do." Inexpensive substitutes for heavily advertised products were suggested, and students practiced making their own toothpaste and face creams. Budgeting was regarded as a device for cutting down on expenditures rather than as a way of planning spending to get the things one wants most.

Product testing

The financial problems of consumers during the Depression were aggravated by a flood of shoddy merchandise at bargain prices. In the first years of the Depression, real bargains were offered by merchants in financial distress and had sold well. As these stocks were exhausted, merchants replaced them with inferior merchandise and played on consumers' belief that real bargains were still available. The clothing items offered were available at low prices only because quality had been cut at every step of production. These false bargains wore out quickly and helped create a widespread belief that the quality of clothing, shoes, and sheets had deteriorated. This feeling created new support for quality testing and grade labeling of consumer products. The widespread demand for product-testing information brought Consumers' Research and Consumers Union into their own. Consumers Union concerned itself with a wide variety of consumer issues beyond product testing, including the labor conditions under which goods were produced. With the founding and growth of CU the consumer movement gained its first stable organizational base—a permanent organization, with a substantial budget, devoted to advancing the ideals of consumer protection.

The reports of the two consumer product-testing organizations stripped away advertising puffery and laid the facts bare for the individual consumer to judge. For the first time the consumer had a reliable source of information independent of the manufacturer.

Antitrust action

The economic position of the large corporations relative to the small ones was further strengthened in the 1920s. The large firms were able to obtain both the capital needed for expansion more easily and to develop and employ new technology. The Depression destroyed many small firms, further strengthening the position of the large ones.

During the early years of Franklin Roosevelt's New Deal administration it was hoped that the economy could be revived by discouraging excessive competition and price cutting. By 1938, however, the government had become interested in trying to stimulate the economy by encouraging business competition. Hearings were held to determine the extent and effects of the concentration of economic power, and the activities of the Antitrust Division of the Justice Department were stepped up. The increasing involvement of the United States in World War II, however, shifted attention away from the antitrust problem.

The main result of the era was to broaden the powers of the FTC. Earlier, the FTC could act only in cases where one competitor injured another by unfair business practices. After the Wheeler-Lea Amendment to the FTC Act in 1938, the FTC also had power to deal with cases in which unfair practices injured consumers. It was also given authority to act against false advertising of food, drugs, and cosmetics.

Consumer representation in government

Consumer interests gained representation in a major governmental agency for the first time in the 1930s. This came about when a Consumer Advisory Board was appointed in the National Recovery Administration (NRA), the government agency set up to coordinate economic recovery efforts. The Board found their role difficult, however. General Hugh Johnson and the other NRA administrators saw no need for the Board, arguing that the consumer interest was the public interest and that they represented the public interest. To meet this argument, the Board countered with the argument that consumers, workers, and sellers each have separate interests and that the public interest is the resolution of conflicts among those different interests. This argument provided a logical basis for consumer representation in government and grew into proposals for a cabinet-level Department of the Consumer. By the end of the 1930s consumer representation in government was taking concrete form, and organizational charts of the proposed department were being drawn up.

Modernizing the Pure Food and Drugs Law

The need for revising the Pure Food and Drugs Law was widely recognized by the early 1930s. The old law had been weakened by court decisions and outdated by new technology. The New Deal administration offered a new bill that would have given the government substantial power, including controls over labeling and advertising. The new bill also proposed placing cosmetics under Food and Drug Administration (FDA) regulation and the creation of a system for grade labeling for food. The need for new legislation was dramatized in a series of exposé books. The first, *100,000,000 Guinea Pigs* (100 million was the size of the United States population at that time), was a bitter report on dangerous products and on advertising and wasteful increases in the number of brands. Another, *The American Chamber of Horrors*, documented the need for new legislation with reports of injuries and deaths resulting from unsafe products.

There was strong opposition to the proposed bill, especially to the portions regulating advertising and calling for the creation of a grade-labeling system for food. Opposition to the bill by special interests gradually drew more and more groups into the fight. The American Home Economics Association and the National Congress of Parents and Teachers were early supporters of new legislation. Later, a number of national women's organizations became involved. Final action came after a tragedy created a demand for action. In 1937, a liquid form of

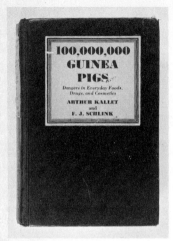

The need for new consumer protection legislation was dramatized in exposé books such as those shown at left.

Courtesy Food and Drug Administration

a new sulfa "wonder drug" was placed on the market without testing. Although the drug was safe in capsule form, its liquid form, Elixir Sulfanilamide, was deadly. Over 100 died after taking it.

The new law passed in 1938 extended FDA control to cosmetics and instituted the requirement that safety be tested for and established before a product was offered on the market. The final legislation was regarded as something of a defeat by the consumer spokesmen who had strongly favored the earlier version of the bill. The new law, however, did update the government's regulatory efforts and brought them into line with advances in technology. Advertising controls were instituted, but responsibility for them was given to the FTC instead of to the FDA. The failure of the proposals for strong controls over labeling and for the creation of a system for grade labeling was, however, a disappointing defeat for the principle of consumers' rights to product information.

The 1930s showed again that major new consumer legislation often comes only after tragedy or scandal dramatizes the need for more consumer protection. The impact of the exposé books showed their importance both in educating consumers in buymanship and in informing them about the need for new legislation. In 1940, public opinion researcher George Gallup reported that, according to a nationwide study of consumer unrest, one-fourth of all adults had read one of the so-called "Guinea Pig" books, and about half of this group said they had changed their buying habits as a result. Gallup concluded that consumer problems were likely to remain an issue because of the concern of teachers, young people, and other opinion-leader groups.

President Kennedy often is credited with beginning the present era of concern for consumer protection with his 1962 Consumer Message to Congress. In it he set forth the now famous consumer bill of rights: (1) the right to choose among a variety of products, (2) the right to be informed, (3) the right to safety, and (4) the right to be heard through representation in government. However, President Kennedy's real influence on concern with consumer protection began even earlier. Arthur Schlesinger has pointed out that during the 1960 presidential campaign Kennedy "communicated . . . a deeply critical attitude toward the ideas and institutions which American society had come in the Fifties to regard with such enormous self satisfaction." The result was an outpouring of critical examinations of the nation's social and economic problems, many of which deeply involved consumers: Michael Harrington's analysis of the situation of the poor, *The Other America* (1962); Jessica Mitford's investigation into the funeral industry, *The American Way of Death* (1963); and David Caplovitz's study of the consumer problems of the poor, *The Poor Pay More* (1963).

Because of international crises, the problems of recession and inflation at home, and congressional resistance, the Kennedy administration had only limited success in getting passage of the legislation that had been outlined in the Consumer Message of 1962. Early in his administration, Lyndon Johnson recognized that increasing public and congressional interest in consumer problems had improved the possibilities for passing legislation, and he offered his own program. In February, 1964, he sent a consumer message to Congress urging passage of 12 new laws, including measures on truth in lending, meat inspection, drug inspection, and pesticide control. President Johnson did not, however, push his program strongly, and there was little action on it.

In 1966, the pressure of rising prices increased consumer unrest. After a gradual increase in the early 1960s, food prices jumped 5 percent in 1966. The increases were especially visible, since they came on frequently purchased items such as beef, pork, eggs, and lettuce. In October, the housewife supermarket boycotts erupted. The buying power of many groups in the population increased only gradually in the early 1960s. With the increasing prices and taxes, these groups were faced with actual declines in their purchasing power. At about this same time President Johnson began to push his consumer legislation proposals more vigorously. One of the appealing features of his program was that it offered important reforms that cost relatively little.

In 1966 consumers angered
by rising prices began picket-
ing supermarkets in various
cities.

United Press International, Inc.

This was an important consideration because of the rapidly increasing costs of the Vietnam war. As a result of Presidential interest and support, a number of new bills were passed in 1966. Their passage created a momentum that continued into the 1970s.

Consumer representation in government

To implement the fourth right of his Consumer Message, the right to be heard, President Kennedy asked the Council of Economic Advisers to appoint a Consumer Advisory Council. Although the functions of the Council were strictly advisory, the consumer interest never before had been represented at so high a level of government. The Council undertook comprehensive studies of consumer needs but had limited impact on Congress and the public during its first year and a half. However, one of its recommendations had particularly important results. This was the recommendation that the President appoint to the White House staff a special adviser on consumer affairs.

President Johnson acted on this recommendation and, in early 1964, created the President's Committee on Consumer Interests and appointed Esther Peterson as Special Assistant to the President for Consumer Affairs. This action brought a consumer representative into the highest levels of government. Mrs. Peterson and her successors, Miss Betty Furness and Mrs. Virginia Knauer, have served a wide variety of functions. They have advised the President about consumer problems and on new legislation affecting the consumer. They have testified before congressional committees on the need for new legislation and rallied support for bills offered by the administration. They have also developed consumer education materials and advised schools on consumer education programs. In addition, they have assisted in the organization and development of state and local consumer organizations throughout the country.

The role of consumer adviser to the President was given a more permanent basis in 1971 by President Nixon. At that time he established the Office of Consumer Affairs in the Executive Office of the President. In setting up the Office, President Nixon expanded its responsibilities to include analyzing and coordinating the activities of all federal agencies concerned with consumer protection.

Product safety

The regulation of food and drugs was one of the areas singled out by President Kennedy for special attention in his 1962 Consumer Message. The weaknesses of the existing laws in ensuring that drugs on the market were both effective and safe had become clear in the course of hearings on the regulation of the drug industry. The new legislation was passed only after news of the tragic affects of a new sleep-inducing drug sold in parts of Europe forced action upon Congress. It was learned that the drug, called thalidomide, could cause malformation in babies whose mothers had used it during the early months of pregnancy. Word of the thalidomide case reached the public in June; by August 1962, legislation expanding the powers of the FDA had been passed and signed into law.

After President Johnson's landslide election in 1964, more new consumer legislation seemed likely. In 1965, hearings began on tire and auto safety. The hearings revealed that there was not any real concern over safety problems in either industry at that time. In the latter portion of the auto safety hearings attention was shifted from the manufacturer's responsibilities for auto safety to the driver. This view was challenged a few months later when Ralph Nader's book *Unsafe at Any Speed* appeared. In it Nader presented evidence of the role of faulty engineering, construction, and design in auto accidents and injuries. Public concern mounted, and in his State of the Union message in January, 1966, President Johnson promised new legislation.

New hearings on the administration's proposed Highway Safety Act began in March, 1966, with Ralph Nader as a key witness. In the course of the hearings news broke that General Motors had hired investigators to check Nader's background and habits. The members of Congress interpreted GM's actions as interference with a congressional witness and were outraged. The auto safety bill passed later that year was far stronger than the original one proposed. The auto safety hearings brought Ralph Nader onto the national scene for the first time and firmly established his position as a reliable and effective spokesman for consumers.

Nader next moved to another area of product safety. After uncovering U.S. Department of Agriculture reports on conditions in meat-packing plants that were not covered by federal inspection since the plants sold only within state boundaries, Nader began a full-scale exposé. Nader and Betty Furness, the Special Assistant to the President for Consumer Affairs, received White House support for new legislation. A strong bill was passed providing for federal intervention in states where inspection procedures fell short of federal standards.

Nader followed with crusades for improved poultry inspection and gas pipeline safety. During this time Nader was doing most of his work single-handed. More recently he has developed a small staff, popularly called "Nader's Raiders." Among the first projects Nader and his staff undertook were investigations of the activities of several government agencies responsible for protecting consumer interests—the Federal Trade Commission, the Interstate Commerce Commission, and the agency responsible for controlling air pollution. Nader and his organization have continued their close watch on both food and auto safety and have also conducted investigations of medical care, nursing homes, water pollution, and occupational safety.

As a result of the relationships he has developed with some members of Congress, Nader has had far greater impact than either the muckrakers of the early 1900s or the authors of the "Guinea Pig" exposés of the 1930s. Nader's concerns include more than just product safety and protecting consumers. His overall goal is to ensure corporate responsibility. This concern is reflected in his interest in aspects of corporate activity including occupational safety for employees and the control of pollution created by manufacturing wastes.

Consumer information

Important gains have been made in the present era in getting recognition of consumers' rights to information. The Truth In Lending Act (1968) forces lenders to spell out credit costs in such a way that interest rates can be compared more easily. The Truth-in-Packaging law (1966) resulted in better label information and an attempt to reduce the number of different package sizes to simplify shopping.

Government as well as business has been forced to provide more information. Under the Truth-in-Information Act, the Veterans Administration was forced to release the results of hearing-aid tests it had conducted. More recently the results of tests by the National Bureau of Standards and the General Services Administration have been adapted and published for use by consumers.

Consumer education

In the early and mid-1960s a new surge of interest in consumer education occurred. Educators and the public both came to recognize that consumer education is an important and useful subject for all students, college-bound and vocational, boys and girls alike. Consumer education, with its real-life problems, was found to be a useful way of arousing interest in topics in English, math, social studies, and science. The new curricula continued to stress both buymanship techniques and money management and also gave new emphasis to the problems and uses of installment credit. New emphasis was also given to the idea that one's spending should reflect personal goals rather than someone else's idea of a good budget.

Consumer organizations

In 1967, a new attempt was made to form a national consumer organization. The new organization, the Consumer Federation of America (CFA), is a national federation of organizations with consumer interests and includes labor unions, state and local consumer organizations, the National Council of Senior Citizens, and the National Consumers League. Its purposes include fact-finding, analysis of consumer issues, and providing an information clearing-house on the consumer-related activities of its members. The new Federation has taken the leadership in the organization of the Consumer Assembly, an annual Washington conference for the discussion of consumer problems and needs. The strength and durability of the CFA remain to be determined.

THE SOCIAL RESPONSIBILITIES OF BUSINESS

It seems clear that concern for consumer problems and consumer protection is likely to be a recurring, and perhaps permanent, feature of the American scene. This concern has arisen as a reaction to three persisting problem areas: (1) ill-considered applications of new technology that result in dangerous or unreliable products, (2) changing views on the social responsibilities of business, and (3) the operations of a dishonest fringe and the occasional lapses of others in the business community. There is little reason to believe that any of these problem areas will ever disappear completely.

The history of the development of consumer protection demonstrates that new technology frequently has been applied without full understanding of or concern for its potential dangers. The automobile had been around for 70 years before Ralph Nader received recognition of the fact that autos included unsafe design features and sometimes were poorly engineered. Although the dangers of incompletely understood new technology have been most dramatic in the area of food and drugs, new legislation to control these dangers has come only after dramatic incidents have focussed public opinion on the problems. This legislation often has come long after the problems were first recognized.

The consumer no longer judges business on its products alone but also on the social costs involved in producing them. The public's ideas of what constitutes a social cost have evolved rapidly in the past 70 years. The passage of the Pure Food and Drugs Act and the Meat Inspection amendment in 1906 was a recognition of the social costs of injurious drugs and adulterated and contaminated food. The work of the consumers' leagues in the early 1900s made the public recognize that unsafe working conditions, long hours, and the exploitation of child and female labor also have social costs. Gradually the public view expanded again to include air pollution and water pollution as social costs. Now new factors, which may seem even less tangible, are coming to be regarded as social costs. These factors include discriminatory hiring practices, decisions about locating factories that ignore areas of high unemployment, neglect of the needs of low-income consumers, and the use of legal tactics and biased laws against poorly educated and powerless installment plan debtors.

Step by step, the concept of the social responsibility of business has been broadened to include not only the relations of business with its stockholders but also the relations of business with its competitors, customers, employees, and neighbors, and it is now coming to include the relations of business with those who are neither its customers nor its employees but perhaps could and should be.

Checking your reading

1. What conditions have characterized the three eras of concern about consumer protection?
2. When was the Federal Trade Commission created, and what powers was it given? What was the main emphasis of the FTC at the time?
3. Trace briefly the history of the attempts to pass a general federal pure food and drugs law. When was the legislation passed? Why was it considered a milestone?
4. How did Consumers' Research and Consumers Union play a significant role in our society in the later years of the 1930s?

5. Explain how the Wheeler-Lea Amendment to the FTC Act expanded the power of the FTC.

6. When did consumer interests first gain representation in a major governmental agency? In what agency?

7. What are the four points of President Kennedy's consumer bill of rights?

8. Mrs. Esther Peterson, Miss Betty Furness, and Mrs. Virginia Knauer served presidents as special assistants for consumer affairs. Summarize the work they have accomplished.

9. When and how did Ralph Nader become firmly established as a consumer spokesman?

10. When was the Consumer Federation of America organized? What are the purposes of the federation?

11. Explain the nature and purpose of the Consumer Assembly.

12. What is meant by the "social costs" of producing products?

Consumer problems and projects

1. Analyze carefully a current issue of *Consumer Reports*. Begin by summarizing information in answer to the following questions (find the answers in the front section of each issue): Who are the educational advisers? What are the purposes of Consumers Union? What type of organization is Consumers Union? How does the magazine rate the products? What do the ratings mean? How are the products tested? Then, describe the various sections of the magazine, including the products tested in the issue you examine.

2. The American economy is based upon a free enterprise system. Does this mean the American businessman can operate without any restrictions upon his business activities? Explain your answer.

3. Write a report on the U.S. Department of Agriculture. Include its history, its various divisions, and some of its functions. Use encyclopedias and other library sources to gather your facts.

4. The United States is a nation governed by laws at the federal, state, and local levels. Cite one law at each level of government, and describe how each law has aided or hurt the American people.

5. Obtain a copy of *The Jungle,* by Upton Beall Sinclair. This book, published in 1906, gives a shocking disclosure of working conditions in the Chicago meat-packing houses at that time. The public was appalled by the book's exposé of this source of food supply. The book was published by O. P. Doubleday, Page. It is now available in paperback from New American Library, 1301 Avenue of the Americas, New York, N.Y. 10019. Report on the contents of the book. Indicate what you think the reaction would be if a book such as this were written about the meat-packing business today.

Chapter 27

Sources of assistance for consumers

In the last few years we have heard a great deal of discussion about consumer problems and complaints. When consumers complain to government and business, what kinds of things do they complain about? The lists of leading consumer complaints received differ somewhat among agencies, but these are some of the problems that appear on most lists:

- Unsatisfactory repairs and service—poor workmanship and excessive charges and difficulties in obtaining spare parts, especially for automobiles, appliances, and televisions.
- Defective merchandise—especially automobiles and appliances.
- Misleading packaging, labeling, and advertising.
- Merchandise that was ordered, paid for, and never received.
- Computerized billings—including complaints about the procedures for calculating interest charges and errors in billing.
- Warranty problems—difficulties in obtaining repairs promised and disagreements about who is responsible for paying for them under the terms of the warranty.

The reason automobiles and appliances are a frequent subject of complaint is that they are expensive items, and difficulties with them usually involve major financial losses. Some tabulations of consumer problems also indicate complaints about purchases from door-to-door salesmen that seem out of proportion to the number of purchases most of us make this way.

COMPLAINING TO GET RESULTS

The consumer who feels a particular firm has not treated him fairly may be torn between a desire for revenge and the hope that by making a complaint he can get better treatment. Seeking revenge is certain to create even more problems and do little to correct the original situation. What is needed is a cool head and an organized plan for correcting the problem.

When should you complain?

You should consider making a complaint whenever you feel dissatisfied with a product and feel that it does not live up to claims or reasonable expectations. If there has been a mistake or a misunderstanding, the honest and reputable merchant will want to know about it. In a real sense, you are helping him when you call a problem to his attention. Reliable dealers and manufacturers want to know about problems customers experience with their products and want to keep their customers satisfied. When you complain to less careful or less honest merchants you are also performing a service by helping to convince them that they cannot afford to mistreat customers.

Before making a formal complaint, it is wise to review product use and care instructions. This may save you both time, embarrassment, and money. A review of the instructions may eliminate the need for returning the product or making a service call. It has been estimated that one-third of all home service calls regarding appliances are unnecessary. Some typical problems are failure to see if the appliance is plugged in, failure to check fuses, failure to check control settings, and failure to read the instruction manual.

To whom should you complain first?

The merchant from whom you made your purchase is the best place to turn first. If he is in your local area, he usually is easier to reach than most other sources of help. In addition, other sources of help expect consumers to try to help themselves by first going directly to the merchant from whom the purchase was made.

Before going to the store think carefully about what is bothering you and what you plan to ask the merchant to do. What is the problem? Can you give a description of what is wrong? What would you like done about the problem? Do you want a refund, a replacement, repairs, or what? Next you should assemble your receipts and records relating to the purchase. It is also helpful to have the original package, tags, and so forth, if the item is a new one.

Find out who in the store you should speak to about your problem; then state your case. Be fair and reasonable, but do not be timid. If the item is left for repairs or for a refund, be sure you do not forget a receipt for it.

What do you do next?

If the merchant cannot or will not help you, you should consider complaining to the manufacturer. Such a step is especially appropriate if the problem concerns defects in the product, problems in getting repairs, or disagreements over warranty terms. Reliable manufacturers want to know how their products perform for customers; they also want to know about customers' problems in getting service in stores that sell their product.

Most products now carry the name of the manufacturer and his address and ZIP code. It may speed things somewhat to write directly to the appropriate official or department. The names of company officers and their addresses are available in several business directories that are available in most local libraries. One standard reference is *Poor's Register of Corporations, Directors and Executives,* which is published annually. If you cannot find this reference, ask the librarian for others. If you do not direct your letter to a particular company officer, send it to the "Consumer Service Department."

What should you include in your letter? Here are some of the things:

- A clear statement of your problem, along with a description of the item, including model and serial numbers, and the date and place of purchase.
- A description of what steps you already have taken to solve your problem, including contacts with the merchant who sold you the item.
- Photocopies of receipts, and canceled checks if appropriate. Keep the originals for your records.
- Your name, address, and phone number. This information is too often forgotten. Be sure to save a copy of your letter in case future correspondence is necessary. One advantage of putting your complaint in letter form is that it gives you a record for future use.

If you return an item and would like a post card receipt as a record that it was received, the service costs only a small fee.

Allow two to three weeks for a reply to your letter. Most major companies have special departments to handle customers' problems more quickly. In the large firms these departments have to handle as many as 1,000 letters a week, so you may need to be patient.

Consumer expert Dr. Marjorie East of Pennsylvania State University favors showing a draft of a complaint letter to the merchant before it is sent. She suggests that the letter writer can ask the merchant to double-check the facts, the model number, and so on. Showing the letter to the merchant this way is obviously a threat, but it does show him you want action and does give him a chance to change his mind if he has not been helpful.

If your problem is a result of misleading advertising or other misrepresentation of the product, your best second step probably is not a letter to the manufacturer. In such cases, a call to your local better business bureau or chamber of commerce is more appropriate. If you suspect out-and-out fraud, contact local law enforcement officials.

What stronger measures should you take?

If you have had no action on your letter within a month, you probably will want to consider some stronger measures. The next step involves a second letter, but this time copies should be sent to a number of government and business agencies that are concerned about consumer problems.

Your second letter should restate your problem and point out that your earlier letter, of such and such a date, has not been answered. In the letter list the agencies to whom you are sending copies. These could include:

- Office of Consumer Affairs (OCA) in the Executive Office of the President
- U.S. Federal Trade Commission
- U.S. Postal Service
- U.S. Food and Drug Administration
- Office of your state's attorney general
- Local law enforcement officials
- Appropriate business trade associations such as the National Automobile Dealers Association, Grocery Manufacturers of America, Association of Home Appliance Manufacturers, Gas Appliance Manufacturers of America, American Movers Conference, and the Mobile Homes Manufacturers Association
- Your senators and representatives in Congress

We will discuss the particular kinds of help that some of these officials and agencies can give in the following section. While some of these agencies can handle a wide variety of problems, others can provide help only on particular kinds of problems. The particular kinds of problems with which each one deals are discussed in the next section of this chapter.

AGENCIES THAT ASSIST CONSUMERS

If the merchant and the manufacturer involved fail to solve the consumer's problem, there are additional sources of help to which he can turn. Some of these sources were mentioned briefly in the section on how to make complaints. The kinds of problems with which each agency deals are set by law or the rules of the organization. A clearer understanding of who can provide help will aid the consumer in reaching the best source more quickly.

The consumer with a problem must, however, be prepared for being told his complaint is unjustified. Some consumers are unreasonable; some misunderstand what was told them; and some are too impatient about deliveries. If you double-check all the details about your purchase before you complain you can be more certain of avoiding the embarrassment of being told your complaint has no grounds.

Better business bureau

The agency that most consumers with problems think of first is the better business bureau. We discussed the informational and educational roles of the better business bureaus in Chapter 5. Another important role of the better business bureaus is handling complaints. The bureaus handle complaints free but insist that they be submitted in writing. Usually a standard form is provided for this purpose. This helps better business bureau staffs to be certain they have the facts straight before they begin action on a problem.

The consumer with a problem should understand the particular types of problems with which the better business bureaus will deal. Their chief concern is in working out misunderstandings and disagreements arising from misleading advertising and misrepresentation. This is the purpose for which they originally were founded. The bureaus will not handle complaints about unsatisfactory merchandise in cases where misleading advertising or misrepresentation is not involved. They refuse to pass judgment on the quality of goods or services or on the fairness of the prices charged for them. They also refuse to give legal advice and will not handle cases involving disagreements over the terms of contracts.

Some local better business bureaus use mobile units to bring information directly to consumers.

Courtesy Council of Better Business Bureaus, Inc.

We discussed some of the variations in the performance of local better business bureaus in Chapter 5. Even though some local organizations are, perhaps, not all they could or should be, the better business bureaus are one of the few local sources of help for consumers. Given the long experience of the bureaus and the new program to improve their services, consumers with problems relating to misleading advertising and misrepresentation should turn first to their local better business bureau. Most smaller towns and cities do not have them. In many cases, local chambers of commerce perform the same types of service for consumers, with the same types of rules.

Office of Consumer Affairs

This office is part of the Executive Office of the President and is located in Washington. It advises and represents the President on matters of consumer interest and is responsible for coordinating all the consumer protection activities of the federal government. While the OCA has no power of its own to use in resolving consumer complaints, it does work through the agencies in whose jurisdiction problems fall. When the OCA receives consumer complaints it may also contact the company involved directly. Many complaints have been resolved in this way. The first Director of the OCA, Mrs. Virginia Knauer, set up a system to ensure that all consumer letters are acknowledged. Each complaint writer is sent a letter informing him of what action the OCA has taken, and a carbon copy of the letter is sent to the business firm involved.

Letters concerning consumer problems may be sent to the Office of Consumer Affairs, Executive Office of the President, Washington, D.C. 20506. Consumers should be sure problems are explained clearly.

Federal Trade Commission

Consumer problems arising out of misleading advertising and illegal business practices fall under the jurisdiction of the Federal Trade Commission. Some typical problems include:

- Deceptive pricing—for example, the advertisement "Brand X Pens—Retail Value $15, Our Price $7.50" when the stores in the trade area are, in fact, charging only $10 for brand X pens.
- Deceptive guarantees—for example, a battery that is guaranteed for 36 months that normally could be expected to last for only 18 months.
- Excessive credit charges and abusive debt collection practices.

The FTC now maintains consumer protection specialists in its field offices throughout the country to assist consumers in making complaints. Both the main FTC offices in Washington and the field offices serve as clearing-houses for consumer complaints. When a problem falls outside the jurisdiction of the FTC, they will forward the problem to the appropriate agency.

The FTC has also played a key role in the formation of consumer protection committees in major cities. These committees typically include representatives of the mayor's office or police department, the office of the state attorney general, the district attorney's office, the local or county bureau of weights and measures, the U.S. Food and Drug Administration, the U.S. Postal Service, and the U.S. Federal Trade Commission. These committees coordinate local attacks on consumer problems and provide a center where a wide variety of consumer complaints can be received. In 1971 committees were operating in Boston, Chicago, Detroit, Philadelphia, Los Angeles, and San Francisco.

U.S. Postal Service

The postal inspectors of the U.S. Postal Service want to know about fraudulent schemes involving use of the mails. The Postal Inspection Service has successfully combatted real estate promoters who have advertised "King-Sized Western Estates" that turned out to be in the middle of the desert and miles from town. They have also staged successful crackdowns on fake contests used as bait to lure the so-called "winners" into making purchases. For example, a promoter using this scheme informs families that they have won a new sewing machine and that all they need to do to get the machine is to buy a cabinet for it. On investigation, the price of the cabinet proves to be more than the usual price of the sewing machine and the cabinet together.

While the Postal Inspection Service has been successful in fighting outright fraud, it has had less success in dealing with mail-order operators responsible for a leading consumer complaint—failure to receive merchandise that has been ordered and paid for. One of the problems seems to be that under existing law it must be proved that the firm knowingly made false claims. Mail-order operators can avoid prosecution by sending out some orders and pocketing the money for others. If questions arise, they can claim a "mistake" has been made.

The Postal Inspection Service has had a record of some success in obtaining refunds for consumers. It is known to make informal inquiries by phone and letter in behalf of consumers and is reported to have had good results. Postal inspectors are stationed in most major cities and can be contacted through your local postmaster.

Other federal agencies

The Office of Consumer Affairs, the Federal Trade Commission, and the U.S. Postal Service are not the only federal agencies concerned with consumers' problems. A great many other agencies also are concerned. Most of these agencies have responsibility for regulating the sale of particular products or services. The U.S. Food and Drug Administration, for example, is concerned with the safety and labeling of food, drugs, and cosmetics. The U.S. Department of Agriculture is concerned with problems related to food inspection and grading, especially for meat and poultry. Instead of regulating a product, the Civil Aeronautics Board regulates a service—airline passenger service—including rates, schedules, and the airlines' treatment of their passengers. These three agencies are only a few of those that protect consumer interests.

There are, in fact, so many different federal agencies serving consumers either by regulating the provision of products and services or by themselves providing services that we will not attempt to discuss them all at this point. We will, instead, devote the next chapter to government agencies that protect the consumer.

State attorney generals

At the state level, the best source of help is the attorney general's department. More than half the states now have special consumer fraud or consumer protection bureaus within this department. The principal concern of these offices is with frauds, misleading advertising, and misrepresentation. Most also serve as clearing-houses for consumer complaints. When a problem does not fall within their jurisdictions they refer it to other agencies.

Some of these agencies have been very effective in helping consumers. The New York State Bureau of Consumer Frauds and Protection has helped thousands of consumers each year since it was organized in 1959 by Attorney General Louis Lefkowitz. Another state agency that has given effective help to consumers is the Illinois attorney general's Consumer Frauds Division. Both the New York and Illinois agencies are able to resolve most problems without court action, and most are settled with a phone call or a hearing in the agency's offices. In Illinois, New York, and other states with effective consumer fraud bureaus, court injunctions are sought against firms that are repeat offenders to prohibit them from continuing operations that are considered fraudulent. The bureaus in New York, Illinois, and the state of Washington are considered to be among the most effective for fighting consumer frauds. They have returned millions of dollars each year to deceived consumers.

State regulatory agencies

In each state there are state agencies responsible for regulating many aspects of business and professional activity. These agencies have the principal responsibility for supervising the conduct of local retail and service firms, independent professionals such as physicians and lawyers, and corporations operating only within the state. Agencies in the various states are organized differently and have different names. Most of the same functions are, however, carried on.

Community Series, University Films/McGraw-Hill

When repeated complaints about a particular repair shop are received, the state regulatory agency places a "rigged" TV set in a nearby private home. The findings of such a test may lead to a hearing.

State regulatory agencies license many independent professionals, such as barbers.

Family Series, University Films/McGraw-Hill

State departments of insurance supervise the activity of insurance firms operating in the state and often can provide assistance on such problems as unexplained cancellations of auto insurance, difficulties in obtaining a settlement with a company, or questions concerning rates. Questions concerning the conduct and operations of banks should go to the state department of banking.

State bureaus of weights of measures deal with questions about the accuracy of grocery scales, gasoline pumps, and other weighing and measuring devices. In many states, this bureau is part of the state department of agriculture.

Consumers' problems in getting honest and competent appliance and auto repairs have led several states and cities to institute systems of licensing repairmen and repair shops. One of the most active agencies of this type is the Bureau of Repair Services in the California Department of Consumer Affairs. This bureau contacts television repair shops, for example, in behalf of consumers with complaints. If it appears that the shop is at fault, the bureau requests the shop to correct the problem. When repeated complaints about a particular shop pile up, the bureau places a "rigged" television set in a private home near the shop under suspicion. All the parts in the set are secretly marked so that when the shop services the set the bureau can quickly determine which parts actually were replaced. If it appears that a shop is cheating, the bureau repeats the check in other homes, with other rigged television sets. When there is sufficient evidence, the bureau conducts a hearing on the case. If the agency concludes a shop has been dishonest, it can cancel its registration, putting it out of business.

Many other types of businesses, businessmen, and professionals are licensed by the state. Some examples are barbers, physicians, and auto dealers. The state agencies regulating their activities usually can provide some assistance or advice on consumer problems.

Local government agencies

In some metropolitan areas the district attorney's office has a separate division to handle complaints about consumer fraud. Some offices, like the one in Philadelphia, have been very successful in getting large numbers of complaints settled without legal action, but they also do take legal action where necessary. The Consumer Fraud Division of the Cook County (Chicago) District Attorney's Office also receives a large volume of complaints—about 40 a day. One of the major weapons of this agency is its power to call offending merchants to informal hearings in its offices. The Los Angeles County District Attorney's Consumer Frauds Division also has, over the years, built a reputation for fighting consumer fraud. In other areas, the district attorneys are too often poorly informed about consumer problems or are understaffed and feel they must devote their time to prosecuting crimes such as robbery and murder.

Several cities and counties have set up special consumer protection offices. The activities of the City of New York Department of Consumer Affairs have attracted national attention. Under Commissioner Bess Myerson, the department instituted a number of new programs including unit pricing—the posting of prices per ounce or per measure for grocery store products. The department is also concerned with such matters as false advertising, improper labeling and pricing, and weights and measures. Other cities with special consumer protection offices include Boston, Chicago, Detroit, and St. Louis. Counties with special county offices include Nassau County in New York (Long Island), Dade County in Florida (Miami area), and Multnomah County in Oregon (Portland area).

Editorial Photocolor Archives, Inc.

Bess Myerson, New York City's Commissioner of Consumer Affairs, has attracted national attention for her work in the areas of unit pricing, false advertising, and improper labeling.

Local news media

As consumer problems have come more and more into the news, many local newspapers and radio and TV stations have established consumer complaint centers. These centers handle consumers' problems with businesses and help in obtaining services from government agencies. Some of the problems handled are reported in a regular column or broadcast. An example of such a complaint center is the one run by the *Evening Star* in Washington, D.C. The center is manned by several full-time staffers, plus others on part-time assignments. Some of the results of the center's efforts are reported daily in the *Star's* "Action Line" column.

DIFFICULTIES IN IDENTIFYING PROBLEMS

We are only now beginning to get a full picture of consumers' problems and complaints. For years consumer problems have been handled on an individual basis with little attempt made to classify them into categories in order to determine what kinds of problems are most frequent. In the past few years, several agencies have begun systematic computerization of consumers' problems in order to get an overview of the situation. We now will have a better idea of the areas in which action is most urgently needed.

Even after the full range of consumer complaints has been analyzed, another problem still remains. This problem is the consumer with a problem who fails to complain—the silent victim. No one is quite sure or can even hazard a guess how many silent victims there are. Some are silent because they do not even know they have been deceived; others are ashamed to admit their problems; some do not know where to turn for help; others do not believe any real relief for their problem is available. All consumers must be encouraged to make complaints they consider valid.

Checking your reading

1. When should you make a complaint about a product or service?
2. Why is it important to review product care and use instructions before making a complaint?
3. In general, to whom should you go first with a complaint? Why?
4. What documents and items should you have with you when returning a product or making a complaint?

5. What sources are available for locating the address of a business firm when you want to make a complaint?

6. List four essential pieces of information that should be included in a letter of complaint.

7. If your letter of complaint is not answered, what follow-up steps should be taken next?

8. What types of consumer problems are better business bureaus principally concerned with? What types of problems do they refuse to handle?

9. How does the Office of Consumer Affairs assist consumers who have complaints?

10. What kinds of consumer problems fall under the jurisdiction of the Federal Trade Commission?

11. To what agency would you complain if you ordered some records through the mail, paid for them, but never received them?

12. Which state agency has chief responsibility for handling complaints about consumer frauds?

13. What kinds of business activities are state regulatory agencies responsible for supervising?

14. On what kind of consumer problems can local district attorney's offices often provide assistance?

15. What kinds of complaints are handled by the consumer complaint centers run by local news media?

 Consumer problems and projects

1. A number of agencies that assist consumers are discussed in this chapter. Prepare a detailed report on the activities of one of them for presentation to your class.

2. What consumer problem have you experienced recently? Draft a letter of complaint to the business firm involved, complete with the address. Be sure you include all the essential information.

3. Prepare a follow-up letter that would be appropriate for use if you did not receive a reply to the complaint letter you prepared. Include a list of agencies to whom copies should be sent.

4. The new hair dryer Jackie Hamilton bought at a local department store broke the first time she used it. She was so angry that she wrapped it up and mailed it back to the manufacturer without even a letter of explanation. "Let them figure it out!" she said. Evaluate the way Jackie handled this problem. What course of action might have been more effective?

5. Some people shop at stores that charge high prices just because they know that if they have a problem or complaint it will be handled quickly and politely. Do you think this makes sense?

Chapter

Government agencies that protect the consumer

Responsibility for protecting consumers is divided among many agencies throughout government. There are more than 70 different agencies in the federal government that provide some sort of direct or indirect service to consumers. We already have discussed the activities of some of these agencies, including the Federal Trade Commission, the Food and Drug Administration, the Department of Agriculture, and the Department of Housing and Urban Development. In this chapter, we will try to get an overview of the full range of consumer services of the federal government and their effectiveness.

EXISTING PROGRAMS

The consumer protection activities of the federal government can be classified in three broad categories. The first includes the direct services to individual consumers such as the home mortgage insurance provided by the Federal Housing Administration—or the recreation facilities in national parks provided by the National Park Service. The second category is the regulation of business activity. This includes a number of different agencies and such activities as control of advertising of investment securities by the Securities and Exchange Commission and the control of airline mergers and competitive practices by the Civil Aeronautics Board. The third category is the representation

Courtesy U.S. Department of the Interior

The recreation facilities in national parks are a direct service to individual consumers provided by the federal government.

in government of the consumer interest. This is an important role of the Office of Consumer Affairs. The major consumer protection programs in the federal government and the agencies responsible for them are summarized in the table on pages 455–457.

Congress has enacted laws that set general policies on consumer protection. At the same time, it assigns the responsibility for administering these laws to particular agencies and leaves the details of regulation up to them. The agencies that protect consumers are in the executive branch of government, but most have power to make new rules and regulations and to enforce them. For this reason, they are said to have *quasi-legislative powers*—that is, law-making powers that are like those of a legislative body. Using these powers, the agencies can set standards of conduct for business firms and determine what they may and may not do. Such regulations usually are issued only after notice is given that the agency plans to issue new rules and hearings have been held on the proposed rules. Many of the consumer protection agencies also have *quasi-judicial powers*—that is, powers like the judicial powers of the courts. On the basis of these powers, agencies can, after conducting investigations and hearings, hand down decisions enforcing their rules.

The agencies responsible for protecting the consumer are both offices within the regular Cabinet departments and independent boards and commissions within the executive branch. Since there are so many different agencies involved in protecting consumers we will focus chief attention on two key ones, the Food and Drug Administration and the Federal Trade Commission. We will also consider the Office of Consumer Affairs, which serves a unique function in representing consumer interests to the President, Congress, and the government agencies.

MAJOR CONSUMER PROTECTION PROGRAMS IN THE FEDERAL GOVERNMENT	
Provision of Direct Services	
Consumer Information	Agricultural Marketing Service, Department of Agriculture—performs grading of meat, poultry, eggs, dairy products, fruits, and vegetables Federal Extension Service—provides publications and educational programs on buymanship and money management Food and Drug Administration, Department of Health, Education and Welfare—provides educational programs on product safety and labeling; takes action against quackery regarding medicines General Services Administration—provides information on services available from government through Federal Information Centers and distributes government consumer information publications through the Consumer Product Information Coordinating Center Government Printing Office—distributes government publications National Bureau of Standards, Department of Commerce—prepares consumer publications based on its testing results Office of Consumer Affairs, Executive Office of the President—handles consumer complaints and prepares consumer educational materials
Insurance	Federal Deposit Insurance Corporation—insures bank deposits Federal Housing Administration—provides home mortgage insurance Federal Savings and Loan Insurance Corporation—insures savings and loan deposits Social Security Administration, Department of Health, Education, and Welfare—provides old-age, survivors, and disability insurance
Recreation Facilities	Forest Service, Department of Agriculture—provides campgrounds and other facilities in national forests National Park Service, Department of the Interior—maintains natural, historical, and recreation areas
Regulation of Business Activity	
Accuracy of Label Information	Agricultural Marketing Service, Department of Agriculture—labeling of meat and poultry products

	Federal Trade Commission—labeling of wool, fur, textile products and products not regulated by other agencies Food and Drug Administration, Department of Health, Education, and Welfare—labeling of food, drugs, cosmetics, and medical devices
Advertising Content	Civil Aeronautics Board—airline advertising Federal Communications Commission—advertising on radio and television Federal Deposit Insurance Corporation—advertising by insured banks Federal Trade Commission—most kinds of deceptive and misleading advertising Food and Drug Administration, Department of Health, Education, and Welfare—advertising of prescription drugs Securities and Exchange Commission—advertising of investment securities U.S. Postal Service—fraudulent advertising sent through mails
Competition, Mergers, and Trade Practices	Civil Aeronautics Board—regulates mergers and competitive practices of airlines Federal Communications Commission—regulates number and type of radio and TV stations and community antenna television (CATV) services Federal Power Commission—regulates activities of interstate electric and natural gas industries and mergers Federal Trade Commission—regulates unfair and deceptive business practices that interfere with competition Interstate Commerce Commission—regulates number of interstate rail, bus, truck, and water carriers and their rates; regulates mergers Justice Department—enforces antitrust laws aimed at preventing restraint of trade and at mergers that lead to monopolistic power
Credit Cost Information (Truth in Lending)	Bureau of Federal Credit Unions, Department of Health, Education, and Welfare—federally charted credit unions Comptroller of the Currency, Treasury Department—national banks Federal Deposit Insurance Corporation—insured state banks that are not members of the Federal Reserve System

**MAJOR CONSUMER PROTECTION PROGRAMS
IN THE FEDERAL GOVERNMENT (Continued)**

	Federal Home Loan Bank Board—savings and loan associations
	Federal Reserve Board—state banks that are members of Federal Reserve System
	Federal Trade Commission—small-loan companies, retail stores, and service establishments
Product Safety	Animal and Plant Health Inspection Service, Department of Agriculture—inspects fresh and processed meat and poultry products
	Federal Trade Commission—prevents sale of extremely flammable clothing and fabrics
	Food and Drug Administration—checks to assure safety of food, drugs, cosmetics, medical devices, and toys; assures that hazardous household chemicals have labeling about safe and proper use
Rates and Quality of Service	Civil Aeronautics Board—regulates airline rates, schedules, passenger booking, and services
	Federal Communications Commission—regulates content of radio and television programs; regulates interstate and foreign telephone rates and services
	Interstate Commerce Commission—regulates movers of household goods
Transportation Safety	Federal Aviation Administration, Department of Transportation—promotes air transport safety and provides air-traffic control services
	National Highway Safety Bureau, Department of Transportation—develops safety performance standards for new vehicles and provides highway safety programs
Representation of Consumer Interest	
	Office of Consumer Affairs, Executive Office of the President—advises President on matters of consumer interest and testifies before congressional committees on legislative needs

Food and Drug Administration

The Food and Drug Administration, along with the Federal Trade Commission, has the greatest share of responsibility for protecting consumers. The FDA is part of the Public Health Service in the

Department of Health, Education, and Welfare. It is responsible for enforcing laws and regulations of several kinds to ensure that

- Food is safe, wholesome, and nutritious
- Drugs are safe and effective
- Medical devices, cosmetics, and household goods are safe to use

The scope of the FDA's responsibilities is reflected in the estimate that 38 cents of every dollar spent by consumers goes for products regulated by the FDA.

In its enforcement activities the FDA uses both in-plant inspections and laboratory testing. FDA inspectors check food-processing plants and warehouses and drug-manufacturing plants engaged in producing products for sale in interstate commerce. In 1970, the FDA had 600 inspectors in the field responsible for checking 80,000 facilities producing food and drugs. Because of its limited inspection manpower, the FDA recently has been placing more emphasis on helping plants to identify potential sources of problems and to develop programs for checking products at these points in the production process. On his inspection visits, the FDA inspector can then review the firm's efforts. This method is felt to provide a better check on a firm's performance than judging the firm solely on problems observed on the particular day of an inspection visit.

In addition to in-plant inspections, the FDA conducts laboratory tests of products obtained from retail stores and from consumers with complaints. It also conducts its own laboratory tests of new drugs and chemical food additives to determine their safety. These tests provide a check on manufacturers' reports of their tests of product safety.

The FDA has a variety of enforcement procedures that it can use. It can ban products from the market, request manufacturers to recall them, seize and destroy products, and, in extreme cases, request the Justice Department to prosecute offenders. In large part, however, the FDA relies on firms to cooperate voluntarily. There is evidence, however, that many firms do not correct the violations observed by the FDA inspectors. Stronger regulatory measures seem to be needed to ensure that needed corrections are made. A former head of the FDA has argued that unless penalties are so severe that no one will risk violations, problems will continue. He suggests that the punishments for violations begin with fines of $100,000 and three years in jail.

The Nader study group that investigated the FDA in 1968 and 1969 criticized the agency for giving insufficient attention to the chemicals that are permitted as food additives. Since these criticisms were made,

FDA inspectors check food processing plants, warehouses, and drug manufacturing plants. At right, an inspector is examining cans of tuna fish.

Courtesy Food and Drug Administration

the FDA has undertaken a systematic study of all food additives and their possibly harmful effects. The Nader group also criticized the FDA's information and education efforts, arguing that they devoted too much time to warning consumers about quack cancer cures and vitamin therapy frauds and neglected more dangerous and costly problems that deserved higher priority, such as food-borne diseases (including food poisoning and botulism). As part of its consumer information efforts, in 1970 the FDA began developing a system for providing nutritional information on food labels, such as calorie content, fat content, and vitamin and mineral content.

The FDA has been given many new responsibilities in recent years, but it is handicapped by limited funds. At least part of the criticisms of the FDA grow out of problems created by an inadequate budget. Improvements will require more funds—some proposals have called for a doubling of the FDA's budget. Consumers and their representatives will have to decide how much improved regulation of product safety is worth to them.

Federal Trade Commission

The Federal Trade Commission is one of the more than 40 independent boards and commissions that operate outside of the regular Cabinet departments. Many of these agencies, like the Interstate Commerce Commission, the Securities and Exchange Commission, and the Civil Aeronautics Board, are involved in consumer protection activities. The independent boards and commissions all have multiple membership; that is, all are headed by a group of board members or commissioners rather than a single administrator. The FTC, for example, has five commissioners, one of which is designated as chairman. In creating these agencies, Congress felt multiple membership was desirable, since it permits the representation of various interests and points of view. The commissioners, or board members, are appointed by the President and must be confirmed by the Senate.

In creating the regulatory boards and commissions, Congress also felt that since the boards have quasi-legislative and quasi-judicial powers, they should not be too much under the control of the President and that they should be protected from other political pressures and from party politics. Board members and commissioners are, to some extent, insulated from such pressures by the long terms of their appointments. FTC commissioners, for example, are appointed for seven-year terms.

The Federal Trade Commission was created in 1914 to control unfair trade practices that affected business competition and to handle related antitrust problems. In 1938 its responsibilities were extended to include deception and other practices that injure consumers. We discussed earlier its activities in handling consumer complaints (page 446).

Because of the limitations on its enforcement powers the FTC must protect consumers by discovering and stopping practices that violate the laws it enforces rather than by using fines or other penalties to deter lawbreakers. The FTC's enforcement power is based chiefly on its power to order firms to cease and desist from unfair or deceptive practices. *Cease-and-desist orders* carry no punishment but do require the firm involved to stop engaging in an objectionable practice. If, however, a firm violates an order, the FTC can seek payment of damages or fines of up to $5,000 a day.

Most cases are settled before they ever reach the stage at which a cease-and-desist order is issued. Most are settled with a *consent order* in which the firm agrees to stop engaging in a particular practice but does not admit any wrongdoing. Consent orders are considered useful, since they save time and effort for the FTC and permit firms to avoid the expense and publicity of formal FTC proceedings.

Many who have examined the FTC and its activities feel its enforcement powers are too weak. Nader's investigative team argued that the FTC's present procedures permit those who use deceptive practices to take "free bites" out of the public, since the FTC has no power to levy fines. The worst thing the FTC can do to a firm that has engaged in

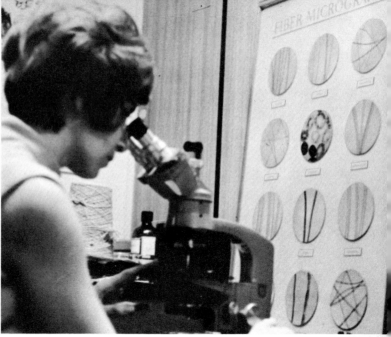

The FTC protects the consumer in many ways. This technologist is using a microscope to examine the fibers of a fabric. Such checks are used to determine whether textiles are labeled correctly.

Courtesy Federal Trade Commission

an objectionable practice is to order it to cease and desist from continuing the practice. The firm is allowed to keep the profits it has made from using the objectionable procedure.

Many people, both inside and outside the FTC, feel that the FTC needs the power to seek *temporary injunctions* to stop deceptive or injurious practices as soon as they are discovered. Temporary injunctions issued by the courts at the FTC's request would permit the FTC to stop the use of a practice until a decision can be reached on whether or not to issue a cease-and-desist order. The FTC already has power to seek temporary injunctions in certain instances, such as cases of false advertising of food, drugs, cosmetics, and medical devices and cases of extremely flammable fabrics. It has not used this power very frequently. The use of temporary injunctions has been limited mostly to cases in which the product was dangerous or in which consumers were likely to suffer substantial and irreparable financial losses. If the FTC's power to seek temporary injunctions in the courts were strengthened, and if the FTC used the new power, consumers could be protected during the months between the detection of a practice that the FTC considered objectionable and the final decision on the practice.

Office of Consumer Affairs

A third key agency serving consumers is the Office of Consumer Affairs, which is part of the Executive Office of the President. The OCA was created in 1971 by President Nixon and replaced the President's Committee on Consumer Interests that had been created by President

Johnson in 1964. The Director of the OCA is also Special Assistant to the President for Consumer Affairs. The first Director appointed was Mrs. Virginia Knauer, who already was serving as Special Assistant to the President at the time the OCA was created.

In the 1971 reorganization, the responsibilities of the earlier office were expanded to include not only advising and representing the President on matters of consumer interest but also analysis and coordination of all consumer protection activities in the federal government. These new responsibilities included establishing priorities for consumer protection programs, resolving conflicts among agencies, and suggesting ways to make programs more effective.

The OCA also has several other responsibilities. We already have noted its role in handling complaints (see page 445). In processing complaints, the OCA refers them to the most appropriate agency. In cases where the problem is not covered by existing laws, the OCA is authorized to contact the firm against whom the complaint is made.

The OCA has encouraged the development of local and state consumer organizations. It has advised them on the principles of organization and on developing their programs. In addition, it has advised state and local school officials on the development of consumer education programs.

Analyses of the mail it receives helps to keep the OCA in contact with the problems of individual consumers. Consumer interests are also represented by the 12-man Consumer Advisory Council, made up of prominent leaders from consumer organizations, labor unions, state attorney generals' offices, and education. The Council advises the OCA on general policy and considers the effectiveness of existing programs and the need for new ones.

It is important to note the limitations on the powers of the OCA. OCA officials can appear and have appeared as witnesses at congressional hearings and at hearings concerning regulations, as representatives of the President. The OCA, however, has no specific power to represent consumers in hearings concerning regulations or to present cases before regulatory agencies or in court. It should also be noted that the OCA is strictly an advisory and informational organization. It has no enforcement powers of any kind. Despite these limitations the OCA serves an important function in representing consumer interests to the President and Congress. Mrs. Knauer and the two earlier Special Assistants for Consumer Affairs have played a key role in calling the attention of the President, Congress, and the public to consumer issues.

Government programs to protect consumers can fail or fall short in several ways. They may fail by neglecting important problems. They may also fail because agencies responsible for regulating particular industries cannot, or do not, police them adequately. In this section we will consider both kinds of failures of consumer protection: failures of coverage and failures of enforcement.

Absence of an overall perspective

Until recently little effort had been made to get an overall perspective of the government's consumer protection activities. Individual agencies worked within the responsibilities outlined for them by Congress, but no one was responsible for systematically examining their activities to find gaps in the government's consumer protection programs. This lack of an overall perspective has resulted in many failures of coverage. The public has become aware of these failures only after scandals such as that created by Sinclair's *The Jungle* in 1906 and tragedies such as the sulfanilamide case in 1937 and the thalidomide case in 1962.

Analyses of the effectiveness and range of government consumer protection activities were begun in the Office of Consumer Affairs after its organization. These studies will prove useful in identifying both gaps in coverage and inadequate enforcement.

Lack of coordination and cooperation among agencies

We have seen that the consumer protection activities of the government are spread among over 70 agencies. It is not surprising, then, that in a number of problem areas more than one agency is involved. For instance, there are nine different agencies responsible for enforcing the Truth In Lending Act and three different agencies enforcing the Truth-in-Packaging law.

This fragmentation of responsibility would not be so serious a problem if the efforts of individual agencies were better coordinated. There are, however, many cases where agencies have not worked well together or have ignored each other. For example, the FTC has complained that the Justice Department has not always cooperated with requests to appeal FTC cases to the Supreme Court and has sometimes refused to compel obedience to FTC subpoenas ordering the appearance of individuals whom the agency wished to question as witnesses. Such problems regarding lack of cooperation have contributed to failures in enforcement.

The fragmentation of the government's consumer protection activities has also made it difficult for consumers with problems to know where to turn for help. The clearing-houses for complaints that recently have been developed within the Federal Trade Commission and the Office of Consumer Affairs have helped ease this problem. Both these offices now have established procedures for referring the complaints they cannot handle themselves to the appropriate agencies.

Shifts from consumer orientation to industry orientation

As we have seen, a number of different government agencies are responsible for regulating business activities in order to protect the public's and consumers' welfare. Over time, however, many of these agencies have tended to forget their responsibilities to the public and have become increasingly concerned with the welfare of the industry they regulate. They begin to regard the industry regulated rather than the public as the "client" whose welfare must be protected. This neglect of the public interest tends to produce failures in enforcement. The shift to an orientation toward industry also makes agencies tend to ignore both new problems that arise in the industry they regulate and gaps in existing laws and rules. This neglect, over time, leads to increasingly serious failures of coverage.

The industry orientation of the regulatory agencies develops for several reasons. Government officials are in constant contact with business representatives. They have many mutual interests, consult each other frequently, and work together on various projects and programs. These close relationships are further strengthened by the movement of executives back and forth between government and business positions.

The views and actions of regulatory agencies are also influenced by lobbyists' activities. The interests of industry groups and of individual firms are represented in Washington by hundreds of lobbyists. This small army is constantly at work emphasizing an industry's or an individual firm's views and problems to congressmen and government executives and reporting government activities back to association members or their firms. In contrast, the consumer interest is served by only a few full-time professionals.

Inadequate representation of consumer interests

As the consumer orientation of a regulatory agency declines it becomes increasingly important for consumers to find ways to represent their interests in its activities. It has, however, proved difficult to do this.

Effective action requires detailed knowledge of the agency's procedures and the rules and laws under which it operates.

Spokesmen for consumer interests have, however, learned ways they can have an important effect on regulatory actions. To do so, they must observe what Commissioner Nicholas Johnson of the Federal Communications Commission has called the "Law of Effective Reform." In his book *How to Talk Back to Your Television Set,* Johnson sets forth the three rules he believes must be observed in order to get corrective action from a regulatory agency. (1) State the facts in the case and the parties involved. (2) Identify some law or regulation that appears to have been violated. (3) Specify exactly what action the agency should take to correct the violation.

The use of these rules can be seen in the case against cigarette advertising presented to the Federal Communications Commission by law professor John Banzhaf. In developing his case, Banzhaf checked the programming of a large New York radio and television station and found that it ran a large number of cigarette commercials. He then filed a letter of complaint with the Federal Communications Commission that this violated the FCC's "fairness doctrine." The *fairness doctrine* is a legal principle developed by the FCC that requires that all sides must be given a hearing when controversial issues of public importance are discussed on the air. Banzhaf argued that commercials

The FCC's application of the "fairness doctrine" required TV stations to carry free antismoking commercials, such as the one shown below. This action paved the way for a complete ban of cigarette advertising on TV.

Courtesy American Cancer Society

ignored the health hazards of cigarettes and that the station was thus obligated under the fairness doctrine to provide information on the health hazards of smoking. The FCC agreed with Banzhaf's arguments, and, as a result, stations began to carry millions of dollars' worth of free antismoking commercials. This action helped pave the way for the removal of all cigarette ads from the air. The fairness doctrine has since been used as the basis for a number of other complaints about advertising content, including cases regarding products that are alleged to cause pollution. It remains to be seen whether the fairness doctrine will also be considered to apply in these cases.

Misplaced priorities and inadequate budgets

Some of the failures of enforcement in the government's consumer protection programs are due to misplaced priorities. Too much effort and money are spent on trivial problems, while important ones are neglected. This results in failures of enforcement. One of the main criticisms of the FTC in the 1969 Nader group report was that the agency spent too much time on minor problems such as inadequate fur and textile labeling and fraudulent schemes such as plans for raising chinchillas at home. At the same time, the study group charged, the agency neglected the consumer problems of the poor, widespread frauds involving home improvements, and other possible violations in which large corporations were involved. This problem of misplaced priorities seems to have been corrected by the revitalization of the FTC that has occurred in recent years.

Many failures of enforcement must, however, be blamed on inadequate funds. The problem of inadequate budgets appears to be most serious in the case of the FDA. One of the key techniques used by the FDA in ensuring product safety is in-plant inspections. The FDA has only 600 field inspectors to check 80,000 facilities producing food and drugs. It is obvious that frequent in-plant checks are impossible with such a small force. Limited funds have also restricted FDA activities in other important areas such as research to check the safety of chemical additives used in foods.

PROPOSALS FOR NEW CONSUMER AGENCIES

The deficiencies in the government's consumer protection programs have resulted in a number of proposals for new agencies to serve consumers. Most of the proposals for new agencies include one or more of the following features:

- A new consumer protection agency that brings together present consumer protection efforts under one roof
- A consumer advocate or consumer counsel who would be empowered to represent consumers' interests in regulatory hearings and in court cases
- An agency that would make available to consumers product-testing information based on its own research, research by other government agencies, or tests conducted by private laboratories under standards that it develops

Some consumer spokesmen including Ralph Nader have taken the position that little will be gained by reorganizing existing regulatory activities under a new agency. They believe that all the same pressures that limit the effectiveness of existing agencies would hamper any new agency with the same functions. These spokesmen believe that a consumer counsel would be more useful and effective. He would present cases or arguments for consumers in hearings and court cases in much the same way an attorney represents private clients. A consumer counsel should, they believe, be a full party in such cases with power to call his own witnesses, to cross-examine witnesses called by other parties, and to present arguments in behalf of consumers. Many who favor the creation of a consumer counsel's office believe that this office should have power to intervene in cases at an early stage while preliminary hearings and investigations are still being conducted. They argue that many important decisions are made at this stage and that if a consumer counsel is to fully represent consumers he must be kept informed from the very early stages of a case. The importance of this provision can be seen when we recall the heavy reliance on voluntary compliance by both the FDA and the FTC and the frequent use of consent orders, agreed to without formal hearings, by the FTC.

There has been a good deal of concern about ensuring that any new agency be insulated from political pressures and from control by the White House. Some proposals attempt to provide this insulation by suggesting that the new organization be an independent agency in the executive branch, headed by a director with a long-term appointment—one proposal suggests a 15-year term. It is felt that such an agency would be more independent than a new Cabinet-level department with a Secretary appointed by the President or an office housed in an existing department.

Bills creating a new consumer agency passed the Senate in 1970 and the House in 1971. New legislation seems likely. It remains to be seen whether the new legislation that is passed will correct the deficiencies we have noted in this chapter. You will be able to evaluate new laws and proposals for yourself by determining how good a job they do in correcting these deficiencies.

Checking your reading

1.   Into what three broad categories can the consumer protection activities of the federal government be classified?
2.   Explain why some federal agencies that protect consumers are said to have "quasi-legislative powers."
3.   When a consumer protection agency has "quasi-judicial powers," what type of power does it have?
4.   The Food and Drug Administration is a part of what executive department?
5.   Because of limited resources, the FDA recently has placed more emphasis on the prevention of problems in the plants it inspects. Explain this program.
6.   What enforcement procedures does the FDA use?
7.   In 1968 and 1969, a Nader study group investigated the FDA. Cite two criticisms of the FDA made by the study group.
8.   How many commissioners serve on the Federal Trade Commission? How are these commissioners selected? How long do they serve?
9.   Explain what is meant by a "cease-and-desist" order.
10.   What is a "consent order" as the term is used in cases in which the FTC is involved? Why are they useful?
11.   Why do some think the FTC's powers to seek temporary injunctions should be strengthened?
12.   When was the Office of Consumer Affairs created? What did it replace?
13.   In general terms, what is the function of the Office of Consumer Affairs?
14.   How many different agencies are responsible for enforcing the Truth In Lending Act? the Truth-in-Packaging law? What can you generalize about this situation?
15.   Explain how the FCC's fairness doctrine resulted in the ultimate removal of cigarette ads from the air.
16.   How many field inspectors does the FDA have? How many facilities must these inspectors check? What generalization can be made about this situation?
17.   List three features often included in proposals for better government consumer protection programs.
18.   List some of the functions that a consumer counsel might serve if such a position were created.

Consumer problems and projects

1.   Over a period of at least one month, collect news stories from newspapers and magazines about the work of federal regulatory agencies. Attach the news items to a bulletin board.

2.   Many of the products and services of some of the largest businesses in the United States are subject to the authority of the Food and Drug Administration. Do you believe this is a good or bad arrangement? Why?

3.   Write a report about the Federal Trade Commission. Include information about its origin, its main purposes, and the principal laws administered by the Commission.

4.   Federal employees work in every community and in every section of our country. Report to the class on some aspect of federal activity in your area. Is the service helpful to the community? If the federal government did not supply the service, would someone else? If no one supplied the service, what would be the effect on your area? on you personally?

5.   Name the federal agency that has jurisdiction over each of the following commodities or activities:

    a. Gas used for cooking or heating
    b. Meat or poultry sold in interstate commerce
    c. Counterfeiting
    d. Broadcast interference
    e. Unfair competition
    f. Registering of newly issued securities

Choose one of the six agencies, and write a report on its power and on the means used to enforce its decisions.

6.   Write a detailed book review of *The Interstate Commerce Omission,* by Robert Fellmeth. The book is available for $1.45 from Grossman Publishers, Inc., 625 Madison Avenue, New York, N.Y. 10022. Include in your report information available in the foreword about who was involved in the study of the Interstate Commerce Commission. After reading this book, do you think any reforms are in order?

Chapter

Principles
of consumer law

In all your dealings with others, you are exposed to various kinds of danger. Human nature and the course of events are such that you need protection from people who would take advantage of you and from circumstances that could harm you.

You get the protection you need from the laws of the land—laws of many kinds that have been worked out over the years, and laws that are even now being drafted for your benefit. This chapter explains the background and the intent of some of the laws that affect consumers. It also shows how businesses operate within the framework of the laws and explains how you as an individual can use the laws for your benefit and protection.

ESSENTIALS OF COMMERCIAL LAW

The following pages describe some essentials of commercial law—the principles that govern it and the rules it follows. Note, however, that this is merely an introduction to the subject. You can gain an understanding of the background of commercial law from this book, but it will not make you a lawyer. If you need or want legal advice, be sure to get it from a licensed attorney. At the end of this chapter, you will be given more information about when, how, and where to get professional legal advice and help.

Even simple transactions, such as paying money in order to ride on a bus, are contracts that can be enforced by law.

B. D. Unsworth

Contracts

Contracts are involved in one form or another in nearly every business transaction. If you buy a suit that requires alterations, you complete an order. You have then actually made a contract by which you promise to pay for the suit and the store promises to deliver it to you, altered to fit you. Even simple transactions such as riding on the bus, going to the movies, or using the lights in your home are contracts that, if necessary, can be enforced by law.

To accomplish its purpose, any contract must be binding upon all parties. No one will be allowed to wriggle out. Another way of putting the same idea is to say the contract must be enforceable; that is, if somebody tries to escape, the courts, under the law, can force him to perform as he promised he would.

Some contracts must be written and signed by all the persons involved so that they are legally binding. This is true of many leases for the rental of property, of agreements for the sale of real estate, and of most installment-plan purchase contracts. Other less formal contracts may be oral and unwritten, and a few may even be unspoken. Still other agreements have no legal significance and thus do not constitute contracts. Personal agreements you make with friends, such as agreeing to go to a party, to attend the movies, or to visit a neighbor are examples of agreements that are not legally enforceable contracts.

Mutual assent

To be legally binding, a contract must be accepted by all parties involved. Actually, there can be no disagreement at all; when disagreement can be shown, this is proof that the parties were not of one mind.

In such situations contracts cannot exist and thus cannot be binding.

In order to show and to prove mutual assent, two elements are required by law, and they are absolutely essential: a valid offer and acceptance. These elements illustrate how useful the commercial laws are in setting up and maintaining a structure for business transactions.

THERE MUST BE AN OFFER   An offer is good only if it is made in such a way that it shows obvious intention on the part of the person making the offer to enter into legal agreement with the person to whom the offer is made.

The offer must be clear and definite, and it must be properly communicated.

A retail store placed an advertisement in the newspaper: Portable TV Sets, $89.50—Today Only. Because the dealer did not have sufficient quantity to meet all demands, there was no *obvious intention* to sell a TV set to everyone who responded to the advertisement. Therefore, the offer was not valid or legally binding; it was more in the nature of an "offer to make an offer."

Henry, who owns several cameras, offered to sell one to Jack for $20. Because Henry did not specify which camera he would sell for $20, the offer was not clear and definite. It could not result in a contract until there was an agreement on the specific camera offered.

Harris posted a public notice offering a reward of $25 for the return of his lost briefcase. Hanson, who had not seen the notice, found the briefcase and returned it. Because the offer was not *communicated* to Hanson, his return of the briefcase was not an acceptance of the offer. The offer was valid but not properly communicated.

A valid offer may be terminated in one of three ways: through lapse of time, through revocation, or through rejection. Only acceptance of the offer results in a contract.

Lapse of time can terminate an offer when a time limit has been set for acceptance.

Bob offered to sell his car to Jim and gave him three days to think it over. Unless Jim accepted the offer within the three-day period, the offer was automatically terminated.

The lapse of a reasonable length of time can terminate an offer when no time limit is specified for acceptance.

Bob offered to sell his car to Jim but set no time limit for the acceptance of his offer. The offer terminated after a reasonable length of time. However, since there can sometimes be disagreement about what constitutes a reasonable length of time, it is usually wise to specify a definite period.

Revocation of an offer terminates it at any time prior to its acceptance. (In the example above, Bob could have decided not to sell his car to Jim at any time before Jim decided to buy or not to buy it.) However, if there is an agreement to keep the offer open for a given period of time—this is called an *option* and is itself a type of contract— the offer cannot be withdrawn during the specified time period. To terminate an offer by withdrawing it, the revocation must be communicated to the offeree prior to acceptance.

The *rejection* of an offer terminates the offer immediately. If Bob had offered to sell his car to Jim and Jim had replied that he was not interested, the rejection would have terminated the offer.

THERE MUST BE AN ACCEPTANCE   Once a valid offer is made, the other parties either reject or accept it. Acceptance of an offer results in a contract. However, the acceptance must be unconditional to survive, and it must fit exactly with the terms of the offer. Finally, the acceptance must be signified by words, actions, or both.

Bob offered to sell his car to Jim if Jim would pick it up from the repair shop and pay the repair bill. If Jim picked up the car and paid for the repairs, he would indicate his acceptance of Bob's offer by this action.

You can accept an offer by mail or by telegram. The time of your acceptance will be that of the postmark on your letter or the time your telegram is accepted by the telegraph company. Some persons may not insist that they have your acceptance in hand to satisfy the acceptance rules, however.

Consideration

To be legally binding, a contract must be supported by valuable consideration from each person. Consideration may be in the form of an object of value, a promise, or a performed act. If one person is to receive something for nothing, the contract cannot be enforced by law.

Jim promised to build a table for Tom if Tom would pay him $10 immediately. Tom paid Jim the $10. Tom could hold Jim to his promise because he had given consideration in the form of the $10, an *object of value*.

In exchange for Addison's promise to sell and deliver his car to Jenkins for $500, Jenkins promised to pay Addison on delivery. In this case, the consideration for Addison's promise to sell and deliver his car was the *promise* made by Jenkins to pay $500 on delivery.

Salazar promised to give his nephew John $2,000 if John would obtain a college degree before his twenty-first birthday. The consideration for Salazar's promise to pay was his nephew's *performed act* of obtaining a degree. An enforceable contract would only arise if John obtained his degree before his twenty-first birthday.

Ralph promised to take Arthur on a three-day hunting trip but failed to do so. There was no contract because no consideration had been given by Arthur. Arthur had given nothing of value, done nothing, nor promised to do anything.

Parties

A contract is enforceable when it is made by two or more persons who can give sane and intelligent assent. This rule protects those who are not able to protect themselves because they are mentally ill or otherwise incapable of knowing what will happen if they agree to do or not to do some action.

MINORS ARE NOT CONSIDERED COMPETENT   At what age are you capable of "looking out for yourself"? The age at which society assumes you are capable is decided by law, and that law varies from state to state. Where formerly it was generally the practice to call people "minors" until they were twenty-one years old, there is now a common lowering of this age. This is indicated by the extension of voting privileges, which were formerly denied to those under twenty-one, to eighteen-year-olds.

No matter what the age ceiling for minors is in your state, until you reach it you have a special status. You can void (cancel) most contracts you make because you are assumed not to have full maturity of mind and judgment until you reach the age of majority. Although minors can walk away from a contract, claiming youth and inexperience as a defense for breaking it, the adult who makes a contract with a youth must perform his obligations. The law assumes that the adult, at least, has the intelligence and the maturity to know and understand what he is doing.

Exceptions to the defense of minors occur when minors contract for necessities such as food, clothing, medical care, and education. Either the minor or his parents must pay for necessities; if this were not so, merchants would be justified in refusing to sell such necessities to minors, fearing that they would suffer financial losses because of irresponsible young customers. If you are a minor, remember this exception to minority defense when you want to buy a wild item of dress.

OTHER PEOPLE MAY BE INCOMPETENT   Persons who are insane or who have faulty reasoning because of illness or other disability are not considered legally competent to make contracts. Just as youth and inexperience can be defenses against unfair contracts, so also can the disabilities resulting from advanced age. Rulings of incompetence serve to protect all parties, of course.

Legality

Contracts must be made for legal purposes. If they are not, they are not legally binding. Contracts that involve actions against the law or public policy are considered illegal. They are not enforceable.

Tom promised to pay Bob $20, if he would steal a typewriter for him. Bob stole the typewriter and gave it to Tom, who refused to pay. Bob could not collect because the agreement was unlawful. It called for a criminal act.

Jim bet Howard $10 that the Midland High School team would beat Rutland High in Saturday's football game. Jim lost the bet but refused to pay. Howard could take no legal action because the law enforces only legalized gambling contracts, such as bets made at race tracks.

DOCUMENTS MUST HAVE THE PROPER ELEMENTS   There is no particular form for written contracts, but they should contain the following elements: the date of the agreement, the names of the contracting parties, the purpose of the contract, the consideration, and the signatures of all parties or their agents.

Although you do not need written contracts for some business arrangements, there are many arrangements that demand written words. Among the arrangements that absolutely demand written contracts are those (1) that cannot be performed within one year, or (2) that involve the sale of real estate or personal property of substantial value, or (3) that guarantee to pay the debt of another person.

Negotiable instruments

Pieces of paper carrying written promises to pay or requests for delivery of money are called *negotiable instruments*. Because so much commerce is carried on with the help of negotiable instruments, it is not in any way surprising that they are also called *commercial paper.*

The kinds of negotiable instruments most often used by consumers are checks and promissory notes.

CHECKS INVOLVE MUTUAL RESPONSIBILITIES   The writer, or *drawer,* of a check is obligated to have enough money in his account to cover the check. The person to whom the drawer makes the check payable is the *payee.* The drawer may also make the check payable to "cash" or to himself as "bearer." The check is then payable to whoever presents it for payment.

The drawer's bank is the *drawee.* It is required to honor or pay any properly drawn check if funds are available to cover it.

There are several plans now available whereby a person can write a check for a sum larger than his account holds. Through the magic of computerized bookkeeping any such overdrafts, which are ordinarily illegal, are very rapidly converted to loans. The secret of such an arrangement is a type of standing promissory note that authorizes the bank to turn any overdraft into a consumer loan. The banks are delighted to have such agreements because they can charge up to 18 percent interest on such loans. Apparently bank customers like the plans, too. For one thing, the plans give the feeling of having a purse that always has at least a little reserve. For another, they are very convenient. Financial counselors may tell you they are too convenient for your own good.

The bank is obligated to refuse payment of any check that has been altered or forged. If the bank allows forged or altered checks to be paid, the bank is required by law to cover the loss. Thus, if you draw a check and then immediately ask the bank to stop payment, you are protected, and the burden of stopping payment falls upon the bank.

Banks are not required to pay postdated checks before the date written on them. If you wrote a check on September 15 and dated it September 20, the bank would not pay the amount on the check until September 20.

CERTIFIED CHECKS PROVIDE ASSURANCE   When you must write a very large check, the payee may ask for a "certified check". *Certified checks* contain a statement by the bank that there is enough money in your account to cover the check and that the bank will honor that particular check. However, the bank does charge a small fee to make a certified check.

The promissory note

A promissory note is a written promise to pay a definite sum of money to the order of a designated person or to the bearer of the note at a specified or determinable time. It is a legal document, and payment can be enforced by law. The person who writes and signs the note is the *maker*. The person to whom it is payable is the *payee*. The promissory note is normally used in borrowing money from a bank, finance company, or credit union.

In some cases, creditors require cosigners or collateral as security for payment of a note. A *cosigner* is a person who promises to pay the note if the maker fails to pay. The cosigner's signature and that of the maker appear on the note. A *collateral note* is a promissory note that permits the payee to hold certain personal property of the maker—usually stocks or bonds—as security for payment of the note. If the maker fails to pay, the payee has the legal right to sell the collateral in lieu of payment.

Legal requirements

In most states, negotiable instruments are governed by a modification of the Uniform Negotiable Instruments Law or by the Uniform Commercial Code. These laws are designed to protect the rights of all parties involved in the use of negotiable instruments. To be negotiable, an instrument must conform to the following requirements:

- It must be in writing and must be signed by the maker or drawer. No particular form of writing or signature is necessary. Any mark regarded by the drawer as his signature is legally valid. An authorized agent may sign the drawer's name followed by "per" or "by" and his own name to indicate that he is the agent and not the drawer.
- It must contain an unconditional promise to pay a definite amount of money.
- It must be payable on demand or at a fixed or determinable future date.
- It must be payable to order of a particular person or to bearer.
- It must be delivered to the payee.

If an instrument meets these requirements, it is negotiable, even if it is not dated or does not specify the value given (consideration) or the place where it is payable.

Negotiation

A large part of the banking industry involves pushing tons of paper back and forth, delivering it to one place or another, as a convenient substitute for money. When a negotiable instrument is turned over from one payee to another, the process is called *negotiation*. This may be carried out in either of two ways: delivery or endorsement.

You can negotiate transfer of funds from yourself to another payee by *delivery* if the check is made payable to "bearer."

If a check is made payable to a specific person, however, that person must *endorse* the check by writing his name on the back before the check can be negotiated.

If Brown gives you a $10 check made out in your name and you want to transfer it to Berkowitz, you must endorse the check and deliver it to Berkowitz in order to transfer the title.

The person who endorses an instrument with intent to transfer the title is the *endorser*. The person to whom the instrument is transferred is the *endorsee* or *holder*. The endorser generally pledges his credit for payment of the instrument if the maker fails to pay. There are several types of endorsements.

Blank Endorsement

Special Endorsement

Qualified Endorsement

Restrictive Endorsement

A *blank endorsement* is merely the signature of the endorser on the back of the instrument without comment or notation. Instruments with a blank endorsement can be negotiated subsequently by delivery from one person to another just as instruments made payable to bearer or cash.

A *special endorsement* is the signature of the endorser preceded by the words "Pay to . . ." or "Pay to the order of . . ." on the back of the instrument. The endorsee, whose name appears after "Pay to" or "Pay to the order of," must then endorse the instrument to negotiate it further or to cash it.

A *qualified endorsement* is one that limits the liability of the endorser. An endorsement is qualified when the endorser writes the words "without recourse" on the back of the instrument before his signature. This means that the endorser assumes no responsibility for payment by the maker or drawer of the instrument.

A *restrictive endorsement* is one that restricts further negotiation of the instrument to the purpose specified by the endorser. Restrictive endorsements reading "For deposit only" with the endorser's signature are frequently used when checks are mailed to a bank to be deposited in the endorser's account.

Using negotiable instruments

Whether you are the maker, drawer, or endorser of a negotiable instrument, your signature on the instrument establishes certain responsibilities and liabilities that you must assume. The following suggestions can help you to protect your own interests in using negotiable instruments.

- When you write checks or promissory notes, write the amount in figures immediately after the dollar sign and the amount in words close to the left margin. Leave no space where words or figures can be added. If there is any difference between the amount in figures and the amount in words, the amount in words is considered valid. Be sure that the amount you have written is correct.
- Avoid making alterations on checks or notes. Negotiable instruments that have been altered in any way are not accepted as valid.
- Act as a cosigner or endorser of a negotiable instrument only if you are willing and able to pay the obligation if the maker fails to pay.

- Use the proper date in writing negotiable instruments. Post-dated checks cannot be honored prior to the date indicated on the instrument.
- Verify your bank statement regularly by comparing deposits and withdrawals listed on the statement with those in your checkbook. Notify the bank promptly of any errors, alterations, or forgeries. (Notice in writing is perferable to oral notice.)
- Use restrictive endorsements when transferring negotiable instruments by mail or messenger. Blank endorsements can be negotiated by anyone who holds the instrument.
- Write negotiable instruments distinctly, without flourishes, and preferably in ink.

WARRANTIES

Warranties are agreements or promises that give you special rights in case something you buy turns out to be defective or in some specified way fails to satisfy you. Whether the warranty is stated (or *express*) or assumed to exist (or *implied*), the warranty is not a safeguard against lack of taste or indecision on your part. It cannot guarantee that you will like what you buy; it can only promise to protect you if the merchandise fails to live up to the specified standards.

A consumer must be very careful to avoid being influenced too much by advertising claims that are merely statements of opinion. "Trade talk" and "puffing" are mildly persuasive ways of describing merchandise to influence the buyer; they are not warranties. Such statements as "This is the best car on the market," "You won't find a better suit for the money," or "This item is moving so fast you had better buy it now" are advertising claims, not warranties; they do not make specific promises regarding title, identity, performance, or quality. Learn to look for the two kinds of warranty, express and implied.

Express warranties

An express warranty is an oral or written guarantee of a specific quality or performance feature. If a manufacturer makes a written promise that a shirt will not shrink more than 1 percent, that is a warranty. If a seller makes an oral promise that a shirt is washable, colorfast, and shrink-proof, and if the shirt fades and shrinks out of size on the first washing, the seller is responsible for the warranty.

It is difficult to prove an oral warranty, so it is preferable to get a written guarantee. This is especially true when you are buying clothes.

Look for the manufacturer's tags specifying the kind of fabric used and the performance to be expected from the fabric.

Implied warranties

An implied warranty is a guarantee that the buyer has a legal right to expect a degree of fitness or quality in what he purchases. There are several kinds of implied warranties. Some of the main ones are warranty of title, warranty of fitness for purpose, warranty of fitness for human consumption, and warranty of salability.

WARRANTY OF TITLE By the very act of selling an item the seller tells his potential customers that he has a right to sell the item and that title will pass to the buyer at the time of sale. If you find that somebody has sold you goods to which he did not have title or to which he had title that was defective, you may claim monetary damages by suing him for breach of warranty of title.

WARRANTY OF FITNESS FOR PURPOSE When you tell a seller your purpose in buying a particular item and rely on his skill and judgment, there is an implied warranty of fitness for purpose. For instance, you tell a seller that you want a heavy-duty vacuum cleaner to clean wall-to-wall carpeting. After buying the cleaner recommended by the seller, you discover that the cleaner is only effective for light cleaning. In this case you can hold the seller liable on an implied warranty of fitness for purpose.

WARRANTY OF FITNESS FOR HUMAN CONSUMPTION When you buy foodstuffs from a food merchant, the food is covered by an implied warranty of fitness for human consumption. Both seller and buyer fully understand that the food is to be eaten. The seller is liable for any illness or injury to the buyer or to his family that results from eating the food. This warranty applies to the sale of drugs as well as to the sale of food. In addition to the obligation imposed by the implied warranty, the seller may be held criminally liable in cases of gross negligence.

Be sure your own food market will take back food that does not live up to your expectations. You may not have a criminal case against the manager if your roast is tough, but if he sold it to you as tender meat he made an implied warranty, and therefore you are entitled to get your money back.

The food that you buy from a merchant is covered by an implied warranty of fitness for human consumption.

Editorial Photocolor Archives, Inc.

WARRANTY OF SALABILITY   By the act of selling goods, merchants imply that what they sell will meet at least minimum standards of acceptability. When the buyer inspects goods and fails to notice defects that an average person could be expected to discover, there is no implied warranty of salability; but for goods that the average buyer cannot be expected to evaluate, such as a radio with complicated parts and construction, buyers are protected by an implied warranty of salability.

OTHER IMPLIED WARRANTIES   Implied warranties are said to exist for goods sold by samples or by description, as in the mail-order catalog. (The copywriters must be extremely careful in their choice of words to ensure accuracy.) The buyer has a legal right to expect the goods he receives to correspond to the sample or to the description used by the seller.

Buying goods "as is"

Secondhand or damaged goods may be sold to consumers without either an express or an implied warranty. To protect his interest, the seller inserts the phrase "as is" into the written contract to warn the purchaser that the articles are being sold in the actual condition in which they are found at the time of sale. The burden of finding out what condition the article is in falls upon the buyer. However, if the seller makes any fraudulent misstatements of facts in describing the "as is" condition, and the buyer relies upon those statements, the contract may be voided by a court. This could happen if you bought a used car in obviously poor condition, and the dealer told you that you would need only to repair the transmission to get the car into perfect running condition. If it turned out that the car needed a new front end, a ring job, four new tires, and a complete electrical system before it would start, the court might be sympathetic to your subsequent claim for damages.

PERSONAL SERVICES

Certain personal services are rendered by individuals who have special skills, knowledge, and experience in a particular field. When you contract for the services of an accountant, a lawyer, a doctor, a painter, an architect, or some other specialist, you usually choose one individual in preference to another because of his performance or reputation in his particular field. For this reason, the contract is valid only when carried out by the chosen specialist. If a patient selects a particular doctor, there can be no substitution of another doctor without the patient's consent. Contracts for personal services do not have to be in writing to be enforceable unless the services to be rendered cannot be performed or completed within one year.

BAILMENTS

Whenever one person delivers personal property to another person for some special purpose with the understanding that the property is to be returned when that purpose is accomplished, a *bailment contract* arises. The person who transfers possession of the property is known as the *bailor*. The person to whom possession is given is known as the *bailee*.

Any kind of personal property, including money, can be the subject of a bailment. A bailment arises at the time the bailor delivers the property and the bailee accepts it. Bailments normally arise in connection with cleaning and repair services, equipment rentals, and storage and safekeeping services. They also arise in connection with the purchase of certain other goods and services.

Cleaning and repair services
A bailee for repairs or cleaning is required by law to exercise ordinary skill in performing the required work. *Ordinary skill* means the degree of skill possessed by a capable and reasonably prudent person engaged

in the same type of business. A dyer, for example, should know that in certain instances a rayon dress will shrink when dyed.

In addition, the bailee must safeguard the bailor's property by taking ordinary care of it; that is, giving the same type of care that the bailee ordinarily would give to his own property.

The bailee is liable for any loss that results from his unsatisfactory performance in repairing or cleaning and for any failure to exercise reasonable care of the bailor's property. Since negligence on the part of the bailee is sometimes difficult to prove, it is advisable to deal with reputable bailees only and, whenever possible, to obtain a written guarantee of services rendered.

When a bailee accepts personal property to repair or alter, he holds a lien, or security interest, on that piece of property to the extent of the value of his services. Accordingly, the bailee has a legal right to keep the property until he has received full payment for his services. The lien is effective only as long as the property is in the possession of the bailee. Once he parts with the property, the lien is forfeited.

Rental services

A bailment for the rental of property is an agreement wherein the bailor, on payment of a set rental fee, rents property to be used by the bailee for a specific purpose. The bailor warrants, either expressly or by implication, that the property is suitable for the purpose of the bailee. Therefore, the bailor is liable for any damage or injury that may be caused by failure of the property to serve the intended purpose. Jones rented a car from Stuart. The brakes on the car failed, and Jones hit and damaged a parked car. He also suffered cuts and bruises as a result of the accident. Stuart was liable for damages because the car was not fit for the bailee's purpose.

In a contract for the rental of property, the bailee is liable for any damages resulting from failure to take reasonable care of the bailor's property or from any use of the property in violation of the contract. He is also responsible for injuries to third persons caused by his negligence in using the bailed article. The bailee must return the article upon termination of the bailment and must pay the agreed rental, unless he has paid in advance. Henry rented a bicycle from a neighborhood bicycle shop and permitted Walter to use it. Walter accidentally damaged the bicycle. Henry was liable for damages because he violated the contract in permitting a third party to use the property. He might also be responsible for any injuries to Walter.

Storage and custody services

When parties agree that, for a consideration, one of them will store or keep specific articles for the other in a garage, warehouse, parking lot, or safe-deposit vault, a bailment for storage or safekeeping is created. The bailee in a contract for storage and safekeeping must return the identical articles to the bailor upon termination of the bailment. He must not use the stored articles for his own purposes. In performing the contract, he must exercise ordinary care and must possess the skill and knowledge ordinarily expected from a bailee of this type. He has a lien on the stored articles for storage charges. If the bailee redelivers the stored articles to the wrong person, he will be liable to the bailor, regardless of his good faith or the degree of care he exercised.

Johnson stored his furniture in a warehouse. A window in the warehouse was left open, and the furniture was damaged during a rainstorm. The owner of the warehouse was liable for damages because he failed to exercise the care and skill ordinarily expected from a warehouse owner.

Generally, a bailment relationship arises when a person leaves his car in a garage or parking lot—especially if the parking lot has attendants on duty at all times. The car owner is given a claim check for the car, and the car must be left unlocked with the keys in it. In this type of bailment, the parking-lot owner is liable for any damages resulting from negligence and is also responsible for failure to exercise reasonable care of the car.

When two parties agree that, for a sum of money, one of them will store the other's car in a garage, a bailment for storage is created.

Editorial Photocolor Archives, Inc.

However, in certain cases, a car owner who leaves his car in a lot or garage formulates a contract for the rental of space rather than a bailment relationship. This is true when a person rents a definite space and habitually parks and removes the car himself. It is also true when a person leaves his car in an outdoor parking space adjacent to a ball park, a public beach, or some similar public place.

Bailments related to other purchases

Occasionally a bailment arises in connection with the sale of other goods and services. When a customer removes a garment to try on clothing at the direction of or with the knowledge and consent of the seller, the seller becomes the bailee of the customer's clothing. A proprietor of a restaurant or a theater is considered a bailee when a customer checks personal belongings with the establishment. However, the liability of the proprietor is usually limited to an amount printed on the claim check or posted in plain sight of the customer. Unless the bailor makes specific arrangements for checking articles of a greater value than the amount guaranteed by the bailee, he can make no claim in excess of the bailee's stated liability.

Mrs. Thompson checked her $800 fur jacket at a restaurant. On the claim check she received, the extent of the bailee's liability was stated as $200. The jacket was picked up by another customer. Mrs. Thompson made no mention of the jacket's value to the checkroom attendant and could recover no more than the $200.

LEGAL SERVICES AND THE CONSUMER

Although consumers are protected by laws, they occasionally require specific legal services to prevent legal problems from arising, to protect their interests, or to enforce their rights. Legal services, in one form or another, are available to every consumer. You will be in a better position to benefit from these services if you know when to seek legal aid and how to obtain it.

When to seek legal aid

Almost everyone occasionally finds himself in a situation in which he wants or needs legal aid. The situations that are listed below normally call for the advice of a legal expert.

- Entering into a contract for the sale or purchase of real estate.
- Entering into a sales contract involving a large sum of money.

- Signing written agreements or contracts that are not presented in standard form.
- Carrying out adoption proceedings.
- Appearing in court as plaintiff or defendant.
- Filing income tax returns if there is any possibility that the return will be questioned or if there are nonstandard deductions involved. (Either an accountant or an attorney can perform this service.)
- Bringing charges or accusations against another person or defending charges brought against you, particularly if there is a possibility that a charge of libel or slander will be raised.
- Drawing up wills, settling estates, or setting up trusts.
- Entering into or setting up any type of business.

How to obtain legal aid

There are several ways to obtain legal aid when you need or want it. Your choice of legal services will depend on the situation, the services available in your area, and the amount you can pay. Legal services are available from many sources, such as lawyers, government agencies, and small claims courts.

LAWYERS You can get help from lawyers, but it takes time, effort, and thought to find the right man to help you. Simply finding a lawyer in the first place can be a puzzling problem to many people. If you have a legal problem, and you have any doubts about its solution at all, your wisest move is to call the local bar association or the lawyers referral service and ask for the name of a lawyer who handles that kind of problem. You can also ask your friends for advice, although it is probably true that a friend's advice on professional recommendations is likely to be so colored by his personal preferences that it may not be wise for you to follow it.

Choose your lawyer carefully; you may want to entrust him with many different problems over the years, just as the doctor you choose equally carefully may help you through several illnesses. Above all, pick a lawyer you feel you can trust.

If you do not have enough money to pay for a lawyer's assistance, call on the local legal aid society—an organization usually sponsored by the local bar association and staffed by volunteers. The legal aid societies do more than provide legal assistance in criminal cases. Their members may give counseling in simple cases. At all times the societies stand ready to refer a person to another agency that can handle his problem more directly or more efficiently.

In any event, if you do work with a lawyer—and the chances are good that you will at several points in your life—be sure to be honest with him; take his advice; leave the professional tactics and work up to him; do not annoy him by anxious telephone calls, but let him work on your problem for you. Finally, be prepared to discuss his fees with him and to pay them. His services are valuable to you (how valuable you may never really know), and the protection he can offer you is one of the most valuable services you can consume.

GOVERNMENT AGENCIES Certain government agencies in your state and city can give you direct legal aid when you need it. These agencies might include the office of the district attorney or the state's attorney, a department of insurance, a department of consumer frauds, and the department of banking. Check in your community to find out what kind of legal services are available through government organizations and officials.

SMALL CLAIMS COURTS If you feel that you have suffered a loss ranging up to $500, you may be able to get a judgment in your case by applying to a small claims court. Such courts are set up to handle cases quickly. You may not even wish to consult an attorney, whose fee could easily be as large as the amount you are trying to recover anyway. Small claims courts do not require that you be represented by an attorney.

Checking your reading

1. What is a contract?
2. What are the essential elements of a valid contract?
3. List the elements generally contained in a written contract.
4. List three types of contracts that must be in writing to be legally binding.
5. Define a negotiable instrument. Give two examples of a negotiable instrument.
6. What term is used to refer to the person who writes a check? The person to whom the check is payable? The bank on which the check is written?
7. What responsibility does a bank have to a person using its checking account service?
8. List four types of endorsements.

9. List seven methods you can use to protect your own interests when using negotiable instruments.

10. What is an express warranty?

11. Name four types of implied warranties.

12. When goods are purchased "as is," what is the responsibility of the seller? The buyer?

13. What is a bailment contract?

14. What is a bailee's lien?

15. Describe the care a bailee must exercise to safeguard a bailor's property.

16. What is a small claims court?

 Consumer problems and projects

1. The laws governing contracts are an outgrowth of man's dependence on other people's promises. How have these laws helped us to handle business matters more effectively? Do these laws restrict us in our daily business transactions? Would fewer laws make it easier to conduct our personal and business affairs?

2. "Put it in writing" is the practice of many businessmen. Is this a sound practice? Is the extra work involved justified, or would an oral agreement be as satisfactory? Does this apply to most of the contracts we make each day? Explain your answer.

3. A minor is unable to make many contracts since, from a legal point of view, he is considered incompetent. Is this to the advantage of a minor? When is it disadvantageous to a minor? Is it fair that an adult must carry out his obligations in a contract even though the minor is not required to carry out his? Explain your answer.

4. Certain contracts must be in writing to be enforceable. Why is this so? Describe two situations in which written contracts would be burdensome or unnecessary.

5. Although a check is a substitute for money, it is not always as readily accepted. Describe the procedure that you would follow in order to make your check as acceptable as money.

6. Would you accept a negotiable instrument endorsed to you by a qualified endorsement? What is the legal effect of this endorsement?

7. If you received a large check with a blank endorsement, what could you do to decrease your risk in carrying it?

8. "Our word is our guarantee" is the advertised statment of a business. Is this an express warranty? Explain your answer.

9. Implied warranties exist for goods sold by samples or description. What action may be taken by the buyer to protect his rights? By the seller?

10. The only legal evidence in many bailment contracts is a claim check. If a very valuable item were involved, what could you do to obtain additional legal protection?

Chapter 30

Consumer problems and prospects

One of the favorite expressions of our time is that we live in a period of change. A politician recently discussed the fact that things are changing, but he reminded us that this has been true down through the centuries. He then observed that the expression "We live in a changing world" was probably first uttered by Adam as he and Eve were being evicted from the Garden of Eden.

Change, of course, has always been a part of the human condition. What is different about change now is its pace and the fact that it will come faster and faster, affecting every part of life. A recent essay in a professional periodical speculated that half of what a graduate engineer knows today will be obsolete ten years from now; half of what he will need to know ten years from now is not yet known.

A LOOK TO THE FUTURE

Although the future for consumers cannot be predicted with certainty, it is possible to look at developments that have already started and piece together a picture of what day-to-day living may be like in the coming years. Population changes, new patterns of earning, and new spending habits will create different problems and different opportunities for consumers.

As the decade of the 1970s began, predictions for population growth indicated that during the decade young adults between 20 and 35 would expand in number twice as fast as the total population; the teen-age group, on the other hand, would decline. By 1980, population in the United States should reach 230 million.

A revolution in transportation

Underground highways could well become popular in the very near future. Because of improved boring methods made possible by such things as laser beams and chemicals, tunneling is becoming cheaper, while land costs are increasing. When new surface highways are built through urban areas, great quantities of land must be acquired, and homes and buildings must be torn down. Thus, one big advantage of underground roads is that they do not displace people from their living areas. Then, too, underground roads are not affected by weather— another point in their favor.

Companies are now experimenting with automated highways or "guideways." In one system a wire is embedded in the road, and two pick-up coils are installed at the front of a car to sense the car's position in relation to that wire. The coils send electrical signals to the steering system to keep the car automatically on course. The system can also control spacing of cars on the highway and can detect obstacles. If an obstacle is detected, the car can be slowed or stopped until the road is clear. Other systems envision vehicles being carried on high-speed conveyers or containers. Automated highways should be vastly safer than the expressways we now have. In addition to the safety factor, the traffic could be moved faster. Experts believe that each lane of an automated highway could move the traffic of three or four of today's conventional lanes.

Home products and furnishings

Homes and things that go in them have changed as modern technology has made possible new products. Self-cleaning electric and gas ovens, color television sets, automatic clothes washers and dryers, automatic

Courtesy HUD Challenge

In the future consumers will see many new and different forms of transportation.

dishwashers, and a host of other appliances are quite commonplace in our society today. Many people consider such appliances as necessities rather than luxuries when they plan their homes. Yet these products were developed recently—most of them within the past twenty-five years. Now new products, such as microwave ovens and water beds, are becoming popular. Will the future bring even different products for the home?

A Dallas department store recently advertised a minicomputer designed for home use. The computer can be used for such things as planning menus and solving business problems.

Believing that many people will prefer in the future to have a home environment that contributes more to peace of mind than a cluttered room in a contemporary home, a growing number of architect-designers have created rooms with little or no furniture. A room might have nothing more than a complex of carpeted, multilevel platforms.

A cashless society

A few decades ago, most people paid cash for the things they bought at drugstores, hardware stores, and clothing stores. They may have charged their groceries, but at the end of the month the grocer was given cash for the amount of the bill.

Then personal checking accounts became popular, and many people began to use checks to pay for the things they bought. In 1971, Americans wrote about 22 billion checks. Many observers believe that another system for paying for goods and services will be needed in the future. They say that if the number of checks written each year continues to increase, the flood of checks may cause breakdowns in the present system.

Credit cards have become increasingly popular, and they reduce the number of checks that are written each month because the cardholder writes just one monthly check for all his credit card purchases. Now experiments are under way to carry credit cards one step further. If a housewife buys $22.80 worth of groceries at a supermarket, she merely presents a bank credit card to the check-out clerk. The clerk places the card on a recorder device that is linked by a telephone line to a bank's computer. When the clerk punches the appropriate buttons on the recorder, the computer transfers $22.80 from the customer's bank account to the supermarket's bank account. Pay-by-computer experiments have been conducted, and the results have been reasonably successful. Merchants like the idea of an instant transfer of money, but apparently consumers have not been quite so enthusiastic about paying immediately. Under the traditional credit card approach, they are billed once a month and then have another 25 days or so to pay. Under the instant transfer approach, they must pay immediately.

YOUR RESPONSIBILITIES AS A CONSUMER

How do all the developments you have been reading about affect you? We live in a changing world, and for this very reason our world is a challenging one. In the coming years, we will all decide, either directly or indirectly, the ways in which America's abundant natural, industrial, and human resources will be channeled to satisfy our needs and wants. We can certainly expect many changes in the future, and with the changes will come new problems to be solved. An increasing population and growing urbanization will present us with problems of city planning. Highly technical consumer products that make our lives more pleasant may also make our lives more harried if we cannot repair them ourselves and if there are not enough servicemen to care for them.

Your political votes

You know, of course, that citizens in a democracy have the privilege of sharing in the making of political decisions. A democracy is dependent for its success on the wisdom of its citizens, and for this reason it would be a serious mistake to consider our political votes lightly. When we stop to think about it, we realize how fortunate we are to be able to help make decisions and how important it is to be well informed about the issues affected by our decisions. How often voters express themselves on important economic issues without really understanding the issues at all! How, for example, can a voter decide intelligently whether we should rely more or less on free markets until he understands the nature and function of market systems? To be good citizens, people in a democracy must learn about their economy.

Your economic votes

Political votes are cast on election days. Economic votes are cast every day. Every time you purchase a commodity or a service, you cast an economic vote. Your preferences of commodities and services and your spending and saving habits all affect our market system and our economy as a whole. If you buy goods from an unethical businessman, you are casting economic votes for that businessman to remain in business. If you buy goods from a firm that offers poor service, you are casting economic votes for the continuance of such poor service. So you see, buying decisions affect others as well as yourself.

Index